Breakthrough Thinking in
Total Quality Management

Glen D. Hoffherr
Markon Inc.

John W. Moran
Organizational Dynamics, Inc.

Gerald Nadler
University of Southern California

P T R Prentice Hall
Englewood Cliffs, NJ 07632

Library of Congress Cataloging-in-Publication Data

Hoffherr, Glen D.
    Breakthrough thinking in total quality management / Glen D.
    Hoffherr, John W. Moran, Gerald Nadler.
      p. cm,
    Includes bibliographical references and index.
    ISBN 0-13-090820-7
    1. Total quality management. 2. Strategic Planning. I. Moran,
    John W., 1944- . II. Nadler, Gerald. III. Title.
HD62.15.H63 1993   93-4328
658.5'2--dc20   CIP

Editorial/production supervision and interior design: *Dit Mosco*
Cover design: *Jerry Votta*
Cover photo: *Rob Saunders / Stockworks*
Manufacturing buyer: *Mary E. McCartney / Alexis Heydt*
Acquisitions editor: *Michael Hays*

Published by P T R Prentice Hall
Prentice-Hall, Inc.
A Paramount Communications Company
Englewood Cliffs, New Jersey 07632

The publisher offers discounts on this book when ordered
in bulk quantities. For more information, contact:

    Corporate Sales Department
    P T R Prentice Hall
    113 Sylvan Avenue
    Englewood Cliffs, NJ 07632

    Phone: 201-592-2863
    Fax: 201-592-2249

Breakthrough Thinking, Full Spectrum Creativity and *A Paradigm Shift in Thinking* are registered trademarks, and *Software of the Mind* and *Breakthrough Thinker* are service marks of The Center for Breakthrough Thinking, Inc., P.O. Box 18A12, Los Angeles, CA 90018

Printed in the United States of America
10 9 8 7 6 5 4 3 2

ISBN 0-13-090820-7

Prentice-Hall International (UK) Limited, *London*
Prentice-Hall of Australia Pty. Limited, *Sydney*
Prentice-Hall Canada Inc., *Toronto*
Prentice-Hall Hispanoamericana, S.A., *Mexico*
Prentice-Hall of India Private Limited, *New Delhi*
Prentice-Hall of Japan, Inc., *Tokyo*
Simon & Schuster Asia Pte. Ltd., *Singapore*
Editora Prentice-Hall do Brasil, Ltda., *Rio de Janeiro*

Contents

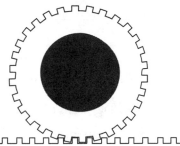

Preface

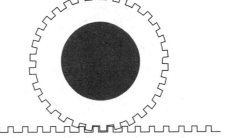

This book combines the power of Breakthrough Thinking with the value of Total Quality Management (TQM). There are many proven examples of the success of both TQM and Breakthrough Thinking; however, the purpose of this book is to show how the principles of Breakthrough Thinking can significantly enhance the results achieved through TQM.

The book is written for senior managers and professionals in TQM providing a full perspective on how to establish a TQM program and how to follow through on any TQM project or activity. Others can get a basic understanding of the concepts by selecting readings in the book.

Our motivation for writing this book comes from a gap that too frequently occurs when trying to translate TQM philosophy into practice; that is, converting all the technology, knowledge, values, goals, and "good ideas" into successful programs. Just proclaiming TQM philosophy is great is far from enough. Just claiming you are doing strategic planning to achieve a total quality and customer focus is quite insufficient. It is *how* you go about doing it that has a major impact on the timeliness, effectiveness, and level of change. To bridge this gap, we propose integrating TQM and the Breakthrough Thinking principles into what we call a Strategic Total Enterprise Management (STEM) model.

STEM represents a significant paradigm shift in organizational planning. Guided by the precepts of Breakthrough Thinking, STEM focuses on results rather than just the creation of activities and teams. In particular, it emphasizes three types of breakthroughs that are central to any effective TQM program:

- Discovering the innovative "ah ha" idea or step-function change usually associated with the word.
- Getting the idea or change implemented.

- Attaining significantly better results in all planning, design, improvement, and problem-solving activities (illustrated, in particular, in the case and research projects presented in Chapter 3).

STEM also addresses the overall needs of the organization in the strategic planning process, ensuring that the quality and business plans are integrated into the strategic plan at the outset. Currently, in most organizations, these three plans are prepared as separate documents, which organizations then spend inordinate amounts of time trying to integrate—usually with little success. This lack of integration typically results in conflicting priorities and mandates, and reinforces the hierarchical, top-down management mentality so common in major organizations today.

However, by applying the principles of Breakthrough Thinking to TQM, the quality, business, and strategic plans are considered collectively—as complementary rather than competing concerns. In short, the STEM model enables the organization to develop a comprehensive plan that encompasses the entire enterprise. In doing so, it simultaneously focuses on the purposes, values, and means for implementing those plans.

Using the STEM model, this book teaches organizations how to become better competitors in today's expanding global market. With the advent of a free marketplace in larger portions of the world, competitive pressures are increasing exponentially. Using traditional TQM methods that focus on small, incremental improvements is no longer sufficient. These increments need to become larger, and breakthroughs to new levels of productivity and new markets are required, as competition for each market grows more intense. Similarly, traditional organizational models and strategies—like continuous improvement, competitive benchmarking, self-managed and empowered teams, zero defects, and others—can no longer move an organization forward rapidly enough to keep abreast of changes in the evolving global marketplace.

In response to these changes, organizations must learn to adapt quickly, and often radically. At the same time, they need to become future-focused, anticipating challenges and solutions to situations that have not even occurred yet (the "Solution-After-Next" principle).

What these needs point to is a dramatic shift in the corporate culture itself. Organizations of the future will need to become dynamic, changing entities, in which management and employees alike seek and embrace change. This cultural shift in organizations will require new structures as well as different methods of rewards and performance appraisal. Perhaps most significantly, it will mean that all employees must comprehend the immediate and larger purposes of their activities, and how these purposes support the enterprise's ability to grow and prosper.

In short, organizations of the future must develop a fluid organizational vision both sensitive to the corporate culture and responsive to the expanding global market. This new kind of vision lies at the center of a Strategic Total Enterprise Management plan. The STEM model breaks down barriers between management and workers, since it enables all members in the organization to understand the uniqueness of their positions and their contributions to accomplishing the organization's vision. STEM also extends the traditional purview of TQM by making an organization future-focused. Continuous improvement methods as they exist in TQM today are not capable of developing future-focused solutions, nor are they capable of catalyzing needed changes in the corporate culture.

The Breakthrough Thinking principles and the STEM model detailed in this book represent the key strategic thinking technologies for organizations of the future.

Central Premises

Underlying the content of this book is the premise that *how* you as an individual or as a group proceed to work on a particular project significantly affects the quality and quantity of the results. Thus, while results (i.e., the three types of breakthroughs listed above) are important indicators of what every organization seeks, the process of attaining those results is just as important. Attention to results alone forgets that (a) a large number of small decisions is made continuously over time on any project; and (b) the assumptions and stereotypes people have significantly influence each decision and the results.

Unless both of these conditions are considered, creativity and innovation are inhibited. To help make over time the many small decisions in (a), a new set of assumptions is needed for (b). A focus on results is indeed critical, but *how* you go about trying to obtain results is what significantly affects the amount and quality.

Another premise is that any individual project or group effort must consider the full range of organizational needs if it is to be successful. Just as a focus on results alone ignores critical dimensions of problem solving and decision making processes, isolating a requirement to the exclusion of the organization's needs as a whole is myopic. An individual or group working on a problem also should approach the task with an open mind, free of a particular bias or predetermined set of objectives so commonly associated with the various "alphabet" programs (TQM, QWL, QC, TEI, TPM, OD, etc.). Finally, the individual or group should not only strive to seek the most effective results now, but clearly identify plans for continuing improvement.

Given these central premises, the set of problem-solving steps outlined in this book differ significantly from conventional approaches. There are several reasons for this difference:

- Conventional approaches set hard and fast goals right away, but Breakthrough Thinking says this could be artificial and constraining if done too early. Immediately setting out such goals limits what you can obtain, and you get only what you expect at that point.

- Conventional approaches often lead to improving what ought not to exist at all. Breakthrough Thinking is an exploration of the context that provides a framework to make certain that the problem you work on is what is needed.

- Conventional approaches assume that dedication and commitment to the short-term problem will produce the most effective results. However, dedication to getting immediate results should in no way inhibit the longer-term benefits of progress building toward bigger purposes and achieving "solutions-after-next."

- Conventional approaches, with their trust in "hard facts," create barriers of rationalism and faith-in-data that can foster antagonistic relations among people. This is despite the fact that such dependence on scientism results in only about 25%-35% of approved recommendations actually being implemented.

Overview of the Book

This book is organized into three parts:

- The Mission and Goals
- The Breakthrough Thinking Process
- The Organization as a Whole

An Appendix with descriptions of many useful tools and techniques is also included.

Part I, *The Mission and Goals*, explains what TQM tries to achieve, and sets forth the need for a different mode of reasoning about the programs, projects, and problems on which individuals and groups work.

Chapter 1, "Total Quality Management Overview," summarizes the TQM philosophy and examines the most prominent TQM models today.

Chapter 2, "TQM in the United States," gives a brief history of the evolution of TQM in the U.S., and describes the kinds of problems and resistance that confront TQM.

Chapter 3, "Modes of Thinking," notes how current assumptions need to be changed about the way to approach planning, designing, and problem solving in TQM.

Chapter 4, "Breakthrough Thinking Overview," summarizes the new set of assumptions in the form of, the seven principles of Breakthrough Thinking.

Chapter 5, "Converting TQM Concepts to Practice," more thoroughly details the Breakthrough Thinking process, and describes how the principles can impact the full spectrum of organizational activities.

Part II, *The Breakthrough Thinking Process*, explains fully how the seven principles are integrated into TQM programs.

Chapter 6, "Designing and Implementing the TQM Program," shows how establishing TQM is in itself a design project where the Breakthrough Thinking process should be applied.

Chapter 7, "Setting up the TQM Project," shows how the same principles can be used to set up any project, especially the priority projects identified in Chapter 6.

Chapter 8, "Developing Purposes," addresses the crucial first step in dealing with any problem, program, or project.

Chapter 9, "Developing Solution-after-Next Options," carries out the Full Spectrum Creativity ideas of Breakthrough Thinking to show how "solutions-after-next" help conceptualize the target system toward which a recommended change should move.

Chapter 10, "Selecting a Solution-after-Next Target," applies decision-making tools to the task of selecting a solution-after-next target.

Chapter 11, "Developing Recommended Changes," explains how to keep recommended changes as close as possible to the solution-after-next target.

Chapter 12, "Detailing the Recommendations," shows how system matrices can guide the group or individual in obtaining the right kind of information.

Chapter 13, "Developing the Installation Plan," shows how the principles can be used to implement recommendations.

Chapter 14, "Incorporating the Solution into the Organization," puts program or project developments into the framework of the entire organization.

Part III, *The Organization as a Whole*, describes the need to bring TQM into alignment with other organizational functions and needs.

Chapter 15, "Integrating the Solution: Processes and Initiatives," explains how TQM and other "alphabet" programs become more effective with the overlay of Breakthrough Thinking.

Chapter 16, "The Future for Total Quality Management," applies the "betterment timeline" principle of Breakthrough Thinking to TQM.

The Appendix details various techniques and tools that can aid the Breakthrough Thinking process. Each technique is described in terms of its results, purposes, inputs, and special characteristics. References for more complete information about each technique are also included.

The authors would like to acknowledge the following individuals for their guidance, help, contributions, and many useful comments:

Doug Anderson
Director of Quality
3M Company

Don Andrews
Manager, Plastics/Design Resins
Dow Chemical Canada

Professor Richard Chase
Director, Center for Operations
Management Education and
  Research
University of Southern California

Henry Klein
H.K. Consultants

John Samuels
Vice President
Conrail

Alan Scharf
President
Scharf & Associates

Dr. Stan Settles
Program Director
National Science Foundation

Dilworth Lyman
Director
International TechneGroup
  Incorporated

Dave Ralston
Ralston & Associates
Organization & Management
  Consultants

John S. Hoffman
Hoffman and Associates

Arvind Malhotra
Industrial & Systems
  Engineering
University of Southern
  California

Joe Thompson
Assistant Regional
  Administrator
U.S. General Services
  Administration

Suzette Rielly
Corporate Training
  Administrator
Polaroid Corporation

We also acknowledge the significant editorial review provided by
Dr. Kathy Landis. Her work improved content as well as understandability.

Much of the material in this book is reproduced with permission
from the following two copyrighted sources: G. Nadler, *The Planning
and Design Approach*, Los Angeles, CA: The Center for Breakthrough
Thinking, Inc., 1982; G. Nadler and S. Hibino, *Breakthrough Thinking:
Why We Must Change the Way We Solve Problems and the Seven Principles
to Achieve This*, Rocklin, CA: Prima Publishing (distributed by St. Martin's Press), 1990–a selection of the Fortune Book Club, Book of the
Month Club, Newbridge (Macmillan) Book Club, FastTrack ("The best
business books summarized on tape"), and one of *Computerworld's* best
books of 1990.

Breakthrough Thinking, Full Spectrum Creativity and *A Paradigm
Shift in Thinking* are registered trademarks, and *Software for the Mind*
and *Breakthrough Thinker* are service marks of The Center for Breakthrough Thinking Inc., P.O. Box 18A12, Los Angeles CA. 90018.

Part I
The Mission and Goals

Total Quality Management Overview

Today billions of dollars annually are wasted through lack of a focus on quality. This waste can stem from something as apparently insignificant as an improperly scheduled meeting that results in a loss of productive human time to a defective product or undelivered service that results in the loss of a customer. This lack of focus on quality results in product and processing systems that lack flexibility,innovativeness, and timeliness to market. The monetary effect of correcting the lack of focus on quality is estimated to be at least 15% of the cost of any product or service.[1]

Imagine the impact on the GNP if every enterprise mastered quality. The GNP and productivity would soar if this waste were reduced.

To eliminate this unnecessary waste, what needs to change is management's approach toward quality. Quality is not something for the quality department. If a corporate culture focuses on the customer, quality control will spring from each employee.

Total Quality Management is a philosophy that is designed to make an organization faster, flexible, focused, and friendly.[2] It leads to a structured system that focuses each employee on the customer. It creates an environment that allows organization-wide participation in planning and implementing a continuous improvement process to meet customer needs.

How would your enterprise appear if it were involved in producing your product or service in a total quality environment? It would be an organization in which:

- The organization would work in a very trusting manner. All decisions would be made at the lowest applicable level.

1. *USA Today,* October 11, 1990, page 13.
2. R. M. Kanter, *When Giants Learn to Dance* (New York: Simon & Schuster, 1989).

- The president and strategic planning team would establish the two or three most important goals for the organization to focus on during the year.
- Every manager and executive would know these yearly goals, and identify the one or two most important tasks needed to achieve the goals.
- Every manager would incorporate quality planning and achievement in all performance evaluations.
- All managers would have measurable milestones of their activities that are audited, documented, and sent up through the organization monthly.
- All employees would not only understand how to do their assigned jobs; they also would be empowered to regularly improve their jobs significantly, generating many suggestions, most of which would be implemented.
- All problems and challenges would be addressed by a team of the most appropriate people, regardless of their level or function within the organization.
- All managers and staff people would use effective and simple planning tools regularly to do a better job.
- Cross-functional teams would be in place to assure that quality, cost, delivery, services, and profit are managed on a consistently high level.
- All employees would be thoroughly familiar with their own specific internal and external customers' needs.
- All employees would know the people who supply them with data and materials.
- All required information would consistently flow smoothly and punctually to the people who need it.
- Improvement activities would be audited regularly at each level of the organization to assure that each employee reaches his or her full potential.

- The organization would know what customers want today and will want in the future. The organization would know what it should do to far exceed customer expectations, and it would seek to maximize those product and service attributes that add value unexpected by the customer.
- Each employee would know what he or she needs to do to make the organization run optimally. In particular, each would know the most important variables of the job to control to ensure customer satisfaction.
- The job responsibilities of each employee would be documented, audited, and updated as needed; changes would be communicated to employees regularly.

There are a variety of ways to transform your current enterprise into an organization focusing on total quality. Some of the more common suggested TQM methods are:

- quality circles
- statistical process control
- time to market
- materials resource planning ("MRP")
- "guru" approaches (Deming, Crosby, Feigenbaum, Juran, Joiner)
- daily management
- quality function deployment
- cycle time reduction

Each method by itself is inadequate. Many organizations are therefore searching for a model that best combines the many TQM methods. The most successful models of this kind today derive from the criteria of two prominent TQM awards–the Deming Prize and the Malcolm Baldrige Award–as well as from Joseph M. Juran's famous "10 Steps to Quality Improvement."

Helpful as these models are, though, one problem has repeatedly surfaced with the Deming Prize and the Baldrige Award. There is a lack of focus on the actual purpose of winning them. Winning either award for the award's sake alone—as has been the objective of too many companies—provides little value to the organization. Rather, the award should be used as a lever to introduce necessary cultural change[3] and new methodologies into the organization. It is in this light that we outline the criteria for each below.

The Deming Prize

Dr. W. Edwards Deming has been enormously influential in starting and advancing the "total quality" revolution. Early in the 1940s, Dr. Deming first developed and promulgated his ideas in the United States. With his developments in Statistical Process Control and the control chart, he is credited for his contributions not only to U.S. business and industry, but also to the U.S. effort in World War II. After the war he turned his attention to Japan, where he launched a thrust towards total quality that many claim should be a model for the rest of the business world to emulate.

In 1962, the Deming Prize was established in Japan to recognize companies that have excelled in TQM. Companies worldwide now compete each year for the Deming Prize, which is based on the following set of criteria.

Deming Prize Criteria

Policies and Objectives

- Policies with regard to management, quality, and quality control
- Methods for determining policies and objectives
- Appropriateness and consistency of objectives
- Use of statistical methods
- Deployment, dissemination, and permeation of objectives
- Assessment of objectives and their implementation

---

3. M. Sashkin and K.J. Kiser, *Putting Total Quality Management to Work*, San Francisco: Berrett-Koehler Publishers, 1993, p. 39.

Operation of the Organization
- A clear-cut line of responsibilities
- Appropriateness of delegation of power
- Cooperation among divisions
- Activities of committees
- Utilization of staff
- Utilization of Quality Circle activities

Education
- Educational plans and accomplishments
- Consciousness about quality and control; understanding of quality control
- Education concerning statistical concepts and methods, and degree of permeation
- Education for subcontractors and outside organizations
- Quality Circle activities
- Suggestion system and its implementation

Information Management
- Information gathering (internal and external)
- Dissemination of information among divisions
- Speed in gathering and disseminating information
- Statistical analysis and utilization of information

Analysis
- Selection of important problems and themes
- Selection of appropriate analytical methods
- Use of statistical methods
- Connections/tie-in with own engineering technology
- Quality analysis; process analysis; results analysis
- Receptivity to suggestions for improvement

Standardization
- System of standardization
- Content of standards

- Methods of establishing and revising standards
- Use of statistical methods
- Accumulation of technology
- Utilization of standards
- Actual records in establishing, revising, and withdrawing standards

Control

- Control systems for quality and related areas such as cost, delivery, and quantity
- Control points and control items
- Utilization of statistical methods
- Contributions from Quality Circle activities
- Actual conditions of control activities

Quality Assurance

- Procedures for new product development
- Safety and product liability prevention
- Process design, control, and improvement
- Process capabilities
- Measurement and inspection
- Control of facilities/equipment, subcontracting, purchasing, services, etc.
- Quality assurance system
- Use of statistical methods
- Evaluation and audit of quality assurance system
- Actual conditions of quality assurance

Results

- Visible results, such as quality, serviceability, date of delivery, cost, profit, safety, environment, etc.
- Invisible results
- Evaluation and audit of results
- Compatibility between predicted and actual results

Future Plans
- Plans for promoting TQM in the future
- Policies adopted to solve shortcomings
- Relationship between short-range and long-range plans

The Baldrige Award

With the Deming Prize based in Japan and awarded almost exclusively to Japanese companies, the Malcolm Baldrige National Quality Award was instituted to recognize U.S. companies that excel in TQM. Begun in 1987, the Baldrige Award promotes:

- awareness of quality as an increasingly important element in competitiveness
- understanding of the requirements for quality excellence
- sharing of information on successful strategies and on the benefits derived from implementing these strategies

Like the criteria for the Deming Prize, the criteria for the Baldrige Award provide a comprehensive list to key TQM components that can help companies assess their progress in TQM against world-class goals.

Baldrige Award Criteria

Leadership
- Senior executives' role–leadership, personal involvement, and visibility–in developing and sustaining an environment for excellence
- Projection and reinforcement of quality values
- Integration of quality into daily management operations
- Extension of quality leadership to the local community

Information and Analysis
- Data systems used to plan, manage, and evaluate quality
- Accuracy, availability, and timeliness of key data
- Timely identification of problems or opportunities; prevention focus

Strategic Quality Planning

- Short- and long-term processes of planning for customer satisfaction and overall operational performance
- Actual short- and long-term quality and operational goals

Human Resource Utilization

- Management's short- and long-term plans for integrating its human resources plans and practices with its overall quality and operational performance goals
- Opportunities for employees to participate in quality improvement; trends in employee involvement
- Quality education and training received by and planned for workers in all employment categories
- Employee recognition for contributions to quality improvement
- Programs and plans for safeguarding the health and safety of employees; trends in employees' well-being

Management of Quality Process

- Design and introduction of new/improved products or services
- Establishment, implementation, and modification of standards for quality and operational performance
- Key business processes and support services are managed for continual quality and operational improvements
- Quality assurance of suppliers of goods and services
- Documentation of quality assessment systems

Quality and Operational Results

- Quality indicators on key measures of product or service; trends compared to competitors
- Operational and business quality measures and trends
- Trends on business processes and support services results
- Supplier quality trend results

Customer Satisfaction
- Knowledge of customer requirements and expectations
- Customer service standards and measures; guarantees; trends in honoring commitments; complaint trends and corrective actions
- Customer commitments evaluated
- Measurement of customer satisfaction; knowledge of competitive data; procedures for monitoring customer gains and losses
- Customer satisfaction trends
- Customer satisfaction comparisons

Joseph M. Juran's "10 Steps To Quality Improvement"

Joseph M. Juran, Chairman Emeritus of the esteemed Juran Institute, has pursued a varied career as engineer, industrial executive, government administrator, university professor, labor arbitrator, corporate director, and management consultant. Spanning almost 70 years, his career has been marked by a search for the underlying principles that are common to all managerial activity. This search has produced much of the leading international reference literature in the area of quality management.

His "10 Steps to Quality Improvement" (listed below) reflect his lifetime pursuit of the key principles and methods by which enterprises can best manage the quality of their products and processes:

1. Build awareness of the need and opportunity for improvement
2. Set goals for improvement
3. Organize to reach the goals (establish a quality council, identify problems, select projects, appoint teams, designate facilitators)
4. Provide training
5. Carry out projects to solve problems
6. Report progress
7. Give recognition

8.   Communicate results

9.   Keep score

10. Maintain momentum by making annual improvement part of the regular systems and processes of the organization

While the criteria for the Deming Prize and Baldrige Award give an excellent, detailed picture of what a TQM system should look like, only Juran's 10 Steps begin to suggest an implementation strategy. There are, however, numerous, well-documented tools available for implementing a TQM system. The most frequently used are divided into a set of quantitative Basic QC Tools, (control charts, pareto diagram, histogram, scatter diagram, flowchart, cause and effect diagram, and design of experiments), a set of qualitative Management and Planning Tools (affinity diagram, interrelationship diagram, free diagram, arrow diagram, matrix chart, matrix data analysis, and process decision program chart), and a set of customer-oriented design tools, Quality Function Deployment matrices. The Appendix includes a brief explanation of the purposes and information sources for many of these tools. In addition, competitive benchmarking is now a popular technique. It searches for the "best in class" as the model of specific operations, processes, and designs that a company can emulate.

Figure 1-1 shows a typical TQM implementation model, listing the sequence of steps that need to be taken, and itemizing the most frequently used techniques and activities for each step.

In summary, TQM is a management philosophy that leads to a structured system involving every employee in planning, running, and improving an organization. Employee involvement at every level is predicated on the needs and wants of the customer, which in turn form the basis of a commonly shared strategic plan that integrates business and quality goals.

Put more simply, a successful TQM system requires an organization to:

• learn *how* to listen to its customers

No.	Step	Techniques and Activities
1	Create TQM awareness among top executives	Research seminars, competitive benchmarks, business environment, market share
2	Decide to proceed	Company visits, management and planning tools
3	Understand the customer	Market research, Kano surveys, focus groups, QFD
4	Assess the organization	Surveys, Baldrige, Deming, brainstorming, management and planning tools
5	Understand critical processes	Daily work management
6	Build pilot teams	Problem solving tools, quality control tools, plan/do/check/act, facilitator, consultants' courses
7	Redefine 5-year plan define annual objectives	Business trends assessment, benchmarking, management and planning tools
8	Utilize breakthrough opportunities	Breakthrough Thinking, market research, critical process analysis
9	Manage day-to-day operations	Critical processes, customer/supplier map, plan/do/check/act, standardize/do/check/act, quality control tools, problem solving tools, planning tools
10	Create functional, cross-functional teams	QFD, company-wide targets, management and planning tools
11	Manage TQM momentum	Audit tools, inter-company communication, activity-based costing, Baldrige criteria, customer feedback, marketplace image survey
12	Review and take action	Scheduled progress reviews, planning tables
13	Give rewards and recognition	Gainsharing, newsletters, awards, luncheons/dinners, bonuses

Figure 1-1. A current total quality management model.

- involve all employees in responding to its customers
- combine the strategic, business, and quality plans into one comprehensive plan

Armand V. Feigenbaum, a quality pioneer at General Systems Company in Pittsfield, Massachusetts, has astutely observed that, "Done right, quality becomes a competitive weapon. Companies that embrace quality have an edge of up to ten cents on every sales dollar over rivals."[4] James Dean of *Business Week*, expanding on Feigenbaum's observation, notes, "That's because fewer defects mean less rework and wasted management time, lower costs, and higher customer-retention rates. Cabot Corporation, for example, saved $1 million a year and freed new production capacity by cutting defects 90% at its Franklin, LA. carbon-black plant over a period of two years."[5]

---

4. *Business Week*, 1991 Special Bonus Issue, October 25, 1991, page 35.
5. *Business Week*, 1991 Special Bonus Issue, October 25, 1992, page 35.

Total Quality Management in the United States

The quality consciousness of American companies has grown consider- ably during the past decade, as businesses have become enlightened and encouraged by the successful implementation of TQM.

As discussed in Chapter 1, one of the most important catalysts behind the TQM movement in the United States is the Malcolm Baldrige Quality Award. It has provided an incentive for United States' enterprises to institute TQM systems.

Other events and trends have propelled the quality movement as well, originating with pre-1900 craftsmen and evolving over the years to its present status. A snapshot of the movement today would show a blend of the innovation found in most contemporary enterprises with the continuous improvement and customer focus found in traditional TQM philosophies. The following chronicle gives a brief history of TQM:

Pre-1900

The industrial revolution supplanted the artisan's individual craftsman ship of the trade guilds. The trade guilds ensured quality through rigorous on the job training and self inspection. It was not unusual for a craftsman to either sign or place his personal mark on the product produced. Pride of workmanship was the standard of the day.

1900-1930

During this time period, the focus changed from individually produced products to mass production. This change brought the need for inspectors who did not have an active hand in producing the product. This new job classification of inspectors were supposed to be there to protect the customer from receiving defective products. Work specialization became necessary to produce mass products which led to many hands producing what one hand used to. With many hands now producing a single product, inspectors began to see variation in the output. Organizations needed to constantly reduce the cost of producing their product. Frederick Taylor was a leader in developing methods that utilized the workers education levels to do specific tasks such as planning, running machines, and inspecting. His whole focus was to increase productivity through specialization. Walter Shewhart developed Statistical Process Control (SPC) Charts to provide a more focused means of tracking variation and ensuring quality output.

1930-1940

Allen Mogensen urged companies to get employees involved in Work Simplification as a means of continual improvement.

1940-1950

During and immediately after World War II production levels were increased dramatically by the application of many of the principles developed by Taylor, Shewhart, Deming and Juran. After the war Japan had to begin anew and rebuild its basic industry. They were helped by two industrial engineers, Homer M. Sarasohn and Charles Protzman, brought in by Gen. MacArthur starting in 1946.

1950-1980

Production in the United States continued to follow its traditional functional methodologies. As Japan's rebuilding and its focus on quality began to impact customer's perception, most companies market shares began to erode. Most US organizations focused on creativity but did not spend the time to develop easily produced consistent high quality products. The functional organizations further entrenched themselves in the US causing barriers to be built between internal departments and functions.

At the same time the Japanese were focusing on cross-functional management, the use of consensus building tools and processes as well as direct worker involvement in making improvements in their daily work.

They focused on educating the workers on controlling their output by using quality circles as a means to engage the worker's intellect as well as their hands. During this time period, the Japanese embraced the philosophies of Dr. Deming and Dr. Juran and made major breakthroughs in productivity and quality.

The Japanese developed a process called Quality Function Deployment (QFD) with Work Design,[1] the concept and principles now embodied in Breakthrough Thinking™ .

During this time the Europeans continued their focus on craftsmanship and thus produced superior quality products, but in smaller quantities than either the United States or Japan.

1980 –

American industry was alarmed by the eroding market share and began in earnest to study the tools and techniques that the Japanese had employed so successfully. The call to arms was the NBC White Paper "If Japan Can Why Can't We?". This documentary highlighted the techniques exported from the United States best quality thinkers such as Dr. Deming, Dr. Juran and Feigenbaum and sparked a renewed interest within the United States. This interest turned into a revolution and is most visibly demonstrated by the national commitment embodied in the Malcolm Baldrige National Quality Award which was created by public law 100-107 and was designed to recognize companies that have successfully implemented total quality management systems. The focus on systems is important since it implies a well coordinated and deployed effort throughout an organization, not just a random collection of tools and techniques. The winners of this prestigious award by year are as follows:

1987

Malcolm Baldrige National Quality Award was created by public law in the United States.

---

1. R. Yoshiya and K. Morooka, *Cases of Work Design Applications,* System Science Institute, Wasedo University, 1972, in Japanese

1988 Baldrige Award winners:
- Motorola
- Westinghouse

1989 Baldrige Award winners:
- Milliken
- Xerox
- Globe Metallurgical Inc.

First U.S. company wins the Deming Prize from Japan:
- Florida Power and Light.

1990 Baldrige Award winners:
- Cadillac
- Federal Express
- IBM Rochester, Minnesota Plant
- Wallace Company

1991 Baldrige Award winners:
- Solectron Corporation
- Zytec Corporation
- Marlow Industries

1992 Baldrige Award winners:
- AT&T Network System Group–New Jersey
- AT&T Universal Card Services
- Texas Instrument, Inc., Defense Systems and Electronic Group–Texas
- The Ritz-Carlton Hotel Corporation
- Granite Rock Company

The Baldrige Award has introduced a quality fever into American enterprises. This is evident in the number of requests for Baldrige Award application guidelines which have soared from 12,000 to over 100,000 in just the first few years. This award has heightened American firms' awareness of quality to levels that years of steadily increasing Japanese competition was unable to do. United States companies are now focused on building quality in rather than inspecting it in after the fact.

How have United States companies fared utilizing Total Quality Management? A GAO survey showed that in each area they studied showed that companies that adopted quality management practices experienced an overall improvement in corporate performance. In nearly all cases, companies that used total quality management practices achieved better employee relations, higher productivity, greater customer satisfaction, increased market share, and improved profitability.[2]

Difficulties that have Surfaced with TQM

While TQM is increasingly commanding the attention of American businesses, the programs it has spawned have yielded mixed results. A number of surveys have shown that the implementation of TQM still has a long way to go in most United States businesses. These difficulties have been documented in surveys printed in leading publications such as *Quality, Quality Progress, Industry Week* and the *Wall Street Journal.*

As a business philosophy, TQM is unquestionably sound and, to use a cliche, makes good business sense. Again, however, the task of translating that philosophy into workable programs is not so easy. For one, failure to embrace *all* of the tenets of TQM inevitably leads to failure in the resultant system. As a case in point, the TQM movement in the U.S. has had considerable success in getting enterprises to focus on their customers. Yet, as vital as this focus is, especially as companies expand into international markets, it rarely is embraced by all members of an organization. Instead, it is seen by many as just another "add-on" program, which like most other "add-on" programs, will come to an end.

Then, too, TQM must frequently be a championed cause, introduced and sustained by one strong leader. If the champion moves on–as usually happens–the TQM momentum falters, and the culture of the organization quickly reverts to its old, customary practices.

---

2. Management Practices U.S. Companies Improve Performance through Quality Efforts, GAO Report to the Honorable Donald Ritter, House of Representatives, GAO/NSIAD-91-190

Even with a strong leader, knowledge about TQM among top executives tends to remain sketchy. Their lack of understanding leads to uncertainty about the benefits of TQM, which in turn leads to their lack of personal involvement and support.

In such situations the success of TQM programs must depend on middle or lower-level managers–which dooms the effort from the start. Those managers who initiate TQM programs quickly become disillusioned and burned out. They soon find the value of the time and energy they are putting into the effort being questioned by their superiors and others: What is the value of TQM? How are their TQM programs contributing to the organization? Are their TQM teams really working on critical issues? To make matters worse, these individuals typically receive no reward for their efforts, while others who remain uninvolved do. A recent Hay Group report summarized these inequities quite well:

> Except for some "leading" companies, most organizations are talking more about quality, but they are not acting effectively to support it. Employees in 1991 do not feel any more empowered or productive than they did in the mid '80s.[3]

Another difficulty with TQM arises when a program is constructed too narrowly. If its purpose is to address a singular concern–like reducing waste and defects, or establishing tighter measurements and controls–its benefits are bound to be limited, both in scope and duration. While such programs may improve quality in the short term, they act to hinder development, innovation, and design improvement. This can have a much larger impact in the long term.

Similarly, if a project team depends exclusively on traditional, "proven" methods for solving problems or developing programs, their efforts may do more harm than good in the long run. Take, for example, the popular technique of competitive benchmarking. The appeal of benchmarking is that it enables a company to learn about the best tech-

---

3. Center for Management Research, 55 Williams Street, Wellesley, MA 02181.

nology or systems available. Yet simply copying what the best are doing can be a serious mistake, for it generates a false sense of catching up while the competitor is already getting better.

In addition, many U.S. organizations, having adopted the values and goals of TQM, become frustrated when they see little or no immediate evidence of improvement. In part, this frustration comes from a culturally ingrained desire for instant gratification and the deceptive promise of a "quick fix." From a business standpoint, it may also stem from an inefficient or outdated accounting system, which lacks the capacity to document changes as they occur (as, for example, Activity Based Costing does). For the most part, though, their frustration stems from the mindset generated by conventional problem-solving approaches.

These difficulties associated with the implementation of TQM programs preface a number of more specific problems that we have repeatedly encountered in our work with organizations. The following questions reflect the central concern of this book—that is, *how* TQM is most productively converted from theory to practice:

How can we avoid the "Quality Bureaucracy" as occurred at, say, Florida Power and Light?

Most organizations believe they need to study the TQM programs elsewhere and then adopt the program structure most appropriate for them. They assume that if they follow the criteria outlined for the Baldrige Award or Deming Prize, their resultant program must be "right." What they often find, though, is that many components of their program conflict with their corporate culture. Confusion about how to proceed, false starts, brooding, and hectic additional data collection then characterize installation and program activities, leading to an unwieldy, ineffective "quality bureaucracy." While investigating successful programs at other companies and studying the requirements for the Baldrige Award or Deming Prize are worthwhile endeavors, they too often detract an organization's attention from critical considerations about its own missions, culture, personnel, and unique product/service/customer mix.

How much of the current system should we study and flow chart?

A common step in process improvement models is defining the project scope. While this makes sense intuitively, how to do it often escapes project teams. A team's "charge," usually handed down from a steering committee, is almost always vague, and typically stated in terms of fixing something undesirable–like reducing the amount of scrap, decreasing the number of misplaced files, or eliminating complaints about the scheduling system. While such statements are a start, they fall short of telling a team how much of the current system to address. Conventional problem-solving approaches provide little guidance, since they focus more on techniques to apply rather than on what data and information are really needed.

What do we analyze if no system/process exists?

Deciding how to proceed in situations like this can be particularly difficult. Common sense says that comprehensive data collection will provide a clear understanding of customer needs, current services, future trends, and the like–all of which will point to obvious solutions. Knowing how to move beyond obvious solutions and beyond using data to prove what is already known at the outset remains elusive. A hospital team, for example, was assigned to plan for outpatient services. After collecting a fair amount of data about present conditions and likely trends, the team was still unable to develop creative or alternative programs. In contrast, when members of a counseling agency undertook a similar task, an examination of purposes moved them from simply adopting another agency's program to designing their own program with flexible treatment characteristics.

Should we work on improving a system or activity that should not exist? How would we know? Where do we start?

By virtue of studying an activity or process, one has already assumed that the activity or process should exist. This is not always an accurate assumption. Without a clear understanding of its purposes, a team may design a better mousetrap when it should have been exploring other methods "to eliminate rodents." Nothing is less efficient than improving what should not exist at all.

How can we be creative with so many constraints and conditions?

Flow charts, cause and effect analyses, interrelationship diagrams, and other data can enlighten participants about how things should ideally work if, for example, the organization were to start again. People also tend to become more accepting of other departments or functions when they learn why certain steps or tasks occur. Unfortunately, the sheer weight of all the data and number of causes and conditions identified in conventional problem-solving approaches can lead to the defeatist attitude of "what's the use?" More significantly, team members may find themselves facing so many constraints that making creative leaps in thinking and exploring of what's really possible may escape them. Time and again teams fall into what we call the "DRIP" trap (Data Rich and Information Poor).

Should we look for breakthroughs only for specific problems, or should each effort to plan, design, improve, or problem-solve be viewed as an opportunity for a breakthrough?

There is no reason to assume that the search for breakthroughs should be limited to certain steps or activities. In fact, *every* activity should be approached to explore the possibility of significant change. Although the TQM model in figure 1-1 lists "Breakthrough Thinking" only in Step 8, almost all the other steps will be shown to benefit from the Breakthrough Thinking principles as well. For example, breakthroughs are needed for:

- Deciding to Proceed (Step 2)
- Understanding the Customer (Step 3)
- Understanding Critical Processes (Step 5)

- Building Pilot Teams (Step 6)
- Refining 5-Year Plan, Defining Annual Objectives (Step 7)
- Managing Day-to-Day Operations (Step 9)
- Creating Cross-Functional Teams (Step 10)
- Reviewing and Taking Action (Step 12)

The ideas of Breakthrough Thinking will also be shown to have value in creating TQM awareness among top executives (Step 1) and in assessing the organization (Step 4).

The list of difficulties could be extended–should other organizational systems such as human resources be changed, should training focus on techniques for TQM or on leadership and facilitation, and so on–but these show why TQM has not achieved all the successes its goals seek.

Added to all these difficulties is what companies bring on themselves by adapting several programs, either concurrently or serially (e.g., Total Employee Involvement, Kaizen, Total Productive Maintenance). As desirable as the goals and values of these programs are in redirecting the attitudes of people in organizations, they all overlap each other. What's more, each one invariably leads to a pilot project to "prove" the effectiveness of the particular program. As each project is set up according to the parameters of the particular program, the participants use almost exclusively the concepts and techniques dictated as "necessary" by that program: the Quality Tools of TQM, the computer information techniques of CIM, the employee empowerment of quality of work life (QWL), and so on. The result is that the *methods* often become the raison d'etre for using the programs, overshadowing the larger issue of why the program was needed in the first place.

Then, too, real world problems are inevitably complicated by a host of factors and issues not necessarily touched on by a particular program's modes of operation. Effective solutions and designs need to embrace *all* factors and issues if they are to lead an organization forward. Again, *how* a project is approached, from whatever source or program it arises, is critical to its ultimate success.

Finally, as alluded to earlier, the interest generated by the Baldrige Award is a mixed blessing. While it has had an unquestionably positive effect on advancing TQM in American companies, the award's cachet masks some disturbing facts:

> Its standards of quality are not broad enough to keep American companies on the leading edge in coming years... Baldrige criteria do not address key elements of success–innovation, financial performance, and long-term planning... Another problem occurs to companies that spend years getting ready to apply for the award and then lose; will the chief executive consign quality improvement to the executive closet–alongside excellence, management by objectives, and other quick-fix management toys of Christmases past?[4]

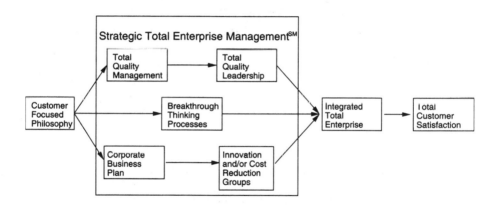

Figure 2-1. Evolution of TQM to STEM.

Changing TQM

To counter the many difficulties that have surfaced with TQM, the authors envision a synergistic evolution of TQM to Strategic Total Enterprise Management (shown in figure 2-1). "STEM" is a comprehensive

---

4. J. Bowles and J. Hammond, "Being Baldrige Eligible Isn't Enough," *New York Times*, Business Section, 9/22/91, p. 13. *Changing TQM.*

planning and design methodology, with the aim of helping an organization achieve the highest level of continuing performance possible.

In the STEM model, TQM begins with the CEO and president and involves the entire organization through an integrated business and quality management plan.

The catalyst to produce this integration is Breakthrough Thinking. Breakthrough Thinking enables an enterprise to see itself as one in which all functions are focused on providing total customer satisfaction. This means much more than the usual idea of quality as "achieving standards" (six-sigma limits, zero defects, etc.). It means even more than the usual idea of "customer satisfaction" (determining what the customer wants and then designing a product or service to meet those needs). Through STEM and Breakthrough Thinking, quality also means addressing the *potential* needs of customers, anticipating what they might value but have not stated or even thought about. To make these changes, an enterprise must learn to overcome its cultural barriers (see figure 2-2) that have impeded an organization-wide acceptance of TQM. The STEM model, therefore, also focuses the organization on the cultural changes needed to ensure ongoing success.

In closing, ask yourself the following questions:

- Where will U.S. enterprises be in the year 2020?
- Will U.S. businesses be relegated to Third World supplier status?
- What will be the U.S. standard of living?
- What will be the definition of a U.S. enterprise?

Unless U.S. enterprises wake up to the fact that they must quickly change their management focus and style, the answers to these questions will not be the ones we will want to hear. In the rapidly developing global economy, organizations must adopt a Strategic Total Enterprise Management model to bolster their long-term competitive existence.

Barriers	Current Enterprise Culture	Change to a Strategic Total Enterprise Management Culture
• Continuity of Purpose	• Changes with the Champion • Uncertain objectives • Short-term perspective	• Clearly defined long-term vision, with milestones, developed through Breakthrough Thinking Process
• Fear of Failure	• Short-term focus requires bottom line mentality • Conservative limited changes	• Long-term organizational survival based on a continuity of purpose
• Manager Role	• Plan, organize, direct, assign, evaluate, and criticize • Results orientation	• Quality leader who removes organizational barriers and promotes a team environment. "A Coach" process orientation with Breakthrough Thinking
• Priorities	• Forced based on the short-term bottom line results focused on the organization	• Team developed, consensus based and focused on the customer and purposes
• Management Structure	• Chain of command with built-in filters • Quality emphasis can be assigned to staff	• Flat organization focused on Employee Empowered Self-Managing Teams guided by the corporate vision and encouraged and supported by management
• Product Design	• Engineering driven with limited input from the customer	• Customer driven design process that will develop products and services that more than satisfy the customer "Customer Enthrallment"
• Training	• Focus on TQM tools and techniques	• Focus will be on the Breakthrough Thinking Process augmented with the TQM tools and techniques as needed
• Physical Environment	• Designed by management to support management style lack of regard for employee "Employee Isolation"	• Physical environment and work rules designed by the employees with their well being in mind, conducive to team development and learning activities "Employee Impact"
• Rewards	• Pay for the job	• Share in the organization's achievements

Figure 2-2. Cultural barriers to TQM (Page 1 of 2)

Barriers	Current Enterprise Culture	Change to a Strategic Total Enterprise Management Culture
• Recognition	• Praise the individual contributor for breakthroughs	• Praise everyone for Continuous Improvement
• Suppliers	• Promote partnerships with caveats that focus on the purchasing company	• Integral part of the organization chain and philosophically aligned to supply "Customer Enthralled Products"
• Mind-set and assumptions about how to approach change	• Data collection and overload, finding fault, modeling, anxiety, expert needed for objectivity	• Breakthrough Thinking Principles, future oriented information

Figure 2-2. Cultural barriers to TQM (Page 2 of 2)

Modes of Thinking

What's to be done? The goals and aims of TQM are worthy, the needs are certainly great, and numerous techniques and tools are available for implementing TQM.

So why are quality, productivity, competitiveness, timeliness, and innovativeness not improving very much? Why are our companies experiencing the difficulties already noted–working on the wrong problems, becoming mired in irrelevant details, creating organizational chaos and low morale, overlooking creative options, making incremental or piecemeal changes at best, to list only a few?

The theme of this book is that each of us and our organizations need a *paradigm shift in thinking*® to accomplish the objectives we seek. That is, how we currently think when we go about converting an abstract goal into a concrete activity, or how (or whether) we use a technique is all based on conventional assumptions that must be challenged.In particular, the thinking that governs the implementation of TQM in organizations needs to change. For the way we think about TQM–in theory and in practice–is bound to affect both the quality and quantity of the results we obtain. In effect, we must improve the *quality* of our thinking.

With TQM, there are many other goals that organizations need to accomplish: time-based management, rapid development of technology-intensive products, education of work force, activity-based costing, customer retention, and so on. To achieve a *paradigm shift in the structures, systems, flow, relationships, and patterns of activity that integrates all the goals,* the organization must also adopt a *paradigm shift in thinking*.

In this period of rapid change, some organizations can adapt quickly and move ahead brilliantly in developing effective, productive solutions to their problems. Books are written describing these successes, and everyone races to copy them.

Unfortunately, adopting such solutions directly does not work. The "answers" for one organization's questions and problems in the past cannot solve another organization's problems now. Even emulating the "best of the best" does not guarantee success, for those solutions, however clever or insightful, were designed for specific, idiosyncratic situations. In short, the most effective leaders today are not trying to replicate what has already been done, but are coming up with new ideas of their own.

Our claim that the thinking process must change stems from these sources:

- Philosophical considerations
- Research investigating how effective and successful people think when they plan, design, improve, and problem-solve
- Comparisons of results using conventional thinking modes with those achieved through Breakthrough Thinking

Albert Einstein said it well, "The significant problems we face cannot be solved at the same level of thinking we were at when we created them."

Philosophical Considerations

It is estimated that a person makes 50,000 decisions in a day. It might be many more if you consider that the choice of each word we speak and write represents a selection from among several alternatives. It would be many less if you say a decision relates only to important choices (however you measure what is important).

A decision is a choice selected from among alternatives. Regardless of the number a person makes in a day, a decision must be related to what precedes the choice, for example, the problem or need that gives rise to the possible alternatives, and to the results obtained from it. Deciding to establish a TQM program, as an illustration, is based on a set of problems, purposes, needs, and desires, as well as an assessment of the consequences that will occur. All aspects of the decision-making process need to be considered if one is to achieve the desired Strategic Total Enterprise Management results.

The aim of a TQM and STEM program is to create or re-structure the systems, products, services, and activities of an organization to achieve the goals and values we have described. This means that it is necessary *to improve the effectiveness and creativity of thinking about each aspect of a problem:* What is the problem? Who should be involved? What are the measures of effectiveness? How are alternatives generated? What information is needed to sketch out and assess each alternative? How is the choice made? How is the selection detailed? How will the recommendation be installed? One should always be prepared to explore these kinds of questions, rather than responding to each situation with a fixed mind-set. The notion that there is only one answer for a situation, even *the* TQM model, is a major cause for any of the difficulties described in Chapter 2.

Thinking is an issue almost everyone ignores. People assume that it is a characteristic of humans, and that some people do it better than others. In all cases, though, we tend to believe that the thinking approach for problem solving we learned in school, for example, the rational, scientific approach, is sufficient for any type of problem. But this is not so. As we shall see, different problems require different modes of thinking.

Problem Areas

The gamut of problems faced by each individual and organization is virtually infinite. In its simplest definition, a problem is a condition or set of circumstances that a person or group *thinks* should be changed. Problems are the product of human dissatisfactions and aspirations.

This is not to say that problems are only a matter of perception. Many are distinctly tangible–a flat tire, a dread disease, an erupting volcano, a military attack. How we look at any problem, how we consider it, is a mental process, and a crucial one. It is the process that is paramount. How we approach a problem shapes the way we deal with it, and determines whether we will have a successful solution, an indifferent result, or possibly bigger trouble.

Although attempting to enumerate the types of problems a person may encounter would be an endless exercise, it may be helpful to note some major areas where problems arise. Each major problem area reflects a basic purpose that an individual or organization seeks to achieve. One person will spend more time dealing with one purpose or problem area than others, based on his or her work and interests, but all of us deal with all of them at some point almost every day.

We all deal with problems of *operation and supervision* in one way or another. The purpose is to keep a good system running well–airline schedules, class schedules, kitchen arrangements, and so on. Parents operate and supervise a system called a family. A student manages a study schedule. A mayor oversees the operation of a city. A manager supervises the distribution system of his or her company.

Professionals tag a vast field of problems with the umbrella label of *planning and design*, which may involve anything from creating the logo on a cereal box to reconfiguring the plumbing system for the city of tomorrow. The purpose is to develop, create, or restructure a system, process, or artifact. Obviously, a wide array of specialists–engineers, architects, urban planners, business strategists, even doctors and travel agents–deal with problems of planning and design. Each of us engages in planning and design whenever we seek to create or restructure anything we are dissatisfied with or aspire to: a vacation, the layout of our house, the traffic flow in the neighborhood, our personal finances. The common thread running through all these activities is the exercise of imagination, vision, and ingenuity to arrive at the most effective solution.

Another big area is *research*. The purpose is to bring together data and observations about a phenomenon to formulate a theory or generalization about it. One does not have to be a scholar to develop a generalization or collect data about some concern. It may be as simple a matter as trying out different fertilizers for a lawn, or discovering which foods affect your allergy. Research is the attempt to satisfy our curiosity about the "why" of some phenomenon: why refrigerators cool and furnaces heat, why earthquakes occur, and so forth.

There are problems of *evaluation*. The purpose is to assess how well a previously selected course of action worked out–a judge determining how equitable his verdicts in lawsuits have been, or a corporate executive determining how well a company has done in choosing among alternative factory sites. Everyone gets into evaluation ultimately because, as we shall see, assessing how well a solution has met the original objective is a step in all intelligent problem solving.

Then there is *learning*, the purpose of which is to acquire skills or knowledge. Civilization would be in sad shape indeed if everyone were forced to do research or gain experience to rediscover all the knowledge and skills previously learned. Learning, of course, depends on people with appropriate information, knowledge, and skills. The *process* of effective learning is a problem area that continually demands solutions.

Modes of Thinking about Problems

Probably the simplest mode of thinking about a problem is exemplified by a jigsaw puzzle. Doing one is largely a matter of trial and error, an exercise even young children can perform.

Unfortunately, the trial-and-error method is too often applied to complex problems that call for a reasoned approach. We have an atavistic urge–perhaps inherited from the caveman's confrontations with animals–to lunge at a problem and grab the first solution that comes to mind; when that doesn't work, we try another, and another, and wind up in confusion and frustration. Most problems have many possible solutions, so the odds of hitting the optimal one on the first try simply are not good.

While other approaches are used, our track record in problem solving is poor, considering how we have responded to the many problems and challenges in education, health care, transportation, business, finance, and many other sectors of society. As we saw in Chapter 2, just to implement TQM in an organization is rife with difficulties, even within the most well-intentioned, forward-thinking companies. For these reasons, we feel some background about basic modes of thinking is in order. That is, we want to examine briefly the mental processes people go through when tackling problems.

While there are many possible problem-solving approaches, all are variations of four basic approaches: do-nothing, chance, affective, and rational.

The *do nothing* approach is based on the belief that people cannot or should not take action to solve a problem. We must ultimately dismiss this notion, since we must assume that people do want to solve their problems and are able to do so. The *chance* approach focuses on the importance of the accidental in finding solutions–like the trial-and-error method. The *affective* approach stresses intuition, insight, and feelings, whereas the *rational* approaches is characterized by structured, methodical, scientific processes.

Each of the latter three approaches has merit, and each has serious flaws. Some are more applicable to specific types of problems than are others. It is important to remember that each approach leads to different types of solutions via different kinds of information. Even more important is that every problem requires a different mind-set and method of inquiry to achieve a successful solution since no two problems are ever identical.

For example, *developing generalizations* involves the rational, scientific approach. It requires detachment, objectivity, astute questioning, and rigid methodology. It entails challenging old ideas and scrutinizing new ones. It assures that new theories are based on evidence, and that the status quo is not summarily rejected. When developing generalizations, a key objective is to make decisions on principles, not values. Principles are based on facts, objective and impersonal, while values are generally subjective.

Operating and *evaluating* likewise require a rational, scientific approach. Maintaining a smoothly operating bus system, for example, necessitates anticipating where difficulties may arise. Evaluation without analyzing and probing would be mere "window dressing" at best.

Affective approaches are most effective when the need is to create or restructure a situation-specific solution, that is, for problems of *planning and design* and for *learning* a skill or field of knowledge. Solving problems in these areas demands a commitment to projection, a willingness to explore what is new, flexibility, and subjective involvement. In short, it requires an openness to searching for ways to make an idea work, along with an ability to work well with other people.

Despite the usefulness of a variety of problem-solving approaches and mind-sets, people still tend to rely almost exclusively on the rational, scientific one. A long history of why this has occurred is described elsewhere (see *The Planning and Design Approach* and *Breakthrough Thinking*), but the result is the 8-step process outlined below. It is the conventional problem-solving approach that organizations take when seeking to create or restructure TQM programs:

1. Identify the problem
2. Gather data about it and use standard techniques to analyze it
3. Describe completely your present system (and, if appropriate, the systems of others)
4. Determine the difficulties and faults
5. Generate alternatives to correct the difficulties and faults
6. Detail the corrections
7. Sell the solution to managers and users
8. Implement the solution

At first glance these steps seem reasonable enough, but their straightforwardness is deceptive. For, while they describe the fundamental process of conventional problem solving, they fail to explain *how* to go about accomplishing any one of the steps: How do you identify the right problem? How much data should you gather? How do you generate creative solutions? How should you evaluate alternative solutions to select the most effective one? How do you assure its implementation?

This problem-solving approach is almost always accompanied by strong statements to "get all the facts" or "be sure you know what is happening now" or "study the present system." This emphasis follows the research model established in the sciences to develop generalizations about phenomena of nature. Far too often, people then look only for what is possible within very limited bounds of their current situation, "satisficing" or settling for just good enough solutions rather than what could be the best possible ones. Yet the need in TQM is to break out of and restructure significantly the current systems, products, and services of organizations.

T. Levitt points out in *Thinking about Management* that "much of the clutter which surrounds change is unnecessary confusion... Change requires a clear view into the future rather than an evaluation of the past."

Research on How Effective People Think

Based on the poor results obtained to date in most organizations (see Chapter 2), the question we raise about thinking is: What is the approach or pattern of thinking used by the effective and successful managers, engineers, planners, and other personnel in the few companies where significant results are being obtained? Studying them would provide us with the essentials of the *paradigm shift in thinking* so desperately needed.

The strange paradox in suggesting that we need *a paradigm shift in thinking* is that almost everyone intuitively knows it is needed and can often describe what such a paradigm shift in thinking would entail. We often present figure 3-1 to audiences to elicit their responses about the conventional mode of thinking as listed below.

For Planning, Designing, Improving, and Problem Solving
Conventional thinking proceeds like this...
Conventional thinking produces...
Conventional thinking sounds like...
Conventional thinking feels like...

Figure 3-1.   Conventional thinking paradigm.   (Page 1 of 2)

For Planning, Designing, Improving, and Problem Solving
Conventional thinking tastes like...
Conventional thinking touches like...
Conventional thinking causes human reactions, such as...

Figure 3-1. Conventional thinking paradigm. (Page 2 of 2)

The answers they provide (figure 3-2) show they are aware of many of the problems noted in this book.

Conventional Thinking	
military	old
control	conservative
data/rich/intensive	analysis/paralysis
defensive/rich/intensive	opposed to change
defensive	male
bureaucratic	top level change with controlled participation
hierarchy of authority	power diminishes downward
linear	power diminishes downward
rule- and policy-oriented	predictable
authoritative	historical
comfortable	answers that emerge must be right
boundaries	focuses on bottom line
sequential	

Figure 3-2. Typical responses to figure 3-1.

Then, when we present figure 3-3 to elicit their responses about what a new paradigm of thinking ought to be, they produce quite a different array of characteristics.

For Planning, Designing, Improving, and Problem Solving
New thinking proceeds like this...
New thinking produces...
New thinking sounds like...
New thinking feels like...
New thinking tastes like...
New thinking touches like...
New thinking causes human reactions, such as...

Figure 3-3. New thinking paradigm.

In figure 3-4 we show some of their different responses.

New Thinking Paradigm	
flexible	innovative
long-term	integrative
warm	exciting
challenge	leads from collective
no limits	mind of all parties
commitment	integrity
free and radical	competitive
multiple viewpoints	intuitive
non-restrictive	helps others to solve
expects full participation	problems
seeks understanding, not just acceptance	changes thinking instead of behavior
interactive	empowers others
change-oriented	obtains creative

Figure 3-4. Typical responses to figure 3-3.

What is most interesting is that their intuitive concepts fit very well with the results of the many studies leading to the *Breakthrough Thinking principles* described in Chapter 4. In other words, people know *what* they ought to be thinking as they plan, design, improve, and problem solve, but they do not know *how* to engage in new ways of thinking.

Reviewing the results of the many studies (figure 3-5) of how effective and successful people think in organizations, shows there is a different approach to brilliant problem solving.

C. Floyd

Details a new approach to the development of software engineering programs, based on an individualized assessment of people, purposes, users, and targets.

B. Snyder

Conducted a longitudinal study of MIT graduates, tracking their thinking processes and problem-solving approaches. Concluded that those who tended to have broad perspectives and considered interrelationships of factors in any setting were most successful.

R. Kasperson

Found that successful engineers seek a wide variety of information when problem solving, rather than confining information to the problem area alone.

D. Schon

Defines the most effective problem solver as the "reflective practitioner"–that is., one who thinks, or "reflects," about purposes first.

C. Argyris

Argues that organizational defensive routines are related to conventional learning and reasoning.

R. Sternberg

Identifies three types of intelligence (analytical, creative, and contextual) that play equally important roles in solving different types of problems.

Figure 3-5. Summary of studies of selected researchers. (Page 1 of 2)

H. Gardner

Identifies seven intelligence types (linguistic, intrapersonal, logical-mathematical, musical interpersonal, spatial, bodily-kinesthetic), expanding on the observations made by Sternberg (above).

W. Bennis and B. Nanus

Outline four strategies that typify business leaders, with vision being the top characteristic.

J. M. Kouzes and B. Z. Posner

Describe five practices of leaders, which include challenging processes, inspiring a shared vision of the future, enabling others to act, and modeling the way.

R. M. Kanter

Advocates integration (seeing the whole, expanding one's perspective) over what she calls the "segmentalism" of conventional problem-solving methods.

R. E. Quinn

Argues that the shift from novice to master manager involves changes in style and assumptions to develop a wide range of perspectives for viewing the world.

D. S. Isenberg

Claims that top-level managers combine intuition and rationality, and see problems as interrelated.

D. F. Heany

Argues that most managers have not excelled at strategy implementation, and need to learn to adopt top-down, team approaches.

O. Harari and L. Mukai

Describe effective managers as change agents, developers, team players, and boundary crossers.

Figure 3-5. Summary of studies of selected researchers. (Page 2 of 2)

The characteristics illustrated in these summaries reflect the same characteristics as those listed in figure 3-4. A closer look at several of the projects mentioned in figure 3-5 will further illustrate the insights that have led to the principles of Breakthrough Thinking.

Dr. Synder studied a sample of MIT graduates over nearly 30 years. He called those people who were technique-oriented and particular about details "Mode 1" reasoners. Those who tended to have larger perspectives and considered interrelationships of factors in any setting were labeled "Mode 2" reasoners. He found that Mode 2 reasoners not only produced more effective results in their careers, but were better adjusted and adaptable in all aspects of their lives. [B. Snyder, "Literacy and Numeracy: Two Ways of Knowing," in Literacy in America, DAEDALUS, *Journal of the American Academy of Arts and Sciences*, Spring 1990, Proceedings of the American Academy of Arts and Sciences, Vol. 119, Number 2.]

Professor Argyris reports from his extensive studies of organizations that the "defensive routines" of people greatly hamper change efforts and restrict people's breadth of learning. Defensive routines are the practices people use to protect their current status or turf-like gathering huge amounts of data in order to mire down any analytic effort, and thus foster the syndrome, "it's too complicated, so we can't really change it." [C. Argyris, "Strategy Implementation: An Experience in Learning," *Organizational Dynamics*, 1989, pp. 5-15.]

Professors Kouzes and Posner studied leaders in many organizations and identified five broad categories to describe how these leaders operated. First, the leaders challenged how things are done, most often by looking to larger ends. Next, they had a vision that they kept relating to the larger ends and to everyone frequently. Third, they delegated authority to others to act in moving toward the vision. Fourth, they performed their own work the way they wanted others to perform. Last, they encouraged the "heart" of those around them through ample recognition and rewards. [J. M. Kouzes and B. Z. Posner, *The Leadership Challenge: How to Get Extraordinary Things Done in Organizations*, San Francisco: Jossey-Bass Publishers, 1987.]

Dr. Peterson had around 200 engineers, planners, architects, and managers in his study. He identified criteria that led to categorizing the sample into effective and less effective professionals. The results, summarized in figure 3-6, are very significant (with discriminant functions of 0.75 to 0.85!).

The thinking process of the effective professional is clearly different from that of the less effective professional, and provides a major clue about the nature of the needed *paradigm shift in thinking.* [J. G. Peterson, "Personal Qualities and Job Characteristics of Expert Engineers and Planners," Ph.D. Dissertation, University of Wisconsin-Madison, 1985.]

The other studies in figure 3-5 similarly point toward different perspectives and ways of approaching assignments to plan, design, improve, or problem-solve. The topics range from types of information sought (Kasperson), combination of perspectives (Isenberg), and different types of intelligence (Sternberg, Gardner), to overall philosophy in software engineering (Floyd) and general concepts of practice (Schon).

Some direct comparisons of the outcomes achieved by conventional thinking and the new thinking methods also help to identify the characteristics needed in a new paradigm of thinking.

Effective Professional	Less Effective Professional
Purpose-oriented to find right problem	Technique-oriented for problem as stated
Copes with soft data	Insists on hard data
Seeks information from a variety of sources	Seeks data bout what exists in the problem area
Involves many other people	Tries to handle problem alone or with just a few people
Tolerant of ambiguity	Insists on firm statement of work, specifications, etc.
Deals with visions of solutions-after-next:	Problem area is the only context with which to deal

Figure 3-6.   Characteristics of effective and less effective professionals when planning, designing, and problem solving.

Comparisons of Results: Conventional and New Thinking Modes

Getting information about such outcomes is not an easy task. Organizations very seldom deliberately try two different thinking approaches with separate groups as a way to evaluate which works better. In too many cases, unfortunately, the comparison occurs after a failure with the conventional approach is followed by success with a different approach—that is, one guided by the principles of Breakthrough Thinking. The following cases and research reports are testimony to the need for *a paradigm shift in thinking,* as embodied in Breakthrough Thinking.

One evaluation from 48 manufacturing companies showed that Breakthrough Thinking produced over twice the amount of yearly economic savings per continuous improvement staff person than did conventional approaches (see figure 3-7). In other words, just *one* person using Breakthrough Thinking produced greater economic savings than *two* persons did using conventional reasoning.[1]

Another example of the power of Breakthrough Thinking comes from a project initiated at Canada Post, the postal service in Canada. The purpose of the project was to design administrative systems that would support one clothing store for the uniforms its employees had to buy, rather than three that were then in operation. A project team of first-line supervisors from various locations across Canada was assembled and given a 5-day workshop on the Breakthrough Thinking process. Upon applying the principles of Breakthrough Thinking to their task, they first produced a detailed system design to satisfy the needs for one clothing store. It was successfully implemented within three months. Looking beyond the immediate needs, they then envisioned the corporation providing a national retail organization (for example, Sears, Bay, Eaton) with Canada Post's clothing standards, and recommended that appropriate Canada Post employees be given credit vouchers to purchase uniforms from the selected firm. This solution eliminated the need for even one

---

1. G. Nadler, "Design Processes and Their Results," *Design Studies,* Vol. 10, No. 2, April 1989, pp 124 - 127.

corporate warehouse and distribution system! Canada Post is now implementing this solution.

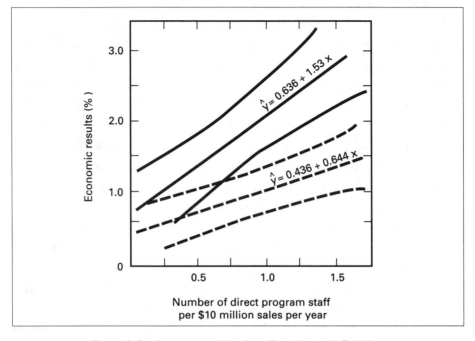

Figure 3-7. Savings resulting from Breakthrough Thinking.

An industrial engineer supplied yet another illustration: "Using the
old methodology in my two-day workshops, we could go only as far as
problem identification. The next step of 'define work process' is labori-
ous, detailed, and cannot be performed in a workshop. Now, using
Breakthrough Thinking, I have taken groups all the way to solution
detailing. In some less complex cases, they are even ready to make recommendations for implementation. This represents a major increase in what
is accomplished by the [Breakthrough Thinking] training groups."

The last illustration arises from a contest that took place among
engineering schools at universities around the country. The assignment
was to reduce the cost of manufacturing a component of a product.
Forty-five entries were submitted. Forty-four were the results of classes of

20 to 25 students each, all of whom used conventional approaches–gathering large quantities of information about current manufacturing processes, the characteristics of the materials used, and the design specifications. One student at the other university used Breakthrough Thinking by himself and submitted an innovative recommendation that did away with most of the materials and design of the old component. He won first prize.

Requirements for a New Thinking Approach

All this background, especially the difficulties faced in TQM activities described in Chapter 2, leads to the major reason for writing this book:

The mode of thinking in organizations–not only about TQM but in all problem-solving situations–needs to change.

The information on thinking in this chapter makes it possible to propose a set of characteristics and factors *a paradigm shift in thinking* should reflect. Figure 3-8 lists these characteristics.

A Paradigm Shift In Thinking Must:
• Identify the uniqueness of each project
• Treat each part of a project as a problem
• Investigate the "problem-as-stated" to determine the "problem-to-work-on"
• Open the solution space
• Define quality and results measures that are important
• Determine what information really needs to be collected
• Get people to participate and develop their own buy-in
• Bring people together from many disciplines and departments
• Build in the concept of continual change
• Lead to plans for implementation at the beginning
• Show impacts of solution ideas on the corporate environment

Figure 3-8. Characteristics and factors.

Breakthrough Thinking Overview

As noted in the previous chapters, the major challenge facing organizations today is *how* to implement TQM. From the vast body of literature about TQM, we may know *what* to focus on, but the pivotal question of *how* still remains. Specifically, how does an organization go about converting all its technology, knowledge, values, goals, and "good ideas" into effective TQM systems and programs?

Fortunately, the answer is not a mystery. The studies in Chapter 3, which document the thought processes and characteristics of successful people, give a fairly good idea of the paradigm shift in thinking that organizations need to make. To codify this shift—and, in turn, to answer the question of *how* an organization can tackle virtually any problem related to TQM—we offer the seven principles of Breakthrough Thinking.

Breakthrough Thinking has a history dating back to the 1960s. Initially developed in the United States as "Work Design," it was used extensively by the Japanese in industry, giving rise to such landmark techniques as Quality Function Deployment (QFD) at Toyota in the late 1960s. Since that time, seven principles of Breakthrough Thinking have emerged from a synthesis of research and program comparisons. These principles enable breakthroughs in problem-solving to occur significantly more often than conventional approaches

While numerous kinds of breakthroughs are made possible by the seven principles of Breakthrough Thinking, three areas in which breakthroughs occur can be defined broadly:

1. Discovering the innovative "ah ha" idea or step-function change usually associated with the word

2.   Attaining significantly better results in all planning, design, improvement, and problem-solving activities (illustrated in cases and research projects presented in Chapter 3)

3.   Getting a major concept or strategy implemented

This last area is particularly crucial for understanding the benefits of Breakthrough Thinking. As an example, one company had two sites four miles apart in one city. A team of people from each site had been working nearly two years to develop plans for improving the performance of the company. Many ideas had been generated, and an architectural firm developed a three-inch report evaluating the ideas and showing the impact on the facilities at each site. However, a lack of financial resources to implement the recommendations of the team led to a rancorous stalemate. A Breakthrough Thinking facilitator was called in. In less than two days, an idea was unanimously endorsed that had been presented in the report but dismissed by both the team and the architect: consolidate all operations at one site! The breakthrough was the implementation of a significantly better idea that had already been identified (but rejected earlier).

This is but one of many success stories illustrating the value of Breakthrough Thinking. Following is an overview of what the seven principles entail:

The Uniqueness Principle

One of the biggest mistakes people make in problem solving is assuming that one problem is identical to another. *It never is.* No matter how alike two problems or situations appear on the surface, they will differ in time (when they happen), place, the people involved, the related circumstances, and the purpose of the solution. For example, two hospitals in similar communities, with the same number of patient beds, types of service, and patient volume, each wanted to improve its medical records library system. The Breakthrough Thinking consultant did not assume that the system developed for the first hospital ten months earlier would work equally well in the second hospital. The *people*, the staff who would use the system, differed in all their myriad characteristics, their social groupings, their organizational roles, and so on. He therefore set up a team in the second hospital to work on the project without even referring to the other hospital's solution.

The first hospital installed a highly acclaimed, automated medical records network in which physicians could enter patient information and orders on a dictation system or at a computer terminal on the patient's floor. Orders were dispatched electronically to pharmacy, radiology, or other departments, and on to patient billing and medical records. The second hospital had a slightly different purpose to achieve, and faced different time and budget constraints and staffing problems. So the project team elected a different system, using existing telephones and more paper, as the most effective way to accomplish their objectives. It was a "breakthrough" for them. Imagine the wasted time and cost if someone had tried to force-fit the first hospital's solution into the second one.

This example of the two hospitals invites a timely warning: Adapting an existing solution (for example, the "best of the best" from competitive benchmarking) to a seemingly similar problem can cost two or three times as much as starting from scratch to create your own solution. Because every problem is unique, every problem requires a unique solution, no matter how many other available components are integrated into the solution.

The Purposes Principle

This principle holds that there is never a single purpose in planning or problem-solving. Identifying the initial purpose is really only the beginning. Scrutiny and creative thinking reveal a whole hierarchy of purposes that expand the scope of the problem—and increase the number of possible solutions. Investigating the range of purposes enables you to seize the opportunity to transform a planning or problem-solving effort into productive change.

To bring into focus the problem that needs to be worked on, you need to ask about purpose at every step:

- What is the purpose of working on this problem?
- What are we trying to accomplish with this information?
- What function does this group of people serve on the task force?
- What is the larger purpose of this purpose? What is the purpose of the external customer, and the customer's customer?

To illustrate the importance of the Purposes Principle, the president and several vice presidents and managers of a manufacturing plant spent eight months studying the problems of late delivery, high overtime costs, decreased quality, and misplaced orders in their company. They then called a Breakthrough Thinking consultant to help them design the new facility they thought they needed to double the factory capacity. By asking the project team to construct a hierarchy of purposes for the project, the consultant led the group to find—after just a couple of hours—that the right problem to work on was the development of management control systems! There is no doubt that a new facility *could* have been designed and built, but it would have been a monumental mistake.

The Solution-After-Next Principle

A common failing among problem solvers is neglecting to look beyond the immediate issue to future needs. Our pragmatism and conventional approach say that if we need to solve a problem, whatever works is right. Just get the job done. However, the implications of a short-term solution need to be considered before you make a commitment to it. This may make alternative solutions look more promising. The change you make now should be based on what the solution might be when you work on the problem, say, three years from now, or when you begin planning in the next cycle.

Applying the Solution-After-Next "SAN" Principle, a department store team developed an ideal solution-after-next conveyor system for receiving and marking all its merchandise, assuming it all came in cardboard containers. When the team found that nearly 85% of the merchandise did arrive in cardboard containers, the company installed almost the whole conveyor system, modifying it only to accommodate wooden crates and plastic containers not suitable for the new system.

As this example illustrates, a long-term and even "ideal" solution gives direction to immediate solutions or "current release" changes by infusing them with larger purposes. Having several alternative solutions-after-next not only stimulates creativity but gets more people involved.

The Systems Principle

No problem exists in a vacuum. Rather, all problems and solutions are like the tip of an iceberg, representing only a small portion of the whole. Thus, for successful problem solving and problem prevention, all the interrelated elements of a business must be considered. To do this, a systems matrix is helpful both for organizing all the elements and for clarifying complex relationships.

Often, a systems matrix is essential for putting a wide variety of data into a workable order and keeping you aware of the larger context of the problem. Most computer-integrated information systems, for example, are so complex that a structured systems matrix of eight elements and six dimensions is one critical way to design one effectively (see figure 4-1). Similarly, strategic planning can be so complex that a series of systems matrices is needed to bring order to all the myriad factors and show inter-relationships among them.

The Limited Information–Collection Principle

The indiscriminate amassing of information and measurements to "find out all there is to know" wastes time, effort, and money. It impedes planning and problem solving by burying you in an avalanche of irrelevant, unmanageable details. It leads to what we call "analysis-paralysis." Furthermore, the information and measures produce a sense of satisfaction about the current situation "just because we know it all." In reality, the data, especially from competitive benchmarking, concerns what may be considered good today even though not performing up to potential.

Elements	Fundamental: basic or physical characteristics—what, how, where, or who	Dimensions				
		Values: goals, motivating beliefs, global desires, ethics, moral matters	Measures: performance (criteria, merit, and worth factors) objectives (how much, when, rates, performance specifications)	Control: how to evaluate and modify element or system as it operates	Interface: relation of all dimensions to the systems or elements	Future: planned changes and research needs for all dimensions
Purpose: mission, aim, need, primary concern, focus						
Inputs: people, things, information to start the sequence						
Outputs: desired (achieves purpose) and undesired outcomes from sequence						
Sequence: steps for processing inputs, flow, layout, unit operations						
Environment: physical and attitudinal, organization, setting, etc.						
Human agents: skills, personnel, responsibilities, rewards, etc.						
Physical catalysts: equipment, facilities, etc.						
Information aids: books, instructions, etc.						

Figure 4-1. Systems matrix.

The Limited Information–Collection Principle is based on the premise that a problem cannot be solved by throwing data at it. Instead, you should only gather information that is useful and relevant to the other principles of Breakthrough Thinking. Probe for the uniqueness of the situation, the larger purposes and the solution-after-next, and the framework for the systems matrix. Continually ask yourself, "What purpose does this information serve?"

Case in point, a project initiated in a large insurance company to locate missing claims folders (about 200 at any one time) would have ordinarily started with the conventional approach of "getting all the facts." However, the project team began by asking about the purpose of such information collecting, which led to a purpose hierarchy. The targeted purpose–at a larger level than the immediate problem–was to keep claims folders available. Obviously, the kind of information collected for this purpose is much different from that for locating missing claims folders. Furthermore, the initial purpose would likely lead to a change which assumes that missing folders are always going to occur, while the larger purpose is much more likely to produce a system in which folders will not be lost.

The People–Design Principle

This principle holds that anyone–not just status players–has the potential to become a valuable contributor. To put this concept into practice, the organization needs to create an atmosphere that encourages contributions from each individual.

People, including external customers, do not resist change per se. They resist change when they don't understand it or when it is imposed on them. They resist change that they see as threatening or that interferes with their other priorities. People also resist change that involves risks greater than the potential benefits.

The People–Design Principle gets people to work on change from the center (themselves) out, rather than from the outside (others) in. This principle works because people are much more motivated by the uniqueness, purposes, solution-after-next, and systems principles than they are by conventional information-overload approaches.

The Betterment-Timeline Principle

No action is ultimate. There is no such thing as "a solution" that will permanently take care of a problem. The change today is just the "current release" (e.g. version 1.1). Solutions should be pictured on a continuum, yielding more and more gratifying rewards as they are continuously fine-tuned. As you implement a design or recommended change, you should also plan to keep changing and improving it. It is even better when a solution carries the seeds of its own later changes.

If you build into a solution a plan for continual modification, you will preserve the solution's vitality and viability. The larger purposes in the hierarchy and the solutions-after-next help to stimulate interest in continuing change and identifying what the next changes should be. Doing this adds value to the benefits of the project as well to what the customer gets.

A Paradigm Shift in the Pattern of Reasoning

Breakthrough Thinking is synergistic: The whole is greater than the sum of the parts. Therefore, trying to apply one principle at a time–or one after another in a preset order–is not as effective as using all of the principles at the same time. This holistic approach means that you consider all the interactions of your organization, rather than narrowing your focus to specific problem areas.

As an illustration of the synergism of Breakthrough Thinking, the president, executive staff, and board of directors of a $300 million company got together to formulate a mission statement for their enterprise. As they worked on developing the statement, they tried to copy, or at least use as a model, several others they liked. Then a Breakthrough Thinking consultant illuminated how the specific "problem" of developing a mission statement needed to be treated as unique, had larger purposes that needed to be defined, and required a solution/

mission-after-next. Putting the mission statement into the context of the company as a whole, the consultant further helped the group realize that, in developing their statement, they needed to seek customer and external condition-scanning information rather than internal data; they needed to get many other people to contribute ideas about the mission; and they needed to have a life-cycle of, say, two years, at which time the mission statement would be done over.

In summary, a general Breakthrough Thinking process or pattern of reasoning consists of the following:

- Examine purposes with the appropriate people, and plan the project and the implementation mechanisms for making it happen.
- Expand the scope of the investigation by examining bigger, more fundamental purposes and goals. Select the biggest purpose (or opportunity or mission) that it is possible to work on.
- Generate ideas for solutions-after-next around the largest purposes you can possibly achieve.
- Form these ideas into several alternate solutions, from which you then choose a solution-after-next or long-range target.
- Using a systems matrix (or matrices), detail the alternative (the "current release") that fits the real world, while coming closest to your ideal solution-after-next.
- Detail the installation plan to carry out that alternative.
- Provide for its continuing change and improvement. Schedule the time to revise the purposes and solutions-after-next.

From this pattern, we can see how the seven principles of Breakthrough Thinking equip people in organizations with the right questions to ask about any problem. Even the most "standard" of activities—such as setting up a task force, running a meeting, doing design, or implementing strategic planning—must be probed with questions about uniqueness, purposes, solutions-after-next, systems, information collection, and people. The results are often dramatic. As just one example, figure 4-2 shows how strategic planning is accomplished much more effectively when it is based on the principles of Breakthrough Thinking. (Note, in particular, how "random" collection of huge amounts of information is avoided.)

---

1. With a team of major stakeholders and implementors, use Breakthrough Thinking principles to design the strategic planning "system" to put in place.

2. Put the strategic planning system into operation: appoint members, schedule meetings, publish milestones and completion dates, and so on.

3. Develop possible mission (purpose) statements and array into a hierarchy of purposes from small to large.

4. Select a mission (purpose) level as the focus, realizing that every mission statement must have larger missions it seeks to achieve.

5. Generate alternative visions (solutions-after-next) to achieve the mission.

6. Select a vision that is an ideal plan of what would be done if you could start all over again.

7. Schedule meetings and review sessions to "try out" the mission and vision on all stakeholders, obtain insights into environmental factors, consider other ideas, acknowledge constraints, and so on.

8. Repeat steps 1 through 7 for developing a strategic resource plan for each of the major needs (e.g., human resources, marketing, finance, organization design, manufacturing or physical resources).

9. Integrate the overall mission and vision with those from the resource areas. Incorporate the knowledge from step 7 into a formal strategic plan that stays as close as possible to the initial vision. A systems matrix perspective provides a workability and reality structure as well as a way of noting future changes.

10. Set up an installation plan and a timeline for stages of change in the organization and for redoing the strategic plan.

Figure 4-2. Strategic planning based on Breakthrough Thinking.

In closing, Breakthrough Thinking is not a solution. It is a paradigm shift in process that replaces conventional wisdom about planning, designing, improving, and problem solving. In particular, it shows *how* to achieve the three major goals of all problem solving in an organizational setting:

- Maximize the effectiveness (creativity, innovativeness, benefit/cost ratio, etc.) of any recommendation.
- Maximize the likelihood of implementing the recommendation or "best" idea.
- Maximize the effectiveness of all resources (people, money, time, facilities, etc.) allocated to planning, design, improvement, and problem solving.

While these goals concern the results obtained from any problem-solving effort–and, indeed, are important guideposts to bear in mind–they still have to be converted into practice. As this chapter has shown, Breakthrough Thinking provides the means to move from abstract goal to concrete practice. It answers the critical question of *how* to proceed that traditional problem-solving approaches fail to address.

Converting TQM Concepts to Practice

5

Total Quality Management engages *all* people in the organization. It challenges their values and beliefs, while demanding new levels of trust, empowerment, and acceptance of responsibility–all of which are channeled toward meeting and exceeding customers' needs.

When an organization embarks upon Total Quality Management, it must understand that TQM is not a "quick fix," but a journey without an end. For TQM not only involves organization-wide participation; it also entails a process of continuous improvement.

Your organization, like every organization, is a complex entity. Look at any management text to review all the interrelated factors and activities–product design, R&D, community relations, marketing, finance, shareholder values, environmental impacts, human resources–to name just a few. Quality enhancements are needed in each of them, yet the variety of functions and needs is very broad–and we haven't even mentioned manufacturing, the arena most people associate with TQM. In reality, the fastest growing segment of organizations implementing TQM is the services sector, particularly financial and health care organizations. Many government agencies are committing to TQM as well.

Added to this complexity are the differences in values, beliefs, and policies from one organization to another, regardless of how "identical" each may appear. A hospital, for example, represents an organization that most people would claim is similar if not identical from one place to another. The typical profile–300 beds, six medical services, nonprofit city ownership, 350,000 population community, and so on–makes such an institution in one state a virtual clone of another in a second state. The Uniqueness Principle of Breakthrough Thinking shows that even this similarity does not exist. Because the people, community, history, economics, and location of each hospital are different, the organizational structure, systems, policies, and values of each will also be different.

57

Furthermore, each function or activity seeks to make its impact more significant and "powerful" by emphasizing its aims as top priority considerations of the organization. The wide variety of "alphabet programs" all reflect this concentration on aims–Total Employee Involvement, Total Productive Maintenance, Value Added Management, Just In Time, and so on. The aims of each program are quite worthy. Adherents are no doubt sincere in promoting their program for the organization.

However, these conditions often pose a series of dilemmas for the organization: Which program is most important? How much support should it receive? When should it be implemented? What are the staffing needs? Unfortunately, in resolving these dilemmas, most organizations adopt one program first as *the* answer to their problems, then adopt another when the first program does not produce the expected results, then a third, and so on. Going from one fad to another is one of the major deficiencies of U.S. management.

These complexities not only highlight the uniqueness of each organization, but also point to the immense task of developing a TQM program that will positively affect an organization's performance. Trying to impose an existing TQM system onto an organization just won't work. Trying to adjust an existing system wastes time, money, and other resources, while minimizing the likelihood of significant breakthroughs. The usual result is a program that yields minimal returns at best (review the comparison studies in Chapter 3).

Some Imperatives for Converting TQM Concepts to Practice

To maximize the effectiveness of TQM in any organization, we offer the following guidelines, which parallel the characteristics of the paradigm shift in thinking outlined earlier (see figure 3-8):

- A system, product design, job, or structure must integrate all factors, not just focus on one or two. System integration means arranging all the organizational factors most effectively, even if the major programmatic thrust (e.g., quality, maintenance, inventory levels) is not at its optimal level.

- Emphasis must be on prevention of errors, or building quality into the products, services, and work. Eliminating the costs of detecting errors or of doing the work over is necessary but not sufficient.

- Both the overall and separate functional strategic plans (e.g., manufacturing, finance, people, marketing, etc.) must include TQM aims and indicators of performance. A TQM central office is insufficient and often unnecessary.

- Simplicity is an essential indicator of internal TQM effectiveness. Conventional wisdom about internal TQM programs must always be challenged to assure that its focus is always simple—for instance, on the organization's customers.

- Time-based competition is a driver in all organizations, and is a key measure of customer satisfaction. It may even be more important than profit, cost, service, new products, and quality! Because of this, all "standard" amounts of time to do anything can no longer go unchecked, but must be continually reassessed. If time-to-delivery is compressed, for instance, all the other measures—profit, cost, service, and so on—will improve.

- All efforts must stay as close as possible to the "ideal." This entails far more than merely reducing variability in current processes. It involves all the performance measures of a system, and translates into making changes (in systems, products, services, and the like) that stay as close as possible to the "ideal" or solution-after-next target. It also includes the Betterment Timeline principle of moving toward the "ideal" as quickly as possible.

- Organizational values and beliefs must be integrated into the TQM process. Although the culture of the organization may need to change to accommodate TQM, focusing on the above imperatives in the current setting will eventually bring the desired changes. In fact, this approach is likely to be far more effective than trying to change the culture directly.

Relating TQM Concepts and Practices

This may be the point to reread Chapters 1 and 2, or briefly review the fundamentals of TQM.

Recalling that the customer–especially the external customer–defines quality, everyone in an organization must be involved and empowered to improve quality. Top management must lead the quality change, realizing that TQM is an ongoing pursuit and that improvements are continuous. The quality process must not center on high performance alone, but strive toward "excitement" attributes (those that the customer does not expect). However, as Chapter 2 points out, we have not been doing too well in attaining these ends nor in identifying the difficulties that must be overcome.

From Chapters 3 and 4, we saw that the biggest challenge facing organizations today–and the primary focus of this book–is *how* to convert all the knowledge, information, and technology available to us into solutions that best achieve the goals of TQM. We also saw that the conventional ways of forging such solutions are largely ineffectual, for they are based on outdated modes of thinking and problem-solving approaches. To develop truly innovative solutions, we need to break away from excessive scientism and embrace the sort of purpose-based problem solving manifested in the seven principles of Breakthrough Thinking.

We also need to disabuse ourselves of the long unchallenged notion that "knowledge is power." As necessary as bodies of knowledge and information are, we must recognize that they are insufficient for solving the diverse problems confronting organizations today. Rather, Breakthrough Thinking suggests a new credo: *Knowing how to use knowledge is power!*

Axioms Governing the Conversion of Knowledge to Practice

The goals of TQM in Chapter 1 and the above imperatives of TQM spell out the conditions we seek in our organizations. In converting these goals and imperatives into practice, Breakthrough Thinking is based on a philosophical foundation, comprised of a set of beliefs we call *axioms*. Axioms are truths that need not be necessarily proved, because people are willing to accept them on face value.

Figure 5-1 lists the axioms that underpin Breakthrough Thinking.

Axiom 1	A continuous (rather than discrete) timeline is the fundamental basis for understanding the past, present, or future of any phenomenon.
Axiom 2	People perform purposeful activities that influence and are influenced by the objectives and goals they seek to attain.
Axiom 3	Everything can be considered a system.
Axiom 4	Each system is part of at least one hierarchy of systems.
	Corollary 4a. Each system is part of at least one larger system.
	Corollary 4b. Each system is composed of smaller systems.
	Corollary 4c. Each system exists parallel to other systems.
Axiom 5	Each system can at any time be identified in one of three conditions: future existence, satisfactory existence, or unsatisfactory existence.
	Corollary 5a. A system tends toward unsatisfactory existence.
Axiom 6	A word is only a representation of a reality, not the real thing.
	Corollary 6a. Models are incomplete representations of real-life phenomena.
	Corollary 6b. A solution on paper is not the desired change or implementation.
Axiom 7	No two situations or things are identical.
	Corollary 7a. There is no such thing as certainty in the future.
	Corollary 7b. A solution for a specific problem in one organization differs from the solution for a similar problem in another organization.
	Corollary 7c. An analogy cannot prove that a premise should be accepted.

Figure 5-1. Axioms for Breakthrough Thinking. (Page 1 of 2)

Axiom 8	A system processes inputs into outputs that achieve a purpose (or purposes) through the use of human, physical, and information resources in a sociological and physical environment.
	Corollary 8a. Each element of a system can be specified or detailed in terms of dimensions, properties, or attributes.
	Corollary 8b. Each element and dimension of a system is itself a system.
	Corollary 8c. Each dimension of each element is a system.

Figure 5-1. Axioms for Breakthrough Thinking. (Page 2 of 2)

Starting the Conversion Process

When translating the knowledge of TQM into practical applications, the most critical starting point is management awareness. That is, executives must know and understand the needs for TQM. Next comes commitment, which means that executives are motivated to take action, realizing that the organization must have TQM to prosper and even survive.

Richard Walton suggests that getting your organization from where it is now to where you would like it to be (i.e., with an outstanding TQM program) is a multiplicative concept: Motivation (or why you want to implement TQM) is multiplied by the vision of what you would like the organization to be, and then by the process (or how you proceed):[1]

Motivation X Vision X Process

Motivation should be strong and broad-based, particularly in light of the difficulties described in Chapter 2. (How to present the case to executives to excite and motivate them is itself an activity in which the Breakthrough Thinking principles can be applied.)

---

1. Richard E. Walton, "Planned Changes to Improve Organizational Effectiveness," *Technology in Society,* Vol. 2, 1980, p. 391-412.

The vision of what you want the organization to be is described in Chapter 1. Even more effective is the Strategic Total Enterprise Management idealization described in Chapter 2.

The methodology for getting TQM implemented is what Breakthrough Thinking provides. This process is the key factor that has been ignored in TQM (and other programs). Everyone assumes that conventional problem-solving approaches are satisfactory, when the studies reviewed in Chapter 3 show clearly how wrong this assumption can be.

Because process is a factor in Walton's formula for obtaining change, it is now easy to understand why motivation and vision alone cannot achieve the objectives of TQM. Even with the greatest motivation and most brilliant vision, the result is bound to be diminished if the process is weak.

It is therefore critical to bring the importance of process to the attention of decision makers, while demonstrating the shortcomings of conventional problem-solving approaches. As mentioned above, the task of developing such a presentation is one that would benefit from the Breakthrough Thinking principles. It is a matter of presenting what is wanted (STEM), so that decision makers see it as an opportunity to strengthen the organization at every level.

Achieving TQM Ends through People

Executives are not the only ones who need motivation and vision if a STEM-based TQM program is to succeed. *All* workers in an organization, despite their rank or job function, must have motivation and vision as well. They need to understand the goals and imperatives of TQM, and they need to accept cross-functional activities, if not formal teams, as the norm of organizational behavior. They also need to appreciate TQM's focus on the customer, whose wants and needs take priority in shaping organizational practices.

To achieve this widespread commitment to TQM, the organization must, in turn, display a new level of commitment to its employees. To get people to take part actively and productively in doing daily work, controlling job activities, solving problems, and contributing to the organization in new ways means they have to be secure in themselves, their job, and even their families.

Labor-management relations under TQM must become a joint endeavor, with members of both groups working together as a team. TQM cannot be handed down by management as a fiat for workers to accept. If it is presented this way, employees will be less likely to embrace the changes required by TQM; and labor unions will be certain to pose formidable roadblocks. Some unions, like the International Association of Machinists, have felt so threatened when TQM programs are mandated from the "top down" that union leaders have issued white papers urging members to challenge all "team concept" programs.

Management personnel must be prepared to grapple with their own problems under TQM. Learning to be responsive to the feelings, beliefs, and values of each employee is no easy task. Changing from a reliance on "our qualifications and history of service" to a continual reassessment of what constitutes value to the customer is often a wrenching experience for managers and executives.

We do not have easy answers for dealing with the difficulties that often arise when an organization moves toward its TQM vision. There are plenty of illustrations in the literature about how some companies have addressed these issues, and we recommend reading about them to learn what has been done.

Conclusion

Developing your STEM/TQM system can take many forms. Chapter 1 detailed the Deming, Baldrige, and Juran frameworks. Yet the concepts presented in this chapter show that those models (and others like them) are far from sufficient—for they all fail to address the question of *how* one goes about developing and implementing TQM.

In Part II of this book, we examine each facet of TQM program development—from pre-program preparation to organizational issues and individual projects—to show how the principles of Breakthrough Thinking provide the methodology that conventional problem-solving approaches fail to include. As just one example of the difference that this methodology makes, figure 5-2 shows how Breakthrough Thinking reshaped an announcement of a continuous quality improvement program at a company. Notice how even the most "standard" of activities–like how you go about establishing a quality council, training facilitators, setting up teams, and so forth–are affected by the changed mode of thinking.

CONTINUOUS IMPROVEMENT
AT _ _ _ _
(with Breakthrough Thinking Modifications)

Goal:
To achieve total customer satisfaction by instilling in each _ _ _ _ employee the desire and initiative to improve -- daily -- the methods and attitudes each uses in performing his/her duties.

Objectives:
1. Provide the managerial support and commitment necessary to achieve the goal and related objectives.

2. Provide adequate training to all employees on the principles of total quality, customer satisfaction, and breakthrough thinking for planning, designing, improving, and problem-solving.

3. Integrate the principles and practices of managing total quality in all daily operations.

The "Goal and Objectives" will be achieved via the following milestones:
1. Expose management to the principles of TQM and breakthrough thinking and the practices of CI through a special half-day orientation training (2/91).

2. Train selected and volunteer staff to serve as breakthrough thinking "quality facilitators" and instructors (4/91).

3. Develop with breakthrough thinking the CI materials for implementation at - - - - (5/91-9/91).

4. Train selected staff managers and volunteer leaders in the "total quality" concept and their roles (7/91).

5. Set up with breakthrough thinking a "quality council" to oversee the training, implementation, and on-going activities of CI (8/91).

6. Integrate CI into the annual planning and budgeting cycle as much as possible (8/91).

7. Begin staff training in principles, practices, and breakthrough thinking for planning, improving and problem solving.

8. Integrate CI into the customer service center" concept, staff to begin to identify internal/external customer requirements, expand purposes of work processes, identify fundamental value-adding or unit operations, and establish measures of effectiveness for the selected purpose level (10/91).

9. Complete initial training, begin to design and establish "teams" for planning, improving, problem solving, and creative actions (12/91).

10. Develop breakthrough thinking illustrative cases, monitor results of training, and take corrective action (12/91 - 2/92).

11. "Quality council" use breakthrough thinking to develop and implement a "reward and recognition" program for outstanding achievement (11/91 - 1/91).

12. Form "first" project team (see milestone 9) (1/92).

Figure 5-2. Breakthrough Thinking methodology.

Part II applies the Breakthrough Thinking pattern of reasoning to all the phases and steps that deal with TQM issues in a specific organization. The General Flow of Reasoning for integrating Breakthrough Thinking with TQM is shown in figure 5-3. The presentation of these phases and steps is arranged to show how the many decisions involved in an activity are made more effectively through Breakthrough Thinking.

Chapter 6 deals with the general design, customization, and implementation of the whole TQM program. Similarly, Chapter 7 deals with the design and implementation of each process or project within the larger TQM system.

Chapters 8 through 13 list the steps to follow for each project. Chapter 14 again deals with the total program, integrating the results of all TQM activities and projects into the Strategic Total Enterprise Management (STEM) system, including the process of setting up a mechanism for continual improvement based on the Betterment Timeline principle. Chapters 8 through 13 explain *how* the pattern of reasoning or steps are done for each problem, improvement plan, installation, opportunity, program, project, design, or activity. The pattern of reasoning is used over and over, almost at every point where a decision is needed. Making decisions, therefore, should always involve developing purposes (Chapter 8), developing options for solutions after next (Chapter 9), assessing the options (Chapter 10), developing the recommendations (Chapter 11), detailing the recommendation (Chapter 12), and developing the implementation plan (Chapter 13).

Step	Activity with • = Results/Outcomes	TQM and Breakthrough Thinking Principles	Related Techniques, Resources, and Considerations*	Chapter
1	Set up TQM systems • System of TQM program • Mission of enterprise • Values and beliefs • Enterprise vision and strategic plan	All Breakthrough Thinking principles and all TQM methodologies	Whole Brain Affinity Diagram, Radar Chart	6
2	Identify pilot and/or primary projects • Initial plan of action and timeline	Uniqueness, Purposes, People Design, Betterment Timeline; transitional timeline	Customer needs, external environment assessment, internal readiness, financial status, corporate performance indicators, GANTT charts, couplet method. Kano survey	7
3	Establish pilot project system • Purpose of project, people on team, resources needed, work program	All Breakthrough Thinking principles; analysis diagram	PLAN	7
4	List possible purposes for system of project	Uniqueness, Purposes; customer focus	Brainstorming, computer recording, survey, questionnaire, PLAN, Whole Brain Affinity Process	8
5	Develop purpose hierarchies	Purposes, People Design	Couplet method, expansion guides, customer purposes, purposes of customer questionnaire, PLAN	8

* See Appendix for an explanation of the techniques.

Figure 5-3. General flow of reasoning for integrating Breakthrough Thinking® in Total Quality Management. (Page 1 of 6)

Step	Activity with • = Results/Outcomes	TQM and Breakthrough Thinking Principles	Related Techniques, Resources, and Considerations*	Chapter
6	Determine criteria to select purpose level	Purpose, Limited Information Collection	Key driving elements, real issue focusing, composite performance indicators, PLAN, couplet method	8
7	Select focus purpose(s) at largest possible level • Focus purpose(s) for problem area or system to be designed or improved	Purpose, Systems, People Design; customer focus, PDCA	Multi-attribute utility evaluation based on one criterion at a time, consensus from largest level to smallest, driving elements, PLAN, couplet method, tree diagram	8
8	Establish measures of effectiveness, (values, goals, objectives) • Factors to indicate amount of success in achieving purpose(s)	Uniqueness, Purpose, Systems, Limited Information Collection; PDCA cycle	Performance indicators, readiness, current status of measures not documented, elimination of unneeded measures currently documented, basic QC tools	8
9	Determine if subgroups on functional components are needed • Subgroups on functional components, each of which starts with Purpose expansion	Uniqueness, Purpose, Systems; critical process analysis, customer supplier map	Functional component inverse hierarchy, couplet method, tree diagram	8
10	Generate many solution-after-next options	Purpose, Solution-After-Next, Systems, Limited Information Collection, People Design; synthesize the opportunity	Stimulator lists, computer programs, synectics, ideal system, bisociation with purpose, force field analysis	9

* See Appendix for an explanation of the techniques.

Figure 5-3.   General flow of reasoning for integrating Breakthrough Thinking® in Total Quality Management.   (Page 2 of 6)

Step	Activity with ● = Results/Outcomes	TQM and Breakthrough Thinking Principles	Related Techniques, Resources, and Considerations*	Chapter
11	Assess solution-after-next options	Uniqueness, Purpose, Systems, Limited Information Collection, People Design, Betterment Timeline	Regularities, irregularities, major components, key tactics, system matrix, couplet method, radar chart, tree diagram	10
12	Select solution-after-next target (Feasible Ideal System Target) for regularity conditions ● Solution-after-next target	Uniqueness, Purpose, Systems, Limited Information Collection, People Design, Betterment Timeline; breakthrough deployment objectives, measures of effectiveness	Decision chart, multi-attribute utility, regularities, workability analysis, system matrix	10
13	Modify the target to incorporate needed irregularity conditions	Uniqueness, Purpose, Systems, Limited Information Collection, People Design, Betterment Timeline; transitional timeline	System matrix, major alternatives, force field analysis, major components, details of system, key metrics	11
14	Choose and specify the recommended changes or system that stays as close as possible to the target ● Recommended actions	All Breakthrough Thinking Principles; customer focus	Decision chart, system matrix, workability analysis	11
15	Prepare proposal for approval (concurrent with step 16)	All Breakthrough Thinking Principles; customer focus, team building	Purpose format, system matrix, presentation tools (e.g., video, slides, etc.)	11

* See Appendix for an explanation of the techniques.

Figure 5-3. General flow of reasoning for integrating Breakthrough Thinking® in Total Quality Management. (Page 3 of 6)

Step	Activity with ● = Results/Outcomes	TQM and Breakthrough Thinking Principles	Related Techniques, Resources, and Considerations*	Chapter
16	Prepare all people not involved to date with background on recommendation, benefits, costs, future changes ● Proposal to implement recommended actions	All Breakthrough Thinking Principles; customer focus, listening and communication	Written and oral presentation, formatting, sequence/review/change, transitional timeline	11
17	Detail the recommendation to have all specifications needed for installation	Systems, Limited Information Collection, People Design, Betterment Timeline; transitional timeline	System matrix, tree diagram, cause and effect diagram, operational plans	12
18	Prepare the installation plan (equipment and material purchases, training, building modifications, resources, etc.) including scheduled betterment dates ● Installation plan	All Breakthrough Thinking Principles; customer focus	System matrix, GANTT chart, operational plans, analysis chart, solution and effect diagram	13
19	Install the recommendations, take necessary actions, and so forth ● Installed system	All Breakthrough Thinking Principles; teaming principles	Technical drawings, computer programs, job training, etc.	14

* See Appendix for an explanation of the techniques.

Figure 5-3. General flow of reasoning for integrating Breakthrough Thinking® in Total Quality Management. (Page 4 of 6)

Step	Activity with • = Results/Outcomes	TQM and Breakthrough Thinking Principles	Related Techniques, Resources, and Considerations*	Chapter
20	Standardize performance on installed system • System performing at or above specified levels	Purposes, Solution-After-Next, Systems, Betterment Timeline; transitional timeline, purposes metrics	All daily management tools and techniques	14
21	Review system at betterment timeline date to seek more changes toward solution-after-next target • Recommended actions and changes to make system better and closer to target	All Breakthrough Thinking Principles; customer focus	PDCA/SDCA, all daily management tools and techniques	14, 15
22	Repeat above step as often as planned in the proposal and installation plan • Further actions and changes to make system better and closer to target	All Breakthrough Thinking Principles; customer focus	All daily management tools and techniques	14, 15
23	Set up project to develop purpose and solutions-after-next again for the system or functional area • New solution-after-next target and action plan for system	All Breakthrough Thinking Principles; customer focus	Methods described in Chapters 8 through 13, PLAN	7

* See Appendix for an explanation of the techniques.

Figure 5-3. General flow of reasoning for integrating Breakthrough Thinking® in Total Quality Management. (Page 5 of 6)

Step	Activity with • = Results/Outcomes	TQM and Breakthrough Thinking Principles	Related Techniques, Resources, and Considerations*	Chapter
24	Set up top management group to develop purposes and solutions-after-next again for the TQM program and its movement toward STEM • "System" of TQM program and STEM process	All Breakthrough Thinking Principles; customer focus, steering committee	Methods described in Chapters 8 through 13, PLAN, STEM	6, 14 15, 16

* See Appendix for an explanation of the techniques.

Figure 5-3. General flow of reasoning for integrating Breakthrough Thinking® in Total Quality Management. (Page 6 of 6)

Part II
The Breakthrough Thinking Process

Designing and Implementing the TQM Program

The complete process for planning and implementing TQM, based on the principles of Breakthrough Thinking, consists of the following steps and results. (The number in parentheses refers to the chapter where the step is described.) Chapter 6 describes methods for and illustrates the Breakthrough Thinking Process (Chapter 5) highlighted below:

Step*	Result
1. Set up TQM program (6)	TQM mission, values, strategic plan
2. Identify primary projects and activities (7)	Initial plan of action and timeline
3. Set up TQM project (7)	Project system (purposes, people, etc.)
4. List possible purposes (8)	
5. Develop purpose hierarchies (8)	
6. Determine criteria to select purpose level (8)	
7. Select purpose(s) (8)	Focus purpose(s) in a hierarchical context
8. Establish measures of purpose accomplishment (8)	Success factors
9. Establish subgroups if needed (8)	Subgroups established

* The number in parentheses after each step refers to the chapter in which the step is described

Step*	Result
10. Generate many solution-after-next options (9)	List of viable alternatives
11. Assess solution-after-next options (10)	
12. Select solution-after-next target (10)	Target solution-after-next
13. Modify target for irregularities (11)	
14. Choose recommended changes (11)	Recommendations
15. Prepare proposal (12)	Proposal
16. Inform people not involved to date (12)	
17. Detail recommendations (12)	Complete recommendation specifications
18. Prepare installation plan (13)	Installation plan
19. Install recommendations (13)	Installed system
20. Standardize performances (13)	System performance measures
21. Review project at betterment timeline date (14-15)	Next recommended changes
22. Repeat step 21 (14-15)	Further actions and changes

* The number in parentheses after each step refers to the chapter in which the step is described

Each organization has its own history, culture, record of performance, and leadership. Such a wide variation from one organization to another means that the assignment of setting up a TQM program is a unique problem that cannot be solved by force-fitting a "standard" model into the organization. Nor can a "standard" set of actions (e.g.

make TQM presentations at all employee levels, set up teams in all parts of the organization, train team members, set up measurements, and do strategic planning) fit every organization. This chapter will show how Breakthrough Thinking can provide the common language and way to proceed to develop the most effective plan for implementing *your* TQM program, leading to a Strategic Total Enterprise Management system–or "STEM" (see Chapter 2).

Awareness

It is very difficult to imagine that people, especially executives and managers, in any organization may not realize how important it is to commit to total quality. In almost all cases, several people come to the conclusion that their organization should have a TQM program, and they even may recognize that a STEM framework ought to be the eventual aim. Yet, there are many ways in which these aims will be interpreted and resultant programs structured, based in large part on the background and knowledge base of the organization and its people.

In any event, the implementation of TQM will involve significant, far-reaching changes in the organization. It will cause a modification in people's attitudes, behaviors, actions, and habits. No one will be untouched.

In short, adopting TQM means transforming the organization's culture. Yet doing this is no easy task. Change is generally viewed as a hostile assault on the system, and a challenge to people's ingrained beliefs. Responding to changes necessitated by TQM, people are likely to have the following defensive reactions:

- Why change?
- Aren't we successful?
- What's wrong?
- This too shall pass–it's just another fad.
- This is too rigid, too structured.

The reason these thoughts and questions arise is that people become comfortable with a system. The system may be imperfect, but it is predictable, and this predictability helps solidify the status quo. Change, even suggested change, begins to rock the boat. Boat rockers are seldom welcome in an established system.

Implementing TQM, organizations must therefore figure out how to make change palatable to those in the system. Change must be planned and introduced in an organized, timely, and sensible manner. Difficulties described here and in Chapter 2 can be avoided.

Unfortunately, in their rush to embrace TQM, most organizations overlook its implementation process as a problem that needs its own design. They hastily choose an approach or adopt someone's prescribed format—convince top-level leaders, create a study group, establish an action task force, train everyone in the techniques, and so on. Then a few months later, they wonder why it did not work. The fact is, just as there is no turnkey TQM program, neither is there a ready-made process for implementing TQM. Both the program and implementation process require hard work, patience, discipline, and a long-range view.

Organizations that chase "quick fix" approaches to TQM are wasting scarce resources, which they should be channeling into the development of their own program and implementation process.

Designing the TQM Process with Breakthrough Thinking

In customizing a plan for implementing a TQM program, the likelihood is very high that the plan will be redone several times as the number of people who become involved at each stage increases. Breakthrough Thinking principles not only anticipate this iteration as a means of keeping the plan continuously up-to-date; they also foster a "buy-in" by all the people as a means of accommodating the uniqueness of each organization.

As useful as Breakthrough Thinking will prove to be for designing your TQM program and implementation process, the formalities of the various techniques described in the next six chapters are often too overwhelming at this early stage. Just adhering to the broad outlines of the principles is what is needed at this point.

The previous paragraphs note how the *Uniqueness Principle* applies in planning a TQM implementation process. It also applies in naming a group to design the TQM program, since the people in one organization will *always* be different from those in another.

As a rule, the individuals selected to design the TQM program should be key senior executives who have the ability, interest, and authority to design and implement organizational change. To bring desired changes, these executives should function as a team in establishing the plan (based on an expansion of purposes, the desired state of the program and organization, the road map or system to achieve it, the people to get involved, the types of TQM training for the rest of the organization, the milestones on a betterment timeline for the program, and the specific types of information to collect about the organization).

While all members of this group need their roles and responsibilities clearly defined, it is particularly important for the group to have a *sponsor*. Ideally either the president or CEO, the sponsor is vitally important to the entire effort, as the following list of duties illustrates:

- Articulate a clear, definable vision and mission for the organization
- Share knowledge to empower others
- Participate in team member selection
- Scope the boundaries of the effort
- Ensure that appropriate and effective training is delivered
- Report group or team performance to the Board of Directors
- Monitor progress
- Provide required resources
- Coach and motivate the group or team
- Empower the group or team to act
- Review recommended changes
- Assist in the implementation of changes
- Recognize and celebrate with the group or team their successes

The group designing the TQM implementation process almost always needs a Breakthrough Thinking or STEM facilitator. The conventional thinking approach is so pervasive that a group without such assistance is almost certain to veer off track by collecting a great deal of information that is not needed. A facilitator keeps the group focused on the key principles, especially *Limited Information Collection*. The facilitator can also provide key assistance to the sponsor or group leader, such as taking notes, getting everyone in the group involved, laying out the pattern of reasoning, and maintaining and setting up schedules.

The *Purposes Principle* gets the group to explore the various missions and aims of the TQM process and expand them into a hierarchy. Each organization will have a different perspective on what it needs to accomplish. The level of the initial purpose selected for the TQM process must be related to the bigger purposes and missions of the organization as identified in the hierarchy.

The *Solution-after-Next Principle* gets the group to generate different visions of how their TQM program and the organization as a whole should operate in, say, three or four years' time. Sorting out these visions leads to a specific target of what the company should be in that time frame. With this target in mind, the group can then determine the format and structure of the TQM program now, while conceptualizing future modifications as the organization moves toward the STEM model.

The *Systems Principle* lets the group detail the elements and dimensions of its installation plan to be sure all features are considered. *Inputs* of information, training, and resources need to be considered, as do the formats, reports, and results of *outputs;* the order and priority of activities and projects in the implementation *sequence;* the desired characteristics and policies of the cultural *environment;* the facilitators, trainers, support staff, operating personnel, executive sponsor, mentors, and other *human agents;* the space, equipment, and location of *physical catalysts;* and *information aids,* such as the library and computer databases.

The *People Design Principle* is partly considered in the Systems Principle. Another part of this principle concerns communications with the whole organization about TQM plans, for it is not possible to get everyone involved at this early stage. The communications strategy can itself be designed with these same principles. It may be undertaken by the primary team or assigned to a secondary team once the basic dimensions of the TQM process have been established.

The *Betterment Timeline Principle* calls for the primary team to maintain responsibility for the overall effort until TQM processes are institutionalized as normal ways of operating. Most desirable would be the transformation of this group into a steering committee for TQM activities. This would keep the key executives continually involved with the efforts, receiving progress reports and initiating changes as needed. It would also help the executives modify their own behavior so that total quality and Breakthrough Thinking become a natural part of everyday performance. The Betterment Timeline Principle also calls for scheduling a complete redesign of the TQM process at some point: What would the TQM process be if it were begun all over again? Each organization needs to consider this basic question at regular intervals.

A Case Illustration

The executive director of a 500-employee county government department decided to install a TQM program. She had heard about TQM from various management conferences, magazines of her professional associations, and trade newsletters. She also was concerned about the perception of the public (the department's customers) concerning her department, for example, the timeliness of providing service, the number of complaints about inaccuracies, the county board's reluctance to provide additional funds, the increasing number of poor performance reports about employees, the lack of space for the number of people who came to the department's offices, and so on. In addition, a multi-million dollar expenditure for a new computer and advanced information system was not producing any results even close to what was projected. Problems included long delays in installation, unavailable software, ineffective results from the software that was available, lack of employee understanding about what to do with the system, and so on. There was also rather high turnover among the top-level managers.

She discussed these concerns with her departmental and county colleagues and others from private organizations for a few months. The administrative group of the department decided to proceed with setting up a TQM system. The executive director eventually called a consultant who had been recommended to her. He was a Breakthrough Thinking facilitator in TQM and other areas.

Her request to him was to "install a TQM program," preferably one of the TQM models she had read and heard about. She assumed, based on conventional reasoning, that the model could just be "shoved" onto her department. She apparently didn't learn from the computer and information disaster how wrong this assumption could be. Unfortunately, she typifies the "quick fix" mentality of too many executives and managers.

In a similar unfortunate vein, almost all consultants are conventional thinkers. They believe their expertise in a particular process, technology, or analysis technique is all that is needed when receiving a request such as this one. They would ordinarily proceed to lay out *the* TQM model as the vision of what should be installed in the department. They would spend large amounts of time collecting information they considered important, despite what the department executives would find useful. They would proudly make elegant presentations about all of the data and the components of *the* TQM model they were about to install.

Sadly, they do not ask about what purposes the organization would like to accomplish through TQM, nor do they investigate the larger purposes or the TQM structure that would move it toward bigger ends. They just assume that "getting all the facts" is sufficient.

The Breakthrough Thinking consultant, however, took a different tack. After an hour-long introduction to the department by the executive director, he explained the importance of having the department customize its own TQM program and installation plan. This took another half an hour. The rest of the three-hour meeting was spent in setting up the procedure for having the department plan its TQM activities. The key executives would comprise the group to do this–the executive director, administrative director, professional director, information system manager, and human resources manager.

The group met for a full afternoon a week later, facilitated by the Breakthrough Thinking consultant. After a very brief review of what was to be done, the group listed the purposes shown in figure 6-1.

1.	Develop proposal to set up TQM and related planning for whole county
2.	Enhance customer service
3.	Solicit internal and external support
4.	Determine if decentralization or regionalization is feasible
5.	Improve quality of professional service
6.	Recruit highly skilled people
7.	Define departmental quality directions
8.	Anticipate increase in workload
9.	Support for citizens and families affected by services
10.	Restructure toward future socioeconomic needs of the county
11.	Take multi-disciplinary approach to TQM
12.	Expedite services
13.	Define criteria for service delivery response in years of severe budget constraints
14.	Get managers to be entrepreneurs
15.	Select and develop mechanism to use
16.	Be better aligned with developmental research in sciences
17.	Market department services
18.	Get private sector funding/donations
19.	Improve residents and educate residents
20.	Become center for training all professionals (labs, social work, etc.)

Figure 6-1. Purposes of TQM program and installation plan
(As actually identified by the Group). (Page 1 of 2)

21. Help us better manage current resources

22. Sophisticate investigative procedures

23. Expand utilization of advanced technological systems tissue harvesting and organ transplantation

24. Expand Trip Reduction Plan

25. Project future needs

26. Prepare for major disasters

27. Identify untapped resources

28. Plan for central facility

29. Avoid waste and duplicate use of resources

30. Develop intra- and interagency training and cooperation. 31.

    Educate county board of the funding sources, sheriff, etc., about TQM and planning

32. Enhance employee morale

33. Identify possible consolidations

34. Incorporate latest technology (information system, operations)

35. Develop better control for spread of poor results and safety to public and employees

36. Improve public relations image and dealings with the media

Figure 6-1. Purposes of TQM program and installation plan
(As actually identified by the Group). (Page 2 of 2)

The group then developed the hierarchy shown in figure 6-2, using the size of the scope of the purpose statement as the way to locate it in the hierarchy (Chapter 8 explains this as one of the alternative ways of developing the purpose hierarchy). The numbers referred to in figure 6-2 are the purposes listed in figure 6-1.

The group developed the statements at each level to capture the intent of the various purpose statements included there. After selecting level *Large* as the focus purpose, the group sketched out a few ideas about how to accomplish that purpose. It then provided details about the idea selected as the most desirable target before using a system matrix (figure 6-3) to state what would be done to get the TQM process under way.

Small	8, 9, 11, 15, 22, 24, 26, 27, 29, 33, 34, 35 To identify, within an interdisciplinary approach, areas for new services, technology, consolidation, waste reduction, and potential environmental, fiscal, and disaster preparation considerations.
Medium Small	1, 10, 20, 21, 23 To define the leadership role in professional service investigation and technological systems utilization with sensitivity toward future cultural and population growth throughout the county.
Medium	4, 6, 13, 19, 28, 30, 32, 36 To provide, under variable budget conditions, effective and high quality human, physical, and organizational resources that make services available with favorable internal and external images.
Medium Large	7 To define departmental and TQM directions.
Large	16, 25 To project future customer and quality needs and to include scientific and technological advancements.
Very Large	3, 5, 14, 17, 18, 31 To identify internal and external support sources to accomplish directions, including management entrepreneurs and marketing efforts.
Extra Large	5, 31 To promote and deliver improved services, including education of the County Board about TQM.
Very Big	2 To enhance citizen services.

Figure 6-2. Purpose hierarchy for county department TQM program.

Inputs	Shareholders, Management, County Board, Chairman, Sheriff, County Counsel, Funeral Directors, Medical Schools, "Significant Others"
Outputs	Monitoring reports, comparison with previous statistics, customer evaluation reports, plans for future TQM activities
Sequence	Implementation plan by ?? (number of months) Method of approach Order of dealing with "inputs" Project schedule Training of employees in Breakthrough Thinking and TQM ideas
Environment	Responsibility and lines of authority. Physical, social, and organizational location–local, off-site, public hearings, and so on
Human Agents	Consultants, internally trained facilitators
Physical Catalysts	Tables, rooms, chairs, computers
Information Aids	Statistics or data group, databases, facilitator's guide

Figure 6-3.   Rough outline of TQM system for county department (Based on deliberations from first session).

The group members had many comments about the process during and after the session:

"I didn't realize that TQM involved that purpose."

"The selected purpose is not what I thought a TQM program would try to accomplish, but I'm glad we found it."

"I am no longer skeptical about setting up a TQM program."

"Now I know how badly we went about the development of the information system."

"This process makes it much easier for me to explain what we're doing to my employees."

These comments respond to areas of concern mentioned in Chapters 1 and 2 as typical pitfalls that encumber many of today's TQM efforts.

Besides the critical decision about what TQM should really be doing, the commitment of the top executives was now complete—and no time was wasted collecting information that would not have even been relevant to what was now the focus.

The system matrix description of the plan to put into operation also noted "blanks" where information might be needed in the future.

Readiness Conditions

How TQM is customized for an organization depends not only on its unique blend of many factors, but also on its level of readiness. The level of an organization's readiness hinges largely on its cultural climate. For example, an autocratic management culture will minimize an organization's readiness for a high level of employee participation in problem solving. In many ways, an organization's readiness factors are surrogate measures of its culture. Low measures on most readiness scales would clearly indicate that a major effort must be made to change the cultural conditions before launching a TQM program. The time it takes to get a product or service from conception to commercialization is also a good indicator of an organization's cultural conditions.

There are two types of readiness conditions that are incumbent to a TQM program: customer factors and internal organizational factors.

Since TQM and STEM deal with strategic processes, we will define initially what we believe are the customer readiness factors or conditions related to customer satisfactions. Then we will define the internal readiness factors that affect customization.

Customer Readiness Factors

- *Quality:* How well the organization meets (or exceeds) customer expectations in a cost competitive manner.

- *Customer demography:*   How knowledgeable the organization is about customer types, customer segmentation, stratified markets, etc.
- *Customer requirements:*   How thoroughly the organization understands what each of its different customer demographics require to meet their needs and expectations.
- *Deliverables:*   How well the organization delivers its products and services (i.e., timeliness, responsiveness, price, etc.).
- *Technologies:*   How well the organization incorporates available technologies into its products and services.
- *Product/Service Development:*   How fast the organization's time to market is for new products and services.

Determining customer readiness conditions also requires an evaluation of the enterprise's direction in relation to its strategic business plan.

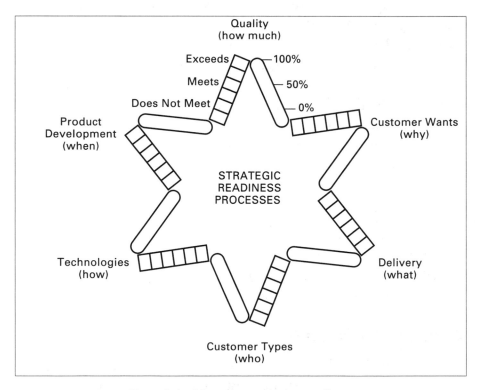

Figure 6-4. Measuring customer readiness.

Two separate measures—one of *corporate* perceptions and the other of *customer* perceptions—could be used to indicate this type of readiness, if the information is found to be needed (as indicated by the Limited Information Collection principle). Figure 6-4 illustrates these two measures in relation to the customer readiness factors.

The thermometer is used to measure *corporate perceptions,* achieved through consensus, of how well your current systems are performing. The ladder is used to measure *customer perceptions* of how the current system is performing in meeting their needs and expectations. The customer perceptions uses a qualitative scale while the corporate perceptions uses a quantitative scale. Both scales are rated through a data-driven consensus process.

This readiness assessment is accomplished initially by having the top executives in the corporation assess through consensus the factors on both scales. Their assessment of the organization's status and customer relations must be frank and honest.[1] The readiness assessment consensus results can be validated in two ways.

The first validation, as depicted on the thermometer, is done by having the top executives repeat the exercise with their staff. Major discrepancies highlighted by this exercise should again be reviewed by the executive team to get a good indication of readiness. This assessment of readiness might also identify the most critical TQM projects to begin working on with Breakthrough Thinking.

The second validation, depicted on the ladder, is done by having representatives from key customer segments, along with members of the executive group, review the initial readiness assessment results (see figure 6-5).

The gaps between perception and reality both in the organization and with the customer are quantified using the matrix shown in figure 6-5.

---

1. During this assessment process, any pockets of excellence that exist in the organization should be documented. These pockets of excellence can be highlighted later to stimulate the development of solution ideas in the solution-after-next (SAN) process. This will also hasten the adaptation of available technology in the organization.

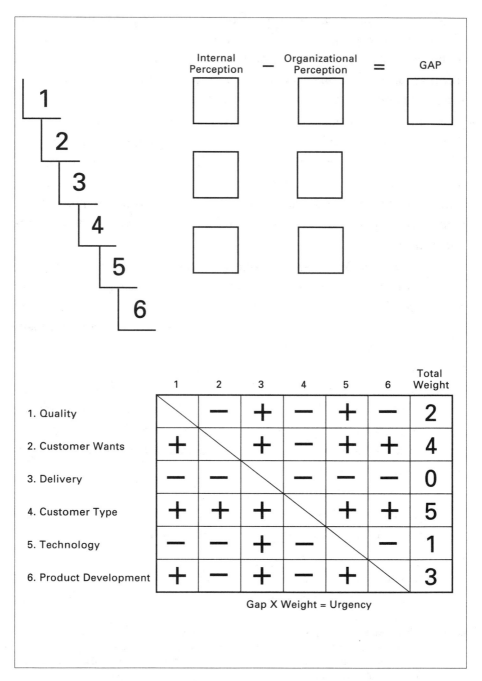

Figure 6-5. Readiness gaps based on customer factors.

This kind of matrix is particularly valuable because it examines key factors from a cause/effect perspective. For example, does Quality *cause* customer wants, or is Quality a *result* of customer wants? In most organizations, customer wants cause Quality, so in the matrix Quality would get a "-" and Customer Wants would get a "+."

As with the thermometer and ladder measures in figure 6-4, the gaps in readiness based on customer factors also help to identify what projects may need work early in the TQM process.

Internal Readiness Factors

The following internal factors and conditions significantly affect the readiness level of an organization in moving toward TQM and STEM.

Commitment to Principles

Management practices of ethics and morality match their statements about them, are understood by all within the enterprise, and form the basis for all decisions. These values raise the organization from the level of laws to one of mutual respect.

Trust

One person can believe what another says. Actions of one person or group are treated with credibility and integrity by others. People are not suspicious of one another.

Employment Conditions

Job security is high; physical working conditions are people-oriented (i.e., noise, dust, heat/cold are greatly minimized); pay levels are competitive; safety is emphasized; career/promotion paths are known.

Policy Commitments

Explicit statements are made to guide actions of all organization members toward seeking improvement in human capabilities and performance, generating interest in continuing change, sharing gains from improvements, lowering the level of decision making, and so forth.

Resource Commitments

The organization is willing to provide professional facilitation services for all organizational roles and functions, allocate top management time to the TQM effort, and coordinate and allocate resources.

Open Communications

People are not threatened; data and information are shared; placing blame is not the objective of communications; decision making is shared; free discussion of uncertainties and ambiguities takes place; confidences are maintained.

Conduct toward Improvement and Change

People perceive change as necessary to organizational health. They are willing to modify organizational structures if needed, focus on purposes and measures of effectiveness, seek to motivate others to search for change, and feel that work produces one form of life's satisfactions. Evaluations of efforts are received favorably; new goals and opportunities are sought to provide control over the change process; people seek to understand the nature and purposes of change in relation to other purposeful activities; and learning of all types is encouraged.

Data and Information

Measures of organizational performance serve as a base of comparison (e.g., cost benefit ratio) for proposals and implemented changes; timelines are prepared to ensure availability of resources; measures describe extent of resource availability; linkages are established with sources of new ideas and research results; and so on.

Organizational Flexibility

People can cope with discontinuities and adapt to technological advances; they are willing to experiment and deal with conflicts of all types. The organization is characterized by a close alignment of customer/client/user needs, a degree of decentralization, complexity of processes and capital investments, compatibility of organizational levels and group norms toward directions and goals, and cohesiveness in actions.

To evaluate an organization on these internal readiness factors, we suggest that executives, managers, and employees be asked to assess each factor, using a scale of 0-100 (undesirable to desirable levels). While no organizational unit will score high (say 70 to 75) on each of the readiness factors, nor will more than just a few soon attain high scores on all of them, the measures will indicate where changes are needed. Specifically, change should be sought for those factors with (1) an average score of 50 or lower from any level of evaluator, (2) scores that differ significantly among each level of evaluators, (3) scores that differ significantly *on average* among the three levels of evaluators, or (4) any combination of these.

Conclusion

The rest of the chapters in Part II of this book, especially Chapters 8 through 13, will explain the techniques that can be useful when customizing a TQM program for your organization. The intent of this chapter was to illustrate what needs to be accomplished right at the start. Following an effective thinking process at the very beginning not only develops a better program, but also serves as an excellent procedural model for all subsequent TQM projects and activities.

In effect, the planning and thinking process for setting up a TQM program are a series of functions to be accomplished, not a set of techniques and tools to be applied nor a standard model to install (see Chapter 5, figure 5-3). These functions are what the Breakthrough Thinking principles address–that is, purposes, solutions after-next, systems details, people involvement, and implementation. The techniques needed to achieve these functions will vary from situation to situation.

Setting Up the TQM Project

The complete process for planning and implementing TQM, based on the principles of Breakthrough Thinking, consists of the following steps and results. Chapter 7 addresses those steps that have to do with setting up the TQM project (highlighted below).

Step*	Result
1. Set up TQM program (6)	TQM mission, values, strategic plan
2. Identify primary projects and activities (7)	Initial plan of action and timeline
3. Set up TQM project (7)	Project system (purposes, people, etc.)
4. List possible purposes (8)	
5. Develop purpose hierarchies (8)	
6. Determine criteria to select purpose level (8)	
7. Select purpose(s) (8)	Focus purpose(s) in a hierarchical context
8. Establish measures of purpose accomplishment (8)	Success factors
9. Establish subgroups if needed (8)	Subgroups established
*The number in parentheses after each step refers to the chapter in which the step is described	

Step*	Result
10. Generate many solution-after-next options (9)	List of viable alternatives
11. Assess solution-after-next options (10)	
12. Select solution-after-next target (10)	Target solution-after-next
13. Modify target for irregularities (11)	
14. Choose recommended changes (11)	Recommendations
15. Prepare proposal (12)	Proposal
16. Inform people not involved to date (12)	
17. Detail recommendations (12)	Complete recommendation specifications
18. Prepare installation plan (13)	Installation plan
19. Install recommendations (13)	Installed system
20. Standardize performances (13)	System performance measures
21. Review project at betterment timeline date (14-15)	Next recommended changes
22. Repeat step 21 (14-15)	Further actions and changes

* The number in parentheses after each step refers to the chapter in which the step is described

Establishing a TQM program does not, by itself, improve quality, satisfy customers, or enhance performance. It is but the beginning of an ongoing process in which change is continuous. Chapter 6 emphasized the importance of designing the TQM program and implementation process so that *movement toward* achieving significant results occurs as quickly as possible.

"The rubber meets the road" when a project established to address a particular problem, issue, or opportunity gets started. It should occur under the most favorable conditions of readiness possible and, ideally, be part of an executive-backed TQM program. That is, a project is best started when it is selected by the TQM steering committee and placed on its priority list (see "sequence" element of the systems description in Chapter 6).

However, projects arise from many other sources as well. A customer may have a special need, a competitor may introduce a new product at a price below yours, the Total Productive Maintenance program may have a high priority need, strategic planning activities may require a marketing plan, or budgetary constraints may require a redesign of the organizational structure–all of which give rise to different types of projects.

Whatever the source of the project, work must proceed in a way that assures all factors and conditions are considered in developing the recommendations. This is as true of a project arising from TQM sponsorship as it is for one arising from any other source. Herein lies another advantage of Breakthrough Thinking–providing a total systems and "full spectrum creativity"[SM] view for every project, as well as obtaining the most effective solutions that best utilize resources (humans, money, time).

Whenever the topic of discussion is a project, many people assume that the extensive literature about project management can be used directly. A great deal of it is valuable and will be used in this chapter, but the aim of this book is to show how Break-through Thinking changes these ordinary perceptions to arrive at more effective results.

For example, a company with rapidly increasing sales faced a myriad of problems: it was experiencing significant delays in shipping its products; the quality of what was shipped caused many customer complaints; the factory was seriously overcrowded; and costs and overtime were high. The president, vice presidents, plant manager, and others met for six to eight months about the problems, and decided to build a facility that would double factory capacity. The president assembled a project team to do this, and called in a consultant to help them. When the consultant met with the team, he asked them right away to "design the project" (that is, treat the project itself as a system). To do this, he had the group identify the purposes of the *project*, not the purposes of the factory or manufacturing system. In just two hours, the group had made a purpose hierarchy and selected the purpose of the project as "to develop management control systems." Doubling the factory capacity was a smaller problem that they might or might not consider only after effective management control systems were developed.

Ordinary project management techniques could have been used in this case, but it would have been wrong to do so. Almost anyone could have designed a factory with double the capacity, but this would have been a tremendous waste of resources, for the best solution to the problem did not require any additional factory space at all!

Once the right purpose to work on had been identified, the project itself could be set up, based on the following elements of the system matrix:

- What *inputs* would be needed?
- What *outputs* could be expected?
- What *sequence* or set of steps should be followed?
- What *environmental conditions* would be required?
- What *human agents* should be included?
- What *physical catalysts* would be needed?
- What *information aids* would be useful?

Project Management[1]

Interestingly, the most important part of project management has nothing to do with the scheduling, budgeting, control, or execution of the work. Certainly all of these issues are critical to successful projects,

---

1. Adapted from Michael Rigg, "Breakthrough Thinking—Improving Project Effectiveness," *Industrial Engineering*, Vol. 23, No. 6, June 1991, p. 19–22.

but they are not sufficient for project excellence. Project excellence is determined primarily by the cost-to-benefit ratio of the chosen solution.

Good project control can help achieve a desirable cost-to-benefit ratio by ensuring excellence in project implementation. Nevertheless, overall project excellence comes from accurately identifying the problem and developing a low-cost, high-benefit solution. Applying a problem-solving method is essential. However, the traditional problem-solving method contains deficiencies that make it difficult to apply (figure 7-1). A close look at this method reveals these deficiencies.

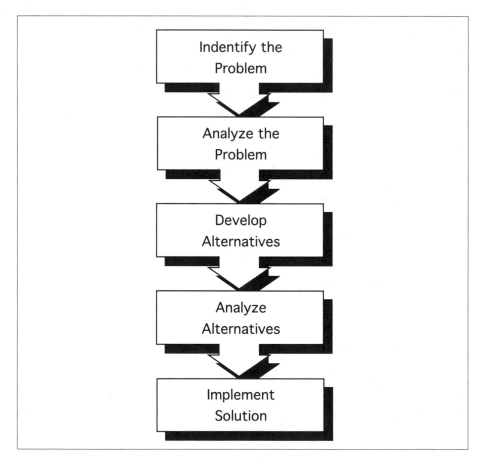

Figure 7-1. Traditional problem-solving methodology.

The task of identifying the problem is the first step in the traditional method. Yet, too often, the project team does not formulate the problem statement at all—or it does so quickly and informally. Either way, the team will not have a clear understanding of the problem.

Also, the team might formulate the problem statement improperly. For example, the problem statement could contain a specified solution, such as doubling the factory capacity, which then would limit the team to that one alternative. It also might be overly broad or narrow. If it is too broad, any solution might be impossible to implement. If it is too narrow, the solution might be unimaginative or fail to address the right issue.

The second step in the traditional method is to analyze the situation. The potential problem here is not one of spending insufficient time on this step, but rather spending too much time—and risking what we call "analysis paralysis." Often, teams fall into this trap because it is easy to collect information on an existing situation. Alternatively, they may feel that great risks result from an incomplete appraisal. A team already understands the situation quite well, especially if it comes from their own work area. In these cases, there is little need for an in-depth assessment of the situation.

The third step in the traditional method is to develop solutions to the problem. If the team avoids the pitfalls of the first two steps, no additional problems should arise at this point. However, the problems with the previous steps make it likely that the team will have problems here too. The team might arrive at this point late, if at all, having spent a good deal of time appraising the situation. Also, a narrow problem statement may limit the creativity of the team at this step.

The next step is to evaluate the possible solutions. Most teams handle this task well, but they need to be aware of other possible pitfalls. First, teams often focus only on the solution itself, rather than the entire system. This "tunnel vision" can result in solutions that might be appealing on the surface, but will not fit well with the overall systems, both technical and human. If so, the organization may eventually have to discard or modify such solutions.

Secondly, most people have a distaste for indecision. They want a clear mental image of the team's direction. As a result, project teams tend to focus quickly on one recommended solution, which then becomes the solution. The result is that many options are not evaluated properly and, of course, the team's creativity is limited.

Fortunately, all of these difficulties arising from the traditional problem-solving method can be circumvented. By incorporating the principles of Breakthrough Thinking into the problem-solving process, project teams will perform more efficiently and generate more efficacious solutions.

The first step of this improved methodology is to identify the problem by developing a purpose statement. A variety of purpose statements should be generated, which the team then organizes into a vertical hierarchy of increasingly larger purposes. These statements, consisting of a verb and direct object, are different from regular problem statements. For example, they do not include change-of-state words such as "improve" or "decrease," just as these words would not appear in the description of an operation.

Once the team develops a purpose hierarchy, it can select the level at which it wants to address the problem. To do this, the team needs to weigh the available resources and choose the broadest feasible statement in the hierarchy. This selected level then becomes the problem statement, and the mission, for the team. The advantage of attacking the problem at the largest level possible is that the solutions generated will be the most comprehensive and creative possible. As we already noted, the problem statement will not generate a broad range of possibilities if it is too narrowly focused.

The second step of the improved methodology skips analyzing the existing situation, and moves directly to generating possible solutions. This is a creative process. The team should not eliminate any ideas at this point, even those that might not work. (That determination should come later.) Following this brain-storming, the team should organize the potential solutions into major categories and add limited details to each: who, what, when, where, how, and how much? The objective is to provide some basic information on how the team would implement the solution, how the solution would address the problem, and how the organization would operate after the changes.

Step three of the improved methodology entails analyzing the possible solutions, and deciding which ones would be best to implement. This step marks an important departure from the traditional methodology, for the target of the analysis is the *solutions* rather than the problem situation. By focusing on solutions, the team becomes more creative and has less difficulty dealing with established paradigms–those mental rules and pre-conceived notions that govern the way things should operate, and so hamper creativity. Analyzing the problem only strengthens existing paradigms. Creativity is fostered when the team formulates a broad problem statement and focuses on the alternatives, not the problem.

The analysis of alternatives, however, must be thorough, particularly since there was no initial analysis of the problem. The team must therefore scrutinize each alternative to determine answers to the following questions:

- Will this solution solve the problem (purpose statement)?
- Will this solution fit into the larger context of the situation, and include any irregular conditions?
- Can the team implement this solution with the given resources?

These, then, are the benefits of the revised problem-solving method using the seven Breakthrough Thinking principles:

- An enhanced method of selecting the problem
- An improved focus on the project's objective
- An expanded set of alternatives
- An increased speed in developing solutions

Two examples illustrate this process. In the first example, the production control manager at a large manufacturing plant wants to improve his department's performance and quality by installing a new inventory control system. A project team is appointed, which analyzes the current situation by documenting the existing manual system and visiting other plants. The team then prepares an engineering package and capital request after several months of study. The request is for equipment to put barcodes on all semi-finished materials and collect data from all work stations in the plant. The cost is high, but the solution is comprehensive and there are some ancillary benefits to the system, such as an improved ability to isolate quality defects.

The proposal goes up the organization. Due to the high cost and consequent risk, management does not make a decision, but rather asks for more information. The team proposes lower-cost tests and a phased implementation. A full year has passed without any action. Some on the team begin to think that a kanban system and a single minute exchange of dies (SMED) program would be a better solution. These individuals are broadening the problem statement without knowing it. Management, still averse to risk, asks the team to analyze the problem again from the start. Despite the doubts of a few individuals, the team again recommends the same solution. Two years after the project start, management finally kills it. The cumulative costs of the team's efforts have been almost as high as the system cost itself.

This example points to several problems, but the primary one is the problem-solving approach that the team uses. The problem statement from the start was assumed to be "to install a new inventory control system." But had the team applied the Break-through Thinking principles, the problem statement would likely have been different (figure 7-2). If it had focused on a problem statement at a bigger level, the alternative solutions would have been much more diverse. Perhaps a more cost-effective solution, such as JIT or SMED, would have emerged earlier, for analyzing solutions instead of the problem generally takes less time. If the team had selected the problem statement and alternatives with a budget in mind, the approval of management would have been easier as well. (This, by the way, is a good argument for establishing a budget range at the beginning of a project. First, management should identify a loose budget and the resources available. Then, the project team should identify the level at which to solve the problem and generate the alternatives.)

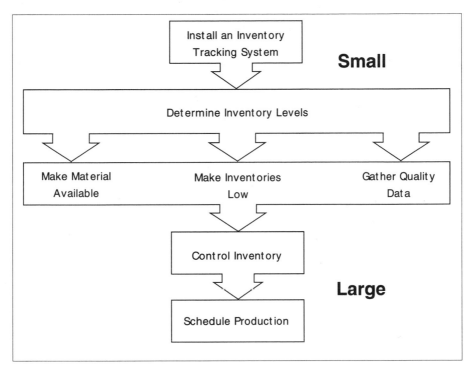

Figure 7-2. The inventory control function hierarchy.

The second example has a better outcome. A company implementing TQM arms its teams with the traditional methodology. The teams begin their projects with a great amount of excitement about the opportunity to make change. The TQM process facilitators counsel to "follow the process by clearly analyzing the current situation." The teams begin to bog down in the process. Many of the teams fail. Those that do persevere take several months to complete their assignments. The reasons are various, from tackling a problem too broad, to spending long periods analyzing the problem, to not receiving sufficient management support. Some facilitators start using the new methodology (figure 7-3), prompted by anecdotal evidence indicating that teams spend much less

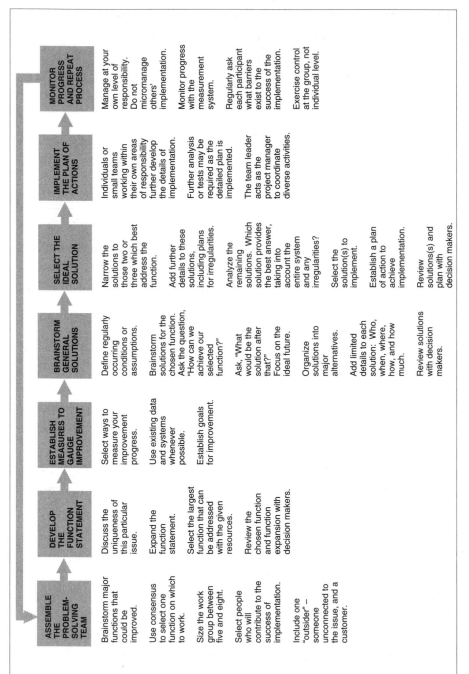

Figure 7-3. A new TQM methodology.

time working through the problem-solving process. The focus on solutions pulls them through the process by giving team members a vision of where they are going. Most of the teams have identified improvements and implemented simple solutions within six weeks, whereas, previously, most teams still were collecting data at that point.

In summary, the key steps of the new problem-solving method incorporating the Breakthrough Thinking principles are as follows:

- Formulate the problem statement by constructing a purpose hierarchy
- Generate alternative solutions early
- Evaluate alternatives for effectiveness and system compatibility

With this new methodology, the creativity and efficiency of project teams should improve substantially.

Case Illustration 7-1

Setting up a TQM project needs to be an integral part of all TQM activities. The steps involved in doing this are the most visibly affected by Breakthrough Thinking, as the following case illustrates. This description of what happened in one company was prepared by one of the TQM managers there:

"The XYZ Continuous Performance Improvement (CPI) Resource Center is a corporate resource of twenty industrial engineers, training professionals, and support personnel. Over the past three years, this $7.5 billion organization has been implementing TQM worldwide through this department. This group first developed its own two-day introduction to TQM by distilling the various TQM philosophies and techniques. We then began presenting TQM in a two-day, introductory workshop. The major components of the workshop included the following:

- Introduction to TQM (the basic philosophy of total quality, continuous improvement, and employee involvement)
- Customer/Supplier Relationships (the internal interdependencies, teamwork, and customer focus)

- Work Processes (the concept of adding value, processes, Deming's 85:15, and waste)
- Analysis Tools (the seven basis problem-solving tools and runcharts. No SPC)
- TQM Implementation (the traditional problem-solving methodology, the policies and procedures of CPI at XYZ)
- Team-building (the Myers-Briggs Type indicator, and team building games)
- Videos (Barker's "Discovering the Future," Gaspari's "Why Quality," Peter's "A Passion for Excellence")

"Additionally, as a last exercise in the class, small work groups brainstormed opportunities for improvement (OFIs) covering their work areas. These were used to form quality improvement teams once the attendees returned to their departments following the workshop. The teams were composed of volunteers who wished to work on a particular OFI. Technical support and team facilitation was available from the Resource Center, although not all TQM teams availed themselves of this opportunity.

"Despite this training, many of the teams struggled. Some teams stopped meeting. Some teams continued to meet, but made little progress. Others got off the topic and ended up addressing a completely different issue. Some teams persevered, but proposed solutions to management which were unacceptable. Some teams were wildly successful, a few saving tens of thousands of dollars. Still, the number of teams having difficulty far outweighed the success stories.

"Just prior to my departure from the CPI Resource Center, I read *Breakthrough Thinking* and saw the implications for our TQM groups. Too much data collection is one reason these teams struggled. I worked with several to reduce the data collection on the current situation. These teams reduced the amount of time required to get to the solutions stage from several weeks to under one week. Breakthrough Thinking helps in almost all cases, and having good management backing and other requirements for success are also part of the whole picture."

The Project Team

Only one person may be assigned to work on a project, but most projects will need a group of people related to the problem and purpose area. Even if one person is assigned to a project, he or she would be very well advised to set up a team, if only an informal one.

Many factors influence the effectiveness of a project team. A system matrix description of the team would illustrate this very quickly. Certain factors, however, remain fixed for all projects–among them, the functions and responsibilities of the team leader, facilitator, and members:

Team Leader

The leader of the TQM project team should be a senior executive who can devote at least half of his time to the role. The responsibilities of the leader of the project are:

- Arrange the meetings (time, place, and agenda)
- Represent the team to the sponsor
- Monitor team activities and progress
- Ensure tasks and activities are completed in a timely and accurate manner
- Establish the team's direction and keep the team focused
- Interact with team members
- Function as a coach

Related factors a good team leader should consider are discussed in the "People to Involve section of "Considerations in Team Operation" below.

Team Facilitator

The facilitator is the group's guide through the team process. The facilitator's duties are:

- Help the team leader
- Keep the group focused on the process
- Help orchestrate the idea flow
- Ensure that everyone is involved

- Summarize and record key points
- Constantly ensure that consensus is reached
- Provide feedback to team members on how they are doing

Related factors a good facilitator should consider are discussed in the "People to Involve section of "Considerations in Team Operation" below.

Team Members

- Attend all scheduled meetings
- Participate in an open and frank manner
- Listen to others
- Respect other views
- Value, not tolerate the ideas of others
- Be receptive to change
- Provide honest feedback on the team's performance
- Complete assignments on time

Table 7-1 expands these ideas by using a system matrix to identify what a person should be doing on a team.

Table 7.1 **Roles of People in the TQM Project** (Page 1 of 2)

Inputs

  People who perceive the problem: Users, clients, consumers, target groups, decision makers, resource controllers and their representatives, activists, lobbyists, those now operating the system

Outputs

  Same people as those for "Inputs," except that they have a solution that is implemented; also, the whole target or impact group affected by the solution

Sequence

  All of the "Input" people follow the problem-solving steps based on the Breakthrough Thinking principles. Key people include the Breakthrough Thinking professional as facilitator and selected experts as information resources

Table 7.1 **Roles of People in the TQM Project** (Page 2 of 2)

Environment
  People who have indirect influence: politicians, religious leaders, administrators and managers, community leaders, bankers and financial executives, taxpayers

Human Agents
  Breakthrough Thinking professionals, experts (scientist, statistician, sociologist, thermodynamics expert, political scientist, etc.), boundary spanners, draftpersons, technicians (measurement specialist, interview technician, data analyst, etc.) See the last section of this chapter for more details

Information Aids
  Specialists with information ordinarily contained in manuals and standard operating procedures (e.g., training, information systems, documentation, evaluation methods, sources of continuing education, maintenance, payroll)

Considerations in Team Operation

Prior to designating a team and holding team meetings, the leader and facilitator need to consider five factors concerning *how* to get the people actively involved. These factors include the step in the problem-solving process, the level of organizational participation, the people to involve, group processes and techniques, and meeting conditions.

Step in Process

The step on which the project team is working is a major consideration. The purpose or function to be achieved by the step is the crucial determinant of which people to involve, as well as when and how to involve them. Compare, for example, the step of determining purposes versus the step of detailing the recommendation.

People's interests and concerns also change. Some who are involved early on may lose interest, particularly if they initially felt threatened by the project but come to realize that their fears were groundless. Conversely, others may become involved later on as the project momentum builds. Then, too, people transfer jobs or terminate, or new people are hired as the project proceeds.

The static generalizations in the literature about the relatively constant group of people to involve in projects should be viewed very skeptically, because the purposes of the many steps are so varied.

Level of Organizational Participation

Determining which people to involve and how to involve them depends on the level of participation and involvement extant in the organization. If, for example, the organization has an authoritarian operating style, trying to get many people involved in a project can be difficult. Similarly, getting workers, supervisors, and others together for meetings in an autocratic-type organization also can be difficult.

Identifying the level of organizational participation is not always easy. Some measures of this are managerial style, organizational climate, readiness for change, and level of involvement (as discussed in Chapter 6). These measures collectively indicate a level of participation that can be described as follows: non-participative, persuasive autocracy, consultative, reactive control, bargaining, anticipatory control, joint determination, supportive, or completely participative.

Of course, each of these descriptions is at best a generalization, derived from information about the behavior and morale of individual people—each of whom is different in terms of style, objectives, and values (as the "Uniqueness Principle" tells us). As such, no description of an organization's general level of participation can predict the specific participatory character of a given division, group, or project team. In addition, an organization's level of participation can change over time, reflecting changes in people and circumstances (e.g., the owner/entrepreneur's relatively autocratic style gives way to collaborative management).

Furthermore, the purposes and objectives of an organization do not necessarily correlate with its participatory style. For example, one hospital does not have the same level of participation as another with supposedly identical size and services. One tool-and-die department does not operate with the same managerial style as another. Nor will one project team or permanent work group operate with identical levels of participation at all times.

The aim of TQM is to move an organization to the level of participation most appropriate for its goals. To get to this target level, however, various participation levels are needed, because in most organizations TQM starts at numerous levels. While this is certainly not a desirable way to begin, efforts must proceed at whatever level the TQM project originates. To facilitate these efforts, the following aspects of groups should be considered whenever a project is organized:

Purpose and Objectives of the Group: Clarity, validity, and flexibility of purpose and objectives; internal vs. external development; organization level to involve (policy, strategic, tactical, operational); measures of effectiveness for group activity.

Source of Legitimization and Reporting: Degree of support, ability to terminate or extend the group, degree of autonomy, lines of reporting.

Membership: Relation to organization level, methods for selecting group members, degree of leadership each seeks to exert, relationships with other members.

Procedures and Participation Patterns: Communication modes, positions of individuals (executives, workers, mixed, etc.), formal and informal operating methods, ability to act as a unit, nonverbal methods of communication, methods of decision making.

Atmosphere and Cohesion: Freedom and friendliness, frankness of discussions, willingness of individual members to speak up, ability to operate effectively as a team, operation under crisis, commitment to purpose.

Timeline: Interrelationships among all project components (standards of operation, cost, external audit control, etc.), and their impact on time schedule.

Subdivision Modes of Organization: Functional components, issue- or product-based subdivisions, coordination among subdivisions.

Leader or Facilitator: Degree of control, facilitator with member as chairman, source of decision making.

Physical Resources: Condition of meeting facilities, ability of computer terminals.

Information Resources: Availability of library and database facilities, access to experts.

If a group is permanent (such as long-range corporate planning self-directed work, or product development teams), additional aspects of group dynamics need to be addressed as well. These include team-building skills, contingency decision methods for switching roles on occasion, and modes of interrelating with other key organizational groups.

Whether permanent or temporary, groups offer a variety of benefits. They invite divergent perceptions and reasoning pat-terns, encourage creativity, and open channels of communication. They produce high-quality solutions with a minimum of errors, and promote "ownership" of a solution to help ensure its acceptance and implementation. New "leaders" or managers are given a chance to "try out" as chairperson of a group, and individuals are able to assess their own interests in a variety of settings.

It is also important to recognize the disadvantages and liabilities of groups. Pressure may be exerted to adopt lower-quality solutions, even by a powerful few. Group members may fall into the "risky-shift" trap, in which they accept an idea, even if it is not good, just to avoid "making waves" amid other group developments. Some groups tend to settle too quickly on a solution, discounting even high-quality ideas once a tentative solution is accepted. Individual goals and "hidden agendas" may push toward "winning" in the group rather than toward finding the best solution. Self-prominence may motivate some rather than organizational benefits. Disagreements on project or substantive topics may lead to personal animosities that manifest themselves in attack, silence, or resignation. Finally, different techniques may be needed if a group is geographically dispersed with insufficient funds for people to travel to a meeting (See "Group Processes and Techniques" section below).

People to Involve

The variety of people who ought to be involved, in terms of their roles and positions, is almost always large, whether or not they are members of the actual project team. Some should be included throughout the entire project, most at various points in time. In addition, many people in and outside of the organization will need to interface with the project area. They may need to accept the solution, change behavior, bargain for scarce resources, authorize a loan, and so on. *Whom* to involve is thus very critical. *How much* to involve them is also critical.

Each person engages in a variety of activities every day, stemming from work, family, recreation, social obligations, civic duties, and so forth. Each one involves roles and produces problems with different purposes. Each activity has an impact on the others. To assume that a factory worker, for example, will deal with an organizational project on its "objective" merits only without considering the other personal roles is shortsighted.

The following is a list of the roles a person could play in relation to a specific project: consumer, purchaser, user, customer, impacted group, client, owner, expert (scientist, engineer, computer, statistical, etc.), person now working in system, manager (first level, middle, top), citizen, opinion leader, lobbyist/activist, representative of constituency, decision maker, source of power (resource controller, politician, board member, etc.). Regardless of the role that applies to an individual, he or she is very likely to play different roles in other projects in the same day or week. The amount of time the person spends on each role will vary too.

The variety of roles and skills needed for a project should be identified before individuals are considered. Then, the various possible roles of each individual should be listed to determine where a person could be utilized in more than one role, and where other roles of the person potentially conflict with the needs of the effort. For example, a person selected for a "citizen" or "consumer" role in a health care planning council may not be effective because a job assignment concerns selling medical supplies.

The major guideline for selecting people for a project should always be improving the probability of arriving at an effective and innovative implemented solution, while effectively using *all* resources. This almost always means that social heterogeneity and lack of conformity are the selection criteria and standards for conduct of a good group.

A project team and work teams are dynamic and need constant change. As noted earlier, many people get new positions or assignments that significantly influence their effectiveness and interest. Others may just lose or change interest as certain steps or phases are completed. As such, it is wise to re-plan the project team every month or so. At the very least, a method should be set up for replacing and bringing in new people.

Actually selecting the people is a decision-making process, based on some general considerations:

- Do the people selected fit the level of the project? Even though a company worker might be involved with policy-level formulation, perhaps a representative of workers would fit better.

- Should the people selected be internal or external to the organization? Internal people who feel the "tension" or difficulties created by the problem are likely to be motivated to seek a solution. However, external people can be vital as well–as, for example, people external to the system who form a pressure group (of consumers, clients, etc.) urging changes.

- How does the nature of the project affect the choice of people to involve? This may vary over time, starting with, say, a correction design need, but becoming bigger through purpose expansion.

- How much time is available for the effort? Less time may mean more people.

- How important will it be to convince others before implementation can take place? A large decentralized organization where a solution influences many may require more people with geographic links.

- What stakeholders need to be included? That is, who is paying for the project? Who stands to gain (or lose) financially from a solution? Who affects its implementation?

- How important is the quality of the solution? Higher quality solutions need broader sets of experts and knowledgeable people.

- What are the range and credibility of skills available internally and externally?

- What are the leadership abilities of the possible leader and/or Breakthrough Thinking facilitator?

- Which affective human characteristics—ego involvement, individual and social aspirations, propensity for risk and for conflict, attitudes toward change, personality type, personal beliefs and values—need to be considered?

- How will the need for changing the group membership be recognized? For example, if the selected level in the purpose hierarchy is bigger than initially expected, the members should be willing to drop out and/or ask others to be involved. Furthermore, the need for various abilities decline (knowledge, technical skill) or grow (estimation, communication) as the project proceeds.

- What person(s) should be included who know where information can be found or inexpensively obtained?

- What other resources are available to support the group efforts?

- In what ways does the group need to accord with legislative mandates?

Along with these considerations, candidates can be identified by asking five or more people in key positions in the organization (or community or region) to nominate people who satisfy these criteria. A person's name appearing on 30%–50% of the lists would likely be a good team member.

A team leader is often named in advance. This selection is critical. The leader must move a group forward, coping with an almost inevitable short timeline for the effort. The leader should be neutral regarding what solution may emerge, and ensure that all ideas are aired, even when personal predilections are challenged. Too often, team members feel they are co-opted into accepting what the leader has already decided.

Qualifications for a leader include the ability to keep the group focused on important issues; the ability to know when consultants, experts, aides, or sounding boards are needed; the ability to gauge which questions, components, or aspects are critical; and the ability to communicate well. The leader also must have a solid understanding of the rules and procedures for running meetings, yet be capable of "bending" them when the group senses it needs to do so.

The facilitator aids the leader and team, very often conducting significant portions of meetings to ensure that the various steps are followed and techniques are utilized effectively. Occasionally, the facilitator assumes the role of leader, setting up the meeting agenda (always in consultation with the key people who collectively might constitute the equivalent of a leader) and generally conducting the meetings on behalf of the group.

Group Processes and Techniques

A team is arranged to achieve certain aims, and it should do so in the most effective manner possible. Many techniques are available to help, as shown in figure 7-4.

Several points are germane when operating a team:

First, having a team does not necessarily mean that meetings will be held. Several techniques (Delphi, electronic mail, opinion polling, telephone conference, interactive TV/computer processes) let groups "meet" without actual meetings.

Second, one or more of the group process techniques in figure 7-4 can be used individually or together in a meeting. Several may be used sequentially (e.g., nominal group for purposes, brain writing for ideal systems, gaming for major alternatives). In addition, each technique, as described in most of the literature, must be adapted to fit Breakthrough Thinking principles. Almost all are presented in conceptual terms—for example, to probe for problems, difficulties, or barriers, instead of purposes, ideal systems, or regularities.

Interacting	Lecture
Nominal	Opinion Poll*
Questionnaires*	Delphi*
Leveling re: likes and dislikes	"We agree"
Honoraria*	Telecommunications*
Interviews*	Role playing
Computer graphics	Matrix diagram*
Game or simulation	Brain writing
Prioritizing matrices*	Short conference
Referendum*	Public hearing
Drop-in-center	Debate
Process decision program chart	Affinity diagram
Future-creating workshop	Team building
Sensitivity training	Arbitration, mediation
Interrelationship digraph	Huddling
Media-based balloting*	Decision worksheet
Multi-attribute utility assessment	Tree diagram
Estimate silently-talk-estimate	Activity network diagram
Dialectical argumentation	Think aloud*

* Techniques that do not require a group to meet formally

Figure 7-4. Common group process techniques.

Third, the techniques can "mix or match" with one another and with various groupings of people. The nominal group technique, for example, would divide a large group of, say, 40 people into four groups of ten people each. Assignment to each small group is usually random. However, the small groups could be organized by roles (users, politicians, operators/workers of current system, etc.). Or they could be organized by personality types (sensation-thinkers, intuition-feeling, sensation-feeling, etc.) if a variety of ideas for a step is desired. Generally though, coalition formulators (e.g. users, politicians) should be avoided. Getting a diverse group to work together is, after all, a key objective of TQM.

Fourth, a technique is always insufficient unto itself. The question to ask or the purpose to be achieved is often far more important than the technique. Using a nominal group technique to elicit assumptions concerning how the quality of department XYZ deteriorated is virtually certain to elicit many statements about a wide variety of present conditions and problems. Asking the group instead to determine the purposes/functions of the components, product(s), and department is far more likely to get the group to identify what really needs to be accomplished in hierarchical terms and how these might be creatively achieved. Good group techniques by themselves will not necessarily be effective, just as participation by itself is not effective without concern for how the questions are posed.

Many techniques and models not included in figure 7-4 could be used in group modes. Some are discussed in Chapters 8 through 13, such as the couplet method, purpose hierarchy construction, regularity development, and solution framework. Many others presented in Appendix A (e.g., interpretive structural modeling, activity matrix, utility assessment, scenario writing) could also become the basis of a group process.

Summarizing and adapting all the ideas about "good meetings" for TQM project purposes results in the following guidelines for the team leader and facilitator:

- Stick to a previously distributed agenda where topics are purpose-oriented. Research shows that structured group activities are far more effective and take no more time than unstructured groups.

- Err toward covering a little too much on an agenda for the available time rather than too little. Parkinson's Law does seem to hold: the work expands to fit the available time. An attitude of parsimony tends to prevail even though every agenda item may not be covered.
- State on the agenda how long the meeting will last.
- Within each agenda topic, control only the process, not the content. Be a gatekeeper: give everyone a chance to contribute by a round-robin process, call on non-speakers, use techniques that assure everyone's participation (e.g., nominal group, brain writing), and be sure everyone understands the meeting rules of order (Robert's Rules of Order are not usually good for TQM project teams).
- Start with statement of expectation of achievements by end of meeting.
- Inform group of developments since last meeting. Individuals responsible for interim activities should inform others of progress.
- Summarize what the meeting has accomplished, what is to be done and by whom before next meeting, and what the next meeting will concern.
- Use majority voting only as last resort when differences are pronounced enough that consensus is not possible. Use the telephone to get information.
- Be enthusiastic about the group's work if you expect the group to be interested and enthusiastic.
- Put any decision that narrowly achieves a majority on the agenda for the next meeting as a means of surfacing new information, obtaining ideas from experts and others in the organization, heeding warnings of moral and ethical consequences, and getting greater group concurrence.
- Reiterate as needed the overall Breakthrough Thinking approach to reinforce the holistic perspective as a basis for

decisions. Encourage members to "listen with their whole being." Because continued practice of the approach will reinforce behavior patterns of individuals for other projects, emphasize purposes/functions for all deliberations and decisions. Check and recapitulate to assure broad understanding among members.

- Avoid spending too much time on a conspicuous idea or the first alternative, and look for other alternatives and broadening information. Avoid the dangers of "groupthink" pressures toward conformity and uniformity.

- If possible, have someone other than a group member take minutes, to be circulated before the next agenda is distributed. Record ideas initially in the way an individual states them.

- Avoid handing out material at the meeting not previously reviewed by the group. This may be difficult to adhere to because the nature of Breakthrough Thinking in TQM projects causes new information to appear on short notice.

- Adhere to time limits and set up future activities on a timeline basis.

- Maintain some flexibility so informality is not cut off when group members seem to need it for building openness, creativity, and trust. Discussion can be encouraged if a hot topic arises affecting the project, even outside the agenda or from outside the group.

- Maintain a positive tone: rephrase ideas positively, offer one or more interpretations, cut off name calling, avoid censoring others establish civility and respect among members regardless of differing viewpoints.

- Recognize that each group is different. Some start as a collection of individuals, an affiliated group from the same organization, supporters of a movement, or class or level of worker. Each should design its own "system."

- If status (organizational level, experience, power, reputation) is highly variable, talk with the high-status people before the meeting to secure their willingness to have equal treatment in the group (advocate first-name basis for everyone; avoid introduction of any status symbols such as "expert" or "doctor"; avoid criticism of ideas during idea generation steps; seat people at random or alphabetically rather than by position or representation).

- Conflicts that arise should be put into a win-win form that aids rather than disrupts the meeting process. Creativity can emerge from conflicting viewpoints. If appropriate, move to bigger-level purposes in the hierarchy, get each person to express the other person's position so it is acceptable to the other one, focus on achieving the purpose and the overall results rather than on defeating a person, give all people all information to avoid coalition formation, and take a little more time rather than moving directly to voting. Breakthrough Thinking principles are particularly useful for conflict resolution because they seek to design a solution to the conflict.

- Refer to the Breakthrough Thinking principles if a person promotes early on the solution the team should support; remind the group that purposes come before solutions, and so on.

- Be alert for problems and difficulties. Some people may act bored, attendance may be low, and some people may attack the leader (self-interest is always present in individuals). Time always seems to run out; team skills and respect may be lacking; facilities may not be good; people may have mistaken expectations or think material presented is too complex, and so on. One difficulty that has arisen in Breakthrough Thinking projects is the frustration a person or two on occasion will feel about not being able to install the solution-after-next target right away. Referring them to the "Betterment Timeline" principle and getting them involved in installation actions may help alleviate this "interesting" development.

• Wait at least three seconds after asking a question, even if there is complete silence, before saying anything else at all. Continued talking or only a short delay after asking a question minimizes greatly the likelihood of responses.

• Be neutral in responding to team members' ideas. Avoid saying, "okay," "good," "great idea," "fine," and so on. Additional questioning and probing stimulates more and better responses, because people do not become subconsciously smug and satisfied as they would with complimentary words.

Meeting Conditions

More often than not, conditions surrounding a meeting do make a difference. One hospital, for example, had just been refused a request by the state for a rate increase. A program to reduce costs and increase productivity while maintaining good quality of care was therefore necessary. Two or three people from five different constituencies were asked to attend a meeting to initiate the program: trustees, administrators, members of the medical and nursing staff, union representatives, and former patients. The board chairman served as the meeting's leader. Three Breakthrough Thinking facilitators were invited to discuss how the program could get started.

Several seemingly trivial decisions had to be made regarding the meeting conditions. Where should it be held? A corner of the cafeteria was selected because it represented "neutral" turf. What seating arrangement should be set up? A large square was formed from several tables so people could sit on all four sides in a non-confrontational mode. How should people be identified during the meeting? Name place cards, 6 x 9 inches and printed on both sides in advance of the meeting, were placed in front of each person. How should seating be arranged around the table? If nothing were done in advance, it is virtually certain that the three union representatives would sit together, the three trustees together, and so on. Coalition formation would be encouraged too early. To prevent this from happening, the name place cards were set up on the tables in advance so that all representations were mixed. Other meeting conditions and features were also addressed: noise was reduced by using sliding partitions; lighting was optimized by setting tables near the window; and the room temperature was set at 70-72 degrees to keep people alert.

Some research suggests that the physical appearance of a meeting place can affect its outcome. Certain wall colors and textures, for example, are seen as being soothing or stimulating. Other physical features can transmit a sense of stillness or inertia, rather than a desired movement and stimulation.

Figure 7-5 lists a variety of conditions that need to be considered when planning a meeting. Some conditions are always present (light, heat, noise, ventilation, etc.), and their inclusion below is to emphasize the need to check them out prior to every meeting. Ventilation, for example, should be checked to determine whether enough is provided, or whether drafts can be avoided. If both smokers and nonsmokers will attend the meeting, thought might be given to seating arrangements so that the two groups are separated.

Office
Conference room
Classroom
Workplace
Table arrangement (round, oval, U, V, and so on)
Location—on or off site
Paper, pencils, easel, chalkboard, and so on
Space zone per person (2 to 4 foot minimum)
Name tags
Place cards

Figure 7-5. Meeting conditions to consider. (Page 1 of 2)

> Lighting
>
> Temperature
>
> Ventilation
>
> Noise level
>
> Group arrangement (random, alphabetical, organized mixing)

Figure 7-5.   Meeting conditions to consider.   (Page 2 of 2)

Case Illustration 7-2

A one-day meeting of 18 key Federal and state officials was held in July 1977 to plan the project system that would be responsible for developing a comprehensive Gypsy Moth Pest Management System (CGMPMS).

First imported to Massachusetts from France in 1869, the gypsy moth had since spread and become a major forest insect pest in 12 Northeastern states, feeding each year on one to two million acres of forest, woodlot, and suburban vegetation. Isolated infestations had been found as far away as Florida, Wisconsin, and California.

Many problems confronted pest managers in their attempts to control the heavy defoliation. Among the most important were the need to develop environmentally sound management techniques, the need to develop "integrated" management approaches that placed maximum reliance on "natural" controls and took into account other kinds of pests and their interrelationships, and the need to coordinate operations with other key agencies. In addition, pest managers were operating in a difficult political and administrative environment, with citizens vociferously complaining about the quality of parks, pest control methods, and property values.

The initial meeting was facilitated by Breakthrough Thinking personnel. By the end of the day, the group had developed a rough purpose hierarchy and identified a list of people from federal and state government agencies, private industry, and the university research community who would be involved in the project. Also identified were responsibilities, detailed planning activities, budget, expected products, and the overall project timeline (figure 7-6). In subsequent stages of the project, the timeline was twice amended and extended to better fit real-world conditions.

September 1977	• Begin planning and design of Comprehensive Gypsy Moth Pest Management System (CGMPMS)
October 1977	• Generate purposes for the Gypsy Moth Pest Task Force (CMPTF) two-day meeting • Establish organizational framework (committees) of GMPTF • Prepare statement of need for CGMPMS • Identify and define functional components of the CGMPMS • Develop alternative Gypsy Moth Pest Management Systems • Establish evaluative criteria for selecting the optimal pest management system • Identify most important conditions of the system • Consolidate ideas from functional component committees • Select pest management system solution
Late October and November 1977	• Hold meetings with state agencies to exchange information • Hold meetings with Federal agencies to obtain feedback • Discuss with or distribute materials to Program Board about GMPTF activities
December 1977 (two-day GMPTF meeting)	• Review details of pest management system solution and incorporate feedback from state and Federal agency meetings
Mid-December 1977	• Hold "National Meeting" on the gypsy moth (tentative)

Figure 7-6. Timeline. (Page 1 of 2)

February 1978 (two-day GMPTF meeting)	• Identify less important conditions (exceptions) that must be considered in the CGMPMS • Identify major categories of the recommended pest management system • Define the broad outlines of the recommended CGMPMS
March 1978	• Review outline of CGMPMS with state and Federal agencies • Review outline with Program Board
April 1978 (two-day GMPTF meeting)	• Define in detail the recommended CGMPMS • Develop initial structure for Gypsy Moth Continuing Planning Committee (GMCPC)
June 1978	• Develop the plan for implementation of the CGMPMS • Identify phases of CGMPMS implementation • Identify future research needs
July 1978	• Discuss CGMPMS and GMCPC with Combined Forest Pest Program Board
August 1978	• Complete final detailing of the CGMPMS and GMCPC
September 1978	• Submit CGMPMS and proposal for a GMCPC to Combined Forest Pest Program Board • Assist Federal and state governments in implementing the CGMPMS and the GMCPC

Figure 7-6. Timeline. (Page 2 of 2)

By October, final preparations and arrangements were complete, and work on the design of the CGMPMS began. The first meeting of 20 people began much as the July meeting had begun—with a great deal of catharsis from group members. It was apparent that they had experienced many frustrations over the past years and felt a need to share them with group members. It was also apparent that this type of activity accounted for much of the time they had spent in other meetings. Facilitators did not try to cut off this discussion, but gradually shifted the focus of conversation from problems and blame to possible purposes of the CGMPMS. At the subsequent meeting, the time devoted to catharsis diminished; after the third meeting, the group no longer seemed to have the need for it.

The first meeting produced solid ground work for the project: possible purposes were identified, a purpose hierarchy was constructed, and consensus was achieved on the selected purpose of the system; "to cope with gypsy moths at all levels of population." Measures of effectiveness for the CGMPMS were identified, and, using the purpose and measures as a guide, the group generated ideas for a target or "ideal" pest management system. A simple model of the CGMPMS for planning purposes was prepared.

By January 1978 the planning group had designed the overall system for the CGMPMS and decided to split up into committees to handle detailed work. Each of the committees treated its area of responsibility as a system and began by identifying purposes, measures, ideas for target systems, and so on.

In June a special group was formed to design a system for gaining approval of the CGMPMS by the states, U.S. Forest Service, Animal and Plant Health Inspection Services, USDA Science and Education Administration, the Secretary of Agriculture's Office, and private groups. This group followed the Breakthrough Thinking approach used by the other groups.

By the end of August 1978, plans for the national level of the CGMPMS were ready for implementation, according to an agreed-upon schedule. The target plan for the national level called for the creation of a National Gypsy Moth Management Board, with responsibility for overall system evaluation, policy formulation, program coordination, and fund raising. The National Board was to have a charter from the USDA, and was to be funded and staffed through the same agency. A Federal pest management coordinator was then designated to coordinate all pest programs in USDA. The reason for creating this position was to deal with problems arising from the many program interfacings.

Over the next eight months the National Gypsy Moth Management Board began operations and planning for the next levels of the system (now under the auspices of the National Board). The three Federal agencies, for the first time in their histories, began to coordinate their gypsy moth work. Although they were cautious at first, positive experiences increasingly brought the agencies closer together, until finally, in 1979, joint programs were undertaken.

By May 1979, the CGMPMS framework was solidly established, and the capability of the National Board and USDA agencies to continue planning and improvement was firmly in place. As a final step in the initial project effort, a report on the status of the CGMPMS was prepared. This, too, was treated as a system and designed using the "General Flow of Reasoning" approach. A meeting with National Board members revealed that the report had to address three different audiences: top-level administrators, middle-level pest managers, and people on the "firing line." Purpose hierarchies were developed for all three groups.

What emerged from this process was a loose-leaf notebook, specifically designed to be expanded and updated regularly, section-by-section. Pages were color-coded for the different audiences, spaces titled and left blank for parts of the system yet to be developed, and a quick-reference table of contents prepared. The report was produced according to a formal timeline of activities developed at the same time as the report plan.

This case offers several unique insights into why the design of the project system is needed. Breakthrough Thinking provided benefits that had been unobtainable before. Participants were afforded the environment and means for interacting and establishing a positive working relationship, developing a unique system to fit their special needs, and creating the right institutional arrangements to carry out their plans. Perhaps most important, the people involved found that a project involves much more than collecting and analyzing data, developing recommendations, and publishing a report, which comprised most of their earlier experiences. Instead, they found that Breakthrough Thinking called for their active participation in a well-organized process aimed at focusing on purposes, developing feasible targets and the means to achieve them, and following through with implementation and continuing planning and improvement.

Central to all these accomplishments was the careful development of the project system. This was the subject of the July 1977 meeting.

Developing a project system at the outset was most likely the key to the successful implementation of the CGMPMS because:

- Practice with Breakthrough Thinking helped the people involved to effectively develop the CGMPMS.

- Frustrations and negative attitudes could be expressed regarding the secondary issue of designing the project system, about which no real positions had been "carved in stone."

- Dealing with large numbers of constituencies and people was treated as an important problem in its own right.

- A focus on implementing change was engendered before people could concentrate on details of the solution (which would have created arguments and defensiveness too early).

- The specifics of the project system were developed to fit the particular people and needs, rather than assuming that a "standard" project team or data collection commitment was required.

Self-Managed Work Teams ("Quality Circles")

Getting all employees involved in improving quality, productivity, and competitiveness is an aim many organizations seek to achieve. Progressive organizations recognize each person's experience and knowledge base as prime resources for helping to achieve such aims. These organizations seek to empower their employees by lowering levels of decision making and by establishing self-directed, self-managed, or self-regulated work teams (often called "Quality Circles"). The key features of such teams is that members do their own control of variances of production or output, they are usually cross-trained to minimize task differentiation, they have expanded perspectives on the "boundaries" of their areas of responsibility, and they get involved in many aspects of planning and designing as well as improving and problem solving.

Many aspects of organizational life have to be restructured to accommodate work teams: aligning human resources policies and self-directed work team practices; redefining the roles of managers, supervisors, and employees; learning to engage in team building practices; opening lines of communication among internal and external stakeholders; training team members in Breakthrough Thinking principles; broadening the organization's overall level of participation (see Section B); incorporating customer-driven and value-added concepts; modifying the change and suggestion systems; and setting up monitoring procedures for the teams.

Like all problems and challenges, changing the organization to support self-directed employee work teams needs a system design of its own, including an implementation plan. Because this type of change is a significant modification in the organization's culture, efforts should be guided by the concepts presented in Chapter 6 about program development.

Regardless of how cross-functional groups or self-directed work teams are established, all of them will work on projects (problems). *How* a team approaches each project will significantly affect the results obtained. Even if a team retains its same membership for all the problems it works on, the concepts of project design, as presented in this chapter, are important for providing a fresh perspective on each problem-solving situation. One danger of ongoing self-directed work teams is the increased likelihood that members will fall into the trap of recommending previous solutions for a current problem. Each team needs to cultivate a continuous entrepreneurial spirit, so that it treats each project as an opportunity for a breakthrough. Therefore, all teams not only need to be well versed in the principles of Breakthrough Thinking; they also should be encouraged to bring in people from the outside (e.g., non-production people for production teams and vice versa). With their training in Breakthrough Thinking, members of such work teams would also be good candidates for TQM projects requiring ad hoc groups.

The message is simple. *Any project to plan, design, improve, or problem solve can benefit from the concepts of Breakthrough Thinking, regardless of the status of the team.* Furthermore, TQM project team members should take a lead in promoting the collaborative arrangements in an organization that are vital to both self-managed work teams and problem-driven TQM efforts.

Computer Support for Teams

The advances in computer hardware and software offer teams a dazzling set of possibilities that far exceed the benefits of word processing, calculations, and access to databases.

New software packages allow a group of people to meet in a room where verbal exchanges can still take place, but where all comments and ideas are entered into a computer, displayed on a screen for all to observe, and then modified by anyone with an audit trail. "Groupware" is the term frequently applied to such systems.

The growth of teleconferencing (audio, video, with two or more people) makes communications possible among people anywhere. Groupware adds computer support, including graphics capabilities, to teleconferencing. In theory, a project team or a self-directed work team would not have to have its members physically located in one place nor have face-to-face meetings. While these are by no means desirable circumstances, the growing availability of technologies is helping to expand the opportunities for effective team work.

At the present time, Groupware resources provide "face-to-face facilitation services, group decision support systems, computer-based extensions of telephony, presentation support, project management, group-authoring, PC screen sharing, group memory management, computer-supported audio or video teleconferences, [and] computer-supported spontaneous interaction," among numerous others catalogued by R. Johansen (*GROUPWARE: Computer Support for Business Teams*, New York: The Free Press, 1988). As one illustration, IBM has developed GroupSystem software, which focuses on room layout and networking to facilitate face-to-face meetings and the decision-making process.

The most critical dimension not addressed by groupware is *how* to proceed. The programs are all based on conventional approaches, seeking information about what exists, forcing the same analytical techniques onto all projects, and providing a wide array of information sources that pique the curiosity of groups, whether or not the information is needed. Even so, the concepts of computer support are critical and will be used more often in the future, especially as they are modified to incorporate the Breakthrough Thinking principles. A simple software program, called PLAN, is already available to help a small group (3-5 people) follow the pattern of reasoning described in Chapters 8 through 13.

How To Go About Setting Up a Project

The planning and thinking process for setting up a TQM project is a series of functions to be accomplished, not a set of techniques and tools to be applied nor a standard model to install. These functions are purposes, solutions-after-next, system matrix details, people involvement, and implementation. The techniques (see Appendix A) needed to achieve these functions will vary from situation to situation.[2]

To conclude, an expanded version of the set of functions to be accomplished when setting up a project team is as follows:

- Identify and expand the purposes of the project, being particularly attentive to integrating the perspectives of all the various programs and initiatives within the organization.
- Select the purpose level(s) on which the project should focus.

---

2. One of the available good books on project management can be reviewed for other techniques which may prove useful. See, for example, S.F. Love, *Achieving Problem Free Project Management*, New York: John Wiley, 1989.

- Develop alternative "ideal" ways to organize the project and team.
- Select the project system.
- Select a leader and facilitator, and define different responsibilities.
- Draft a project time schedule and list of needed resources.
- Select the members of the team.
- Provide recording and data management resources.
- Define the roles of each member.
- Train the team members in Breakthrough Thinking (if not done previously).
- Set up all meetings with essentially the same mode of reasoning (i.e., uniqueness of each meeting, purposes of meeting, etc.). Distribute agenda of topics beforehand, and ask each person to come with at least two ideas for each topic.

Developing Purposes 8

The complete process for planning and implementing TQM, based on the principles of Breakthrough Thinking, consists of the following steps and results. Chapter 8 addresses those steps that concern *purposes* (highlighted below).

Step*	Result
1. Set up TQM program (6)	TQM mission, values, strategic plan
2. Identify primary projects and activities (7)	Initial plan of action and timeline
3. Set up TQM project (7)	Project system (purposes, people, etc.)
4. List possible purposes (8)	
5. Develop purpose hierarchies (8)	
6. Determine criteria to select purpose level (8)	
7. Select purpose(s) (8)	Focus purpose(s) in a hierarchical context
8. Establish measures of purpose accomplishment (8)	Success factors
9. Establish subgroups if needed (8)	Subgroups established

* The number in parentheses after each step refers to the chapter in which the step is described

Step*	Result
10. Generate many solution-after-next options (9)	List of viable alternatives
11. Assess solution-after-next options (10)	
12. Select solution-after-next target (10)	Target solution-after-next
13. Modify target for irregularities (11)	
14. Choose recommended changes (11)	Recommendations
15. Prepare proposal (12)	Proposal
16. Inform people not involved to date (12)	
17. Detail recommendations (12)	Complete recommendation specifications
18. Prepare installation plan (13)	Installation plan
19. Install recommendations (13)	Installed system
20. Standardize performances (13)	System performance measures
21. Review project at betterment timeline date (14-15)	Next recommended changes
22. Repeat step 21 (14-15)	Further actions and changes

* The number in parentheses after each step refers to the chapter in which the step is described

As mentioned above, this chapter focuses on the *purposes* for whatever the concern is. Whether your concern is the whole TQM program (Chapter 6), a specific TQM project (Chapter 7), or any "standard" activity (setting up a meeting, making a telephone call, determining employee performance expectations, etc.), you should always start with purposes. Doing this helps ensure that all your efforts target the right problem. The concept is simple; the execution is hard but rewarding.

Your initial tasks are to identify as many purposes as possible that ought to be achieved for the problem area, and then expand them from small to large scope to determine the level on which to focus—that is, to determine the "focus purpose." This process forces you to continually keep in mind the following questions:

- What is the purpose of this system (or area, or unit, or problem)?
- What is the purpose of this purpose?
- What does this purpose accomplish?
- What is the purpose of the customer (and of the customer's customer) that this purpose addresses?

As you go about these tasks, you will find that obvious purposes expand into less obvious ones, and that all, in turn, expand into strategic intents and missions. By arranging them hierarchically, you take into account the needs and goals of the entire organization, for you cannot consider any *one* purpose without also considering related larger (and smaller) purposes in the hierarchy.

Purposes of Developing Purposes

Finding the right purpose to achieve is a powerful reason for this step. Doing very well what ought not be done is obviously undesirable. Other major benefits of exploring and expanding purposes are equally compelling. Explain why you should do this step even if everyone agrees on the focus purpose is.

Developing purposes enables you to:

- Put each focus purpose into the context of its larger purposes, including those of the customer. It is insufficient just to say that you know the purpose. When clients tell us about the mission (purpose) of their organization, we often surprise them by asking, "What is the mission of that mission?" There are always larger missions that everyone should consider when planning, designing, improving, and problem solving.

- Challenge everyone's assumptions about the ends to be achieved. A project or problem may appear straightforward, but many breakthroughs occur when the "obvious" is expanded to find the real purpose or to identify the larger context.

- Achieve independence from techniques to be applied. Conventional approaches rely on many techniques that are supposed to be used on all projects, as noted in Chapter 1. Facilitators (and groups) should be familiar with such techniques, but they should also be wary, because quantification often seems to reduce the complexity of the problem. The mere fact that new techniques appear like "flavors of the month" is a clear indication that they should not be the basis for approaching any problem or project. Being "comfortable" with techniques is a sure sign that results will be limited or nonexistent. Getting bulky analyses does virtually nothing for the conceptual flexibility and quickness needed in TQM efforts.

- Develop collaboration among the different disciplines and organizational functions impacting the problem. People who promote their own solutions often "war" among themselves, as many cases illustrate. Getting these people to relate their specific purposes to larger purposes generally brings them together and leads to discovering even more effective solutions.

- Bring order to chaos. Every problem is surrounded by the many perspectives, special concerns, and circumstances of the people involved. Each person has a favorite technique or two. Each has several internal "customers" and one or two external customer linkages. Every system has many elements and dimensions that must be balanced. Dwelling on purposes and their expansion enables the group to establish interrelation-

ships among these seemingly chaotic conditions, while opening avenues for attaining major changes and improvements.

- Relate effectively to external customers and suppliers. Customer satisfaction, a major hallmark of TQM, is the most
important measure of quality for all organizational products,
services, and activities. However, just meeting customer needs
is not enough. The goal of TQM is to *exceed* those needs–for
external and "internal" customers alike. Any request from an
"internal customer" is best tied to a purposes exploration and
expansion, that will relate the request to external customers
(and suppliers) to determine its usefulness and need. Because
external factors are almost always going to be the major determinants in effective problem solving and strategic planning,
purpose expansions are critical to establish external customer
linkages.

- Consider the needs and concerns of the many stakeholders.
Saving lead time is one important advantage gained from an
early agreement on purposes; also, critical guidance for all parties is provided from the outset as they work individually on
project tasks and activities.

- Set the stage for making the biggest effective change possible.
Creativity is almost always viewed as the process of finding
brilliant solution ideas. Breakthrough Thinking encourages
"Full Spectrum Creativity"^{SM} by finding the right purpose for
such solution ideas, and by enlarging the solution space within
which creativity is sought. To illustrate how this works, try the
following exercise: First, list all the solution ideas you can
think of for the purpose "to drill a hole." Then, list all the
ideas to achieve the next larger purpose in the hierarchy, "to
make a hole." Finally, list all the ideas to achieve the following
larger purpose in the hierarchy, "to create a void." At each level
of the hierarchy, there are numerous possible solutions; however, "make a hole" elicits many more possible solutions than

does "drill a hole." When you think of creating a void, even more solutions arise. In fact, the basic premise of what your are doing might no longer be the same. For example, when you think of *drilling a hole*, a specific tool usually comes to mind. *Making a hole* brings to mind an assortment of tools, while *creating a void* may take you to outer space–or inside a light bulb. Creating a hierarchy of purposes helps you to broaden your perspective and invites insights into the problem that conventional problem-solving methods do not. In short, the purposes orientation fosters an expansive critical thinking mode to plan, design, improve, and problem-solve in any circumstance.

- Turn problems into opportunities. Literature is filled with suggestions to turn the problem-solving process into an "opportunity-solving" process. Such suggestions are not useful without the purposes view. A purpose expansion identifies opportunities for organizational improvements and product/service innovations. It also provides for the prevention of errors as solutions are sought, building quality assurance into the problem-solving process.

- Consider implementation of the proposed recommendation right at the beginning. Expanding purposes enables people to immediately anticipate and understand the implications of possible proposed changes. Also, identifying the focus purpose dictates which people ought to be involved, since the system to be developed may be much different from the existing one. Finally, agreeing on purposes prepares people emotionally for forthcoming changes (see Chapter 13), and helps build a commitment to the long term through a shared vision of bigger purposes.

- Recognize the uniqueness of the company, organization, group, project, or individual. The Uniqueness Principle of Breakthrough Thinking points out that analogies and solutions from elsewhere are inappropriate initially in any project. Good analogies are hard to find and bad ones are misleading. Even the most sophisticated executive or leader can go astray with an irrelevant similarity. Because end-users and other related people can get involved in the exploration and expansion of purposes, assurances are far greater that they will buy-in to the unique focus purpose regarding products, marketing, service and support, brand or image positioning, or net purchase price and cost savings, through use of the resulting solution.[1]

- Relate the project or activity to the TQM program (Chapter 6) and the mission of the company. Even though the mission (broad purpose) is found using the methods described in this chapter, each effort involved in planning, designing, improving, or problem-solving needs a purpose expansion to clarify its relation to the organization's mission and customers. This not only gives direction and meaning to each effort; it also engenders a commitment to larger strategic plans.

- Integrate the project or activity with other projects and organizational functions. Each problem (or opportunity) exists in the context of other problems and organizational activities. For example, a project in the manufacturing area will impact and be influenced by marketing, distribution, procurement, human resources, customer service, and numerous other company operations. A purposes exploration, expansion, and hierarchy provide a way of reasoning that interrelates all the critical facets and functions of an organization.

- Think like executives. Effective leaders intuitively approach problems from a contextual, "bigger purpose" perspective (Chapter 3). They stress values and ends to be achieved, and map unknown territory by exploring purposes. They base their

---

1. G. A. Getz and F. D. Sturdivant, "The Nuts and Bolts of Formulating Differentiation Strategy," *Planning Review,* September-October 1989, p. 4-9.

decisions on a limited amount of information, guided more by their vision of an ideal system or solution-after-next target. Approaching problems by looking first at purposes trains a person in these concentrated thought processes that leaders intuitively use.

- Enhance situation awareness. Because every problem and project exists as part of a larger whole, a group needs to understand the larger environment within a framework of scope, time, meaning, and future projections. External factors beyond those arising from customers are likely to be driving forces that will shape solutions and systems. A purpose expansion increases awareness of this "bigger picture."

- Determine the level of risk. Working on the problem-as-stated is close to taking no risks on the assignment. However, risk-takers usually achieve higher degrees of success than risk-averters. A purpose hierarchy provides an effective way both to determine the focus purpose and to assess risk propensity, to obtain the most successful outcomes from the effort and resources invested.

- Know what information to collect. No effort involved in planning, designing, improving, or problem-solving can ever proceed without some information collection. Because information of any sort always contains some falsehoods or omits some truths, collecting information about the wrong item can radically skew results. Asking pertinent questions that stem from an investigation of purposes is far more likely to yield relevant, accurate data than blindly applying analytical techniques and collecting information.

The rest of this chapter provides details about how a person or group might go about determining the focus purpose to be achieved (or the "problem to work on" as opposed to the "problem as stated"). All efforts involved in planning, designing, improving, or problem-solving need to do this because of what the Uniqueness Principle tells us: that no matter how similar or analogous one problem may appear to another, the people involved and the technology available are bound to be different.

Most projects will not need most of the following techniques because the concepts explained to this point will be sufficient for "talking through" an expansion to establish a context and select a purpose level. Instead, the technical material which follows is presented to let everyone know how the process can work, and to give facilitators a grab-bag of techniques from which to select a tool when needed.

Definition of Purpose and Purpose Hierarchy

The term *purpose* has certain characteristics that you need to understand before trying to develop a purpose hierarchy.

First, every purpose has four components: (a) a mission, aim, primary concern, or need (function); (b) desired conditions (values, beliefs, motivators, etc.); (c) goals (measures of performance, success factors, and the like); and (d) objectives (specific amounts of the goals to be achieved in specific time frames). *Purpose* will be used in this book for (a) because it has a broader sense of a real-life end to achieve than does the technically oriented *function.* Table 8-1 illustrates the differences among the four components.

Table 8.1   **Illustrations of Word Distinction** (Page 1 of 2)

Components of Purpose	
Radiology Department	
Purpose (or function)	to produce x-rays of various body sections
Values	improve diagnostic ability, make people well, increase health care quality, provide patient care (higher level functions)
Goals	number per day, accuracy, cost
Objectives	(measurable performance specifications) 30 per day without error
Example activities	place patient, turn on machine, interpret x-ray

Table 8.1   **Illustrations of Word Distinction** (Page 2 of 2)

Components of Purpose	
Hospital Maintenance Engineering Department	
Purpose (or function)	to keep equipment in optimum operating condition
Values	improve equipment efficiency, increase quality capability of hospital, ensure efficient use of resources
Goals	percent of machines that are operating
Objectives	95% in operating order per week
Example activities	repair of machines, preventive testing
Personnel Department	
Purpose (or function)	to have necessary people available
Values	hire capable personnel, reduce turnover, provide employment
Goals	percent of people requirements satisfied
Objectives	90% requirements satisfied
Example activities	screen, hire, train, fire
Automobile Manufacturing Company	
Purpose (or function)	to produce vehicles for transporting people and objects
Values	make a profit, be stylish, have quality dealers, meet energy requirements
Goals	earnings per share, return on investment, market share
Objectives	20% improvement in earnings in 1981, 15% in return on investment
Example activities	purchase, weld, paint

Second, the precision or clarity of a purpose statement depends on a shared understanding that the people involved have about it. That is, what might appear vague to an outsider (or to a semantic purist) would still elicit common images, definitions, and perceptions on the part of those involved. Third, a purpose statement is composed of an action verb and a subject. The action verb should be prescriptive and address the total set of conditions (for example, *to provide, to have, to establish*), rather than specifying the amount of change or incremental goals (*to increase, to minimize, to reduce*). Thus, the simplest purpose statement has few substantive words—*to establish a group.*

Fourth, a purpose statement should be specific but non-limiting. Every added word reduces the possible solution space with a limitation, even though it may appear needed at the time it is formulated. Compare, for example, *to establish a project group* with *to establish a well-knit project group.* Many purpose statements have modifiers (like *well-knit*), even though they are not really needed. These generally represent values, measures, controls, or interface dimensions derived from the purpose element of a system matrix (Chapters 4 and 12), which will be factored into the recommendation.

Table 8-2 presents various questions and guides to help structure a purpose statement and develop a hierarchy.

The substeps in table 8-3 should help put the guidelines in table 8-2 into perspective for arriving at a hierarchy of purposes. An explanation of each substep in table 8-3 follows.

Table 8.2 **Structuring Purpose Statements and Hierarchies** (Page 1 of 3)

Questions for Purpose Expansion
1.   What are we really trying to do when we perform this function?
2.   What bigger purpose has caused this purpose to come into being?
3.   Why is it necessary for this purpose to be achieved?
Guidelines for Formulating a Purpose Statement and Developing a Purpose Hierarchy
1.   Start with the perceived needs of the group or organization.

Table 8.2 **Structuring Purpose Statements and Hierarchies** (Page 2 of 3)

2. Select the initial statement for the purpose hierarchy based on its uniqueness to the originating system. One way to start an expansion is to create a list of many possible purposes, and then choose one with the smallest scope as the starting point. A small purpose theoretically elicits a fewer number of ideas regarding how it might be accomplished than would a larger or more profound purpose.

3. Make purpose statements prescriptive and specific but non-limiting, using only a few words.

4. Write purpose statements in active verb-noun forms, referring to complete states rather than changes in states. See table 8-1 for examples.

5. Exclude incremental verbs from the purpose statement (like "reduce," "improve," and "increase"), and avoid qualifying adverbs and adjectives, unless they are necessary locational modifiers (e.g., "to measure temperature of human body"). If you tell a friend that you are trying to "decrease costs," "improve quality," or "reduce defects" and he or she has to ask "about what," you have a goal, objective, or measure rather than a purpose. (It is not possible to define a system matrix (inputs, outputs, etc.) for such goals, whereas this can be done with a purpose.) If possible, convert such value or goal statements to purposes (e.g., see figure 8-1: "improve inventory control" becomes "to control inventory"; "improve communication among management" becomes "to communicate among managers"). Some are measures only and cannot be converted; these should be set aside for possible use later in this step.

6. Proceed in small rather than large increments (jumps) when expanding purposes into a hierarchy.

7. Select statements for the hierarchy from a list of possible purposes or generate additional purposes as necessary.

8. Make sure that each bigger-level purpose statement is still part of the originating project or system. (One way to do this is to generate many ideas about the possible next level, and then choose the smallest.)

Table 8.2　**Structuring Purpose Statements and Hierarchies**　(Page 3 of 3)

9.	Construct the hierarchy in terms of purposes rather than a sequence of activities or explanations.
10.	Choose the most regularly occurring purpose if more than one is a likely candidate for the next bigger level.
11.	Relate purposes to the organizational unit or audience of concern.
12.	Expand purposes well beyond any possibility for selecting that largest level, and always expand enough to include customer needs and wants.
13.	It should actually be possible to design a means or system that can achieve the selected purpose without reference to some other need or purpose.

Table 8.3　**Developing Purposes**

A.	Generate a list of possible purposes.
B.	Choose a small-scope purpose as the beginning of the hierarchy.
C.	Expand the initial purpose into a hierarchy.
D.	Set up criteria for selecting the focus purpose(s).
E.	Select the purpose level(s).
F.	Identify measures of purpose accomplishment.
G.	Determine functional components.
H.	Select components if needed.

Generate a List of Possible Purposes

Record all suggested functions, preferably on an easel pad or board so group members can always see the list. As an example, figure 8-1 illustrates the very first list developed by a *facilities study group* project. The following techniques can be used to help generate possible purposes:

- Discuss purposes, brainstorm purposes, "mess around" with and talk about purpose ideas.

1. Better procedure/methods for raw material flow (inspection, incoming inventory, how and where stored, primary operations, etc.).

2. Determine facilities to meet customer requirements for products and service.

3. Determine plan expansion needs.

4. Organize work (material) flow.

5. Be able to change with the changing times (energy).

6. Provide an environment (envelope) for better flow of material and manpower and arrive at finished state and shipment.

7. Determine plant reorganization, facility- wise.

8. Establish (or plan) a workable design (system) for the "shop."

9. Determine nees for proper material handling and storage.

10. Establish status of parts – current, representative, etc..

11. Look at difficulties throughout shop from start to finish.

12. Maximize* production and shipments while developing and implementing item 6 (short-range goals).

13. Utilize* to a greater degree the available computer facilities (potential users).

14. Same as 7.

15. Improve* inventory control.

16. Improve* communication among management – up and down.

17. Maximize* ROI.

18. Determine long and short range marketing goals.

19. Satisfy our customers.

20. Schedule and coordinateproduction needs closely with sales forecast.

21. Reduce* lead times.

22. Improve* procedural planning.

23. Same as 20.

24. Improve* flow of new produt changes/releases, etc..

25. Increase* production capacity.

26. Create ability to give a good (delivery) shipping date.

27. Improve* product quality.

28. Improve* forecasting methods.

29. Improve* service, repair parts shipping (forecasting, handling, etc.).

30. Be able to change with marketing changes.

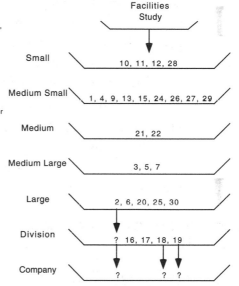

Facilities Study

Small   10, 11, 12, 28

Medium Small   1, 4, 9, 13, 15, 24, 26, 27, 29

Medium   21, 22

Medium Large   3, 5, 7

Large   2, 6, 20, 25, 30

Division   ? 16, 17, 18, 19

Company   ?   ? ?

* Guides 4 and 5 in Table 8-2 are "violated" by the verbs marked with an asterisk. However, this list is reproduced as actually developed by a group, and these types of violations almost always occur. The P&D professional with a group goes along initially with it because of the proposes of thw whole P&D scenario. "Correcting" the group takes place only as needed and when the group perceptions can accept them.

Possible purposes/functions as actually listed by a study group.

Figure 8-1.   Possible purposes/functions as actually listed by a study group.

- Send a questionnaire to various individuals or groups. What purposes do customers, clients, or users want achieved? What purposes do the operators/managers perceive as necessary? What purposes do sister departments or organizations expect? What purposes does society expect? Stakeholders? What need is served by the problem area? What new needs may emerge? What purposes are stimulated by competitors or the coming of a new technology?

- Use the nominal group technique with the initiating statement: "List as many purposes as possible you think ought to be accomplished (by name of system or area of problem)." (See Appendix A.) If the group has ten members or less, all can take part in classifying and sorting the resulting list of purposes. If more people are involved, small groups of two to four people should be formed to clarify and sort purposes. Each subgroup should then be treated as an individual in a round-robin presentation of purposes.

- Set up a Delphi technique survey. (See Appendix.)

- Have an individual or small group use PLAN on a personal computer. This program poses various questions on the screen to stimulate purpose responses, and has the computer keep track of the responses.

Choose a Small-scope Purpose as the Beginning of the Hierarchy

A small-scope purpose is unique to the problem, and points to the most direct or irreducible function within the problem area. That is, it cannot apply to any other system in the organizational unit, and has the fewest number of ways of being accomplished. Some statements may need to be converted from objectives/goals to purposes (e.g., "increase space available" to "have space available," reduce citizens' complaints about recreation to "facilitate use of recreational resources"). Possible methods for selecting the smallest-scope purpose include the following:

- Just pick one from the list by consensus of the group.

- Select likely candidates for smallest-scope purpose from the list. Then select one from the shortened list by consensus or by the couplet method.

- Use the couplet method. Compare the first statement with the second. Ask which one is smaller. Does purpose one accomplish purpose two (one is smaller), or does purpose two accomplish purpose one (two is smaller)? If we achieve purpose A, would we need B (B is smaller)? Is purpose A the purpose of purpose B (B is smaller)? Then compare whichever purpose statement is selected as smallest with the next purpose statement using the same set of questions. Continue the couplet questioning until all purpose statements have been examined. The purpose statement selected as smallest in the last couplet is the start of the hierarchy.

- Use the pair comparison technique (the full technique from which the couplet method was extracted). When the number of purpose statements is 15 or less, compare each one with every other one using the same questions as in the couplet method. Arrange the list of purposes in rows and columns of a matrix to help compare each pair and to record the answers to the questions about each. The purpose statement selected most often as the smallest from all the pair comparisons is the start of the hierarchy.

- Review each one. Classify it as small scope, medium-small scope, and so on (see figure 8-1). Each scope level can then be assigned a summarizing purpose statement or two, or expanded into an actual hierarchy. The person-card or KJ method could also be used to sort by scope. (see Appendix).

- Put each statement on an index card or Post-It™ slip. The group can move the cards or slips around to establish a hierarchy. For a more systematic way of categorizing the purposes, a matrix could be set up with the purpose statements as rows and the size of scope–S (small), SM (small-medium), M (medium), and so on–as columns.

Expand the Initial Purpose into a Hierarchy

Once the smallest-scope purpose is selected, all of the remaining entries on the list become candidates for bigger-level purposes. Many purpose statements not on the list are also possibilities. The following verbs and their synonyms (see any thesaurus) can be used as prompts to help identify possible purpose statements for each successive level:

To acquire	To design	To plan
To accept	To exchange	To prepare
To advise	To exercise	To produce
To analyze	To have	To promote
To consume	To investigate	To provide
To control	To learn	To research
To cultivate	To manage	To select
To do	To operate	To sell

More than one purpose can usually describe each successive level. Selecting one can be done with a technique from the previous section.

What should you do if two or more purpose statements are equally likely candidates for a particular level? You have a number of options:

- According to Guideline 10 in table 8-2, select the purpose related to conditions that occur most frequently or regularly.
- Following Guideline 11, pick the purpose that is most closely related to the organizational unit of concern. (For example, when a railroad company designed a system for an ore-mining company to move materials from the pits to processors, it

selected purposes based on the ore-mining company's needs–
the customer–rather than its own needs.)

- Ask, "If we develop a system for purpose one, will we still want
  one for purpose two?"

- Do two or more separate purpose expansions from the point
  where the question arises, and select the most regular one or
  the one most closely related to the organizational unit of concern.

- Do two or more expansions and keep them in a multiple-
  channel hierarchy. Continue to expand each one at least three
  to five levels beyond the point where the channels unite to
  form a single hierarchy. Figure 8-2 illustrates a multi-channeled expansion.

How can a big jump in expansion be avoided (Guideline 6 of table
8-2)? This was a problem for a group of workers in a manufacturing
company, who listed "to make tables" as their smallest-level purpose. In
developing a hierarchy, some members of the group identified the next
larger purpose as "to have objects supported." Others, however, felt this
was too big a jump, because it extended too far outside their organization. One way to avoid this kind of jump is to change the wording of the
initial statement so that the purpose becomes broader. Thus, "to make
tables" might become "to produce tables," followed by "to have tables
available," "to have flat surfaces supported in space," "to have flat surfaces
parallel to the floor," and, finally, "to have objects supported." Large
jumps are undesirable because they obscure a host of intermediate purposes, one of which might be the focus purpose of your project. In addition, the gaps in the hierarchy caused by such jumps lessen the chances
of stimulators (like the verb prompts above) generating more creative
ideas.

How do you know if you have the right hierarchy? You can never
know, for there is no *right* hierarchy in terms of accuracy and precision.
But we can tell you that the first hierarchy is seldom the final one. It is
not unusual for project teams to develop two or three hierarchies and

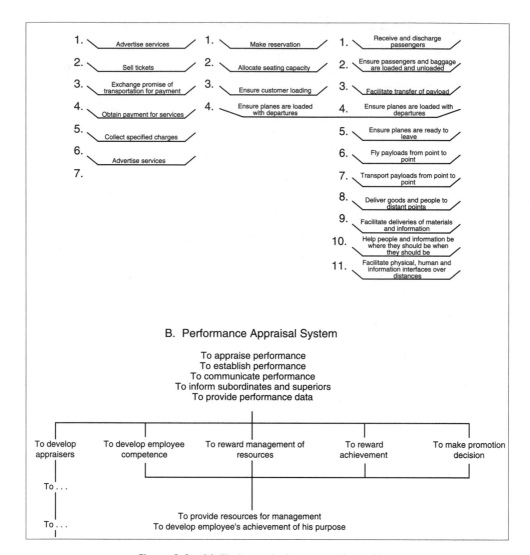

1. Advertise services
2. Sell tickets
3. Exchange promise of transportation for payment
4. Obtain payment for services
5. Collect specified charges
6. Advertise services
7.

1. Make reservation
2. Allocate seating capacity
3. Ensure customer loading
4. Ensure planes are loaded with departures

1. Receive and discharge passengers
2. Ensure passengers and baggage are loaded and unloaded
3. Facilitate transfer of payload
4. Ensure planes are loaded with departures
5. Ensure planes are ready to leave
6. Fly payloads from point to point
7. Transport payloads from point to point
8. Deliver goods and people to distant points
9. Facilitate deliveries of materials and information
10. Help people and information be where they should be when they should be
11. Facilitate physical, human and information interfaces over distances

B. Performance Appraisal System

To appraise performance
To establish performance
To communicate performance
To inform subordinates and superiors
To provide performance data

To develop appraisers

To develop employee competence

To reward management of resources

To reward achievement

To make promotion decision

To . . .

To . . .

To provide resources for management
To develop employee's achievement of his purpose

Figure 8-2. Multi-channeled purpose hierarchies.

compare them before selecting the one that captures most of what the people involved believe. Instead of seeking *the* right purpose level and hierarchy, then, a group should spend time discussing the alternatives, agreeing to "see what happens" before deciding what hierarchy or level to use. "Messing around" with hierarchies is an apt way to describe this substep. It gets a group to view purposes from different perspectives, during which time mental sets are being expanded and contexts worked out.

Figure 8-3 and 8-4 illustrate lists of possible purposes and hierarchies. (Also see figures 8-7 through 8-10 at the end of this chapter for other illustrations of TQM purpose hierarchies.)

What can you do if a group decides that developing a hierarchy is not necessary because "everyone knows what the purpose is"? If the group is adamant, one or more actions might be taken:

- Get the group to agree on a statement of the purpose that "everyone knows." (The usual variety of purposes from the group members convinces them that they do not know it.)
- Develop what they think the system ought to be in five (or one or three) years if they could have "their own way."
- Identify measures of effectiveness for judging the quality or success of the eventual recommendation for achieving the purpose "everyone knows."
- Generate a list of purposes and have group members bring alterative hierarchies to the next meeting.
- Determine functional components for the purpose "everyone knows."

Any one of these may cause a group to decide that determining the purposes and a hierarchy is needed first.

Set Up Criteria for Selecting the Focus Purpose(s)

Several techniques can be used to generate possible criteria: discussions, questionnaires, nominal group exercises, interviews, Delphi procedures, and so on (see Appendix A). Organizing the criteria can be done by grouping like criteria together, rating and ranking each criterion, or

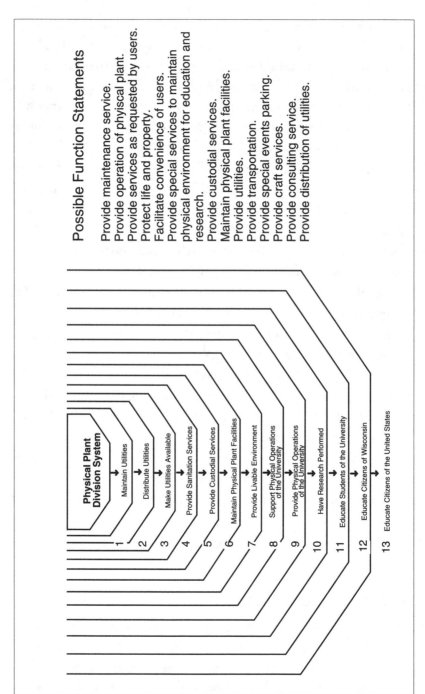

Possible Function Statements

Provide maintenance service.
Provide operation of phyiscal plant.
Provide services as requested by users.
Protect life and property.
Facilitate convenience of users.
Provide special services to maintain physical environment for education and research.
Provide custodial services.
Maintain physical plant facilities.
Provide utilities.
Provide transportation.
Provide special events parking.
Provide craft services.
Provide consulting service.
Provide distribution of utilities.

Physical Plant Division System

1 Maintain Utilities
2 Distribute Utilities
3 Make Utilities Available
4 Provide Sanitation Services
5 Provide Custodial Services
6 Maintain Physical Plant Facilities
7 Provide Livable Environment
8 Support Physical Operations of the University
9 Provide Physical Operations of the University
10 Have Research Performed
11 Educate Students of the University
12 Educate Citizens of Wisconsin
13 Educate Citizens of the United States

Figure 8-3. Possible function statements.

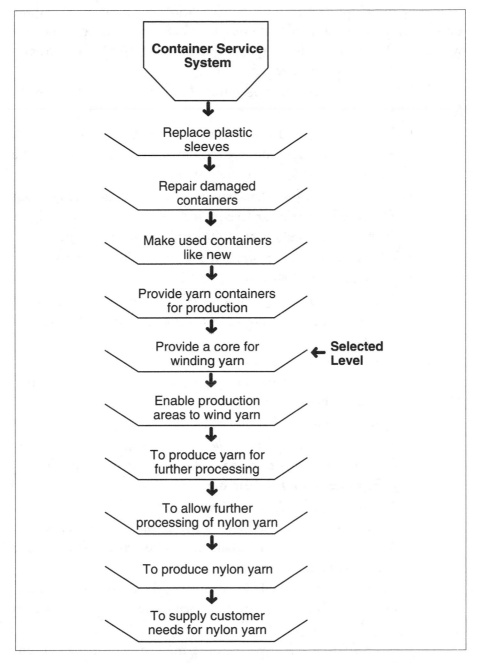

Figure 8-4.   Function expansion worksheet. Container is a spool-like receptacle for yarn. Problem statement: reduce costs of container service.

setting up a multi-attribute utility model. Selecting criteria can be done by voting, by applying predetermined measures, or by using a decision worksheet. You may decide to try out (mess around with) a level or two to get the "feel" of several criteria.

The following criteria have been found useful in several, but not all, focus purpose selection situations:

- *Potential benefits.* These include the quality and costs of all resources (human, information, and physical), as well as the whole system targeted by the purpose.

- *Management biases.* Management may insist that a project not go beyond a particular level, which, in their view, would put the project beyond the capabilities of the organization.

- *Potential impact on the strategic plan.* See STEM concepts.

- *Potential positive impact on customers.*

- *Political factors.* The opinions of those who are expressing urgency and exerting pressures for change may need to be considered.

- *Time factors.* A project to be completed in six months can generally involve a bigger focus purpose than one with a time limit of 24 hours.

- *Possible costs of a project at a given level.*

- *Complexity associated with the purpose level.* Each larger purpose involves a bigger system, which may involve significantly greater interactions and factors.

- *Organizational and jurisdictional factors.* A project in manufacturing may not compare with a related purpose in accounting. A change in group members may often avoid limiting the selection of a larger purpose.

- *Control factors.* Regulations and controls from the government, associations, or other external sources may conflict with a particular purpose level.

- *Capital factors.* These refer to the amount of capital a particular purpose is likely to need for its possible solution. Also of concern is the impact of capital-intensive solutions on flexibility.

- *Future resource needs.* Considerations here include people, equipment, space, capital, and so on.

- *Potential risks.* Some risks will become apparent when other criteria are considered, such as political factors, time factors, and project costs. Another common risk concerns the ability to maintain deliveries while changes are being made.

- *Other factors of significance in purpose selection.* Included here would be relationship to other projects, availability of technology within or even outside the organization, workability, actions of competitors, patent situation, compatibility with company history, liquidity, market position, and adequacy of facilities.

Select the Focus Purpose Level(s)

Several slightly different procedures may be of help in accomplishing this step:

- *Reverse steps of expansion.* Starting with the biggest level, the group evaluates each purpose according to the criteria. If that level is not selected, then the next smallest level is reviewed with the criteria, and so on. Another way to evaluate the hierarchy is to determine which purposes best suit each criterion, considered one at a time. The purpose selected is based on the "average" of the different levels–if five criteria were involved, and the purpose levels selected by each criterion considered by itself were 6, 7, 8, 7 and 10, the 7.6 "average" would suggest using both purpose 7 and 8 as the focus purpose(s).

- *Decision worksheet.* See figure 10-3: alternative column one would be the smallest purpose, alternative column two would be the next larger purpose, etc. The criteria rows would be defined by those selected, mainly from the possibilities listed above. Weighting of criteria is rarely done to select the focus purpose.

- *Delphi procedure.* Outside experts set up methods of measurement, evaluate purposes, and select the purpose level.
- *Nominal group technique.* Ratings and rankings are often used with this technique.
- *Subjective judgment.* When hierarchies are poorly structured or independent criteria are difficult to identify, sometimes subjective judgment is the best way to select the focus purpose level.

Although *one* purpose level is usually sought, it is not at all unusual for a group to agree that two or even three adjacent levels will serve as the focuses. Quite small increments between levels often lead to a focus on two or three purposes. The group which developed the hierarchy in figure 8-3, for example, decided on two focus purposes, the second one being the next bigger level, while the group involved with the figure 8-4 project decided that their focus needed to include the next smaller level as well.

Identify Measures of Purpose Accomplishment

Factors guiding the selection of a purpose level combine with the selected level itself to establish *measures of purpose accomplishment,* or MPAs. MPAs are instrumental in evaluating the alternative solutions that will be proposed to achieve the purposes. As such, MPAs should reflect not only the expectations of the group but also critical factors the organization believes lead to success (often stated in the strategic plan).

MPAs are thus not established–nor exist–in a vacuum. They are shaped by a great deal of careful thought as well as subsequent reconsideration and assessment. While they should relate specifically to the selected larger purposes, some may concern the initial tensions, desires, and values that led to the problem. Also, MPAs often change as later steps give rise to new suggestions, reconsideration of purposes, and detailed design specifications. Such developments may turn some seemingly unimportant MPAs into significant ones, and vice versa. MPAs may be used at different points in the Breakthrough Thinking process to clarify the focus purpose, select objectives, or set goals.

MPAs stem from the values and motivations of people in an organizational setting. They especially should incorporate performance factors the "boss" will use to gauge the effectiveness of recommendations for achieving the purpose. Whether a project needs or should have the usual specific objectives (e.g., reduce costs by 25% by the end of one year) depends on the circumstances. That is, what is needed can only be determined within a specific project, so measures of effectiveness will be the focus here. The important test at this point is whether an objective can be measured now and after the project's conclusion.

A measure can be:

- dichotomous (either/or, yes/no, go/no-go)
- continuous (several or many possible values)
- continuous threshold (a minimum "either/or" level must be attained, and then many values are possible)

However, no measure is ever complete, unequivocal, or entirely accurate. Nor is it possible that the eventual solution will be optimal to all the stakeholders. Therefore, setting up MPAs requires a trade-off among objectives that are project-related and those that are related to the eventual recommended solution. Trade-offs also occur when the various MPAs are weighted to establish the importance of each one (as used, for example, in a decision worksheet).

Desirable characteristics of MPAs are that they be:

- complete (i.e., they cover all the important aspects of the focus purpose)
- operational (they can be meaningfully used)
- decomposable (aspects of evaluation can be simplified by breaking the MPA into parts)
- non-redundant (they avoid double counting of impacts)
- simple and easy to obtain data about

In addition, everyone concerned should be able to understand the MPAs and agree that each *directly* measures achievement of the purposes.

That is, a measure should not just *assume* the link to purpose exists. (As an example, a Federal government agency selected the management-by-objectives technique to increase its productivity, but the objective concerned the number of MBO programs installed rather than effective services rendered.) MPAs should also provide some assurance that the group can actually control or influence the factors used for determining success.

Determining which MPAs to use is a decision-making process, as sketched out in table 8-4. The second column, "Organizing Alternative Measures," gives a sequential list of techniques for assessing the usual large number of possible measures: first you divide the measures into "go/no-go" categories, then determine desired levels, relate the measures to basic values, and so on as needed. Once the measures are identified and arranged, Column 3 lists techniques that can help you select which measures to actually use.

Before finally selecting MPAs, you need to determine whether currently available and continually collected data establish the levels or amounts of desirable measures. If present levels of a measure cannot be identified, then the group should seriously consider finding alternative measures or delay the effort until such data can be collected and continuing measurements established. (Collecting such information can be a project in itself.) Measurements to be made at the end of a project need a base point of pre-project conditions so that the effectiveness of proposed solutions can be gauged. Whether or not productivity, for example, is improved by changes at the end of the project can be assessed only if current productivity measures are adequate.

Because not every project can be expected to succeed, you should include MPAs that would indicate when a project ought to be stopped. Some signals of this include:

- the project is taking too much time
- the project is 50% over budget
- no solution proposed would result in an improvement of 15% over what exists

Table 8.4　**Selecting Measures of Purpose Accomplishment (Step F)*** (Page 1 of 3)

Generating Ideas for Measures of Purpose Accomplishment ⟶	Organizing Alternative Measures ⟶	Selection of Set of Measures
Results sought: List of prospective measures of purpose accomplishment to gauge possible solutions and eventual success of implemented solution	Results sought: Similar and related measures appropriately identified and arranged	Results sought: A set of measures hopefully ranked or even weighted to use for evaluating possible and implemented solutions
Methods, Techniques, and Resources to Attain Results*	Methods, Techniques, and Resources to Attain Results*	Methods, Techniques, and Resources to Attain Results*
Stimulators (ask: What MPA does this stimulator suggest in your mind for the selected or bigger function or purpose?)	• Go-no go (discrete—what must be present in a solution or the solution alternative is automatically rejected? vs. continuous grouping	• Prioritizing 　Importance 　Data availability 　Prospect of getting data
Stated values of decision makers	• Deterministic (a specific amount) or probabilistic (a minimum/maximum desired level with a certain confidence)	• Decision worksheet for purpose/function measures
Checklist of objective ties to purpose hierarchy		
Client initial charge to facilitator or group	• Related measures to basic values (safe, low cost, low detail times, etc.) to have several branches	• Rate trade-off categories (subjective measures)

*Many items in column 1 may be organized by one or two of the smaller number of items in column 2, and a selection made by one or more of the still smaller number of items in column number 3.

Table 8.4　**Selecting Measures of Purpose Accomplishment (Step F)*** (Page 2 of 3)

Generating Ideas for Measures of Purpose Accomplishment	Organizing Alternative Measures	Selection of Set of Measures
Results sought: List of prospective measures of purpose accomplishment to gauge possible solutions and eventual success of implemented solution	Results sought: Similar and related measures appropriately identified and arranged	Results sought: A set of measures hopefully ranked or even weighted to use for evaluating possible and implemented solutions
Methods, Techniques, and Resources to Attain Results*	Methods, Techniques, and Resources to Attain Results*	Methods, Techniques, and Resources to Attain Results*
Review list of purposes for objectives included therein	• Objectives tree or hierarchy. Broad at top to specific at bottom. Each smaller level is part of next larger branch level. Put branches together into tree.	• Must exist vs. measurable amount categories
List factors by which the solution will be judged as satisfactory	• Level of data availability for each possible measurement	
Determine which suggested restrictions, givens, or limitations, or government regulations are possible MPAs	• Array of measures which could be assigned to each level of the purpose hierarchy	
Nominal group technique	• Array of measures which are related to each major word of the purpose/function level statement	

*Many items in column 1 may be organized by one or two of the smaller number of items in column 2, and a selection made by one or more of the still smaller number of items in column number 3.

Table 8.4 **Selecting Measures of Purpose Accomplishment (Step F)*** (Page 3 of 3)

Generating Ideas for Measures of Purpose Accomplishment ⟶	Organizing Alternative Measures ⟵ ⟶	Selection of Set of Measures
Results sought: List of prospective measures of purpose accomplishment to gauge possible solutions and eventual success of implemented solution	Results sought: Similar and related measures appropriately identified and arranged	Results sought: A set of measures hopefully ranked or even weighted to use for evaluating possible and implemented solutions
Methods, Techniques, and Resources to Attain Results*	Methods, Techniques, and Resources to Attain Results*	Methods, Techniques, and Resources to Attain Results*
Interview of key individuals	• Trade-off categories	
Literature sources (what others have identified as critical values within which this project solution should fit)—especially specific fields (information systems, manufacturing company, quality of working life, development, etc.)	• Utility vs. measurability	
Questionnaires, Delphi surveys	• Understandability vs. completeness	
Policy statements of organization	• Simple vs. complex	
Define performance specifications desired (e.g., portable, adjustable, comfortable for four hours)	• Motivation vs. objectivity • Test of importance—would possible solution be altered if factored omitted?	

*Many items in column 1 may be organized by one or two of the smaller number of items in column 2, and a selection made by one or more of the still smaller number of items in column number 3.

Objectives and measures are unique to each situation. Yet, some general goals are often stated for broad categories of organizations or projects. They illustrate the "literature sources" entry in the first column of table 8-4 and serve the purpose of providing stimulators for a specific project. Examples of the values, objectives, goals, or measures that can serve as stimulators in several fields are shown in table 8-5.

Table 8.5 **Illustrative Stimulators for Developing Measures in Projects**
(Page 1 of 2)

Business Organization

Resource utilization (efficiency), innovation, adaptiveness to environment, morale, goal achievement (effectiveness).

Another Version for Business

Market share, return on investment, amount of sales, cost reduction expectation, number of customer complaints, material utilization, absenteeism and turnover rates, timing of new product introductions, cost of grievances and industrial disputes, productivity ratios.

Hospital View of Performance

Community relationship (number of community educational programs, score on community attitudes toward and reputation of hospital), staff and patient satisfactions (comfort level, staff morale, consideration of social as well as medical condition of patient, information supplied to patient and family), efficiency of operation (length of stay, medical staff time utilization, material utilization, cost per service), effectiveness of operation (mortality, morbidity, readmittance numbers, community awareness levels).

Engineering Design

Go/no-go (physical laws, nature with or without physical laws), societal laws (Constitution, standards of technical associations, codes of communities), safety standards (underwriters' laboratory, insurance companies), resource availability (materials, energy, equipment, and/or capital, labor), amount of capital and operating costs (reliability, maintenance, quality), and marketability.

Table 8.5 **Illustrative Stimulators for Developing Measures in Projects**
(Page 2 of 2)

Appropriate or Intermediate Technology

Utilization of renewable energy resources, labor intensiveness, utilization of
locally available materials, compatibility with local labor skills, simplicity of
installation and maintenance, use of decentralized technologies, satisfaction
of local needs, environmental soundness, durability of solution.

User Benefits in Environmental and Architectural Design

Conformance of user requirements to environmental form on basis of
facilitating behavioral needs (overall, functional, operational, stimulus,
spatial, and contingent), physiological maintenance (support, climate,
hazards, and physical endurance), perceptual maintenance (consonance,
operational, and sensory), and social facilitation (territoriality, organizational
orientation, convergence, social isolation, and social accommodation).

Urban Planning

Economic, environmental, political, and social considerations; impact on
organizational structure; degree of value agreement; need for coalition
development; impact on resource allocation; technical difficulty; and level of
environmental stability.

Product Design

Viability (are benefits greater than costs?), acceptance, validation (does the
system achieve purpose or solve the problem?), evaluation (does system meet
requirements, demonstration (how do observers react to system?),
verification (does system run as planned?).

Costs of Quality

Cost of appraisal (testing, inspection), cost of failure (internal or external,
reworking), cost of prevention (assuring work is done right).

Determine Purpose Components

Often projects are so large or complex that doing work in parallel
on parts of the project is desirable. Setting up purpose components (or
sub-purposes) is an effective way of doing this. Concurrent or sequential

projects for sub-purposes generally result in a more effective use of time and resources. Sometimes several alternative *sets* of sub-purposes need to be developed, from which you then select the "best-fitting" ones.

Purpose components should be independent of each other. However, complete independence is not possible; otherwise, the components would not be part of the focus purpose.

Size and complexity are relative matters. A system may be considered large or complex if one person or group would be unable to do it alone, or if the cost and number of people involved are high. Several criteria, such as total cost, number of output items, number of employees, size of area, and number of locations, may be used to determine a project's complexity. Components also may be required if the number of facilitators is limited and a prioritizing of efforts is needed.

Figure 8-5 puts the idea of purpose components into the context of the purpose hierarchy. If a project starts with the "hopper" shown with an asterisk, the purpose expansion proceeds as shown.(Figure 8-2 illustrates how purpose components may be developed while doing the expansion.) Turning figure 8-5 upside down portrays a system "pyramid" that defines the sub-purposes. Figure 8-6 shows a completed graph of functional components used in a nurse utilization project. It also contains notes stating which components need work and which will be left as they are.

Table 8-6 provides questions, guides, and suggestions for identifying purpose components. They all start with the focus purpose level. The Quality Function Deployment (QFD) technique or Fishbone Diagram, both described in Appendix A, might also be used with the selected focus purpose level to identify components.

Select Purpose Component(s) if Needed

Either identify a purpose component for which the remaining steps are followed, or concurrently assign components to individuals or groups. The latter situation is more desirable because the focus purpose will be accomplished sooner. Even though each sub-purpose becomes its own project, the overall approach should be continued for the focus pur-

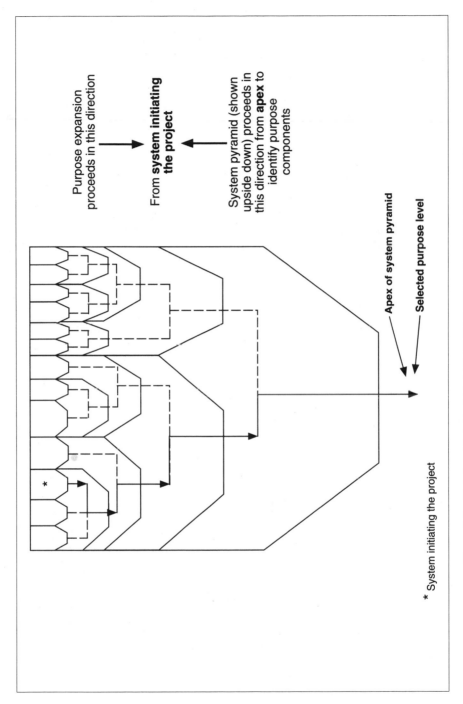

Figure 8-5. Relationship between purpose hierarchy and purpose components.

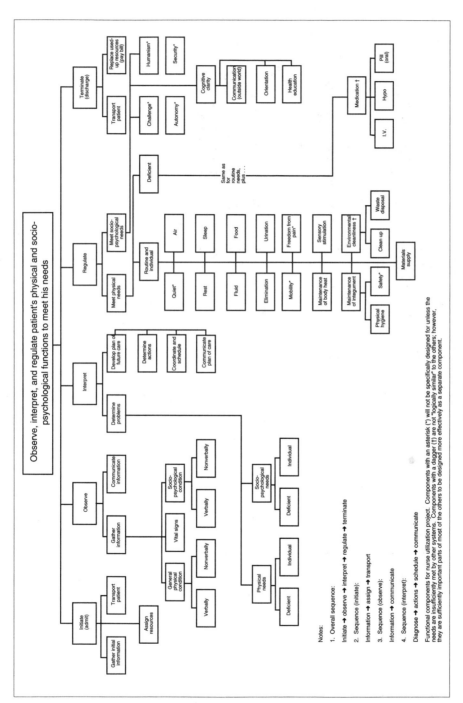

Notes:

1. Overall sequence:

Initiate → observe → interpret → regulate → terminate

2. Sequence (initiate):

Information → assign → transport

3. Sequence (observe):

Information → communicate

4. Sequence (interpret):

Diagnose → actions → schedule → communicate

Functional components for nurse utilization project. Components with an asterisk (*) will not be specifically designed for unless the needs are insufficiently met by other systems. Components with a dagger (†) are not "logically similar" to the others; however, they are sufficiently important parts of most of the others to be designed more effectively as a separate component.

Figure 8-6. Functional components.

Table 8.6 **Questions and Guides for Identifying Sub-purposes or Purpose Components**

- What are the purpose components or sub-purposes of _____? Insert the focus purpose in the blank space. Repeat the question for each functional component.

- What linkages are relatively fixed between the focus purpose and its component sub-purposes?

- What minimum number of constants make up the focus purpose level?

- What minimum set of sub-purposes or purpose components, when each one is achieved and coordinated with the others, will effectively achieve the selected level?

- What minimum number of sub purposes will be likely to remain present throughout the time horizon of the focus purpose?

- Are possible sets of purpose components of similar scope and significance?

- Is each pair in a level of purpose components relatively independent? Or does one conflict with or overlap the other?

- What criteria might help align possible purpose components: equal "size" components, number of people or organizational units per component, minimum numbers of components?

- Would mathematical decomposition or partitioning be useful? Some measurable criteria might be cost, saturated information links, minimal information flow between clusters (purpose components), connectivity, or the ratio of the number of links at a node to the maximum number possible, and relational or reachable matrices based on linkage needs and possible transitivity conditions (if A is bigger than B, and B is bigger than C, then A is bigger than C).

- Can other features such as probability of occurrence and risk factors help separate components?

- Can various techniques (e.g., questionnaires, Delphi procedure, nominal group technique) be used, especially for systems not yet in existence where subjective opinions are needed?

- Might purpose sampling (instead of activity sampling) of *stable* sub-purposes (i.e., there is a high likelihood the sub-purposes will remain during the longest possible time horizon of the project) or QFD customer terms and views uncover *importance* factors with regard to the components? (A nurse walking, for example, is recorded in purpose sampling not as walking, but as the purpose the nurse seeks to accomplish by walking, such as administering medicine, recording blood pressure, or obtaining a treatment tray.)

pose to ensure the best possible "whole system" design and interrelation-ship of the parts of the plan.

Criteria in addition to those for selecting the focus purpose are needed. One is the availability of personnel; another is the amount of time available for completing design of the total system. Given enough personnel, several purpose components can be designed concurrently. Teams may need to be set up for each one. Added resource commitments will often be required. Conversely, given sufficient time to design a sys-tem for the focus purpose, there may be no need for separate sub-pur-pose projects.

Each purpose component is approached by developing its purpose hierarchy first. Each sub-purpose project represents an opportunity that should be explored to ensure its purpose is necessary. Measures of pur-pose achievement for each purpose component are usually sub-factors or partial measures of the overall set.

Illustrations of Purpose Hierarchies

A variety of TQM projects have benefitted from the insights initi-ated by developing and reviewing a purpose hierarchy. In addition to those presented in this chapter thus far, several others are illustrated here.

Figure 8-7 was developed at a large international petroleum com-pany. The management requested a study of "Using Technology To Improve Existing Businesses as well as Developing New Businesses." Starting the project with a purpose expansion and hierarchy led the group to select the first statement related to "value and utilize technol-ogy." The real purpose of the study was uncovered by building a purpose hierarchy. The purpose the study team selected was to have a technology component in the strategic plan. The next higher level purpose was to impact and build technology into the business plan. At the current time the study team felt that its efforts were best concentrated at the purpose of having a technology component in the strategic plan since they had the contacts and resources to accomplish it. Once this was accomplished, they felt they would have built a foundation to move into the next bigger level purpose. If the original problem statement "value and utilize technology" had been pursued in its nebulous form, the team would have developed solutions to the wrong problem.

• To value knowledge and technical expertise
• To recognize technology in the corporation
• To utilize and use technology
• To profile technology and its rate of return
• To raise the profile of technology in the strategic plan
• To have a technology component in the strategic plan*
• To develop a strategic technology planning process
• To use technology as a strategic weapon
• To ensure the use of technology in the business plan
• To impact and build technology into the business plan
*Selected focus purpose

Figure 8-7. Purpose hierarchy using technology to improve existing businesses as well as developing new businesses.

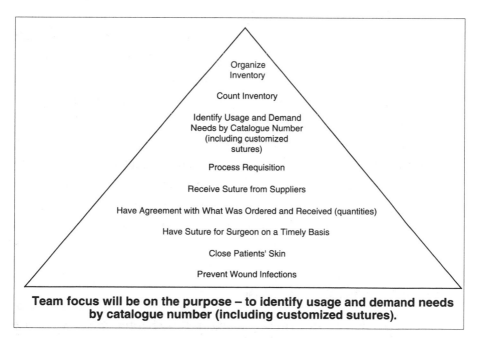

Organize
Inventory

Count Inventory

Identify Usage and Demand
Needs by Catalogue Number
(including customized
sutures)

Process Requisition

Receive Suture from Suppliers

Have Agreement with What Was Ordered and Received (quantities)

Have Suture for Surgeon on a Timely Basis

Close Patients' Skin

Prevent Wound Infections

Team focus will be on the purpose – to identify usage and demand needs by catalogue number (including customized sutures).

Figure 8-8. Purpose hierarchy for the process of procuring suture products.

Most Narrow
• To create a flexible schedule • To staff nursing units according to needs • To schedule nurses to meet staffing requirements • To provide timely staff scheduling in meeting needs of management and staff • To ensure all nursing staff understands staffing/scheduling process • To facilitate alternative staffing and scheduling system to improve patient care • To attract and retain more nurses to Bethesda through flexible staffing and scheduling plan • To facilitate adequate nursing care for patients • To schedule appropriate staff for patient care • To provide patient care at Bethesda
Most Broad

Figure 8-9. Nursing staffing and scheduling purpose hierarchy.

Figures 8-8, 8-9, and 8-10 illustrate three of many projects in the QUALITY #1 program at Bethesda Hospitals in Cincinnati, Ohio. Each of the figures is relatively self-explanatory. They show how projects in any arena can bring together the thoughts and perceptions of the diverse members of each group and put them together in a mind-opening frame of reference. Even if you believe the selected purpose level is "obvious," note the great advantage of establishing the larger context for each. The larger purposes help tremendously in stimulating creative ideas that will be much more acceptable than before to the group members. In actuality, the selected focus purpose was almost always different (and bigger) than what each group would have worked on if no hierarchy had been made.

Cases for Chapters 8 through 13

Two cases will be described starting in this chapter, to show the use of the Breakthrough Thinking process (Chapter 5) for TQM projects.

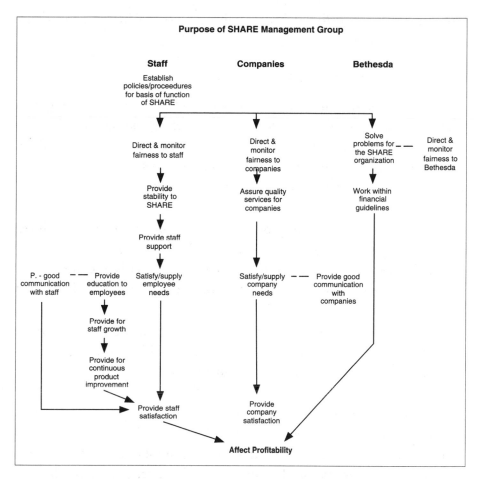

Figure 8-10. Purpose hierarchy Share Management, November 1, 1991.

The remaining steps for each case will be reviewed in the appropriate chapters that follow.

Case A: Package Tracking

A national and international package delivery company sought to improve accuracy quality and cost reduction of its package tracking system (PTS). Packages are received either by customers bringing them directly to a service center or by requesting pickup service. In the receiving area of the hub center, air packages are separated from ground packages, and they are roughly sorted by zip codes.

Throughout the entire process, packages are scanned three times. They are prepared for shipping, separating U.S. packages from International. The receipt of packages to an origin hub center is documented by scanning the barcoded tracking number on the package label. This is the Origin Scanning.

Packages are shipped to the proper destination hub center, where their receipt is also documented by scanning. This is the Destination Scanning. Here, packages are sorted out into delivery areas and they are finally delivered to their destination by trucks.

Most of the problems occur during the scanning process internal to the destination hub center. The portable data collectors used for the scanning fail to pick up or read off a tracking number either because the maintenance of batteries in the unit is not adequate, or because the unit has been damaged somehow in the process.

Most of the damaged units are a consequence of the heavy flow of packages handled by scanners which requires them to constantly move around the operation area and, therefore, they inevitably bump up against the units.

At the end of a scan, when data collector units are turned in for transmittal of records to the Central Computer Center, the statistical figures reported do not match those actually transmitted. This problem is possibly generated by bugs in the software used. Some of the major and more critical problems were:

- Labels fall off between scans
- Packages missing labels
- Packages not scanned
- Frozen/lost records of data due to damaged scanner hardware
- Labels not turned in by drivers after delivery
- Bugs in software that cause unmatching statistical figures

The team began by generating a list of possible purposes for the system. After studying all the different functions of the package tracking system, the following list of purposes was developed:

1. To track every package
2. To sort every package
3. To scan every package
4. To route every package
5. To match up origin and destination tracking numbers
6. To deliver packages to customers
7. To provide parcel service to customers
8. To deliver goods
9. To provide the status of packages upon request of customers

The Couplet Method was used to find the purpose statement to start the purpose hierarchy (compare the first purpose with the second to determine which one is smallest in scope). The smallest one is compared in the next purpose, and so on: $1 > 2, 2 > 3, 3 < 4, 3 < 5, 3 < 6, 3 < 7, 3 < 8, 3 < 9$. Therefore, purpose 3 starts the hierarchy. Comparing all the other purposes led to the following hierarchy.

1. To scan every package
2. To match up origin and destination tracking numbers
3. To sort every package
4. To track every package
5. To provide the status of packages upon request of customers
6. To route every package
7. To deliver packages to customers
8. To provide parcel service to customers
9. To deliver goods

The following criteria were used to select the focus purpose for the project:

Potential Benefits

Improving the operations of the whole system will benefit and satisfy: Management's desires and expectations, customers' needs, human and physical factors of the actual process and costs to the company will be reduced.

Management Desires

Project sponsor desires not to exceed or to go beyond the capabilities of the company. Any real world implementation has to take place within available resources and should create and achieve the desired purpose.

Customers' Needs

Customers' telephone inquiries for undelivered packages. Customers' main concern is to be informed on:
- location of their packages
- has delivery been attempted?

Time Limitations

Purpose level to be attained within a four-month period.

Political Factors

There is an urgency for change on the management's part mainly due to pressures coming from customers complaints and costs incurred.

Project Cost

Any capital investment is available as long as return on investment proves to satisfy or to be better than management's expectations.

Based on the criteria set up for selecting the purpose level, the selected focus purpose is noted in boldface in the hierarchy: **"TO PROVIDE THE STATUS OF PACKAGES UPON REQUEST OF CUSTOMERS."**

The measures of purpose accomplishment were set up with managers, using major stakeholders as the stimulus for identifying possible specific objective, (table 8-7).

Table 8.7   **Measures of Purpose Accomplishment for Package Tracking System**

Stakeholders	Values	Goals	MPA (Objectives)
Scanners	To maximize scanning efficiency	To scan every package	No. of packages not scanned (1 out of 50)
On-line supervisors	To maximize scanning efficiency	To scan every package	No. of packages not scanned/80
Management	To reduce costs of complaints/day	To reduce complaints	No. of complaints/day (0)
Customers	To obtain quick service To receive packages	To receive packages on time To locate packages	Percentage of satisfied customers/day (99.5%) No. of packages lost/day (0)
Scan clerk	To have an efficient transmit system	To transmit 100% of scanned packages	Percentage of packages transmitted (100%)
Drivers	To maximize no. of deliveries	To deliver on time	Percentage of on-time deliveries (99.5%)
Phone operators	To answer all customer inquiries	To provide information of packages	Percentage of packages with requested information unanswered/day (0%)

Case B: Emergency Operations Center

"Where Uncomfortable Officials Meet in Unaccustomed Surroundings to Play Unfamiliar Roles Making Unpopular Decisions Based on Inadequate Information in Much Too Little Time."

The Long Beach Department of Public Service wanted a facility layout which would effectively house a future Emergency Operations Center (EOC). n EOC is a centralized location where various officials can converge to coordinate, manage and efficiently employ resources in response to a major disaster. This center will collect, sort, prioritize and disseminate information. The EOC will operate under the Incident Command System (ICS) with each department carrying out their prescribed procedures. Considerations for the layout included facility location, proximity with the Communications Center, placement of each department with respect to their functions, and quality of results and process of operations. However, the EOC is only fully activated at times of a large-scale disaster, such as an 8.3 measured earthquake. Therefore, the design of the rooms and placement of furniture and equipment should facilitate a multipurpose role.

The Incident Command System (ICS) was developed as a consequence of fires that consumed large portions of Southern California in 1970. As a result of those fires, a need was identified to develop a system whereby different agencies could work together toward a common goal in an effective and efficient manner. The system consisted of procedures for controlling personnel, facilities, equipment, and communications.

The Incident Command System is a system designed to begin developing from the time an incident occurs until the requirement for management and operations no longer exists. The incident commander is a title which can apply equally to an engine company captain or to the chief of a department, depending upon the situation. The structure of the Incident Command System can be established and expanded based upon the changing conditions of the incident. This means that in only disasters of major proportions will the entire ICS system be fully activated. It is intended to be staffed and operated by qualified personnel from any emergency services agency and may involve personnel from a variety of agencies.

The ICS consists of six sections:

   1.   Incident Command

2. Public Information Officer

3. Operations

4. Logistics

5. Plans

6. Finance

There is another entity not now included in the ICS: the Policy group. The Policy group will be included in the EOC since it meets the needs of the City of Long Beach for strategic planning and setting priorities for the EOC mission. The Incident Command System organizational chart is shown in figure 8-11.

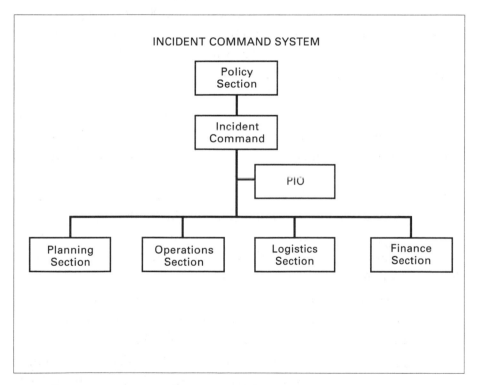

INCIDENT COMMAND SYSTEM

Figure 8-11. Incident Command System organization chart.

The Incident Command section works hand in hand with the Policy group. It is imperative that Incident Command be near the Policy group because they are in constant communication with each other. Primarily, Incident Command is the section that disseminates information and decisions made by the Policy group to other sections of the EOC. One can say that the Incident Commander is the "voice" of the Policy group. The Policy group communicates with other sections of the EOC through the Incident Command section.

The Public Information Officer's (PIO) function is to develop accurate and complete information regarding the incident cause, size, current situation, resources committed, and other matters of importance. The information officer will normally be the point of contact for the media and other governmental agencies that desire information directly about the incident.

The operations section is the heart of the EOC. It is the place where all decisions made by Policy, Plans and the IC are carried out. The operations section is responsible for all tactical command and coordinating the assets assigned to incident response in accordance with the approved Incident Action Plan.

Overall resources support for the containment and control of the incident would be coordinated and provided by the Logistics Section. Any personnel, equipment, supplies, services or any other type of resources whether public safety, mutual aid, or private sector assets, expendable materials, and so on, which are required would be routed to the Logistics Section for acquisition. The mission of the Logistics Section is to know what resources are on hand, where additional resources are available, and to keep track of these resources in order to supply them effectively to operations.

The planning section is responsible for the collection, evaluation, and dissemination of tactical information about the incident. They also perform the preparation and documentation of action plans.

The finance section is established on incidents when the agency(s) who are involved have a specific need for financial services. In the ICS, not all agencies will require the establishment of a separate finance section. In some cases where only one specific function is required like cost analysis, a position could be established as a technical specialist in the plans section.

The Policy Section ultimately provides direction and control for EOC operations. The section is made up of the Mayor, Vice Mayor and eight other Council Members. Therefore the Policy room is a place where these officials can meet without interruption to establish strategic plans and set priorities for the EOC mission.

The purpose hierarchy developed for this project is shown in figure 8-12.

1. To have an EOC
2. To provide an appropriate and efficient workspace for the required staff
3. To collect, evaluate, prioritize (validate), sort, and disseminate information
4. To determine strategies
5. To assign resources
6. To coordinate activities
7. To facilitate the response to a major emergency
8. To save lives and property

Figure 8-12. Purpose hierarchy.

With consent of all those involved, the purpose level was defined as:

To provide a single focal point for centralized management of information during a disaster response, in order to improve communications and coordination.

The measures of purpose accomplishment are shown in figure 8-13.

Values	Measures of Purpose Accomplishment	Goals	Objectives
Effective management of emergencies and major incidents	No. of deaths	Preserve life and property	0
	Property loss/damage ($)	Restore normalcy	0
Efficient, safe and survivable environment	Damage ($)	Provide security, structural integrity, proper ergonomics, and staff needs necessary to support/care for ICS organization	0
	No. of security violations		0
	No. of injuries		0
	No. of complaints		0

Figure 8-13. EOC measures of purpose accomplishment. (Page 1 of 2)

Values	Measures of Purpose Accomplishment	Goals	Objectives
Accurate and efficient decision making, evaluation, priority sorting processing, and dissemination of information and coordination of responses	Reaction time	Minimize response times according to established priorities Maximize resources Centralize decision making	<10 min.
	Percentage of incidents responded with proper resources		100%
Cost effective facility	Percentage of available hours used	Multipurpose	100
	No. of different users		>1

Figure 8-13. EOC measures of purpose accomplishment. (Page 2 of 2)

Developing Solution-after-Next Options

Chapter 9 focuses on the step in the Breakthrough Thinking process highlighted below.(The numbers in parentheses refer to the chapter in which the step is described. The Breakthrough Thinking process is detailed in Chapter 5.)

Step*	Result
1. Set up TQM program (6)	TQM mission, values, strategic plan
2. Identify primary projects and activities (7)	Initial plan of action and timeline
3. Set up TQM project (7)	Project system (purposes, people, etc.)
4. List possible purposes (8)	
5. Develop purpose hierarchies (8)	
6. Determine criteria to select purpose level (8)	
7. Select purpose(s) (8)	Focus purpose(s) in a hierarchical context
8. Establish measures of purpose accomplishment (8)	Success factors
9. Establish subgroups if needed (8)	Subgroups established
10. Generate many solution-after-next options (9)	List of viable alternatives
11. Assess solution-after-next options (10)	
* The number in parentheses after each step refers to the chapter in which the step is described	

Step*	Result
12. Select solution-after-next target (10)	Target solution-after-next
13. Modify target for irregularities (11)	
14. Choose recommended changes (11)	Recommendations
15. Prepare proposal (12)	Proposal
16. Inform people not involved to date (12)	
17. Detail recommendations (12)	Complete recommendation specifications
18. Prepare installation plan (13)	Installation plan
19. Install recommendations (13)	Installed system
20. Standardize performances (13)	System performance measures
21. Review project at betterment timeline date (14-15)	Next recommended changes
22. Repeat step 21 (14-15)	Further actions and changes

* The number in parentheses after each step refers to the chapter in which the step is described

If you know what purpose(s) needs to be achieved, you open immense possibilities for developing an effective, innovative solution– as long as you are guided by the "most ideal" or "solution-after-next" targets. That is, you constantly need to ask: How would we achieve the purpose if we could start from scratch? What solution would we likely use in three (or five or two) years if we worked on the problem then? Dealing with purposeful "best" alternatives leads to ideas that can bring significant changes.

The title of this chapter signals an important difference in the approach to TQM from what typically exists today. Currently, most organizations pursue a single solution option to accomplish their TQM objective, such as:

- Just-In-Time (JIT)
- Statistical Process Control (SPC)

- Total Participation
- Six Sigma
- Quality Circles
- Socio-Technical Work Systems
- Employee Owners
- Time-to-Market

Many organizations have thought they were being creative by putting a few of these options under an umbrella and calling it TQM. Later they became frustrated and disillusioned since the techniques did not produce the expected results. Instead, they often found they had created a bigger problem than the one they started out to solve, proving the saying that:

Yesterday's Solution = Today's Problem

Unfortunately, the very thinking that underpins successful systems operations and research is often to blame for our failures in developing innovative and implementable ideas. In pursuing the quest for the "one right answer" with the same old methodologies, many organizations only create TQM bureaucracies. Short-sighted vision and entrenched patterns of thinking can lead to "solutions" that do far more damage than the good they were intended to accomplish.

To break out of this cycle, first the purpose hierarchy opens the solution space available to the TQM team or individual. It carves out the perspective of "what we want to accomplish." The other Breakthrough Thinking principles then come into play:

- Solution-After-Next Principle, the subject of this chapter, (seeking the most effective "how" to achieve the focus purpose)
- Betterment Timeline Principle (considering larger purposes and creative solutions-after-next in structuring a built-in process of continual improvement)
- Limited Information Collection Principle (making certain time and effort are expended only on data collection geared to

the focus purpose, its implementation, and the betterment timeline)

The creative process–how innovative ideas emerge in the human mind–remains largely a mystery. We do know, however, that creativity involves much more than generating unusual or far-reaching ideas. We have already seen, for example, how an assessment of purposes is essential preparation for developing outstanding solution ideas, and the methods used to implement a solution are equally critical. That's why we use the term *Full Spectrum Creativity*^{SM} when talking about the Breakthrough Thinking process. We will use the word creativity extensively in this chapter to refer to the process of developing solution options because it occurs so much in the literature. However, the whole approach described in Chapters 6 through 14 constitute what we mean by *Full Spectrum Creativity.*

It should be quite understandable why we do not know how innovative or creative ideas develop in the mind. After all, we do not know how the brain works for all human activities, let alone how it produces a creative concept. That is why the approach of this book is so exciting: It provides a challenging way of searching for major breakthroughs and the most effective answers, knowing that there is no promise of certainty.

The critical guide in the search for solution options is the concept of purposes, which sets up the problem. As Albert Einstein once said, "The *formulation* of a problem is often more essential than its solution...To raise new questions, new problems, to regard old problems from a new angle, requires creative imagination and makes real advances..." The focus purpose, the hierarchy in which it is located, and even other purpose statements not used in the hierarchy provide the important mind-opening start. Developing a solution-after-next or ideal system for the future is the next step. ("Solution-after-next" and "ideal system" are used inter-changeably here.)

Guidelines and Rationales for Developing Ideal Solutions

- Avoid early convergence on a solution for the focus purpose, even though it would most likely be better than any solution found with the conventional analytical and segmental approach. Getting real breakthroughs needs openness to consider many possibilities. As such, divergent thinking is best at the beginning of the process. We have already seen this when developing purposes. Seeking as many ideal systems or solution-after-next ideas continues this expansive kind of thinking.

- Bring out the innovative thinking everyone possesses. Ideas and objects labelled *creative*–that is, original and useful to or valued by society–are often chalked up to divine inspiration or individual talent. There are some people, of course, who do exhibit a propensity for creativity. Many studies, however, show that each individual is able to can develop unusual ideas (and get better at it with practice), if the setting is appropriate. While exploring purposes starts this favorable opening of the mind, seeking solutions-after-next and ideal systems gives people faith in their own abilities to generate ideas. They focus their attention on innovation with penetrating and searching questions. It gives people the opportunity to explore new ideas, experiment by combining ideas in new ways, and probe ways to improve what they have always felt should be changed.

- Focus initially on idea generation, not evaluation. Aiming at the "best" or "most ideal" helps people to use this long-standing idea in the creativity literature. Conventional problem-solving approaches tend to let people poke holes in an idea as it is presented, because the ideas are random and of highly variable consequences. Seeking solutions-after-next also provides a way of getting a wide variety of background perspectives involved, because people need an opening for proposing unusual thoughts without feeling foolish.

- Seek the biggest change possible. Everyone knows that most changes are incremental. Continuous improvement is based on this concept. This does not mean that each incremental improvement has to be a small one. Seeking the biggest change possible is especially important in today's world where dramatic political and social changes almost always require a "return to square one" for most problems–defense, social services, corporate organization, health care delivery, education, insurance, banking, and so on. What should be sought is not simply what might solve the *immediate* problem, but what goes beyond the immediacy and the accomplishment of the singular purpose. The solution chosen to achieve a purpose should be as close as possible to the solution-after-next target (SANT) or feasible ideal system target (FIST). The ideal will serve as a long-term guide to stimulate continuing improvements. Call it building castles in the air, or needing a clear long-term view, or desiring to take things to the next level as a never-ending process, the approach is a critical way to achieve the dictum of Alan Kay, an Apple computer scientist: "The best way to predict the future is to invent it."

- Experiment with ideas. Fiddling around with many solution-after-next options is a necessary part of creativity. Even when time is short, keeping options open as long as possible helps provide experimenting space for a group. Experimenting creates an intellectual "incubator" for ideas to germinate, some of which might otherwise not be considered. Additional knowledge gained in toying with the ideas gives some of the more fragile ideas a chance to unfold.

- Expand the group's awareness of the situation. The purposes hierarchy explored different "situations" and provided insights into the larger framework in which solutions should be sought. Now solutions-after-next and ideal systems provide another mechanism for making people aware of the full range of alternatives (from competitors, new technologies, customer desires, etc.) that might impact their proposed solutions.

- Learn to think like effective problem-solvers. Envisioning solutions a group would use if it could begin again replicates the thinking processes of the most creative problem-solvers in business and industry.

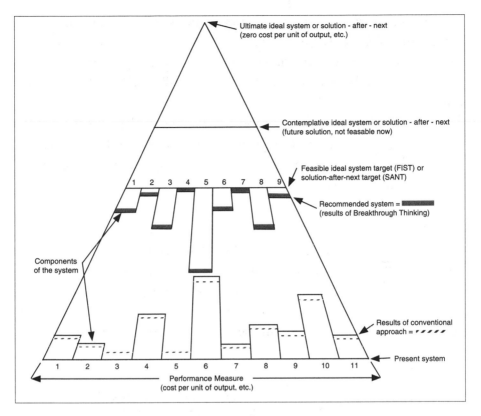

Figure 9-1. Levels of ideal systems for a necessary purpose.

Meaning of Solution-after-Next or Ideal System

A solution-after-next or an ideal system depends largely on the situation. A FIST or SANT for a luxury car manufacturer, for example, is very likely to be significantly different from that of a mass-market compact producer. This section explains the general concepts behind such targets so that they are easier to apply to specific settings.

"Ideal" might be defined as perfect, absolute, consummate, best, faultless, flawless, pure, unblemished, choice, quintessential, or prime. The concept of "ideal" can be likened to a compass on a ship, in that the compass points the ship toward a desired destination. You may experience difficulties with the voyage, but there is at least an excellent chance of reaching the desired destination.

A positive way to use the experience and knowledge of people is to ask continually, "What are some ideal and purposeful solutions from which a target can be selected?" The target will cause people to seek and accept changes. Satisfaction with a solution should not deter further changes.

The simple representation shown in figure 9-1 identifies three levels of a solution-after-next or ideal system. Assume that each line connecting two equidistant points along the legs of the angle defines a performance measure of importance.

Ultimate

The apex of the triangle in figure 9-1 represents zero cost per unit, no scrap, no energy needs per unit, or zero time per service (the infinity level). Of course, an ultimate level *for a necessary purpose* can never be reached, and no attempt is ever made to design an ultimate ideal system. Yet the ultimate level is important because it represents the absolute best.

Contemplative

This term refers to a solution that could not be installed until further developments rendered it feasible. Contemplative ideal systems present visionary and utopian challenges: How *can* the metal be made to shrink more as it cools? How *can* the product be distributed automatically? How *can* the traffic flow be arranged without any stops? As the result of a contemplative ideal system proposal in a meat processing firm, an entirely new product was suggested, investigated, found feasible to produce, and then marketed successfully.

Feasible

A feasible ideal system is one that could be installed assuming only *regularity conditions* actually prevailed. For example, the most frequently ordered mechanical pencil out of, say, 53 styles and 14 colors may comprise only 17% of all sales, but ideal systems and solutions-after-next should be developed as if this style and color comprised 100% of the orders. (Regularity may also concern conditions in the outside world over which you have no control, but which are nonetheless considered most important with regard to the focus purpose.)

In figure 9-1, a feasible solution-after-next target (SANT) has been selected to guide the development of the recommended solution—which, in this case, consists of nine components (a frequent breakthrough in solutions is the reduction in the number of components in the new system, compared in this example to the present number of eleven). Each component has a certain cost per output unit. The need for 14 colors of mechanical pencils instead of one, for example, causes the development of other ideas that would seek to modify component 1 as little as possible. Component 3, when examined, may involve a capital expenditure far beyond the resources and borrowing capacity of the organization. Therefore, the alternative involves a greater cost per unit than the target component, but at a proportion that may be different from component 1. The same examination goes on for each component in the system. Some of the components, such as numbers 4 and 7, are used directly as designed in the target. The recommended system then includes the selected alternative of each component that stays as close as possible to the target component.

Groups should be encouraged to consider many ideas before reaching closure on a recommendation. Developing many alternative ideas, even if not ideal, is far more likely to lead to a creative "best" or "most effective" solution. In addition, discussions and even arguments about ideal systems and targets are preferable to looking for who is to blame for a problem or what are the "real" facts about the problem. This carries on the process begun with purposes, where many alternatives are generated as well.

All such alternatives, regardless of how crudely they may be stated, should be considered for as long as possible. There is no way to anticipate in advance if a breakthrough solution is possible, so developing many creative and ideal alternatives increases markedly the probability of finding a breakthrough.

Concepts of Idea Generation

Many studies have reported on personality characteristics of creative people, organizational conditions that spawned creative ideas, group dynamics that fostered creativity, and other topics that report about *past* creative situations. But none of these offers prescriptions for generating new ideas or being creative, let alone explains *how* creative ideas are generated.

We have found most helpful the "bisociation" explanation of what happens in the human mind when purposeful and creative ideas emerge. Bisociation postulates that ideas occur in the human brain when two thoughts, two concepts, two models, two "things," two abstractions, or two unrelated items are mentally forced to intersect. It is at this juncture that creative and purposeful ideas emerge, whether or not they can consciously be traced back to the forced relationship. Nor does it make much difference if an idea can or cannot be related to two specific items.

A prescriptive version of bisociation asks that a person think of two planes "floating" in space, each one representing one of the two items. The forced relationship between the two can be visualized as a line along which the two planes intersect, and along which the idea is structured and turned into a recognizable form.

Figure 9-2 illustrates the two bisociation planes. One of the planes represents the focus purpose(s). The secondary plane represents the concept, or thought, that is forced to intersect with the primary purpose plane. The two planes are forced to intersect many times, each time with a different thought, technique, or concept forming the secondary plane. The forced intersection can benefit from different perspectives juxtaposed with the purpose plane. The major items that could comprise the secondary plane are noted in figure 9-2.

Moving from the individual mind to conditions that help a group generate ideas leads to several suggestions. To improve group generation of creative ideas, we suggest the following:

- Rule out criticism when ideas are being generated. Assessing ideas occurs separately, in the next step.

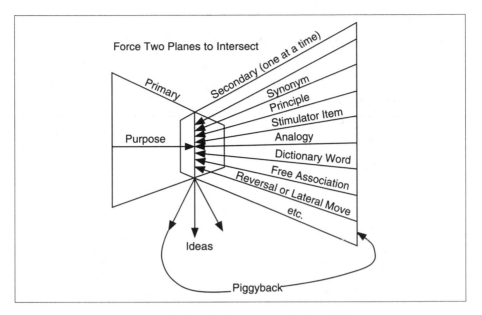

Figure 9-2. Bisociation concept of creativity.

- Encourage freewheeling, no matter how wild the ideas may seem. Even fantasies should be encouraged.
- Use different techniques to suit the different forces that stimulate different people.
- Try to improve an idea by building on it or by combining it with other ideas. Piggybacking can help. Ask, "What if?" Probe how the idea could be made to work.
- Consider everyone "equal" (i.e., forbid status differences during meetings).
- Secure top-level commitment to policies that support continuing change and improvement.
- Be persistent in achieving purposes.
- Get the participation of other people in applying the Breakthrough Thinking principles.
- Involve people not connected with the project.
- Consider brain resting. Stop idea generation for an hour (or a day) and then return to it.

- Record all ideas about how to achieve the purpose(s).

- Put aside specific times outside of formal meetings to generate ideas.

- Build teams. Dealing with purposes is a critical team-building activity. So is developing solutions-after-next, because the process helps build a shared vision while conducive to openness and team learning.

- Maintain a positive attitude.

- Learn to listen.

- Let intuition have its day. Follow up values and preferences with explorations of ideal ways to accomplish them.

- Have fun. Let the humor of some solutions-after-next and ideal systems engage participants.

- Handle ideas gingerly. Change negatives to positive possibilities (e.g., ask, "How can we make the idea workable," rather than seeking reasons why it wouldn't work). Scale down expensive ideas. Never say "never." Have an advocacy team for each idea.

- Seek simplicity. Use this statement as a stimulus for trying to develop the workability of a complex idea.

- Encourage risk-taking ideas. Claiming an idea represents too much of a risk is a deadly form of negativism, often cloaked in the garb of safeguarding the organization's existence.

- Set up a partnership or alliance. This is a more formal way of getting outsiders involved. Large projects may need such joint ventures as a way of encouraging the development of unusual ideas.

- Keep options open as long as possible. Premature closure on solution ideas is just as dangerous as deciding that you already know the purpose of the project or system that initiates the effort. Instead of ignoring an idea, invest some time or even place a "call option" on a promising but unknown solution.

There are literally hundreds of techniques and methods for developing creative ideas. They all seek to stimulate the human mind in some way as a way to elicit ideas. Some are simple, depending on one basic prod, while others are more extensive, using lists of questions, words, and/or frameworks of interrelation-ships. Both types need the "primary purposes" plane of figure 9-2, with which the particular "technique" plane intersects. Almost all the techniques overlap, but using several still provides different stimuli that help foster idea development. Figure 9-2 includes a few techniques that stimulate the generation of creative ideas. They all use questioning as the means of turning problem-solving into an occasion for opportunity-solving. An explanation of these and other techniques follows (see Appendix for references for most of them).

Some of the simple tools are reviewed first. All techniques should be repeated several times to generate as many ideas as possible.

Visualize the future: How would a system work in, say, 10 to 15 years to achieve the focus and bigger purposes?

Ideal competition: How do you imagine your ideal competitor would set up a system or solution that would achieve the focus and bigger purposes? If your product or service didn't exist, what would your customers buy? What would your product have to be like to attract customers?

Perfect product or system: How would the ideal product or system be specified to achieve the focus and bigger purposes?

Re-engineering: Set up initially for computing and information systems, this technique is virtually the same as asking how you could achieve the focus and bigger purposes if you started again.

Paradigm change: Similar to re-engineering, this technique asks how a product or system would work to achieve the focus and bigger purposes if the conventional paradigm were discarded in favor of a new one (i.e., using aluminum instead of steel, tying the customer's computer system to yours, having suppliers design components for your product instead of you). This technique is related to the "Pretend" technique, in which you imagine how your aims are met.

Technologies for the future: New technologies are always emerging. How would a solution-after-next for the focus or bigger purposes of your product or system be affected by gene engineering or photonics or digital taping? If current trends in robotics (or any other technology) continue, what system might be available in five years to accomplish the purpose?

Prototyping: Rapid prototyping of products is available for product development. How could an ideal system be conceptually prototyped to achieve its focus and bigger purposes? Imaging or envisioning the elements of a solution is similar.

Customer satisfaction requirements: How would a solution-after-next or ideal system for your product or business work if it met the product, sales, after-sales, and corporate culture requirements of your customers? Ask your customers (and suppliers) what their versions of an ideal system would be. Learn from your customers and suppliers instead of doing market research and setting standards.

Core competencies: How would you ideally use and build on the basic skills and advantages you now have as a means of achieving the focus and bigger purposes?

Synonyms: Develop a list of synonyms (or antonyms) for each major word or phrase in the purpose statement (a thesaurus is helpful). Use each one, one at a time, as the secondary plane to intersect with the purpose plane: "What does (purpose x) and (synonym/antonym y) bring to mind?" "How would an ideal system or solution-after-next work to achieve the focus or bigger purposes by means of (synonym/antonym y)?"

Principles: Virtually every area of an organization is governed by a set of principles that represent ideal or desirable conditions. Here is a sampling of the areas in which such principles apply:

- Plant layout
- Packaging
- Automation
- Computer systems
- Organization design
- Office layout

- Machine and tool engineering
- Materials handling
- Instrument design
- Accident prevention
- Electronic devices
- Job design
- Appropriate technology
- Human factors
- Product design
- Information handling
- Physiological distress
- Anthropometric measurement
- Production processing
- Forms design
- Motion economy
- Counseling
- Inventory control
- Warehousing
- Ergonomics
- Production processing
- Chemical processing
- Cybernetics
- Urban planning

Table 9-1 lists the principles used in developing ideal systems. Often these principles are given different terms, such as checklists, laws, theories, precepts, maxims, guidelines, ideologies, or postulates. Key words sometimes signal the principles: adapt, modify, magnify, minify, rearrange, reverse, substitute, invert, combine, and so on. However they are worded, the principles are used one at a time as the secondary plane to intersect with the purpose plane: "How would an ideal system or solution-after-next work to achieve (focus purpose x) by means of (principle/law/precept/ checklist item y)?"

Table 9.1 **Principles for Designing Ideal Systems**

• Eliminate the need for the purpose.

• Specify one low-cost input.

• Specify one low-cost output.

• Put related knowledge/experience/information together when action is needed.

• Use automated techniques–automation, electronic data processing, and so on.

• Deal with variances at their point of origin–adaptive control.

• Utilize each resource 100%.

• Deal with regularity factors before exceptions.

• Consider each measure of purpose accomplishment one at a time.

• Ask, "How would you do it if you started all over again? With the technology of five years from now: If only a scientific breakthrough were made in gene engineering (or some other field)?"

Stimulator Items: Every subject area has many illustrations of previously successful ideas or solutions that can be turned into stimulators or prods for discovering new ideas. One excellent format for organizing such discoveries is the system matrix. Table 9-2 shows the arrays that might be put together for just two of the eight elements in a manufacturing setting. Sometimes the stimulators are put on cards that can be used systematically or at random to prompt a group or individual.

Analogy and Metaphor: Use innovative solutions in a completely different field as the basis of the secondary plane. Or try to turn what is strange into something familiar (or vice versa). Or select a completely different field in which the same type of purpose may be needed and develop alternatives for that field, then use the solution from the second field as the basis for adaptation in the initial field: "How would an ideal system or solution-after-next work to achieve (focus purpose *x*) by means of (analogy *y*)?" Such questions and methods avoid the spurious and slipshod analogies conventional thinking often produces.

Table 9.2 **Sample Manufacturing Stimulators for
System Inputs and Sequence** (Page 1 of 3)

(See Chapter 4 for all eight system elements.)

Inputs: What ideal input specifications can you design for the purpose/function by considering:

New material	Scrap
Another material	Packaging
Frill elimination	Standardized parts
Standardized forms	Purchased items
Parts manufacturing	Size of part
Positioning devices	Received size (length, width, etc.)
Shelf life	Finish specifications (colors, etc.)
Shape	Product design to eliminate a material
Small parts	Modular construction
Packing material	One-time carbons
Non-tangling parts	Supplier performing additional work
Weight of parts	Auxiliary materials (oils, etc.)
Strong material	Reverse of cause and effect
Quantities shipped light-gauge material (also heavy-gauge)	Strict specifications of incoming quality
Palletized loads	Number of output components
Quantities packaged	Enlarged parts
Packing rearrangement	Composite materials
Acceptance sampling	Programmed instruction
Parts redundancy	No parts redundancy
Time to obsolescence	Prepacking to specifications

Table 9.2 **Sample Manufacturing Stimulators for System Inputs and Sequence** (Page 2 of 3)

(See Chapter 4 for all eight system elements.)	
Analogy with completely different system	Piggybacking of one input with another

Sequence: What ideal sequence specifications can you design for the purpose/function by considering:

Order of performance	Combination jigs
Rebalance of work	Physical processing technique
Scrap handling procedure	People receiving form or report
Lot size	New processing techniques
Two operations combined into one	One operation turned into two
Operation in another department	Services (air, gas, water, etc.)
Number of steps	Sliding, rotating, and fixed parts
Requirements for preceding and succeeding jobs	Performance during machine time on another job
Dispatch of material from central point	Magnetic circular fields (microscopic) or bubbles in metal
Unit loads	Processing more than one at a time
No controls	Two or more operations
Controls established sooner or later	Large quantities
Real-time response	Omission of operations
Sensors	Number of steps
Microfilm	Resource allocation
Parts redundancy	Reporting directly to worker
No parts redundancy	Department size
Additional package uses	Level of decision making
Handlings	Electronic devices

Table 9.2 **Sample Manufacturing Stimulators for System Inputs and Sequence** (Page 3 of 3)

(See Chapter 4 for all eight system elements.)	
New equipment	Continuous flow processing
Piggybacking one sequence with another	Relocation and rearrangement of operations
Programmed instruction	Homogeneous activities
Digital control	Requirements for succeeding jobs
Reverse order	Work while parts are in transition
Alikes and unalikes	Location of performance
Steps in best order	Training of operator
Multispindle setup	Reprocessed scrap
Performance after more operations than at present	Computer-aided design and manufacturing
Two operations at one place	Modular construction
Material changes (see "input" list)	Computer-based training
Combination machinery or equipment	Correct performance or method on previous jobs
Operation(s) on another machine(s)	Site requirements
Heuristic decision-making process	Telemetering
Slack in critical and other parts	Inventory levels
Electronic teaching devices	Span of control
Proper point for verification	Shipment from storage
Number of controls	Regenerating answers with logic
In-process inventory	Analogy with a different system
Direct shipment	Location of storage
Delegation of authority and decision-making	

Dictionary Words: Thumb through a dictionary and pick out a word at random, then pose the same question: "How could we possibly achieve (purpose *x*) by means of (dictionary word *y*)?" This is a lot of fun for any group.

Free Association: A variant of the dictionary word method, this technique uses a thought, object, or vision as the basis of a question. Notes and forms drawn on paper are often used to start a chain of associations that may lead to ideas.

Reversal or Lateral Move: Sometimes called zigzag thinking, this method borrows from some of the others. A reversal might look at smaller purposes in the hierarchy as the secondary plane (instead of the "frontal" attack of using larger purposes only), and a lateral move might be an analogy or stimulator. Both are represented in thinking about how to accomplish the "opposite" purpose, or how *not* to achieve the focus purpose, or piggybacking on another idea and thinking about its "opposite."

Imaging or Future Perfect Thinking: Use the measures of purpose accomplishment as the secondary plane to visualize what the solution might be if that measure were achieved "completely." Then use each measure in the same way. Both the measures and the images serve as stimulators to determine how that future might be reached.

Scenario Planning: This technique for describing a solution-after-next has two levels: first write out the scenes of what is desired, and, second, write out the actions needed (administrative "moves," resource acquisition, possible "games" of people, etc.) to implement the first scenario. Scenario writing brings out multiple perspectives, and the system matrix can be a guide in stimulating thoughts about factors, elements, and dimensions to consider. Scenarios help rid the mind of the desire to have a single point or line forecast of any specific factor. They let people pursue the "what if" questions: "What if we had a 100-megabyte computer that fit in a watch-size container for your wrist?" Then, "How would an ideal system work to achieve the purpose(s) using that development?" Preparing several scenarios with the involvement of many people inside and outside the organization avoids the illusion of certainty so many people seek in forecasts, and reduces vulnerability to surprises.

Morphological Analysis: A morphological matrix, box, tree, or array are other terms that represent the essence of this technique. Various values, dimensions, examples, characteristics, conditions, properties, or attributes of a relatively independent variable become the columns, while the aspects of another variable constitute the rows. Each cell becomes a forced relationship between the two variables to generate ideas. The two variables can be one or more of several sets available in the organization: purpose hierarchy and measures of effectiveness, inputs and outputs, regularities and functional components, business strengths and industry attractiveness, levels of people involved and values, product mix and market served, and so on.

Computer-Assisted Stimulators: Many of the word lists, checklists, principles, and stimulator words and phrases are now available on a large number of computer programs to help generate creative ideas. For example, IdeaFisher has over 705,000 words and phrases that can be presented within selected categories in a relational form to stimulate the viewer(s) to think up ideas. Presenting one word or phrase in relation to a second reflects the bisociation concept of forcing an intersection. These computer programs could use the focus or other purpose statements as one of the phrases. The output of such programs is a list of ideas that can be recorded in the computer. The PLAN computer software, developed specifically to take you by the hand through the Breakthrough Thinking process, includes a section on developing solution-after-next options. The above computer techniques can be used to supplement this section of PLAN.

Group Techniques: Delphi, nominal group, brainstorming, brain writing, telephone conferences, and individual interviews are just some of the techniques that are useful in generating ideas, used alone or with others. Asking each person to generate ideas away from a meeting for group discussion also can be quite effective. Some of these techniques, such as nominal group and brainwriting, are facilitated with computer-based group decision-support systems (GDSS). In such cases, each person in a group meeting has a networked computer that permits his or her entries to be entered and displayed as needed on a projection screen or individual monitors. Manipulation of the ideas, as well as full record keeping, is an advantage of GDSS.

Asking People Outside Your Organization, Discipline, or Profession: In addition to customers and suppliers, ask friends and experts from completely different fields, products, or services how they would envision an ideal system working that would achieve the focus purpose(s).

Heuristics: Many fields such as engineering design, systems architecting, and urban and regional planning, have developed a set of heuristics[1] or insights that can be used to stimulate ideas. Examples of heuristics are "The product and process must match," "An element good enough in a small system is unlikely to be good enough in a more complex one," and "To be tested, a system must be designed to be tested."

Table 9-3 suggests a number of ways to generate solutions-after-next, using the techniques described above. Item B makes specific reference to them, but all of the items can benefit from the techniques. In any event, your overriding goal should to be to seek as many ideas as possible.

Each item in table 9-3 is stated in a form that fits the bisociation concept. Item A, for instance, puts the bigger purpose levels onto the secondary plane, forcing an intersection of it with the primary plane concerning the selected purpose level. Item D puts regularity conditions onto the secondary plane and Item F uses measures of purpose accomplishment. Except for Item G, the suggestions listed can be done in any order.

---

1. E. R. Rechtin, *Systems Architecting*, Englewood Cliffs, NJ: Prentice Hall, 1991.

**Table 9.3   Generating Alternative Solutions-after-Next
(or Ideal Systems)**

A. Develop ideal systems that would eliminate the need for the focus purpose. What ideas achieve a bigger purpose?

B. Develop ideal systems for achieving the selected (and bigger) purpose by applying creativity techniques.

C. Develop ideal systems for achieving the selected (and bigger) purpose that eliminate the need for any assumed limitation.

D. Develop ideal systems for regularity conditions.

E. Develop ideal systems by reviewing the initial list of purposes and using suggestions contained therein.

F. Develop ideal systems that focus on satisfying only one measure of effectiveness. Repeat for end measure.

G. Review the list of ideas generated. For each clearly unachievable idea, develop proposals for the nearest approximation that is close to being feasible.

It is not likely that every technique will be used for each project. Selecting which tools to use depends on the preferences of the group and facilitator. A facilitator will probably select five to eight favorites to use, as figure 9-3 shows for one reviewer of this book.

Draw a picture
• Prototyping

Imagining the future
• Paradigm change
• Ideal competition
• Technologies for the future
• Imagining of "future perfect" thinking
• Perfect product or system

Figure 9-3.   Sample list of a facilitator's favorite tools for generating solutions-after-next. (Page 1 of 2)

Stimulators
• Dictionary words
• Stimulator items
• Check items
• Computer stimulators

Analogy and Metaphor

Morphological Analysis

Reversal or Lateral Move

Principles
• Principles
• Core competencies

Figure 9-3. Sample list of a facilitator's favorite tools for
generating solutions-after-next. (Page 2 of 2)

The critical outcome of this step is a list of as many specific ideas as possible of solutions-after-next and ideal systems for achieving the selected or bigger purposes in the hierarchy. A *specific* idea is one that does not merely reiterate with similar or other words the stimulator or principle being used. For example, an ideal system for preparing invoices should not be stated as "use electronic data processing"; this merely restates Principle 5 of table 9-1. A specific statement might be: "The customer's order is entered on the computer, which deducts the quantities from the inventory memory, adds them to the computer sales analysis register, and automatically types the combination production order-shipping copy for file, bill of lading-invoice form..." When principle reiteration or very general statements occur, the proposer should be asked, "What do you mean by that?" or "How can you/we make that idea work?"

A second outcome, not always attained or necessary, is a list of questions for which information may need to be collected. Seeking ideal systems is probably the best source of such prospective unknowns about which information will need to be sought. It is virtually certain that not all potential sources of knowledge and latest developments will be known to everyone on the project team, even if some of them are "experts" in the field. Not all questions will need a serious information-gathering effort, but the right questions are likely to be asked through this process.

The Solution-After-Next Principle teaches us to stay close to the next solution and to go beyond the obvious. The design team should be planning changes now based on what might be the solution of the future. The team needs to think ideally and freshly. Ask, "What would we do next if what we have identified today were fully implemented now? What would we do after that to move the organization forwards?"

The solution-after-next approach focuses the TQM design team on exciting potential solutions that can be implemented now or in the near future.

In short, solution-after-next thinking moves the organization ahead of its competition.

Case Illustrations

Case A: Package Tracking

Possible solutions were developed for the package tracking system (introduced in Chapter 8) by using several methods:

First Method Used: Principles Technique

Possible solutions were generated from the following questions:
- What is the best way to achieve the selected purpose level?
- What ideal system would best fit the selected purpose level?
- What are some of the regularity conditions we have to keep in mind when generating ideas?

Second Method Used: Free Association

The key word used for this technique was "efficiency." Each member of the team took part in "brainwriting." Afterwards, team members discussed each of the ideas. All the ideas were then collected and each one discussed and further expanded.

Ideal Systems

To review briefly, the goal here is to find ultimate but unattainable ideal solutions. his assumes a perfect system in which start-up costs and overhead are not of immediate concern. It is understood that these factors play a major role at later stages of the project, but to avoid certain biases they were neglected now. Later, some of the ideas were modified to accommodate those very factors. Some of the potential solutions in their original form seemed unfeasible at first, but later were considered feasible after adjustments were made.

The list of ideas, including partial and complete solutions, was organized in the following ways:

Major Alternative: An idea that in itself would, if implemented, achieve the selected purpose level. Of those generated, only one is selected as the target solution. A major alternative should consist of several components and details (explained below).

Component: A smaller solution than a major alternative, which cannot achieve the selected purpose by itself. A major alternative can be achieved by using several components.

Detail: Any remaining ideas that are not large enough to be components, and that can be used in either components or major alternatives.

After sorting all inputs from the group, the ideas were classified as follows:

Major Alternatives
- Photograph tracking
- Triple label method
- Current system

Components
- Manual tracking
- Dot code tracking
- Add-on information on bar code labels
- Conveyor belt scanning
- Use of diads

Details
- Fixed position scanners
- Use of three different color-coded shipping forms (next day, second day, international)

- Bar code labels with address
- Imaging within hub
- Increased staff

Details were pieced together in several ways in order to create more solutions. By using details and components, expanding on them and modifying them, ten alternative solutions were developed. These solutions are briefly described in the next few pages.

The following alternatives, components, and details were generated, keeping all of the following system regularities in mind:

Package is received.

- A driver may pick up a package and deliver it to the hub.
- The customer may bring the package directly to the hub for shipping.

Tracking label is affixed to package by company or customer.

- The customer must keep tracking number so package can be identified later on.

A preliminary sort is done to determine general region where package is sent.

Package is prepared for shipping.

- Small items are packaged in multiples in a bag (a package is small if it can fit through a coat hanger).
- Normal packages are loaded directly into the shipping igloo.
- Bulky items are packaged separately.

Package is transported to its destination hub.

Package is sorted for delivery.

Package is delivered to its destination.

List of Alternatives (composed of major alternatives, components, and details listed above)

- Photograph tracking
- Radar tracking
- Triple label method, imaging within hub
- Dot code tracking system with add-on information bar code labels

- Calculator tracking with current system and fixed position scanners
- Conveyor belt scanning, imaging within hub
- Manual tracking with increased staff
- Current system with fixed scanners and diads
- Conveyor belt scanning and the use of diads
- Paperless system with diads

Each of these alternatives was briefly described in scenario and system matrix formats to permit assessment, as illustrated in Chapter 10.

Case B: Emergency Operations Center

Two major considerations guided the development of alternatives for the Emergency Operations Center (introduced in Chapter 8):

- site location
- facility layout

Site Location

The Long Beach Department of Public Service was open to suggestions of where to place the EOC. In the beginning the Public Service team thought the EOC would be best situated. But the land there turned out to be hazardous because of an earthquake fault. Through more searching, the team found an infrequently used auditorium of the Gas Department. In addition to offering this site, the Gas Department suggested the possibility of building on a site on which now sits a pipe and wrapping storage building. More investigation of the grounds prompted the team to consider a covered parking structure and a compressor building as yet other potential sites. Although the Gas Department had not offered these, they were included as possible EOC sites.

In summary, the Public Service team settled on four alternative sites for the EOC, all located on the grounds of the Gas Department. The map (figure 9-4) of the Gas Department shows the entire parcel of land. These four sites are:

- Alternative 1: The compressor building
- Alternative 2: The covered parking garage

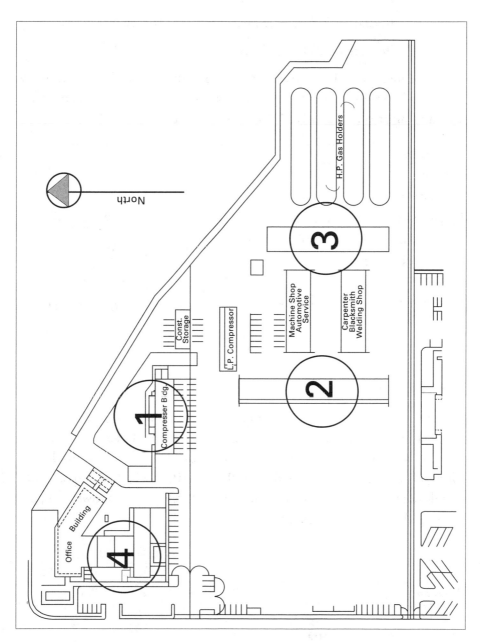

Figure 9-4. Four alternative sites.

- Alternative 3: The pipe and wrapping storage warehouse

- Alternative 4: The auditorium

The measures of purpose accomplishment for the site selection are shown in figure 9-5, and the decision matrix in figure 9-6. The compressor building area (Alternative 1) was chosen as the site.

Measures	Unit	Worst	Best
Total area	sq. ft.	0	15,500
Distance from nearest hp gas holder	feet	0	760
Distance from nearest entrance	feet	845	280
Distance to middle of natural gas holder (future parking lot)	feet	540	140
Area per person	sq. ft.	0, 250	125
Distance from line of fire (high pressure gas holders)	feet	0	414

Figure 9-5. Site measures of purpose accomplishment.

Facility Layout

The team developed a Relationship Chart (figure 9-7) before identifying various configurations of the EOC's functions. Layout measures of purpose accomplishment are shown in figure 9-8. The various layout configurations are shown in figures 9-9, 9-10, 9-11, and 9-12. Additional information for each alternative was developed, as shown in figure 9-13 for Alternative 2 (figure 9-10).

Criteria	Alternatives				
	WT	Alt 1	Alt 2	Alt 3	Alt 4
Total area	3	9.5	8.5	8.5	2
Distance from nearest hp gas holder	4	8	8	1	9
Distance from nearest entrance	5	9	6	1	10
Ratings: 5 = Best ⟶ 1 = Worst					

Figure 9-6. Site decision matrix. (Page 1 of 2)

Criteria	Alternatives				
	WT	Alt 1	Alt 2	Alt 3	Alt 4
Distance to middle of natural gas holder (future parking lot)	4	8	9	1	7
Area per person	4	8	7	10	2
Distance from line of fire (high pressure gas holders)	5	6	1	1	8
Total	270	199.5	156.5	83.5	168
Ratings: 5 = Best ⟶ 1 = Worst					

Figure 9-6. Site decision matrix. (Page 2 of 2)

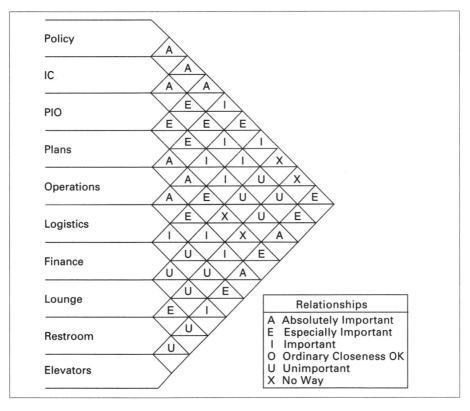

Figure 9-7. Activity relationship chart for each department.

Measures	Unit	Worst	Best
Optimum use of workspace	%	0	100

Hallway space:
  Aisle width
  Aisle space
	
	feet
	%
		
		3.5
		0
			
			6
			20

Area per person:
  Policy
  IC
  PIO
  Plans
  Operations
  Logistics
  Finance
	sq. ft.	
		0
		0
		0
		0
		0
		0
		0
			
			50
			80
			50
			100
			100
			70
			50

Distance from elevator:	feet	145	0
Distance from nearest stair	feet	145	0
Number of exits	no.	0	3
Number of entrances	no.	0	2
Total area used	**sq. ft.**	**0**	**11,500**

Figure 9-8. Layout measures of purpose accomplishment.

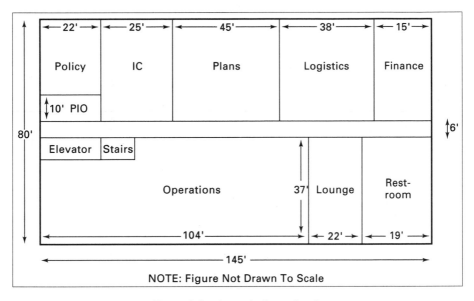

Figure 9-9. Layout alternative 1.

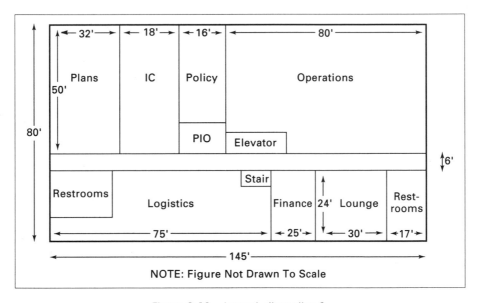

Figure 9-10. Layout alternative 2.

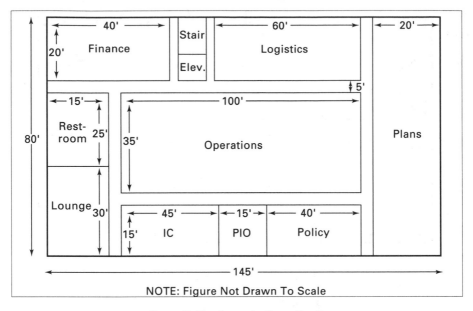

Figure 9-11. Layout alternative 3.

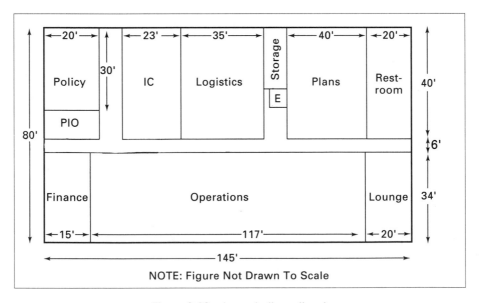

Figure 9-12. Layout alternative 4.

Measure	Amount	Percent
Amount of workspace used: (excluding the restroom, lounge, aisles, elevators and stairs)	9,106 sq. ft. of 11,600 sq. ft.	78.5
Hallway space: Main aisle width Percentage of aisle space over total EOC area	6 feet 864 sq. ft. of 11,600 sq. ft.	7.45
Square feet per person: Policy IC PIO Plans Operations Logistics Finance	60.0 81.8 66.67 80.0 107.3 69.6 110.4	
Distance of elevators from each section: (ft.) Policy IC PIO Plans Operations Logistics Finance	50.25 61.0 25.25 86.0 68.0 42.0 35.5	
Distance to the closest stair: (ft.) Policy IC PIO Plans Operations Logistics Finance	49.25 60.0 24.25 85.0 67.0 55.0 36.0	
Number of exits	3	
Number of entrances	2	
Total area used	**11,600 sq. ft.**	**100**

Figure 9-13. Statistics for layout alternative 2 (figure 9-10.)

Selecting a Solution-after-Next Target

Chapter 10 focuses on the step in the Breakthrough Thinking process highlighted below. (The numbers in parentheses refer to the chapter in which the step is described. The Breakthrough Thinking process is detailed in Chapter 5.)

Step*	Result
1. Set up TQM program (6)	TQM mission, values, strategic plan
2. Identify primary projects and activities (7)	Initial plan of action and timeline
3. Set up TQM project (7)	Project system (purposes, people, etc.)
4. List possible purposes (8)	
5. Develop purpose hierarchies (8)	
6. Determine criteria to select purpose level (8)	
7. Select purpose(s) (8)	Focus purpose(s) in a hierarchical context
8. Establish measures of purpose accomplishment (8)	Success factors
9. Establish subgroups if needed (8)	Subgroups established
10. Generate many solution-after-next options (9)	List of viable alternatives
11. Assess solution-after-next options (10)	

* The number in parentheses after each step refers to the chapter in which the step is described

Step*	Result
12. Select solution-after-next target (10)	Target solution-after-next
13. Modify target for irregularities (11)	
14. Choose recommended changes (11)	Recommendations
15. Prepare proposal (12)	Proposal
16. Inform people not involved to date (12)	
17. Detail recommendations (12)	Complete recommendation specifications
18. Prepare installation plan (13)	Installation plan
19. Install recommendations (13)	Installed system
20. Standardize performances (13)	System performance measures
21. Review project at betterment timeline date (14-15)	Next recommended changes
22. Repeat step 21 (14-15)	Further actions and changes

* The number in parentheses after each step refers to the chapter in which the step is described

Chapters 6 through 9 detail the initial steps of the Breakthrough Thinking process, in which idea generation and divergent thinking are key factors. Beginning with this chapter, the mode of thinking changes from a divergent to a convergent mode. Creativity, however, will continue to play a critical role. Selecting a solution-after-next, modifying it to become a recommendation, getting approval for it, detailing it, setting up an installation plan, installing the change, and following up with a continuous betterment plan all demand creativity—and all flesh out what we mean by "Full Spectrum Creativity." Methods for remaining creative while accommodating the realities of the situation will be the focus of this and subsequent chapters.

In particular, this chapter will unfold a process for arriving at a target solution-after-next. Because the ideas developed in Chapter 9 will vary in terms of understandability and completeness, our aim in Chapter

10 is to show you how to hone the ideas so that they suit the unique needs of your TQM endeavor. The process of selecting a solution-after-next will also continue to encourage the search for even better solutions and ideal systems.

One way to do this is to view each idea or solution option as potentially useful for as long as possible. Yet at some point you will need to settle on a target to guide the development of a recommended solution.

Table 10-1 lists the steps in moving toward an idealized target solution that is not overly explicit in all details. You will find that moving through these steps is almost always an iterative process, or one that involves jumping ahead some steps and then returning to earlier ones.(Iteration may also occur between developing options in Chapter 9 and selecting a target or vision in this chapter.)

Table 10.1   **Selecting a Solution-after-Next Target**

Identify regularities for the target.
Separate ideas into major alternatives and incorporate as many component ideas as possible into each.
Provide details for each major alternative to ensure workability and allow assessment of effectiveness.
Identify each major alternative as contemplative or feasible.
Select the solution-after-next target (SANT) or feasible ideal system target (FIST) (see figure 9-1) for regularities by evaluating the major alternatives with measures of purpose accomplishment.
Make the SANT more ideal and as operational as possible.
Save other ideas.

Identify Regularities for the Target Design

Anyone who tries to specify the details of a solution too early tends to get bogged down in coping with all the circumstances surrounding the situation. When this happens they are likely to reject any new ideas (because they are more difficult to work out) and go back to old ways or "proven" ideas. If this happens, the creativity needed to develop solution-after-next options is lost and even the selected purpose may not be achieved.

You can resolve these difficulties by developing *initially* a solution that applies *only* to the regularity conditions (as discussed briefly in Chapter 9). The ideas are sorted into a target solution that would achieve the purpose only for the most important, regular, or usual conditions. Then later exceptions to these "regularities" are incorporated. This lets people assimilate ideas, real-world conditions, and complexities at a rate they can handle.

In effect, this process develops a feasible, workable, usable, and, it is hoped, creative target solution or central theme to fit relatively "ideal" conditions, those defined by the regularity factors. Such a target solution often leads to the eventual installation of a composite, multichanneled, or pluralistic system that handles the irregularities or exceptions, yet retains most of the benefits of the target solution itself. A pluralistic or multichanneled solution also sets up a "continuing change" mind set in the people involved, for it is easier to change one well-defined channel of a solution than it is to change a part of a monolithic, single-channel solution that fits all conditions.

A regularity condition is a factor or circumstance that occurs most frequently, or is biggest, longest, most critical, or most important. It may be a situation in the "outside" world over which the group has no control in relation to the focus purpose(s). It may be a condition or circumstance that is expected to remain relatively the same over the long term (perhaps three to five years). In actuality, it can be just about anything that a group or individual wants it to be.

The most important feature of a regularity condition is that it is considered to exist 100% of the time for the purpose of developing the target. "Real" regularities are preferable to assumed ones, even though a regularity could represent an important though less frequently occurring condition. Heart attack patients in an emergency room, for example, are a small percentage of all admissions but are considered a regularity condition because of their critical nature.

More than one regularity condition may be put together in a set, which collectively constitutes the 100% condition. For example, group technology in manufacturing seeks families of similar parts for developing "ideal" systems. A family of parts is a regularity condition that could be assumed to exist 100% of the time.

There are a number of ways to identify possible regularity conditions. Each major word or phrase (verb, subject, modifier) in the selected or bigger purpose level in the hierarchy can serve as the basis for identifying them. In this method, review each to determine what real-world factors will be constants, basics, or invariables, even well beyond the time horizon for the project. As an illustration, consider "to ship standard products to dealers." The major words or phrases, are *ship, standard products,* and *dealers.* For the word *ship,* these factors may be considered as regularities: mode of shipment, destinations, form and size of shipment, shipping materials, and costs. *Standard products* might include types, styles, sizes, and quantities. *Dealers* may include wholesaler/retailer, size of city, type of dealership, total quantities purchased, and level of service provided by dealer.

In many cases, the conditions of regularity are tied to words that represent primarily inputs or outputs of the eventual solution. Inputs and outputs deal with larger systems or factors in the external environment that are less likely to change for the project, however large or small it may be. In other words, identifying conceivable input and output conditions regarding each word of the purpose statement is another way to discover regularities.

Another way to identify regularities relates to the functional components that may have been included as part of the purpose development (Chapter 8). A purpose level decomposed into a system pyramid or tree diagram establishes conditions from which one or a set of components can be selected as most regular. Similar techniques, such as the relationship chart or interaction matrix, portray frequency or importance of activities, which may be viewed as possible regularity conditions.

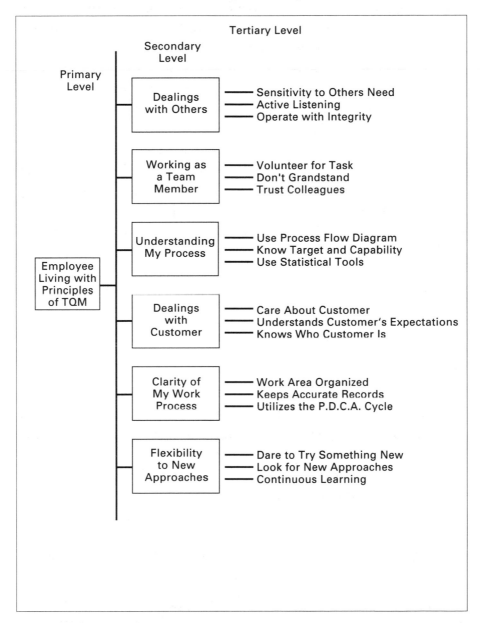

Figure 10-1. Tree diagram of employee living the principles of TQM.

As an example, one regularity frequently assumed for TQM programs is *to have employees live the principles of TQM*.[1] This purpose is quite large, and it usually needs functional components, in this case illustrated with the tree diagram shown in figure 10-1. The tree diagram was developed using brainstorming and details from an affinity process.

As we fill in the tree diagram from left to right, we ask the following question at each level: "What needs to happen for this to be accomplished?" Through this question the diagram expands in a logical sequence, preventing the tendency to make large leaps in the detailing process. As a safeguard against such leaps, a second question is asked from right to left: "If these items happen, will the next level occur?" If we have made large leaps in detail, we will see the discontinuity very quickly. (In figure 10-1 the tree diagram has been detailed in three levels in order to identify what needs to occur for employees to live the principles of TQM.)

Next, we need to develop regularities from the functional components or tasks based on the order of importance. Figure 10-2 shows a prioritization matrix used to evaluate the components, which have been assigned the following values:

1: The components are of equal importance in accomplishing the purpose.

5: One component is significantly more important than another component in accomplishing the purpose.

10: One component is exceedingly more important than another component in accomplishing the purpose.

1/5: One component is significantly less important than another component in accomplishing the purpose.

1/10: One component is exceedingly less important than another component in accomplishing the purpose.

(Other values and methods of assigning greater or lesser weightings may change the results.)

---

1. G. Hoffherr, J. Moran, and R. Talbot, "The Whole-Brain Affinity Model: A Synthesized Approach to Surfacing Creative Concepts" *Competitive Times*, Issue 3, November 3, 1991.

Employee Living Principle of TQM	1	2	3	4	5	6	Total	Priority
Dealing with others		1	5	1	10	5	22	1
Working as a team member	1		10	1	5	5	22	1
Understanding my process	1/5	1/10		10	5	5	20.3	3
Dealings with customer	1	1	1/10		10	5	17.1	4
Clarity of my work process	1/10	1/5	1/5	1/10		1/5	.8	6
Flexibility to new approaches	1/5	1/5	1/5	1/5	5		5.8	5

Figure 10-2. Prioritization matrix.

Prioritizing tasks is accomplished by comparing pairs, as illustrated in figure 10-2. Results of this comparison are shown in the far right-hand column of figure 10-2. The larger the numerical score, the higher the priority ranking. The last column on the right shows the prioritization number of each task identified in the tree diagram.

Two components are tied, so they become the regularity conditions governing development of the target. Various options explained in Chapter 9 are then followed for these two regularity conditions. (Note that the prioritization matrix can easily produce a different result if the judgments are changed ever so slightly. All techniques must be used very carefully!)

Still another method of identifying regularities is to select a distant point in time as the "regularity." This permits people to think in terms of ideal conditions: "What would be an ideal gypsy moth pest management system for the United States five years from now?" "How would the downtown area look four years from now after the urban development project is completed?" "How do you think the manufacturing division would be best organized ten years from now?" Each of these time-based conditions may also require "smaller" regularity decisions, but they are often much easier to make in this context. Those factors or circumstances that would be regularity conditions in five or ten years time are easy to consider because people's personal concerns *now* are not at stake.

However, no factor should be accepted as a regularity if it in any way limits creativity. For example, the most frequently occurring mode of shipment *can* be identified (railroads 40%, trucks 35%, air freight 20%, and customer pickup 5%; see Pareto technique in the Appendix). Assuming that railroads are 100% of the conditions may well cut off innovative ideas about air shipments. One way to avoid this trap is to make successive assumptions: first air, then trucks, and last customer pickup constitutes 100% of the shipment conditions.

Thus, regularities are not an end in themselves, but rather a means toward the end of developing a solution-after-next target (SANT). Even though the concept of regularities represents a significant breakthrough in actually designing "ideal" systems, just listing regularity possibilities does not mean any of them should be used. Some regularities may need further study before you can make decisions about them. The determining factor is whether precise data would change any conclusions based on estimated data.

Selecting the regularity conditions for a specific project is often accomplished on a trial-and-error basis. Objective criteria might be used, such as suitability, importance to management, and proportion of cost in the whole system, but for the most part decisions about regularities are subjective. In some cases, the design of ideal systems can use one regularity condition at a time. A Pareto diagram is a technique that summarizes some of these regularity concepts.

If more than one regularity condition is selected, and each becomes the basis of its own feasible ideal system target (FIST), then the best features of all of them could be combined.

Separate Ideas into Major Alternatives

The objective in Chapter 9 was simply to generate ideas of any type or scope: minimal improvements over what exists, "wild" ideas, solutions others have used successfully, vague scenarios, custom-made systems, complete and self-explanatory ideas, incomplete kernels of an idea, or adaptations of what others are doing. Generating more such ideas is encouraged even now.

As mentioned earlier, commitment to any one concept should be avoided until the last possible moment in order to give idea generation free rein. One way to generate more ideas is through "competing" alternatives. A helpful tactic is to develop an optimistic and a pessimistic scenario for each alternative. This also helps to overcome the propensity for an organization to develop very early only one solution idea more completely than others. By setting up your major alternatives this way, you not only avoid premature closure on any one idea; you also invite as many good ideas as possible about each alternative.

As the last chapter explained, a *major alternative* is a broad and complete idea that, if implemented, would *in itself* achieve the selected purpose for regularity conditions. In general, major alternatives are mutually exclusive. That is, only *one* of them is selected as the target for achieving a purpose, even though a "small" idea may appear in several of the alternatives. A *component* is an incomplete or partial solution. It may be part of one or more major alternatives, and combined with others can produce a major alternative. Any remaining ideas are *details* that may fit many major alternatives or components.

You need to review each idea to determine its status as a major alternative, component, or detail. If you cannot identify any major alternatives, try putting components together. You might also want to redo the purpose expansion or re-use creativity techniques.

Provide More Detail for Each Major Alternative

Each major alternative will need different kinds and amounts of detail. At this stage, however, you should seek only those details that are needed to assure the organization that an alternative is workable and to assess it sufficiently in terms of the MPAs. The need for details really comes later, when specific tasks are undertaken. For example, the amount of detail needed to conduct a feasibility study is far less than that needed to develop construction plans for bidding. Similarly, less detail is needed for determining marketing policies than for locating warehouses–or for determining user information needs than for designing a computer program.

A system matrix can be a useful guide in determining the details needed for each alternative. Certain factors (purpose hierarchy, selected function level, MPAs, human agents, etc.) may remain the same for each alternative, but the remaining cells can elicit more than enough questions about other necessary details. A system matrix also makes it easy to determine the technology and resources needed (people, equipment, money, etc.).

Following are other guides to help you determine the level of detail needed for each major alternative:

- Adhere to the basic principles of Chapter 9–ideal system concepts, regularities, and so forth. For each principle, ask, "How can an ideal system be developed from the major alternative using this principle?"

- Incorporate some exceptions. Ask, "How can the major alternative stay 'ideal' while incorporating this particular exception?" One particularly good exception to inquire about concerns the control dimension. These questions are usually addressed after the fundamental parts of the alternative are detailed, but control details often go hand in hand iteratively with fundamental ones, so that workability and effectiveness might be better assessed.

- Use the MPAs (or other significant parameters or variables) to uncover needed details. Ask, "How much additional detail do we need about Alternative X so we can assess it against MPA number1? Against MPA number 2? number 3?" And so on. The same questions are then asked for all of the other major alternatives.

- Play the "believing game" with each major alternative. That is, believe the first major alternative is the FIST and ask, "What is needed to make it work?" Then believe the second major alternative is the FIST and ask the same question. Continue with all of the alternatives.

- Use the techniques and models listed in the Appendix to provide details. When combined with the system matrix, these techniques and models enable you to test each alternative to determine how it would work in a "real-world" setting, how it relates to other systems, how it might respond to changes, and what types of organizational consequences it might cause. Here are some examples:

  Solution Impact Assessment: Construct a matrix with purpose statements from the hierarchy as rows and each of the major alternatives (MA) as columns. What impact would each MA have on each purpose level, and what details could be added to the MA to make it achieve the focus and bigger purposes? Another version of this matrix would use current organizational functions as the rows (marketing, distribution, manufacturing, procurement, human resources, engineering, etc.). What impact would each MA have on each function, and what details could be added to either the MA or the organizational function to make it more effective?

  Systems Approach: This technique is very often cited as necessary in detailing solutions. For example, one article on a systems approach to TQM suggests that the integration of quality functions must deal with process control, facility management, operations planning, product design, marketing, training, financing, management, forecasting, supplies, customer relations, technology adaptation, production, and quality assurance.[2] These all could be the rows in a system matrix cre-

---

2. W. E. Roth, Jr., *A Systems Approach to Quality Improvement,* New York: Praeger Publishing, 1992.

ated for a solution impact assessment. Also, as each is a "system" of its own, each could be described through a system matrix, providing far more specificity than just listing organizational functions does.

Influence Diagram, Tree Diagram, or Reverse Cause-Effect Diagram: Each of these begins with a major alternative as the subject to be delineated according to factors that affect it. The elements and dimensions of a system matrix can be used to start the diagramming process, or factors can be selected based on the particular situation. For example, a critical factor might be the health impact of the work on the people involved in the solution. People have fewer heart diseases when they have a high degree of control over their own work.

Computer Aids: Almost every technique is computerized both to stimulate ideas and to record data. Most are very effective, but they are no substitute for thinking about the needed information and talking with others about the possible ways to achieve the purpose.

The following guidelines also are helpful in detailing activities:

- Be sure a specification will help to achieve the purpose.
- Specify only a minimum amount of details, and let people in the system add the rest.
- Include multiple modes for achieving the purpose and objectives whenever appropriate.
- Put information and control requirements at points close to the origin of difficulty, and at points where actions can be taken.
- Include transitional and change over specifications.
- Build a betterment timeline into all specifications.
- Be sure the specifications make sense to readers and users of the solution.
- Provide specifications that are complete, operational, decomposable, and non-redundant.

- Relate specifications to performance expectations (costs, time, life cycle, quality of work life, etc.).

Many questions naturally arise when such detailing gets underway. However, every question should not necessarily lead to an information-gathering project. Instead, each question should first be assessed to determine if answers are, in fact, needed at this point. Often they are not.

Broad and sometimes specific performance characteristics are frequently needed to analyze the effectiveness of each major alternative before you can select the FIST. In most cases the MPAs can serve as these performance indicators, but they may also include critical operational components, such as forms of control, social interactions, legal conditions, and environmental impact. The values, measures, and control dimensions of each alternative's system matrix can generate yet other performance characteristics. Estimating amounts for the MPAs, operational components, and other performance measures will yield valuable information about each alternative. To perform these estimates, many techniques are available: reliability distributions, overhead rates, progress functions for learning curves, predetermined motion-time data, time series analysis, multiple regression, Taguchi methods, sensitivity analysis, simulation with or without computers, and many others (see the Appendix).

As the list of techniques demonstrates, there is no end to the amount of information that can be collected about a situation. In addition, a huge number of databases both inside and outside the organization can literally overwhelm a project as well as help it. No doubt, a major issue facing virtually every project is just what information should be collected. A group "cops out" on this basic question if it says, "Well, collect it all." It abdicates its responsibility to be effective in finding the best solution (see Chapter 3). Gathering so much data also significantly hampers the likelihood that the group will be able to break out of conventional ways of problem solving.

The Limited Information Collection principle should be the guide for this issue. Every suggestion to get information or collect data should be greeted with the same questions: What is the purpose of getting information XYZ? What are its larger purposes? What is the most ideal way of achieving whatever focus purpose is selected? (And so on.) Not only do these questions minimize the amount of information to collect; they also provide much better guidance on how the organization should invest its data collection, R&D, and intelligence gathering resources.

Identify Each Major Alternative as Contemplative or Feasible

The purpose of this step is to categorize the major alternatives as either "contemplative" or "feasible." Changes and additions to the major alternatives often occur in this step. Some weeding out of less effective ones also takes place, even though there is no urgency to do this yet. Another outcome is a list of ideas for which additional research and development might be started.

A major alternative is *contemplative* if several of its components are not now capable of implementation. The alternative is considered *feasible* if all components for the regularities could be implemented immediately, without regard to costs.

All contemplative alternatives should be reviewed with experts (e.g., customers, suppliers, manufacturers, R&D organizations, government information centers, libraries, technical specialists). Experts are usually able to provide sound estimates for the timing of a breakthrough that the FIST might need to anticipate. They also can estimate how long it may take to get needed information about feasibility and workability questions.

This step makes it possible for groups with varying amounts of knowledge and ability to be successful. Someone not knowledgeable in all the latest technology is likely to call a major alternative contemplative when it is really feasible. Reviewing your alternatives with others can ascertain the actual feasibility of each.

Select the Target Solution For Regularities

In this step you actually choose your target solution. Even though the target is considered workable, economic, beneficial, and compatible only for regularity conditions, it will be an important beacon as you develop the recommendation for *all* conditions.

Arriving at a target solution is essentially a decision-making process. That is, a choice must be made from among the major alternatives. Although decisions have been required all along, "formal" methods for making these decisions have not been necessary, since it is fairly simple to go back and redo them if later they appear to be unsuitable. Selecting the SANT, however, deserves more formality because it sets the stage for a great deal more effort and commitment of resources (if not already done by the selection of a much bigger-than-expected focus purpose).

However formal the decision process may be, it still entails using a model. All models should be treated with a modicum of skepticism. After all, models are *representations* of reality, not reality itself. A decision-making model or framework will always have some errors, and most will be time-bound.

With this caveat in mind, the rest of this section details the decision-making process as it applies to selecting the SANT (or FIST). The concepts can be applied to almost all other decision-making situations, but selecting a SANT requires amplifications in two particular areas:

- The factors about which information is needed in order to make a selection
- Ways to utilize the factors in making a selection

Factors About Which Information Is Needed

The decision worksheet illustrated in figure 10-3 lists the basic factors: (1) the criteria, value scales, or measures of purpose accomplishment for assessing each major alternative; (2) the weighting or importance of each criterion; (3) methods of measuring the criteria; and (4) the alternatives to be assessed.

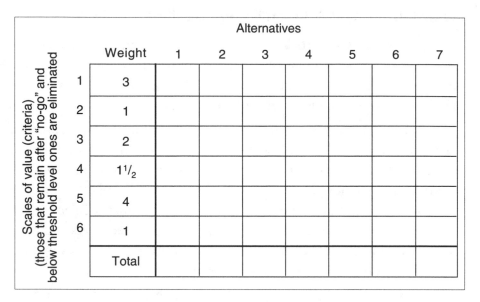

Figure 10-3. Decision worksheet.

1. On the basis of the dichotomous and threshold measures of
    purpose accomplishment (see Chapter 8), an alternative will
    be rejected for further consideration if it does not meet the
    desired conditions. Continuous criteria use the performance
    characteristics to assess an alternative (e.g., dollars, customer
    requirements, job satisfaction, time, number of people).
    MPAs will most likely have to be reviewed for additions, dele-
    tions, and modifications. The very nature of exploring ideal
    system options, discussing ideas with others, identifying regu-
    larity conditions, and getting information about how to
    make major alternatives workable almost certainly introduces
    a different view of what MPAs are needed. For example, crite-
    ria related to user reactions, testability, fit with core compe-
    tencies of the organization, social impact, concordance with
    organization values, or flexibility to accommodate change
    may now be considered quite important. New measures will
    need to be added to the previously defined ones, or the whole
    set may need to be done over.

2.   Assigning weightings or values to the criteria is necessary so that they can be used in conjunction with all other measurements for each alternative. One quite simple method of assigning value to criteria is to pick out the least important one and give it a weighting of 1. Then assign a numeric value to every other criterion to express how much more important it is (two times, five times, one-and-a-half times, etc.). Other techniques to help in evaluation include utility theory, subjective judgment, questionnaires, nominal group technique, the Delphi technique, and voting (see Appendix).

3.   Measuring the amount of a criterion is often already accomplished when performance characteristics are determined (e.g., the alternative will have a capital cost of $15,000; it includes ramps for the handicapped; an audit will take place once a year; four hours will be needed to process the inputs into outputs; and so on). Other criteria will ordinarily need to be measured at this point, like aesthetic appeal, capability for continued change, monotony, flexibility, maintainability, safety level, conduciveness to political climate, and so on. Several subjective techniques may be used, all of them variants of utility theory. A simple subjective tool involves a scale from 0 to 100, with 0 representing absolutely none of the criterion or absolutely the worst condition (e.g., infinite costs, no reliability, infinite time, no flexibility), and 100 representing absolutely all of the criterion or absolutely the best condition (e.g., zero costs, complete reliability, complete flexibility).

The 0-to-100 scale can be used for each criterion in evaluating the alternatives. Start with criterion A, for example, and determine how much of criterion A–from 0 to 100–is present in alternative 1, then in alternative 2, and so on. Then how much of criterion B is in each alternative? And so on. Another form of the question is, "What performance from 0 to 100 would we expect from alternative 1 in terms of criterion A?"

A more theoretically "correct" method assigns, say, 100 points to each measure of effectiveness. The 100 points are then divided up among all the alternatives according to the expected performance of each.

Almost every major alternative will have a great deal of uncertainty surrounding its performances on the various measures of purpose accomplishment as well as its assumptions about conditions within and outside of the organization. This is why probabilities and likelihoods of occurrence and performance will enter into the deliberations about selecting a SANT. They help nail down the risks associated with every proposed change.

When probabilities of occurrence (or utilities of external conditions or states of nature) influence the level of an MPA in an alternative, and information is available about the occurrences, a group can either calculate or estimate the probability, using the 0-to-100 scaling technique. Multiplying the amount of an MPA present in an alternative by its weighting (and, if necessary, by a probability of a state of nature) produces the "number" that goes in a cell.

Computer programs are available to structure the questioning, measurement, and recording of information, and even to make the decision regarding the SANT. However, you should avoid relying too much on such computerized processes. A research project found that the performance of a computer-aided group was significantly lower than the performance of another group that did not use such computer programs.

Ways to Use Factors in Selecting the Target

The decision worksheet in figure 10-3 puts all of the weightings, measurements, and probabilities together by multiplication in each cell, where the criterion row and alternative column intersect. The alternative with the highest total is supposedly the one to be selected. It presumably represents the solution that most effectively makes trade-offs among the various criteria and values that conflict with each other (e.g., cost and aesthetics, practicality and innovation).

Yet that alternative should never be accepted as the FIST on the basis of this total alone. Errors, differences of opinion, and other uncertainties cause the numerical scores to vary widely. A change in just a few of the measurements could affect which alternative is selected. When added to the impossibility of ever having *all* the criteria clearly stated, this variability only points to the alternative that should start discussions among the people involved, until one alternative is finally settled on. In addition, all criteria, weightings, and measures should be reviewed so that everyone agrees on their meanings.

The literature on decision making often refers to the process in terms of a mathematical equation or criterion function. The difficulties in developing a completely quantitative selection of the target solution suggests that some simplified techniques might well be as effective.

One is the index or ratio value that divides the measures into two groups: benefit/risk ratio, effectiveness/cost ratio, benefit/cost ratio, and so on. However, some factors may not fit into either category and may thus be neglected, so this technique is not always wise to use.

Another simplified technique is the lexicographic model, which ranks each alternative on the basis of the most important criterion. Those with the same "highest" value are then measured against the second most important criterion. Those with the same score are measured against the third most important criterion, and so on until only one alternative remains. However, this alternative should not be accepted only on the basis of this technique.

A decision tree is another simplified technique for relatively large projects. (figure 10-1 would have probabilities of occurrence and payoffs for each alternative to make it a decision tree). Each functional component has several possible alternatives, and an alternative selected for one component will fit any alternative selected for another component. Thus, the functional components are relatively independent (e.g., for a new metropolitan mass transit system, the type of buses, form of schedule, personnel selection). Another kind of decision tree starts with a project in which the sequence of activities is important. How one activity is performed sets up a range of alternatives somewhat different from the range stemming from another activity. Still another version translates the lexicographic model into a visual tree in which each level concerns only one criterion. Probabilities are also easily portrayed on this kind of tree.

Some projects may not need much of the formalism described to this point. Consensus may just emerge. A simple vote may suffice, or people could be asked to write down their top three preferences, which would then be tabulated for the whole group. After some discussion, the group could be asked to repeat their listing then more discussion would follow. This could be repeated until consensus emerges.

Many computer aids are available in the decision-making area. They are primarily interactive, prompting the user to respond to questions. The information is recorded (in a format similar to the decision worksheet in figure 10-3) and processed to present the alternative the group has selected. Some programs use a decision tree format, while others "hide" the format. Discussion can still take place, primarily to modify the numerical inputs and then see if there is a different solution. Of course, changes may also be made in the alternatives themselves to enhance a characteristic or performance factor and thus its overall evaluation. Computer aids, however, should be treated only as a tool to help you explore all the issues. Remember, at least one study has shown that people relying too much on computer techniques for making decisions significantly under-perform those who do not use them!

It is not unusual to find that new alternatives emerge in the decision-making process. They are almost always combinations of parts of existing ones. They are pieced together as the evaluation of the MPAs show that one part of an MA (major alternative) is very good, while the rest is not. How can the good part be used? Simply merge it with another MA and spell out the resulting new MA. Ordinarily, there is an element of indifference about the specifications of almost every MA that permits such developments.

All measurements and evaluations are also subject to time constraints and windows of opportunity. Probabilities are always changing, as are the weightings and assessments that make up a decision framework. These are additional reasons for not trusting *the* answer provided by any model, technique, or computer program purporting to make the decision. Just pay attention to the insights they offer.

Some projects might end up with several FISTs, one for each of the regularity conditions or relatively independent functional components. This most likely occurs if each regularity condition was treated as if it occurred 100% of the time, and ideal systems were developed for each one. The next step would combine all of the FISTs into one recommended solution, while staying as close as possible to each original FIST.

Multiple FISTs may also be needed when the same project is performed in several locations. A letter we received describes this possibility:

"I have been working with three project teams—one from each of our three main plants. All three were given the same problem: to design a new hog cut [the initial processing of hogs in a meat-packing company] for each of their respective plants. Our original thought was that we would have a common target system for all three plants. As the Uniqueness Principle indicates, however, we found that a separate target system was required for each of the three plants. Even slight differences in such things as product mix, local specifications, and so on, meant that a common target was not practical. On the other hand, it may well be that the differences that eventually showed up in the recommended systems will be blessings in disguise. Because of this we were forced to design a better control and information system that will do a better job of evaluating the performance of the proposed system as well as better information in future systems. Corporate management is very enthusiastic about the proposed systems. The estimated cost reductions and returns on the investments are far better than they expected and even better than I had guaranteed before the project was undertaken."

One measure of purpose accomplishment that almost never appears in assessing the major alternatives is "simplicity." Yet it may be one of the most critical in gaining acceptance as a guide for the recommendation. It is a very difficult factor to measure and depends almost completely on subjective judgments. However, this could ultimately be the most important measure for it influences most of the others—costs, understandability, user-friendliness, maintainability, reliability, and so on.

The probability is very high that every person associated with a project will have a *favorite* part of an MA. Sometimes a person will even try to hold on to a mediocre alternative because of a particular element in it. That is when the more formal decision-making tools are useful: they proceed in a way that lets the particular person back off graciously if another MA is selected as the target.

Make the Target as Ideal and Operational as Possible

The first part of this step is simple: always seek an ideal result. Be a thief. Steal what is good from B, C, and D, even though A has been selected. Constantly try to refine the SANT to an even more *ideal* state, regardless of the resources allocated or time available. It is always possible that compromises along the way have reduced the SANT to a "nearest semi-feasible solution" or to a "somewhat creative" level, so you should always strive for improvement.

Clues as to how this might be achieved are furnished when you measure the alternatives against the criteria as described above. A criterion on which the FIST did not measure well offers a good potential area for making it better. If, for example, the capital cost criterion showed that the FIST may involve a high initial expenditure, you might seek a better ideal system with a lower capital expenditure.

You also need to remember that, in a year or two, the SANT or FIST will need to be developed again to take advantage of new knowledge and technology—no matter how valuable the SANT is now. That means you should avoid associating finality with the target; like recommended solutions, it has to change or stagnation will set in. Keep the target moving ahead.

Developing a *better* SANT (or set of SANTs) is not always necessary, but you should consider doing it as a way to help the implementation process. Providing greater assurance of workability can go a long way toward getting decision-makers and implementors to accept the value of a target that will guide the rest of the effort. In addition, being alert to questions about workability and operations can help minimize the delays of decision-makers and others in accepting and moving toward the eventual recommendation. Even though regularities are involved, decision-makers and others often want to know how the SANT will "actually work," who will be able to do it, when it will be done, and from where the resources will come. Anticipating such questions by preparing scenarios in advance helps speed up implementation.

One other consideration may arise: the timing of the project. The more innovative the FIST and thus the likely recommendation, the more the client or organization needs to be ready to accept it. You may need to make certain that the real world's perceptions are moved along. This is not a deliberate delay so much as it is reflective anticipation of user and customer needs.

Save Other Ideas

Retaining all major alternatives, components, and other suggestions may help later in the project or in other projects. The possibility always exists that the SANT may be rejected later, and a new target needed. To keep all of the project ideas on file, a computerized arrangement of key words could be used, or a filing system could be established in which the various ideal systems are categorized by organizational unit, technology involved, components used, and project number (including suppliers).

Case Illustrations

Case A: Package Tracking

The team assigned to this project screened ten major alternatives, using the filtering worksheet shown in figure 10-4. In doing this they eliminated alternatives 1, 2, 5, and 7. Alternatives 3, 4, 6, 8, 9, and 10 remained as the possible SANT. The group described its reasons for eliminating four alternatives in its report so others could review the ideas.

The measures of purpose accomplishment were given weights based on the level of importance for each assigned by the managers. The weights, along with the score (from 1 to 10, 10 being the best) given to each alternative for each criterion are shown in figure 10-5. The total for each alternative is found by summing the products of the weights and scores. Alternative 10 had the highest score and was chosen by the FIST.

Alternate Solutions	Solution Accomplish Purpose?	Solution Workable?	Handle Key Regularities?	Cover Criteria Objectives?
1	Yes	No		
2	Yes	No		
3	Yes	Yes	Yes	Yes
4	Yes	Yes	Yes	Yes
5	Yes	Yes	No	
6	Yes	Yes	Yes	Yes
7	Yes	Yes	No	
8	Yes	Yes	Yes	Yes
9	Yes	Yes	Yes	Yes
10	Yes	Yes	Yes	Yes

Figure 10-4. Filtering worksheet.

The criteria (or MPA) listed in the decision worksheet (figure 10-5) are simplified from those initially developed for the project (see Chapter 8). To illustrate, each criterion or MPA is defined in terms of the specific measures used: (1) Costs are reduced (reduce complaints measured by number of complaints/day, and improve the PTS system, measured by percentage of match among origin, destination, and delivery codes); (2) Customer gets packages quickly (receive packages on time measured by percentage of customers receiving packages on time/day); (3) Customer receives packages (reduce lost packages measured by number of packages lost/day); and (4) All inquiries answered (obtain status of packages measured by number of packages with requested information unanswered).

To help display the advantages of the SANT (FIST) compared to the current system, table 10-4 was prepared as part of the report.

Case B: Emergency Operations Center

This project team identified regularities and irregularities (figure 10-6), but they did not find it necessary to assign numerical values to the factors, because identifying the important issues was the only critical reason for doing this step.

Criterion	Weight (%)	Alternative					
		3	4	6	8	9	10
Costs are reduced	15	9	6	6	7	7	8
Customer get pkgs quickly	30	5	7	7	6	8	9
Customer receives pkgs	15	8	8	8	7	8	7
All inquiries answered	40	9	7	7	8	8	9
Total	100	765	700	700	710	785	855

Figure 10-5. Decision worksheet, FIST: alternate solution 10.

The former alternatives (see Chapter 9) were evaluated with the decision matrix shown in figure 10-7. The resulting SANT layout is shown in figure 10-8 (a modified version of figure 9-9).

Regularities:
• Incident Command System
• Decision making
• Constant coordination between the policy, operations, logistics, plans and finance groups
• Management of information
• Use of equipment
• Management resources
• Setup of EOC facility and ICS
• Information flow
• Tension an stress

Irregularities:
• Use of EOC facility for another purpose
• Change in government policies and procedures
• Maintenance, training and exercise

Figure 10-6. EOC regularities and irregularities.

Criteria	Alternatives				
	WT	Alt 1	Alt 3	Alt 5a	Alt 6
Optimum use of workspace	4	8	8	7.5	7.5
Hallway space:					
Aisle width	3	10	10	8.5	10
Percent aisle space	3	6	6.5	3	6
Square feet per person:					
Policy	3	8	8	8.5	9
IC	4	9.5	9.5	7.5	10
PIO	2	4.5	6.5	5	7
Plans	3	8.5	8	8	8
Operations	5	10	9	9.5	10
Logistics	4	9.5	10	8.5	10
Finance	2	1	1	1	1
Distance from elevator:					
Policy	2	8	6.5	1	1
IC	3	6.5	6	1.5	4
PIO	4	9.5	8.5	1	1
Plans	3	4	4	3	6
Operations	5	5.5	5.5	7	5
Logistics	3	1	8	6.5	7
Finance	2	1	7	7.5	1
Distance to stairs:					
Policy	2	7.5	6.5	7	6
IC	3	7.5	6	3	6
PIO	4	8.5	8.5	5	9
Plans	3	5	4	6.5	6
Operations	5	6.5	5.5	5.5	5
Logistics	3	6	6	5	5
Finance	2	8	7.5	7	7
Number of exits	3	10	5	10	10
Number of entrances	4	10	5	10	10
Total area required	4	9.5	9.5	10	5
Total	**880**	**644.5**	**620.5**	**555.5**	**641**
Ratings: 5 = Best ⟶ 1 = Worst					

Figure 10-7. Layout decision matrix.

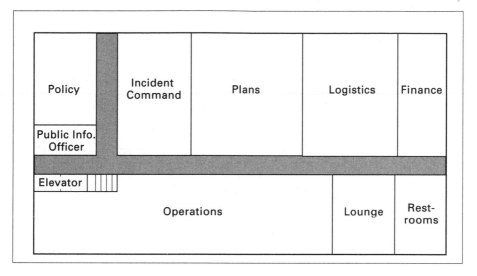

Figure 10-8. Solution-after-next target.

Table 10.4   **Current System vs. SANT** (Page 1 of 2)

Information	Current System	SANT
Package Size		
Maximum size	130 Girth (inch) (Dimension + length)	42 x 33 x 30 (inch)
Minimum size	None	8 x 6 x 1 (inch)
Average size	12 x 12 x 18 (inch)	
Package Weight		
Maximum weight	70 lbs.	100 lbs.
Minimum weight	None	1 lb.
Average weight	10 to 15 lbs	

Table 10.4 **Current System vs. SANT** (Page 2 of 2)

Information	Current System	SANT
Conveyor Belt		
Package spacing	No specification	Required 8 inches
Belt speed	100 to 125 ft./min. (adjustable)	500 ft./min.
Noise level	Noisy	Cogged belt drive for noise reduction
Width	22 to 60 inches Use 42 or 48 inches as average	Adjustable

Developing Recommended Changes

Chapter 11 focuses on the step in the Breakthrough Thinking process highlighted below. (The numbers in parentheses refer to the chapter in which the step is described. The Breakthrough Thinking process is detailed in Chapter 5.)

Step*	Result
1. Set up TQM program (6)	TQM mission, values, strategic plan
2. Identify primary projects and activities (7)	Initial plan of action and timeline
3. Set up TQM project (7)	Project system (purposes, people, etc.)
4. List possible purposes (8)	
5. Develop purpose hierarchies (8)	
6. Determine criteria to select purpose level (8)	
7. Select purpose(s) (8)	Focus purpose(s) in a hierarchical context
8. Establish measures of purpose accomplishment (8)	Success factors
9. Establish subgroups if needed (8)	Subgroups established
10. Generate many solution-after-next options (9)	List of viable alternatives
11. Assess solution-after-next options (10)	
* The number in parentheses after each step refers to the chapter in which the step is described	

Step*	Result
12. Select solution-after-next target (10)	Target solution-after-next
13. Modify target for irregularities (11)	
14. Choose recommended changes (11)	Recommendations
15. Prepare proposal (12)	Proposal
16. Inform people not involved to date (12)	
17. Detail recommendations (12)	Complete recommendation specifications
18. Prepare installation plan (13)	Installation plan
19. Install recommendations (13)	Installed system
20. Standardize performances (13)	System performance measures
21. Review project at betterment timeline date (14-15)	Next recommended changes
22. Repeat step 21 (14-15)	Further actions and changes

* The number in parentheses after each step refers to the chapter in which the step is described

The SANT is an important milestone in the Breakthrough Thinking process. In the short term it guides the development of the recommended solution; in the intermediate term it guides the many small decisions that come into play as the solution is installed. In the long term, it can stimulate the continuous improvement aspects of TQM.

The SANT, however, is but one of *many* milestones. Once you settle on it, the next step is to develop a recommendation that accommodates *all* conditions–that is, regularities and irregularities alike–while staying as close as possible to the SANT.

A simple illustration demonstrates this. One of us was helping a retail clothing company develop a warehouse to serve its nine stores in a metropolitan area. The group had just arrived at a SANT, as shown in figure 11-1 (demarcated by the solid lines and capital letters). There was only one regularity condition–that the merchandise be marked with tags

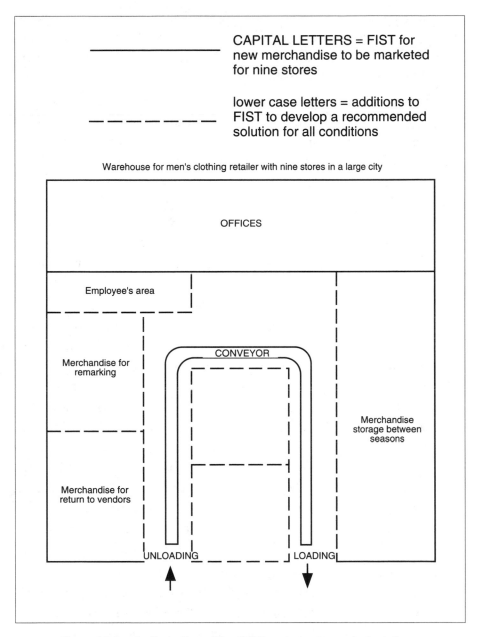

Figure 11-1. An illustration of the SANT and recommended solutions.

for shipment to the stores (a condition which, in actuality, applied to 60% of the arrivals at the warehouse). In the solution that the group envisioned, the merchandise would be unloaded onto a conveyor where it would be tagged, and then loaded onto trucks for delivery to the stores.

The president of the company happened to walk by the group just as the SANT was being drawn on a big sheet of paper. After learning about the purposes, the measures of purpose accomplishment, and possible solution ideas, the president exclaimed, "But you can't do that," pointing to the SANT. "It won't handle the merchandise to be returned to the vendors." In other words, he was immediately willing to throw away a solution that would work for 60% of what occurred, because it would not work for 8%. He was displaying the syndrome of "one route" or "one process" for everything (as happens in most projects handled with conventional methods).

The group had searched very diligently for ways to adjust the SANT to include the irregularities, but they had found (as the president intuitively noted) that the irregularity of merchandise to be returned to vendors really could not be incorporated into the conveyor concept of the SANT. But that did not cause the group to discard the SANT and related SAN options. Instead, they developed SANTs for the major exceptions, and where compatibility with the primary SANT could not be developed, they set up separate channels or *systems* (shown with *dashed lines* in figure 11-1). They had determined that the conveyor concept should be retained in the recommended solution, but saw no reason to have just one *system* to handle everything. They thus produced a set of recommendations that could accommodate both regularities and irregularities, while adhering to the SANT as much as possible.

The steps involved in moving from the SANT to the recommended solution are summarized in table 11-1. This process can be quite extensive, since several of the activities can become projects of their own.

All kinds of probing will be needed as you develop the recommended solution. Going back to previous steps of the process will be needed: What bigger purposes might suggest a way of handling an irregularity? What other ideal systems might incorporate the regularities and irregularities, and even be better than the SANT? Calling on each person's vast storehouse of knowledge to find some workable ideas will be needed. Searching databases for clues to technology that might be useful will be needed. Experimenting with combinations of components will be needed.

Table 11.1 **Developing the Recommended Solution**

Develop alternatives for irregularities, exceptions and additional conditions while staying as close as possible to the SANT.

Estimate performances, outcomes, and consequences of each alternative.

Modify the SANT as little as possible by incorporating the desired alternatives to create a workable solution that will be recommended for adoption.

Develop Alternatives for SANT Components

The SANT is comprised of functional units or components, represented by a model or set of specifications. Figure 11-2 illustrates one such model–in this case, a layout in which the components are identified by letters. Figure 11-3 illustrates the same SANT but through an information flow chart (in which the components are once again identified by letters).

This step generates as many additional ways as possible to achieve each component when irregularities are included. Some components (C in figure 11-2, for example) may need no alternatives because the FIST suits all conditions. Conversely, no alternatives may be found for a component that needs some. In this case, the solution will probably involve multiple channels (as in figure 11-1), or the project team may need to return to an earlier step in the process.

There are several ways to find alternatives that address irregular conditions:

- *Apply the Breakthrough Thinking Process.* Because each component is a system, ask the questions associated with Breakthrough Thinking: What is the purpose of the component?

What are ideal systems for achieving this purpose? Some of the ideas might even improve the SANT while incorporating ways to cope with irregularities.

- *Adhere to Principles and Special Checklists.* Principles and stimulator lists in appropriate fields (e.g., human factors, numerical control, facility planning, job design for older workers, learning, nursing care, group behavior) can prompt the development of new alternatives: How could Principle X be turned into a way of achieving the purpose of Component Y, while staying as close as possible to its target? Special considerations, such as appropriate technology in developing countries, might be incorporated: What ideal solution would achieve the purpose of the component with 100% local labor or local resources?

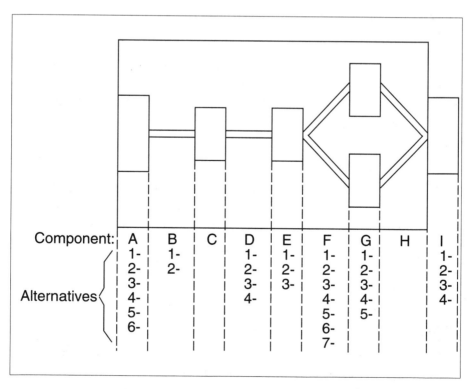

Figure 11-2. Illustrative layout model of a SANT

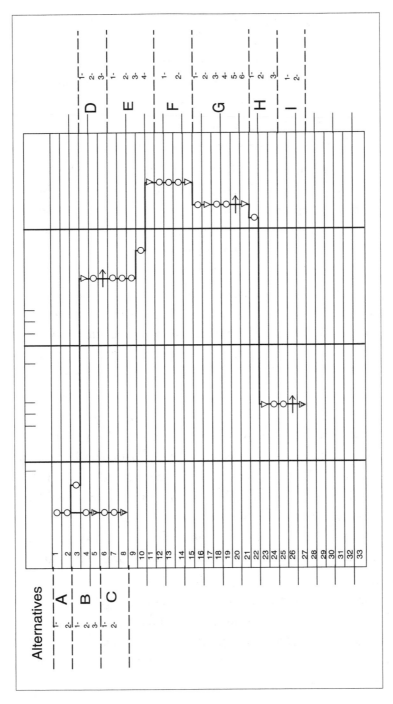

Figure 11-3. Illustrative information flow chart of a SANT.

- *Use Idea Generation Techniques.* As reviewed in Chapter 9, persist in achieving purposes: brainstorm, talk aloud, involve someone not at all connected with the project, etc.
- *Check File of FISTs.* Other ideal system ideas on file, as well as those recorded at the end of Chapter 9, may be helpful.
- *Get People to Participate.* Without any of the other aids, this alone could achieve the purpose of this step.
- *Try Contrary Concepts.* If the core concept of the SANT is computer-integrated manufacturing (CIM), explore how human integrated manufacturing (HIM) might develop different alternatives. If a mainframe computer system is at the center of the SANT, what alternatives might work if networked personal computers were used?
- *Examine Customer Expectations and Opportunities.* What requirements of the customer(s) might stimulate alternatives for this component? What feature could be added to the component to give the customer unexpected value? Bigger purpose levels in the hierarchy might provide additional insights here as well.

Figure 11-2 shows how there can be a differing number of ideas for accomplishing each component. Combinations of the various components can give rise to many alternative solutions. Alter-native 1 could be A1 + B + C + D1 + E1; alternative 2 could be A2 + B + C + D1 + E1; and so on. Each possible combination of components could be identified (especially on a computer) to provide a complete set of alternative solutions for evaluation in C below. Through such a list, additional ideas also could be generated, as well as patently unworkable ones eliminated.

Another strategy is to develop a SANT for each set of regularities or for each functional component. Multiple SANTs are generally helpful in large-scale projects, such as planning a hospital or doing regional irrigation planning. One project recalling military personnel from leave in an emergency, for example, had six functional components, each of which had a separate SANT.

Estimate Performances, Outcomes, and Consequences

Detailing of these alternatives should really precede any effort to estimate performances and consequences. Doing this will help assure that the alternatives are workable before you spend time assessing them. It also will get you thinking about their consequences and implications. In fact, thinking about the full implications of the alternatives is more important than getting all the details.

To this end, a *systems* approach should be taken when detailing each alternative. You should already have dealt with the issue of breadth when setting up the project (Chapters 6 and 7), at which point the concept of a system matrix was introduced. You should review the *Systems* principle again now (see Chapters 4 and 12), and apply the basic elements of inputs, outputs, sequence, physical and organizational environment, human agents, physical catalysts, equipment, and information aids to each alternative.

Organizing information about each alternative in a system matrix is an effective way to identify what estimates and other specifications may be needed. It also can pinpoint where trade-offs among the alternatives might be needed (e.g., greater centralization of the gypsy moth pest management system must be balanced against the need for a fast response time when an infestation occurs), and where more (or fewer or different) measurements are required.

Without a system matrix, there is no way to tell just how much detail will be needed for any one alternative. In some cases, it may be necessary to set up some experiments (with, say, Taguchi methods) comparing different levels of detail for an alternative. In other cases, outside sources (like the marketing department) can supply you with important details. The Appendix lists many techniques that can help you gather details for the alternatives. Just remember that the amount of information needed for this step is determined by its purpose: to obtain estimates of performances, outcomes, and consequences of each alternative.

These estimates will likely be more accurate than the ones you used when selecting the SANT, but they will not be as precise as the measurements you will eventually need for the operators and supervisors of the system. Several techniques may be of help as you formulate your estimates. They are listed in the Purposes/ Functions section of the Appendix under the following headings:

- Analyze job methods and motions
- Appraise/assess investments
- Appraise/assess alternative options/plans/policies/programs
- Appraise/assess systems
- Collect data and/or information
- Describe/establish/measure relationships
- Estimate budget and dollar requirements
- Evaluate alternatives
- Measure errors

Getting the variety of estimates needed–performance, consequences, labor needs, learning and progress curves, reliability, benefits, advantages, cash flow and costs (direct, indirect, capital), time, outcomes–for each alternative to the FIST may be done by looking at similar types of activities or projects, for which historical data are available. Quite often you will need to conduct a study of your own or collect special data. The general flow of reasoning described in Chapter 5 will help you design the needed information/data collection *system.*

In summary, this flow of reasoning leads to the following guidelines that should govern your information-gathering efforts:

Keep asking what the purpose/function is of the information collection system. Even if the purpose is necessary when information gathering starts, a group of specialists can easily get sidetracked. Also, continually assess if the information or measures being sought must be obtained so accurately.

Seek an ideal system target to guide information collection. Think in terms of the ideal when developing your information gathering system: What information would be ideal to collect? What would be ideal ways to get and prioritize it? Also, keep in mind the principle of zero data collection as a guideline. Ask if subjective estimates would suffice, or if a few measures rather than many would work. And so on.

Be sure the population base and data sample are representative for the purpose to be achieved. "Good" data about the wrong set of conditions, population, or time period are useless. Starting with a nonrepresentative base can almost never be corrected by any type of prediction or forecasting.

Bear in mind that the accuracy of data collection should be driven only by the needs of the decision to be made, and not by normal statistical requirements [confidence level?]. This is often a question of sensitivity. What impact will a lack of data (or lack of accuracy) have on the decision to be made? If a slight error affects the decision, then more data or greater accuracy is needed. Would the decision be modified if the data were, say, negative? This idea emphasizes the value of sketching out the estimates needed, simulating the values to be obtained, and manipulating the information hypothetically to pinpoint areas where accurate decisions need to be made.

Get people involved in providing estimates and in obtaining information. People involved in the project, as well as others outside of it, can contribute significantly to its eventual implementation by being a part of this decision-making process. The Appendix includes some techniques for getting "good" measures and data from people.

Select Workable Solution to be Recommended

The ideas presented in Chapter 10 for selecting the SANT are applicable here as well, though there may be some differences in the MPAs, weightings of criteria, and related measurements. Changes in the MPAs are not at all unusual at this point in a project. The inclusion of irregularity conditions may modify the SANT enough that other factors need to be considered. For example, customer service after product or service sale may become critical or the need to demonstrate the effectiveness, validity, and viability of the recommendation may loom large. whether or not the organization has the core competencies to support an alternative also may need to be considered (including such questions as "Should the organization invest in the new competencies?" and "Can it afford *not* to?"). A list of the revised MPAs and their weightings will result from such deliberations, and, as the following paragraphs explain, even this list will likely change as the project proceeds.

A frequent difficulty in selecting a solution is evaluating *how well* each alternative accomplishes the purpose. For example, the purpose of one telephone company system was to initiate action when a customer called requesting service for a telephone. Time and cost were obvious MPAs, but an intangible measure of how well the purpose was accomplished was the voice image, or pleasantness, the customer experienced when making the call. An alternative may be less costly and take less time, but its coldly efficient performance may destroy a valuable source of information about the company as a whole. A company lending library for nonfiction books may have an automatic system to procure, check out, and return books to achieve least cost and time goals. But the critical factor in determining how well the purpose is accomplished may be the enthusiasm a reader develops by discussing various titles with a knowledgeable librarian.

Psychological and organizational factors are major considerations here, especially when compounded by other factors—social, political, legal, and even technical. Different skills and levels of complexity influence the way people react to an alternative. For example, most people think that their performance already represents the highest level of their capacity. So when a solution would require a higher level of performance, they are bound to wonder how they could achieve the new level, and often reject the solution because of this apprehension.

People's attitudes may not be sympathetic for other reasons as well. A suggestion for change, for example, will hardly be welcomed by someone with the attitude that "my system is outstanding as it is." In other situations, persons from whom authority and information must be obtained may have personality characteristics that make them difficult with whom to work.

Consideration must extend beyond the alternative itself, then, to its probable effect on the people involved. What will current workers do with their extra time? Is more work available? What will happen to workers removed from jobs? Are any important social groupings involved with the change? What effect will local and national economic conditions have on people if the change is made now? Chapters 13 through 16 address many of these important questions.

Judgment and non-quantitative factors play a big role in selecting the solution, primarily because so many trade-offs are needed. One trade-off in choosing among alternatives, for example, asks, "Which one promises to achieve the highest number of the values described in Chapters 1, 2, and 3, with the fewest number or lowest probability of risks (no risk is an impossibility)?" Also, external factors very often affect the decision (e.g., availability of money, interest rates, personal relationships of the chief executive officer and financial institutions, area wage differentials).

To help you deal with all the factors and variables, a decision worksheet like the one illustrated in table 11-2 is often useful. However, in actually selecting a solution, formal decision-making techniques (like the worksheet or multi-attribute utility assessment) may have very little use. Even though you may present a lot of data with one or more of these techniques, a manager is likely to select an alternative by his or her own mental trade-offs.

When you use a decision-making tool, short cuts will inevitably occur. For example, an alternative is likely to be judged in the aggregate rather than selectively, in terms of individual factors. Such short cuts are not bad, and at times are even more useful than precise measures. The truth is, *all* modes are needed to be effective in arriving at a solution.

Bargaining is another way of selecting a recommended solution. Individuals, either singly or in small groups, represent perspectives or constituencies with differing values. The conflicts can be small (e.g., among people with different responsibilities in a company who must make the decision) or large (between labor and management, between the company and suppliers, etc.). A project group may be quite formal in its analysis of the alternatives, but the bargained solution may combine parts of several previously and newly developed alternatives.

Table 11.2 **Illustration of Evaluation Work Sheet Selection of Workable System** (Page 1 of 2)

		System No. 1, 3, Forklift	System No. 1, 4, 5	System No. 2*
System or Operation: Door for Burner (handling) Department:			*Project No.:* C-100 series *Date:* September 1980	
How much installation cost?				
1	New machines	$10,000	50 trucks @ $50 = $2,500	Conveyor $20/ft. x 700 = $14,000 Motors $800
2	New tools, material, labor	—		
3	New designs		4-wheel hand trucks	
4	Installation	$50		Hangers (200)
5	Overhead			$2,000
6	Scrap of machinery, tooks, and materials			
7	Misc. (loss of production, wages, etc.)			
8	New cost	$10,050		$16,800
9	Less salvage			
10	Total cost (a) Depreciated cost per year	10,050 $2,010	2,500 $500	16,800 $3,360
How much operating cost?				
11	Present system, labor, material, machine rate, overhead, and misc.	—	—	
12	Total			
13	Proposed system			

Table 11.2 **Illustration of Evaluation Work Sheet
Selection of Workable System** (Page 2 of 2)

		System No. 1, 3, Forklift	System No. 1, 4, 5	System No. 2*
	System or Operation: Door for Burner (handling) Department:		Project No.: C-100 series Date: September 1980	
	Labor	$3 x 500 hrs = $1,500 (for door line)	$2.50 x 1,000 hrs. = $2,500	
	Material			Power $500 Maintenance $300
	Machine rate, overhead, and misc.	$2 x 500 = $1,000	$1.50 x 1,000 hrs. = $1,500	
14	Total	$2,500	$4,000	800
15	Cost per unit or $ sales	—	—	
16	Expected volume per year			
17	Total operating cost per year	$2,500	$4,000	800
18	Present operating cost per year			
19	Gross savings/year (10 or 10a less cost)	$2,010 + 25% utilities	$500	$3,360
20	Net savings/year	Total cost/year = $3,000	Total cost/year = $4,500	Total cost/year = $4,160
21	Rate of return			
22	Hazard factor	Need wider aisles– greater safety problem	Creates poor housekeeping	—
23	Control factor	Flexible	Can cause too much damage to parts through handling	Closer to ideal system target
24	Psychological factor	—	—	—

Even though a single recommendation is typically sought at this stage, it is not surprising to find that more than one alternative is still a potential solution. There is nothing wrong at this point in recommending that two (or more) viable alternatives be investigated further. Perhaps they may eventually be useful because the technologies involved in each lead to different types of competitive positions in the market. The recommendation may then include a small investment in each technology for a limited period of time to determine which should be selected or whether to follow up with both.

Case Illustrations

Case A: Package Tracking

Chapter 10 detailed the decision-making process that this project team underwent to arrive at their SANT. After studying six alternatives, the team had settled on a SANT that entailed a *paperless* electronic system using a fixed position laser scanner in the hub and portable DIAD scanners. This SANT, however, was designed only for regularity conditions.

Their task now was to modify the SANT to accommodate the irregularities. The irregularities they cited fell into two categories: those that affected package pick-ups and deliveries, and those that affected the sorting/scanning system at the hub.

Modifying the SANT to Handle Pick-up and Delivery Irregularities

Three irregularities were identified for the pick-up and delivery phases of the PTS: breakdown of the portable DIAD scanners and related scanning problems, truck breakdowns, and printer/software problems that would prevent business clients from printing their own tracking labels. These irregularities are addressed below.

DIAD Scanner Breakdown and Related Problems: In each truck, there should be a backup scanner to use in case of any breakdown. If an unusually large number of packages makes it too difficult for the driver to hand-scan every one, then the driver should take the packages directly to the hub, where they would then be scanned. The drivers should never spend too much time on this hand-scanning procedure; otherwise the whole operation would be delayed.

Truck Breakdown: Drivers should immediately contact the hub if their trucks break down, so that a backup truck can arrive as soon as possible. Another option is to have nearby drivers pick up the packages from the broken-down truck.

Printer or Software Problems: For commercial packages, the companies could make their own tracking labels with equipment supplied by the PTS company. If, however, malfunctioning in the printer or software prevented the companies from printing their own labels, the driver who picks up the packages must make sure they are entered into the DIAD. Again, if there are too many packages to be entered into the DIAD, it would be more efficient for the packages to be scanned later at the hub.

Modifying the SANT to Handle Irregularities of Hub Sorting/ Scanning System

The irregularities of the SANT for sorting and scanning packages at the hub included the following:

- Irregular (small) or damaged packages
- Damaged or lost/sheared off labels
- Hub scanning/sorting system downtime
- Packages jamming on conveyor belt
- Overload of incoming packages
- Inaccuracy of the system

Each of these irregularities became a component for which several alternative ideas were generated. Alternative solutions for the first three irregularities are given below. The last three irregularities are not included because the selected SANT already handled them.

Component Definitions

A: Irregular (small) or damaged packages

B: Damaged or lost/sheared off labels

C: Hub scanning/sorting system downtime

Component Alternatives

A1: Place an employee next to the hub scanning/sorting

A2: Train unloaders to identify such packages

B1: Place an employee next to the hub scanning/sorting

B2: Train unloaders to identify such packages

C1: Build in frequent or timely maintenance checks

C2: Switch over to manual scanning and sorting

Components

Alternatives	A	B	C
	1	1	1
	2	2	2

List of all the possible alternative solutions

A1-B1-C1	A1-B1-C2
A2-B1-C1	A2-B1-C2
A1-B2-C1	A2-B2-C1
A2-B2-C2	A1-B2-C2

Explanations of Components and Their Alternatives

Component A refers to any irregular or damaged package that might pass through the conveyor belt, making the system non-operative. irregular packages are those that cannot be read, scanned, and sorted by the system because they are either too big or too small. Since the proposed paperless system would only be able to sort and scan packages with the "right" measurements, extremely large and small packages would be bypassed. According to the list of Component Alternatives, there were two ways to solve this problem: (1) Place an employee next to the hub scanning/sorting, or (2) Have well-trained unloaders.

Alternative 1 would place an employee along the conveyor belt to spot irregular packages. If an irregular or damaged package happened to go down the conveyor belt that the system could not pick up, this employee would immediately spot the package and simply set it aside.

Alternative 2 would rely on well-trained unloaders to prevent irregular or damaged packages from coming through the system. If one were to trace back where these irregular packages came from, it would have to be the unloaders, for they are the ones who place every package on the conveyor belt. It would be possible, then, to train the unloaders to recognize packages that would not be picked up by the automated sort/scan system, and to place those packages aside. The unloaders would need to be trained in a way that they could still perform their jobs efficiently while keeping an eye on irregular packages at the same time.

Component B, the irregularity concerning damaged or lost/sheared off labels, could be handled the same way. Again, placing an employee next to the hub scanning/sorting area or having trained unloaders were the two solutions from which to pick.

Component C refers to the special circumstance when the automated scanning/sorting system might break down. This would be a great disaster, causing the whole hub to shut down since the system could not scan or sort any packages. As shown on the Component Alternatives list, there were two options to prevent this catastrophe from ever happening: (1) Have frequent or preventive maintenance checks, or (2) Switch over to manual scanning and sorting.

The first alternative would have a technician check over the automated sorting/scanning system at least once a day. These inspections would take no more than 15 minutes, and would ideally be done in the morning to make sure everything was all right before the day's operations began. This small investment would likely save a great deal of time and money later.

The other alternative to handling system downtime was to switch over to manual scanning and sorting if this emergency ever happened. A manual scanning and sorting system (consisting of trained, available workers) would have to be planned well ahead of time. An ideal situation would be to have workers ready to scan and sort as though the automated system never existed in the first place. If this manual scanning and sorting system were well planned, the delay time would be minimal and the business would still operate until the automated system was fixed.

Modifications to Make the SANT More Ideal

Using the decision worksheet, the team first evaluated the alternatives for each component according to the following criteria: speed, cost, acceptance, and ease of implementation.

Criteria	Weight	A1	A2	B1	B2	C1	C2
Speed	10	9	8	9	8	8	3
Cost	30	8	6	8	6	8	3
Acceptance	25	8	9	8	9	7	5
Ease of Implementation	35	9	8	9	8	9	2
Total	100	845	765	845	765	810	315

Taking the highest-scoring alternative for each component, the team then found an alternative workable solution that would incorporate the irregular conditions. Thus, the SANT with necessary modifications consisted of the following:

A1 + B1 + C1

This meant placing an employee next to the automated scanning/sorting conveyor belt, while having frequent checks to make sure the whole system was operating according to plans. These component alternatives would allow the system to handle any irregularities that might surface in the best possible way.

Case B: Emergency Operations Center

Various types of information were assembled to help in developing the recommended system. Because there was no previous system, organization charts were developed to provide a framework for clarifying exactly how a quality-oriented EOC would perform. Figures 11-4 and 11-5 show two of them.

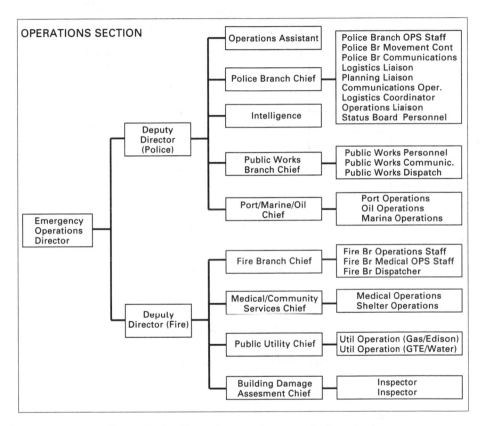

Figure 11-4. Operations section organization chart.

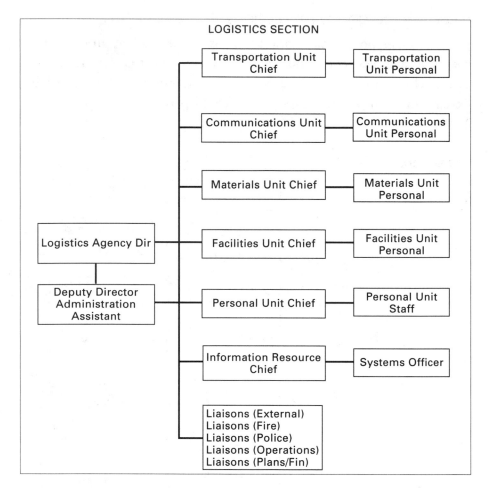

Figure 11-5. Logistics section organization chart.

Detailing the
Recommendations

Chapter 12 focuses on the step in the Breakthrough Thinking process highlighted below. (The numbers in parentheses refer to the chapter in which the step is described. The Breakthrough Thinking process is detailed in Chapter 5.)

Step*	Result
1. Set up TQM program (6)	TQM mission, values, strategic plan
2. Identify primary projects and activities (7)	Initial plan of action and timeline
3. Set up TQM project (7)	Project system (purposes, people, etc.)
4. List possible purposes (8)	
5. Develop purpose hierarchies (8)	
6. Determine criteria to select purpose level (8)	
7. Select purpose(s) (8)	Focus purpose(s) in a hierarchical context
8. Establish measures of purpose accomplishment (8)	Success factors
9. Establish subgroups if needed (8)	Subgroups established
10. Generate many solution-after-next options (9)	List of viable alternatives
11. Assess solution-after-next options (10)	

* The number in parentheses after each step refers to the chapter in which the step is described

Step*	Result
12. Select solution-after-next target (10)	Target solution-after-next
13. Modify target for irregularities (11)	
14. Choose recommended changes (11)	Recommendations
15. Prepare proposal (12)	Proposal
16. Inform people not involved to date (12)	
17. Detail recommendations (12)	Complete recommendation specifications
18. Prepare installation plan (13)	Installation plan
19. Install recommendations (13)	Installed system
20. Standardize performances (13)	System performance measures
21. Review project at betterment timeline date (14-15)	Next recommended changes
22. Repeat step 21 (14-15)	Further actions and changes

* The number in parentheses after each step refers to the chapter in which the step is described

The level of detail needed for the recommended solution will vary from project to project. The complexity of the system, the scope of the purpose, the amount of resources allocated to the project, and many other factors all impact the available detail. We will thus discuss fairly thoroughly in this chapter some methods for specifying solution recommendations, hoping you will call on these ideas whenever you need them as you work your way through the detailing process.

One of the most important variables that comes into play at this point in a project concerns the approval of the recommendation. Some projects need only one approval, while others need a series of approvals. Still others may need approvals at various levels in the organization–from foreman to supervisor, engineer, facility manager, vice-president, president, and even board of directors. Some approvals may have been obtained long before the project reaches this stage. In all cases, getting approval is best served by assuming that the process is a *system* that needs to be *designed* using the general flow of reasoning.

Furthermore, the recommendation needs to be interrelated with the overall TQM program and business plan. Although effective detailing methods should address these interrelationships, they tend to look inward to the system itself. The techniques described in this chapter will provide a major way to incorporate both the minor details and the broad perspectives.

All of these conditions mean that the actual process of detailing a recommendation and getting it approved will proceed in many different ways. While setting out steps identifies the functions you should accomplish sometime in a project, the order in which you move from step to step is by no means rigid. Those listed in table 12-1 could quite easily be switched around. As you read about how to accomplish each step, therefore, keep in mind that they may apply at much different points.

Table 12.1   **Detailing and Getting Approval of Recommendation**

• Formulate plans to get final approval of the recommended solution

• Detail the solution as much as needed to permit its installation or movement to the next stage of protocol. Use the elements and dimensions of the system matrix

• Review the recommended solution and system matrix with knowledgable people to assure its implementability

---

Formulate Plans to Get Final Approval

The recommended solution usually needs to get at least one approval, and the authority to grant approval is often given to people outside of the project. This is most likely to occur when the project:

- involves capital expenditures beyond what the individual, group, or manager can authorize.
- requires the reallocation of limited resources.
- is rather large and complex.

- needs external approval from regulatory boards or commissions.

- impacts or interfaces with several departments or constituencies.

- needs to be installed in several parallel departments or locations.

Approvals are also desirable, even if not really necessary, as a way of building a group of favorably disposed intermediaries throughout the organization. This helps to minimize the risk and expedite the implementation. Even the most outstanding recommendation may become useless if enough people are not convinced of its benefits. This situation should not arise, however, if the Breakthrough Thinking process is followed.

Approval will be needed at as many levels as the organization requires for decisions involving major expenditures or organizational changes. A recommended solution for a new machine to improve quality in a manufacturing plant, for example, was selected from several alternatives by a project team that included the plant supervisor. But the $40,000 expenditure required the approval of the plant manager and the director of manufacturing. Then, because 24 plants would each need a comparable capital expenditure, the corporate manufacturing vice-president had to approve it. Lateral as well as hierarchical approvals also may be necessary.

Such multiple approvals will almost always involve people who are not familiar with the solution, its details, and the competing alternatives from which it was chosen. In addition, people who think they will be negatively influenced will seek protection through negotiation or politicking. Continual interaction with people outside the team can help overcome this lack of under-standing so that this step is accomplished much more easily.

Even so, "political" and emotional forces–even clever lobbying within a company as well as in government–are part of gaining approval.

How a proposal is put together, who promotes it, and how and when it is presented are just as critical as what the proposal is all about.

As mentioned above, the plan for obtaining approvals should be designed for the specific situation following the general flow of reasoning: What is the purpose of the approval plan (to get final approval, to go ahead with next stage, to set up pilot effort, to conduct exploratory tests, etc.)? What are some ideal systems for achieving the selected purpose (report, videotape, oral presentation, etc.)? What are the regularities? Each report and presentation, even within a well-established process, should also be developed with the Breakthrough Thinking process. Idea generation should be encouraged because this is a crucial point in almost all project efforts.

Above all, in developing your approval plan, you want to make it easy for decision-makers to say *yes*. Obviously, then, your proposal should stress the opportunities and benefits that the solution holds for the organization. But you will probably have to address additional needs and concerns as well. You may need to clarify the solution, for example, or translate it into a more thorough installation plan. You may need to relate the solution more closely to the abilities of current (and possibly new) personnel to carry out the solution if it were installed. You may find that the solution needs to be modified to diffuse feelings of tension or to better reflect the culture of the organization. Often, too, you will need to design your approval plan in such a way that it elicits the motivational commitment necessary to see the solution through the usually difficult installation and into full operating status.

Regardless of the presentation format and approval strategies you choose, you will undoubtedly have to document the recommendation in a formal report. The following guidelines will help make this report strong—and, in turn, bolster your efforts to get the solution approved:

- A report has a rhetorical purpose (inform, persuade, and induce action) that is different from the technical purpose of the project (design, explore, formulate, solve, etc.).

- A report is usually addressed to the primary decision-makers. People or groups affected by the recommendation are addressed through other materials (training, presentations, manuals, etc.) in later steps.

- A report should be written from the perspective of the reader, and should normally move from the specific to the general. In some cases, the Breakthrough Thinking process can help you summarize what happened in the project. Redundancy, selectively used, can make it easier for different audiences to find what they need.

- Reports in the form of working papers should be submitted at several points during a project. They help move perceptions of people along the timeline and allow you to address questions at an early point.

- A report submitted by the project team is better than one submitted by only a facilitator or manager.

- The report should justify the recommended solution in terms of its advantages over what currently exists, or over other alternatives if nothing now exists. Benefit/cost ratios should be prominently displayed, along with what should be done about any proposed personnel changes (reductions, retraining, relocation, etc.).

- A description of the SANT should be included as the target toward which the recommended system is aiming. Betterment dates for the next steps toward the SANT should also be included.

- The report should explain why the SANT is not being recommended in its entirety. The decision maker(s) may well find that a limitation perceived by project team members or managers really does not exist, thus leading to a better solution. Also, the report should include comments about following up on the SANT components not now being recommended, and about research projects set up to investigate the contemplative ideal systems.

Getting approval of a proposal almost always involves comparing it to other proposals or activities in the organization. For example, a capital expenditure request is likely to be one of several proposed to a board of directors, or a proposal for a new Federal-state management board is usually one of several alternatives the agencies involved have considered. The resulting inevitable bargaining or negotiations almost always concern matters of much broader scope than the actual proposal itself. As disappointing as it may be to you, an outstanding recommendation may become a pawn or chip, and so a rejection may have nothing to do with the natural merits of the proposal–regardless of how well its benefits are spelled out. Not all of the reasons decision makers give to explain a rejection or request for modification will satisfy a project team, but the team will be less disappointed if members understand the nature of the negotiation process and why ongoing relationships among various individuals and constituencies are so essential.

The process of getting approval illustrates why many projects are aborted at this point. New products, proposed buildings, changed information systems, improved marketing ideas, or proven health care measures are often abandoned because of a lack of support, if not outright disapproval. However, approval of the proposal should be far more likely if the Breakthrough Thinking process is followed.

Develop Details of the Solution as Much as Needed

Starting with this step, it is virtually impossible to be specific. Each project is now so different that our discussion will shift from operational details about the steps to the pertinent functions and outcomes that ought to be considered. (A few process ideas will be suggested for getting to the outcome and accomplishing the functions.)

This step seeks to develop sufficient details to assure the initial and continued workability of the solution. A secondary aim is to keep the solution as close as possible to the SANT for achieving the purpose.

Detailing often involves careful specification in two areas not usually thought out too well beforehand: mechanical and physical items (inputs, outputs, circuitry, environment, automation, physical devices, and catalysts) and sequence and human agents (work balancing, organizational arrangement, equipment location, software, personnel planning, information-flow aids, training needs). An interaction matrix between, say, needed unit transformation operations (sequence) and technical factors (temperature, noise, chemical reactions) illustrates one technique for detailing. These specifications may lead to revisions and details in the budget proposed for the solution. The projected budget should be continually updated through these last two phases.

Another outcome started here is the schedule of events needed to put the recommended solution into operation. This is actually a system that could be designed with the general flow of reasoning.

A project team can use several processes to develop details. Visualization, or what the mind's eye sees, is probably most critical. This calls up a mental image of the solution from which descriptive details can be drawn. Visualization usually includes *seeing* the interrelationship of the mechanical and physical items within the sequence, and with users and other human agents. Visualizations are frequently recorded by means of models (see Appendix). Most of these techniques help in the analytical and experimental processes of arriving at detail specifications. Table 12-2 lists some of the guidelines for detailing once you have worked through these processes.

Table 12.2 **Guidelines for Detailing** (Page 1 of 2)

• Be sure a specification will help achieve the focus and bigger purpose
• Specify only the minimum amount of detail, and let people in the system add the rest
• Include multiple modes for achieving purposes and objectives whenever appropriate

Table 12.2 **Guidelines for Detailing** (Page 2 of 2)

• Put information and control requirements at points close to the origin of difficulty and at points where actions can be taken

• Include transitional and changeover specifications

• Build into the details a betterment timeline

• Determine if the specifications make sense to readers and users of the solution

• Provide operational, decomposable, and non-redundant specifications

• Relate specifications to performance expectations (costs, time, life cycle, quality of work life, etc.)

The large number of handbooks on very specific details and performance specifications provide a rich resource for this step. So, too, do the many techniques included in the Appendix. The purposes to be achieved by detailing a solution will determine which of the many models and techniques are best suited to your particular needs.

If the solution consists of several independent functional components, the task of detailing each could be assigned to subgroups or individuals as separate projects of their own. For example, a regional urban planning team that sets up a five-year plan may organize another group to detail the housing component. Or the invoicing component of an accounts receivable system may be detailed as a separate project. Likewise, detailing the gear for an engine transmission could be a separate project.

In addition to the guidelines shown in table 12-2, solution details should also exhibit the following attributes:

Details of the fundamental structure that is to exist when installation is complete: A structure refers to an arrangement, configuration, organization chart, relationship, or physical model that describes what the recommended solution should "look like." It also concerns the SANT version of the structure and the adaptive routes that may be pursued in moving toward the SANT.

The way the structure will operate once it is in place. This scenario of how operations will proceed should include steps to improve the whole solution and to periodically update the SANT.

The major activities and events needed to move from approval of the recommended solution to actual operations (the installation plan, described in the next step).

These three attributes are illustrated in the following statement of what would be needed in detailing a corporate strategic plan:(1) Purposes of the company, new product developments, facility improvements, human resource developments, financial status sought, organizational chart, five-year plan in all categories (SANT), and so on. (2) Appointment of project teams or individuals for one-time efforts (new product development, program initiations, etc.), organizational changes in operations or supervision, timing for capital expenditures, financial arrangements, and so on. (3) Preparation of monthly budget allocations by cost/profit centers, obtaining warranty claims printouts, scheduling departmental meetings to review budget implications, and so on.

Solution Frameworks

Because changes have always been proposed in organizations, frameworks tend to emerge over time that dictate how a solution should be detailed. However, because such frameworks are usually developed through conventional approaches, most have only limited use. For example, conventional approaches usually assume that the techniques used for analysis purposes (e.g., subdivision, fact gathering, modeling) are more than sufficient for specifying the solution. If layout space and flow analysis was done initially, then a layout space and flow model can describe the solution. If a control equation summarized the facts about the present methods, then it can model the solution. One eight-step systems approach uses the first seven steps to analyze the problem with a variety of techniques and models (e.g., Delphi, scenarios, game-based models, Bayesian-type *a priori* subjective probability models). Then, in the eighth step, the aim is to develop a solution model by drawing on these techniques to find "a system model that gradually finds modularity, [or] partitioning giving way to integration"[1](a perfect illustration of the limited thinking described in Chapter 3).

With many of these conventional frameworks providing some insights into what might be used in your projects, here is a brief review of several:

Playing by Ear. This label implies little prescriptiveness, but it does partially encourage an integrated view encompassing a gestalt or whole view framework.

Experience. This category, based on accumulated knowledge or experience, concerns the "raw" experience of sorting out what *appeared* to be satisfactory *in the past.* If engineering drawing (or architectural program statements) seemed sufficient for the last 25 years, then it should suffice now; if apparently successful policy statements comprised eight factors in the past, then all policy statements today should include eight factors. Most of the modeling techniques described in the Appendix would fit in this category.

Criteria for a Good Solution. Often organizations use checklists that incorporate the *good* features of solutions. A project outcome is therefore supposed to state the levels of features used or, in effect, how much each criterion is met. Those developing automation solutions, for example, would use criteria for good automation in checking the solution details.

Science Basis. Mathematical, statistical, or predictive equations are often considered sufficient as a solution framework. In addition, three forms of scientific knowledge are frequently considered sufficient frameworks: "Descriptions are viewed as recounts of what happened in a situation... Frameworks represent gross prescriptions for behavior. They can be very broad, as in the Marxian framework for economic behavior, or open to varied interpretations, as in the 'systems approach.' Algorithms represent specific prescriptions for behavior, down to the level of the [individual action]."[1]

---

1. J. N. Warfield, *Societal Systems,* New York: Wiley, 1976.

Professional Education. Each profession trains practitioners in its own solution framework. Typically, the framework is presented without any explanation, just as "the way it is done." Most often, some particular concept or set of techniques is presented as *the* current "all-you-need-to-know" idea: control models, information processing, decision making, networks, computer simulation, operations research models, sketches or line drawings, and so on.

In addition, technical communications courses and seminars tend to enforce rigid frameworks through prescriptive instructions about the content and arrangement of written reports (i.e., reports must have a purpose statement, executive summary, introduction, recommendation, etc.). More recently, professional education has emphasized optimization. That is, the solution specification is assumed complete once the most desirable and sensitivity calculations are done.

Questions and Checklists. The factors, concepts, or principles of any solution framework are sometimes put into checklists and questions. This makes them useful primarily as creativity stimulators. They tend to lack the flexibility, comprehensiveness, and especially prescriptiveness to be effective solution frameworks. For example, "What will be the result of the technological change" and "Do we have enough information to answer the previous questions?" hardly identify what solution characteristics are needed.

Whatever their shortcomings, solution frameworks have the benefit of providing reality to the recommended solution in ways that the individual or project team usually has difficulty doing. Those people charged to study the problem situation tend to lose their objectivity as the project progresses. So if objectivity is to be maintained–so far as this is ever possible–team members must internalize the concepts and values that lead to specifying and presenting the recommendations. This is what a good solution framework enables them to do.

Using the System Matrix as a Framework

Good ideas for a solution framework are present in almost all of the previous methods. Yet the desired attributes and criteria of a good solution framework point to the need for something much more effective. The system matrix appears to offer this opportunity while making use of whatever benefits the other frameworks supply.

Among its diverse uses in this respect, a system matrix is a good way to check interfaces, consequences, impacts, computer programs and databases, performance specifications, flows and layouts, and so on. It provides the type of insights needed for a "worst case analysis" of a solution through the measures, control, and interface dimensions of all the elements. It helps to avoid the difficulty of enthusiastic team members forgetting to include details that must be substituted for assumed workability. The future dimension can help turn up specifications to avoid the usual distortions that often beset solutions. It also encourages contingency planning for the solution and helps to anticipate questions from managers, installers, and users of the solution.

There are several reasons why a system matrix is so effective as a solution framework. First, it represents an open perspective along at least two continuum: time (figure 12-1, indicated by "Future") and level of detail (figures 12-2 and 12-3). The time continuum shows how the SANT (say, F on figure 12-1) and recommended solution (A on figure 12-1) can be interrelated in terms of time. A documentation of what is actually implemented might be represented by B or C in figure 12-1. Figures 12-2 and 12-3 show the level of detail continuum. They illustrate how infinitely small or large descriptions of any solution can be. Although seldom carried very far in either direction, the recursive characteristics of this kind of framework can handle real-world complexities, transforming ideas into informal, formal, and reality states. Figures 12-2 and 12-3 also display a basic concept in the Quality Function Deployment (QFD) technique—that of portraying various levels (or systems) of a product or service at which the responsibility for each quality function can be assigned (see Appendix for an explanation of QFD).

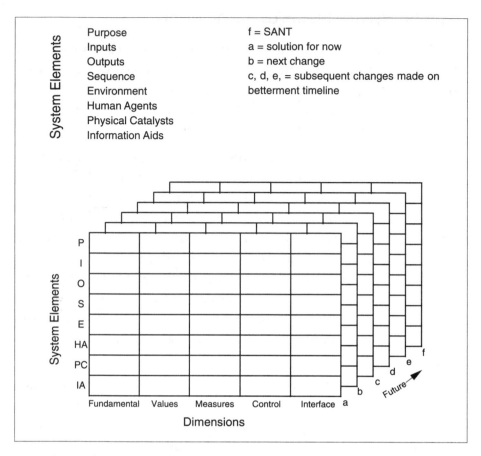

Figure 12-1. Another form of solution grid. Overlap and interrelationships exist among the cells.

Second, a system matrix provides a "deliberate orientation that enables *realization* of solutions, rather than just a *retroactive* [view]... that the organization wakes up to find itself with."[2] The system matrix format can embody the developmental drifts of the past while making more tolerable any "conflicts of interest" and fostering the embodiment of "shared values" for the future.

---

2. R. A. Rettig, Review of *Fish Protein Concentrate*, in *Science*, Vol. 203, January 26, 1979, p. 349.

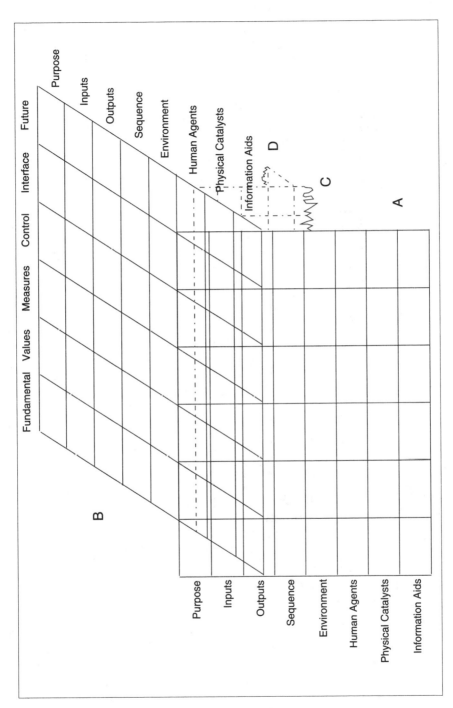

Figure 12-2. A system view of each element.

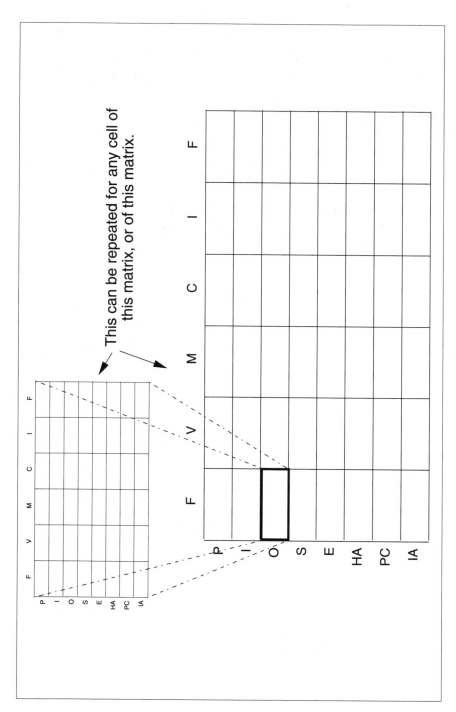

Figure 12-3. A system view of each cell of a system matrix.

Third, because of the reasons above, the system matrix offers advantages in concurrent engineering or simultaneous design. Reducing the lead time for product and service designs means many previously separate and sequential functions are considered together in the planning and design process–engineering, manufacturing, industrial design, marketing, suppliers, and so on. The system matrix perspectives in figures 12-1, 12-2 and 12-3 show how the overall system can serve as the integrative and communication bases for all the disciplines involved, each of which may then be responsible for one or more *systems* of its own.

Fourth, a system matrix significantly advances the principle of objectification, or making a solution understandable. The matrix and its interpretive extensions both uncover places where details are needed and enhance retention of information about the system. There should be far less chance than with usual solution frameworks, for example, of having cultural, social, economic, and political determinants overlooked by a technological fixation.

Fifth, the large number of questions raised in each cell of the matrix at each detail level significantly increases the probability of providing a total solution (needed parts of a total solution, such as control features, can be designed in advance). The questions raised by the system matrix also enforce the Limited Information Collection principle–that is, to get only *needed* data.

Sixth, each cell can encompass all of the various conditions in which a solution specification may be forthcoming: designed with singular specifications, with or without risk; designed with probability of occurrence specifications, with or without risk; designed for uncertainty, or a limitation or constraint of any type.

Because the system matrix may represent a "small" or "large" solution situation (e.g., a drill press operation vs. a national health insurance program), the entries in the cells in the system matrix and any of its recursive matrices can vary widely in scope and content. Yet some additional insights into the meaning of each cell might help in using the system matrix in actual projects. Table 12-3 lists illustrative items and

Table 12.3   **Specification Matrix** (Page 1 of 8)

	Fundamental	Values	Measures	Control	Interface/ Consequences	Future
Purpose	1. Primary concern, aim. Purpose hierarchy. Priorities of function. Mission statement, "What business are we in?"	2. Increase effectiveness and innovativeness. Attain better quality of life. Enhance human dignity. Encourage individual betterment. Convert problems to opportunities. Assumptions underlying purposes. Maximize organizational effectiveness. Sensible.	3. Profit (discretionary income). Market share. Return on investment. Debt-equity ratios. Dividend. Number of complaints. Earnings per share. Degree of risk.	$. Stakeholders/ board of directors review. Review timing for changing plans. Profit/loss operating statements. Balance sheet. Review trigger. Points to change to contingency plans (22).	5. External environment (27). Diversification of objectives. Mergers/ acquisitions prospects. Dividend policy. Corporate and governmental planning agencies. Pragmatic effects of information (43). Organizational myths.	6. Bigger purposeful level in three years. Betterment schedule. Profit and other measures forecasts for five years. Problems/ opportunities, priorities. Status of each specification in cells 1-5 at n, n + 1, n + 2 (time periods in the future).

Table 12.3 **Specification Matrix** (Page 2 of 8)

	Fundamental	Values	Measures	Control	Interface/Consequences	Future
Inputs	7. Problems, needs. Clients, users, etc. Raw materials, parts, etc. Forms, cards, tapes, verbal information. Cash, checks. Raw data. Reports. Previous outputs.	8. Minimum loans. Frequent changes in needs. Customer/user expectations. Material efficiency (local, sufficient, etc.). Preferences/utilities.	9. Rate of problems. Cost per unit. Amount of cash per day. Reaction time to order. Number of customers. Material yield. Number of users involved. Arrival times. Product mix.	10. Incoming inspection control. Orders/requests monitoring. Invoice/accounts payable control. Variance reports. Consumer attitude study. Data entry control.	11. Relate changed orders/requests to adaptive plans. Relate to expectations (30). Planning/design assumptions. Market being served. Interest/tax rates. Info display to users. Decision support system (43). Material Suppliers.	12. Different sources of supplies. Demographic/population analysis and trends. Status of each specification in cells 7-11 at n, n + 1, n +2 (time periods in the future).

Table 12.3 **Specification Matrix** (Page 3 of 8)

	Fundamental	Values	Measures	Control	Interface/Consequences	Future
Outputs	13. Policy statements. Drawings/products. Programs. Marketing plans. Actual service, conference class, meeting, etc. Corporate plan (policy, strategic, tactical, operating, structural, contingency). Product diversification plan. Models (iconic, analog, symbolic). Transformed information. Individual outcomes (study, personal life, relationships, etc.). Reports and memos. Environmental impact statements (29). Sketch plan.	14. Quality outcomes. Flexible. Comprehensive coverage. Effective product/service (pluralistic). Pricing/costing policies. Interesting/elegant/inspiring/esthetic. Simple (one-page report). Appropriate technology based. Satisfy user. Difference between desired, undesired (waste), spurious (poor quality), and incidental. Equity. Products are designed with manufacturing capability. Stylish.	15. Timing of installation or production, priorities. Market share. Cash flow. Break-even quantity. Sales per assets, employee. Cost per unit. Number of on-time deliveries or services. Selling costs. Sales price. Warranty expense. Operating margin. Dividend payments. Product/service mix. Occupancy rate. User satisfactions. Number of beneficiaries (or losers). Amount of incentives to adopt.	16. Credit investigation. Monitor warranty requests. Final inspection/evaluation. Accounts receivable control. Reports control. Failure rate assessment. Sensor for indicators. Compliance with instruction. Cost control. Accident assessment.	17. Market analysis. Competitive analysis. Product/service reputation. Patent condition. Relate to expectations (30). Advertising. External certification. Distributors/retailers/users. Securities Exchange Commission Form 10K. Implementation game plan. Semantic meaningfulness of information displays (43). Contingency plans. Inventory levels (21). Regional integration of services. Coalitions of supporters.	18. New product R&D. Sales growth. New domestic/international markets. Availability of new products. Projections of old and new products to provide future sales. Financial forecasts. Different projections. Maintain freedom of choice for future users (open-endedness). Status of each specification in cells 13-17 at n, $n + 1$, $n + 2$, (time periods in the future).

Table 12.3 **Specification Matrix** (Page 4 of 8)

	Fundamental	Values	Measures	Control	Interface/ Consequences	Future
Sequence	19. Implementation network. Set unit of operations. Information system. Distribution system. Scenarios for up and down inputs (orders/requests). Decision processes. Storage methods (material, information). Maintenance system. Flow pattern.	20. Minimum (optimum) time lag between input and output. Be able to handle emergency cases. Facilitate normal operating changes. Easy communications. Use only available resources. Meet deadlines. Make sense to people. Multi-channeled capability. Avoid controls that are "worse than the disease." Minimize energy use.	21. Rate of service, priorities. Cost per unit operation. Inventory turns. Free cash flow. Capacity of system. Conversion efficiency. Distribution costs. Specific scheduled updating. Schedule of implementation. Amount of working capital. Budgets (overall cost centers). Storage capacities. Productivity ration. In-process time/order. Risk probabilities. Work hours. Vacation schedules.	22. Inventory report and action. Budget versus performance. Quality control. Production control. Variance reports. Contingency processes. Maintenance activities. Upside/downside budget with triggering points. Accident control. Sensor for indicators.	23. Physical catalysts (37 and 39). Communications net. Facility layout. New product development protocol. Seasonal variations. Person/machine allocations. Integrated logistics support. Interaction with user. Routinization. "What if" questions. Accident prevention. Internal audits.	24. Future processes. Expected free cash flow. Feasible ideal solution target. Labor skills of future. New facilities. Target date for new component or product. Budget updating. Technological forecasting. Status of each specification in cells, 19-23 at n, n + 1, n + 2 (time periods in the future).

Table 12.3 **Specification Matrix** (Page 5 of 8)

	Fundamental	Values	Measures	Control	Interface/Consequences	Future
Environment	25. Strategic policies. Regulations. Competitors. Threats and opportunities. Labor supply. Organization structure. Management style/philosophy. Union contract. Temperature/humidity/noise/dust/light level. Technological character of organization.	26. Pleasant. Quiet. Organizational development. Consultative management style. Ecological awareness. Social accommodation. Organizational myths and beliefs (ambience). Organizational value type (output, motivation, flexible, image, administrative). Legal conditions and style.	27. Probability of event. Risk (±) with event. Capital resources. Overhead budget/expenses. Amount of formalization. Lowered level of decision making. Social indicators (mobility, info access, political participation, cohesiveness, etc.). Rate of ventilation.	28. Person assigned to monitor events. Report to cells 1 and 3. Management depth. Standard operating procedures. Physical environment controls.	29. Impact on location and vice versa. When to reorganize. Disturbances. Decision processes (19). World conditions. Sociopolitical conditions. Chamber of Commerce. Departmental jurisdiction and linkages. Impact statement (13). Wave patterns of enthusiasm.	30. Expected future events and disturbances. Futures studies research. Transportation improvements. Advanced scanning. Status of each specification in cells, 25-29 at n, n + 1, n + 2 (time periods in the future).

Table 12.3 **Specification Matrix** (Page 6 of 8)

	Fundamental	Values	Measures	Control	Interface/Consequences	Future
Human Agents	31. Workers, operators, supervisors, etc. Responsibility assignments. Technicians, professionals. Training program. Work grouping. Leadership style. Skill, power control requirements. Group autonomy levels.	32. Good quality of working life (autonomy, decision making). Personal development and growth. Individuality within groups. Maintain territorial integrity. Respect of affective beliefs. Civil liberties and rights. Reward monetarily to fit good performance. Personal values. Equitable treatment. Safe work conditions.	33. Allowed time per operation. Percent idle, delays. Accident rate. Ratio administrative to "line" personnel. Compensation system at all levels. Turnover rate. Training costs. Wage/salary rates. Education level. Job satisfaction. Age distribution. Productivity level. Liability rates. Health status.	34. Productivity comparisons. Quality control charts. Conflict resolution methods. Payroll verification. Contingency assignments. Personnel policies. Bonus triggers. Management and person can measure.	35. More productive equipment (7 and 39). Accidents (39). Labor market. Wage surveys. Professional licensing, regulations, and associations. Union organization. Family leisure, community life. Experience levels. Boundary spanning. Linkages, internal and external. Job security. Vacation schedules.	36. New professional/technological skills. Manpower problems/trends. Bureaucratization trends. Maintain freedom of choice of methods. Status of each specification in cells 31-35 at n, n + 1, n + 2 (time periods in the future).

Table 12.3 **Specification Matrix** (Page 7 of 8)

	Fundamental	Values	Measures	Control	Interface/Consequences	Future
Physical Catalysts	37. Machines/tools. Space, physical facility. Facility location. Workplaces. Desks, chairs, etc. Equipment. Computers. Power, liquids.	38. Clean, well maintained, safe. Secure information. Use available physical resources.	39. Capacity per machine. Age of each item. Percent downtime/utilization. Accident rate. Capital expenditure budget. Depreciation methods. Time of access. Maintenance cost. Memory/CPU capacity.	40. Timeliness of delivery. Quality control charts. Performance reports.	41. Sequence needs (19 and 21). Location with cells 25 and 27. Accidents (35). Maintenance activities (22). Equipment supplies.	42. New technological breakthroughs. Space for expansion. Status of each specification in cells 37–41 at n, n + 2 (time periods in the future).

Table 12.3 **Specification Matrix** (Page 8 of 8)

Information Aids	Fundamental	Values	Measures	Control	Interface/ Consequences	Future
	43. Training manuals. Service and maintenance manuals. Library sources. Equipment references. Computer programing languages. Physical laws and properties. Measurement theories and techniques. Syntactic structure of display. Decision support system. Models (iconic, analog, symbolic). Data bases.	44. Readily available. Complete. Security.	45. Time response. Cost overall and per unit. Number/type of inquiries.	46. Security monitoring. Transmission control. Quality assessment. Check in/out.	47. Categories of knowledge. Central info banks. Linguistic forms. Levels of technology. Display formats. P&D data bases. User and human agent satisfactions.	48. Coding research. Status of each specification in cells 43–47 at n, n + 1, n + 2 (time periods in the future).

questions for each cell, many of which reflect the solution frameworks described above.

Each item in each cell can be turned into one or more questions for which details *may* be needed in a specific project. For example, what is the specification or detail, if needed, for the measures of inputs (cell 9 in table 12-3) in the solution? What is the cost per unit of input material? What is the amount of cash input per day? How many customers or users will there be? Using such questions as prompts, the individual or group decides whether something needs to be specified, or whether additional information needs to be collected.

Our experiences using the system matrix in table 12-3 as a solution framework can be summarized to show other aspects of its great flexibility. A very broadly stated solution may need very rough details about only the fundamental dimensions of purpose, inputs, outputs, and sequence. This is the minimum level of detail. Additional detail may involve physical catalysts, human agents, information aids, or any additional dimensions for several of the elements.

The system matrix can be easily modified to become an excellent basis for developing the situation-specific solution framework. For one, the element and dimension names are just words. They represent ideas and meanings that can be easily expressed in other ways to suit the specific situation. The order in which the elements and dimensions appear can also be changed to fit the situation. An architectural project, for example, used nine elements ("environment" was split), calling the "fundamental" dimension "conceptual" and the "values" and "measures" dimensions "quantitative." A Canadian colleague, Alan D. Scharf, periodically includes a "finance" element to consolidate the monetary and financial details otherwise located in various elements.

A manufacturing company adapted the matrix to incorporate key aspects of the strategy, such as regularities, as shown in figure 12-4. Each unit operation is then described separately in terms of the SANT and the recommended solution.

| Unit Operation:_____ | Subunit: _____ | Output: |
| Inputs: | Main Functions: | |

Element	Unit	Physical Regularities	Physical Irregularities	Additional Information (including what might be future of*)
Size Weight Shape Material } *				
From: Handling method* Quantity/run Total weight Frequency				Including safety
Time: Set up Operation				Including safety
Space: Operation Storage				
Inspection:				
Facilities: Workplace } * Storage Tools Utilities Machinery Information sources				Other items Interaction with other work Percentage of utilization
To: Handling method* Quantity/run Total weight Frequency				
Who: Skills, etc.				Including human resource development Quality of working life

Flow chart	Sketched layout

Figure 12-4. Adaptation of a system matrix in a manufacturing company.

Projects that focus on management information systems can redefine the "information" element by replacing "physical catalysts" and "information aids" with "display media" and "attention catalysts" (aspects for understanding and using the information), while the "measures" dimension is replaced by "time" (chronology or intervals).

As valuable as a system matrix is for static documentation and for portraying the "results" of a project, knowledge about the elements and dimensions is a critical benefit in all steps of the approach. Perhaps the key benefit stems from the system perspective that must be considered in each step. Questions about interrelationships are raised at all times, not just at the end of a project. The infinity concepts of the system matrix invite the openness at any point to detail virtually any component for review and assessment.

In the train of thought that guides the development of a system matrix, the system is "empty" (i.e., with no specifications) in the beginning. At the end of the process, it is completely "filled in" with all the needed details. Specifications are added as each step is completed and decisions are made. More than one system matrix may be involved at the same time, as when several alternatives are being considered before the SANT is selected. Different elements receive different amounts of emphasis at different times. Desired outcomes, for example, are normally considered early while undesired outcomes are considered later.

Saying that the system matrix is empty at the start is obviously a technicality. As every project is always part of a larger system, some specifications automatically exist. But because the Breakthrough Thinking approach stresses the importance of identifying the "right" purpose at the outset, trying to figure out early on what these larger system specifications are could be a waste of time. They may well be much different when the purpose level is selected. Thus, you should always start with a clean slate–or operationally, an empty system matrix.

Table 12-4 skips over several steps in the Breakthrough Thinking process to illustrate this strategy. The steps can occur in several orders, the "values" dimension may be specified before others, and so forth. The solution framework can also be used as a stimulus to answer questions raised by the strategy: What possible areas or cells should be searched to find regularities? What is meant by alternatives for the SANT? What factors should govern testing? Other formats could be used in the right-hand column of table 12-4: element-by-element narratives, a description developed with questions from the system matrix, and so on. A small amount of detail is developed in the first two or three phases, while much more is incorporated in later phases. This keeps options open for even better solution ideas. When the project gets to the SANT or beyond, certain cells will require much more detail than others, such as working drawings and specifications for a building in a shopping center for the "fundamental" dimension of the "physical catalysts" element.

Table 12.4 **Time Interrelationships of System Matrix and Breakthrough Thinking Process** (Page 1 of 2)

Step	Expected Outcome	Status of System Matrix (SM) (illustrations of specifications that are developed)
:		"Empty" SM
5 :	Purpose/hierarchy and selected level	Fundamental dimension of purpose. Some future and interface dimensions of purpose
8	Measures of purpose accomplishment	Values and measures dimensions of purpose, also some control. Some values and measures dimensions of output
9		Several system matrices, one per component. Priorities for components in *overall* SM purpose element

Table 12.4 **Time Interrelationships of System Matrix and Breakthrough Thinking Process** (Page 2 of 2)

Step	Expected Outcome	Status of System Matrix (SM) (illustrations of specifications that are developed)
10	Generate many solution-after-next options	Each component matrix and the overall SM repeated as many times as there are ideas. At least start with sketches of possible operational timelines and structures. Each matrix with an idea serves as a "straw man"
11	Major alternatives	One system matrix for each major alternative "straw man" (and for each functional component), each one containing all of the previous specifications. Desired levels preferred.
12	Select SANT	SM with broad details for most cells. Desired outputs only.
13	Alternatives for SANT components to accommodate irregularities	SANT SM repeated with additional details, one for each alternative
14 :	Selected recommended solution	SM with more specific details. May have separate SF for each multiple channel for irregularities. How to cope with undesirable outputs.
18 :	Prepare installation plan	SM with still more details, working drawings, and specifications, etc.
20	Standardize performance	SM with documentation details plus future dimension re: betterment review and changeover
:		"Completed" SM

Figure 12-5 shows the system matrix array for a statewide natural resources data classification system (the "A" system). The coding to find the specifications is contained in each cell. The "B" data entry system is shown as an input to the "A" system, "C" as the accounting or control system for the data entry system, and "D" as the data input control system. Several system matrices can be used to detail multichanneled or pluralistic solutions that occur as irregularities.

Many techniques, tools, and models are available to help with the process of detailing, even though they vary a great deal from one field to another. A few general techniques are explained in the Appendix. Also, each organization will have its own ways to detail the various cells in a system matrix. Just as an example, one type of model is used to portray the specifications of the solution. These include prototype forms that will be needed, cost/price models, engineering drawings of products, flow charts, bills of material, office layout diagrams, and the like.

Other models and techniques that aid the process of detailing include computer simulations, activity sampling, Delphi surveys, decision worksheets, physical item operational modeling (e.g., heat transfer through a wall), and attitude questionnaires. An activity sampling study, for example, can help determine the location of equipment in an office layout model. A Delphi survey can help decide what information to include on prototype forms. A heat transfer operational model can help determine the thickness of metal to specify on engineering product drawings. A computer simulation of surgery patient arrivals and service in a hospital's recovery room can help pinpoint the number of beds needed.

Some techniques and models may become a continuing part of the solution. Examples include forecasting models, job descriptions, pro forma profit-and-loss statements, computerized decision support models, and marketing surveys. Because these models are part of the solution, they should be re-evaluated and possibly redesigned at regular intervals. For example, a sales forecasting model may be very effective in designing a new system, but a betterment design should be planned every year or so to update the model.

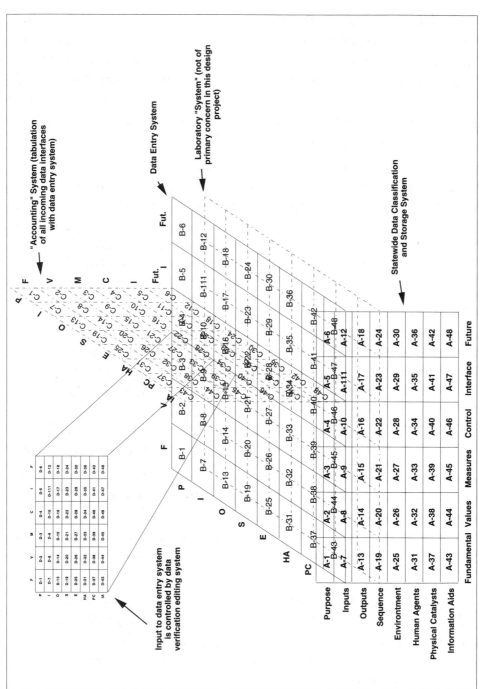

Figure 12-5. Statewide data classification and storage system.

The flexibility of the system matrix illustrated by figure 12-5 allows ideas and specifications to be "filed" in the proper location(s) in any order. The framework sets up a systems "crossword" structure in which entries can be made anywhere initially and subsequently. The relationships are clear in whatever order the entries are made, and each entry is likely to identify other system aspects needing clarification or strengthening. The system matrix concept is particularly important in the complex world of computerized systems. Without the smaller and larger perspectives of the system matrix, no one would be able to comprehend the whole. The elements and dimensions in each system matrix in such complex applications allow conceptual, physical, spatial, directional, chronological, locational, and many other aspects of a system to be appropriately handled as specification density increases.

Review Solution Details with Others

As noted above, continual involvement in a project can easily obscure the vision, or objectivity, of the people most closely associated with it. They may fail to discern potential roadblocks in the installation plan, or in their enthusiasm they may overlook many fine design details. One advantage of the system matrix, we saw, is that it helps to maintain an objective perspective. Still, it is wise at this point to stand back a moment and review the solution details, particularly with people who are not directly involved with the project.

The time needed for this step may appear to some as an unnecessary delay. If a team has worked a long time in isolation, members may feel that their understanding of how to make the solution work is all that is needed, regardless of what others think. Stopping at this point to review the recommendation may also breed impatience in members who want "instant gratification" after all their work.

However, we cannot stress the importance of this step enough. Far from being a delay or superfluous activity, the review plays a critical role in ensuring a project's success. As it fosters objectivity and heightens attention to detail, it serves as a powerful way to thwart Murphy's Law ("anything that can go wrong will"). With studies showing that 50 to 75 percent of advanced manufacturing systems fail after installation (Majchrzak), a review seems especially worthwhile–even if a system matrix has been thoroughly detailed. As one team of researchers has observed, "The greatest costs stem from unforeseen mismatches between the new technology's capabilities and needs, and the existing process and organization" (Chew, Leonard-Barton, Bohn).

While the need to review is a constant in this step, its format, length, and complexity are variable. The biggest criterion for judging how to structure a review or how much time to devote to it is the amount of evidence needed to sway people into accepting the recommended solution. Previous meetings with key decision makers and representatives of constituencies may mean less time is needed for the review. In general, the larger the solution, the more likely is the need for a thorough review.

In most cases, reviews are structured as a series of questions. These questions arise from general considerations of what a review should entail as well as from expressions of uncertainty and inquiry raised by the decision maker(s) in the approval step. The following questions are only a sample of what you may need to ask in a review:

- Can the recommended solution be brought closer to the SANT? Can it be improved? Additional small changes in specifications should be made before installation to avoid the reaction, "Why weren't all the changes installed at the same time?" or "If you don't have time to do it right, when will you have time to do it over?"

- Are *needed* specifications included in the recommended solution? Will it actually work? You might not want to include all specifications so that the people working in the system will have some flexibility.

- What components and subsystems need testing? What type of testing would be effective?

- Should priorities be set up or redone for the next stages of the project? What effort over the next five years should be earmarked for the project? Which components of the solution should be installed first?

- Who should be responsible for actual installation? Options here are to let the project team supervise the installation, set up a transition management group, or give the responsibility to the managers who would be in charge of the solution after its installation.

- Should other organizations, departments, groups, or associations adopt the solution, or should they start their own project? The latter is usually preferable because of the Uniqueness Principle, but then many large organizations require standardization in their policies, systems, and operations.

- What possible conflicts can be anticipated? What actions need to be taken to minimize or eliminate their impact on achieving successful implementation?

- Have users/customers/clients/recipients/citizens been adequately involved or informed, so that their reactions can be legitimately considered?

- What sensitivity does the set of specifications have in relation to the desired workability? Who should do the review and how might they proceed?

- Has some other individual or group who simulated the new system found it workable and detailed sufficiently?

In conjunction with these questions, some of the following people should be able to contribute valuable insights and opinions about the recommended solution:

People involved in the operation of the system, but not involved in the project. These people may be found at all levels, from top management to supervisory and operating personnel. They can participate most productively at this point by going over each step in the Breakthrough Thinking process.

Workshop groups and project teams. The original group could conduct a "review" by approaching the solution as a betterment project.

Separate review committee. Various personnel such as foremen, administrators, board members, supervisors, workers, and technical staff could constitute such a committee (even if they have been consulted previously).

Outside audit committee or evaluator. An external "inspector general" is good, especially when a group has been relatively isolated during the project. Consultants could even be used.

One last note: Reviews need not always be framed as a series of questions. One very effective alternative is simply to submit the proposal for approval. This tactic works particularly well with open-minded, flexible groups, such as health system agencies and corporate planning departments. Another alternative is to have an outside staff person use the system pyramid to test the feasibility and workability of all functional components.

Case Illustrations

Case A: Package Tracking

Once this project team developed alternatives to handle the irregularities in their package tracking system, they were ready to detail the solution. The SANT, you may recall from Chapters 10 and 11, was a "paperless" system consisting of fixed position laser scanners in each hub and hand-held scanners (DIADs) primarily for drivers to use.

A major part of the team's detailing activities was to identify specific points in the existing system where problems were occurring. Although the purpose of the project was "to inform customers about the status of packages," the purpose stemmed from poor record keeping and scanning problems in the hubs.

Following is an overview of the team's investigation into these problems, which traced the problems to employee errors and so led to their recommendation to install a completely electronic system. To begin their investigation, the team looked first at equipment and then at employees.

Equipment

The equipment used in the existing package tracking system included hand-held scanners, personal computers, and host computers at both the head office and hubs. Transmitting data about each package required four steps:

- Bar code label to hand-held scanner
- Scanner to PC
- PC to host computer in hub
- Host computer in hub to host computer in head office

Of these steps, the only one that proved to be working well (with an error rate of approximately 4%) was the last one, when information went from the hub to the head office. The project team thus narrowed their investigation to the remaining three steps, focusing primarily on the equipment but also on employees' actions.

Bar Code to Scanner

Hypothesis	• Workers miss the scan. • Faulty bar code labels or scanning devices.
Test Environment	• A number of bar codes will be scanned by an "average" operator who will perform at his/her normal rate.
Data Collection	• Check scanner's memory to see if registered bar code numbers match original list of bar codes. • Check to see if there are problems with the listening device.

Scanner to PC

Hypothesis	• Equipment is not compatible.

| Test Environment | • All registered bar codes will be uploaded to PC by an operator in a selected hub. |
| Data Collection | • Print list of bar codes after information has been uploaded to PC and check these numbers against those on original list. |

PC to Host Computer in Hub

Hypothesis	• Software is not transmitting data accurately. • PCs and host computers are not compatible.
Test Environment	• Data will be transmitted from PCs to host computer in hub.
Data Collection	• Check results by comparing data from PCs with data received by host computer.

People

After finding equipment to be in working order, the team turned exclusively to the people involved. These included:

Hub Operation:
- Scanning Operators
- Drivers
- PC Operators
- Host Computer Operators

Head Office:
- Host Computer Operators

Because transmission of data from hubs to the head office was practically error-free, host computer operators at both hubs and the head office were eliminated from further study. PC operators were also eliminated since similar problems were occurring in almost all hubs. That narrowed the problem down to scanning operators and drivers.

Scanning Operators: In the existing system each scanning operator had a hand-held scanner, which came with a scanning pen, a laser gun for reading the label, and a headphone through which the operator heard a beep when the bar code was read.

The possible mistakes these operators made were:

- Failing to scan every package
- Failing to re-scan packages if they did not hear the beep from the headphone
- Handling the scanning devices improperly

Drivers: Drivers in the existing system were responsible for removing the stubs from the package labels after delivering the packages, and then bringing the stubs to the hub for image scanning.

The most common mistakes the drivers made were:

- Forgetting to return the stubs
- Losing the stubs

Destination Scanning Operators: At the destination hub, operators scanned and highlighted package labels with a specific color to indicate the day of the week:

Monday	Yellow
Tuesday	Pink
Wednesday	Green
Thursday	Purple
Friday	Blue

The main purpose of this color system was to remind drivers to turn in the stubs after their shift. If a driver returned the stubs the next day, the supervisor would know they were late just by looking at the color.

Possible errors made by the destination scanning operators were:

- Using wrong color code
- Failing to scan and highlight every package

"Triple Label" Test

The main purpose of this test was to make the operators and drivers understand the basic concepts behind the package tracking system and to enable them to check each other's work. The test also helped to determine whether scanning operators and drivers understood their assigned roles and how well they performed them.

For the purposes of this test, labels were divided into three detachable sections. The white section was removed at the hub for the Origin Scan; the gray one was detached at the destination hub for the Destination Scan; and the final sections–red for "Next Day Air" and brown for "Second Day Air"–were detached when the packages were delivered.

With the color codes, it was fairly easy for workers to determine the status of each package and to check each other's work. For example, if a supervisor found a package with, say, a pink label on a Thursday, he would know that the package was two days late in getting delivered, and he would also know who was responsible for the delay.

Fixed Position Scanners

When the Triple Label test showed that employees were causing all the problems, the team had most of the evidence needed to put forth their recommendation for the paperless tracking system. In their proposal to management, they outlined the problems, summarized test results, and then argued for their solution. Portions of their argument are excerpted here:

> "We recommend that fixed laser scanners be installed in each hub. The only drawback to this idea is that the operation environment needs to be controlled. For example, the speed of the conveyor, the orientation of the packages, and the space between packages must meet the criteria for the scanner. This will restrict the flexibility of the scanners somewhat. However, it should completely eliminate human errors by eliminating the need for the scanning operators. Most importantly, the overhead scanners will entail a minimum of change in the current system, thus solving the problems in the existing system immediately.

> "The overhead scanner is like a 'tunnel' in which the laser will scan three sides of a package for the bar code. An indication light will be installed right next to the scanner. A green light will signal that the bar code on a package has

been read; a red light will indicate that the bar code has not been read. A visual indicator is preferred over the aural beep because the hub environment is very noisy and sometimes the beep is hard to hear. Furthermore, *all* workers can see the lights, whereas only one worker can hear the beep."

Handling Irregularities

Because of the laser scanner's restricted flexibility, the team recommended manual scanning for very small and large packages. In the event of a power failure, the overhead scanners would not be able to work. In such cases, the battery-operated portable scanners would be used. Finally, inspectors would be assigned at strategic points along the conveyor system to inspect the conveyor belts and repackage any damaged or opened items.

Cost Analysis–Benefits

- Scanning operators would be eliminated. A few would be relocated as inspectors, and several others would tend to manual sorting.

- Costs to maintains and repair the tracking system would be reduced substantially.

- Sorting and scanning processes would be expedited.

- Both employee productivity and scanning accuracy would improve.

Case B: Emergency Operations Center

The layout sketches were successively refined to arrive at some details for actual operation. Figure 12-6 shows one of the drawings for the recommended system. A comparison with the SANT (figure 10-6) illustrates how the recommendation is based on, but differs from the SANT.

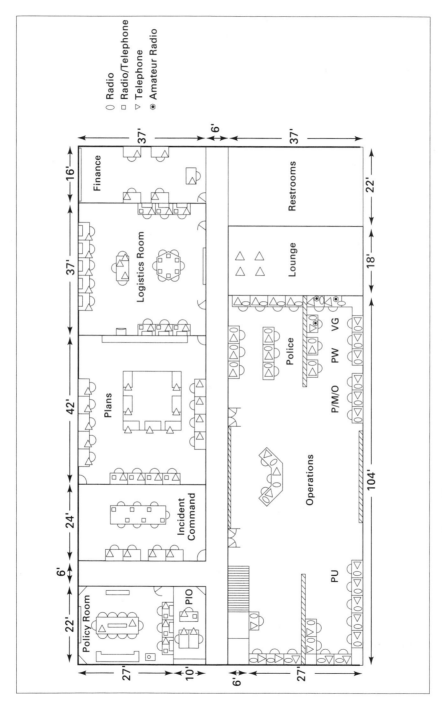

Figure 12-6. Detailed layout with radio/telephone communications.

Developing the
Installation Plan

Chapter 13 focuses on the steps in the Breakthrough Thinking process highlighted below. (The numbers in parentheses refer to the chapter in which the step is described. The Breakthrough Thinking process is detailed in Chapter 5.)

Step*	Result
1. Set up TQM program (6)	TQM mission, values, strategic plan
2. Identify primary projects and activities (7)	Initial plan of action and timeline
3. Set up TQM project (7)	Project system (purposes, people, etc.)
4. List possible purposes (8)	
5. Develop purpose hierarchies (8)	
6. Determine criteria to select purpose level (8)	
7. Select purpose(s) (8)	Focus purpose(s) in a hierarchical context
8. Establish measures of purpose accomplishment (8)	Success factors
9. Establish subgroups if needed (8)	Subgroups established
10. Generate many solution-after-next options (9)	List of viable alternatives
11. Assess solution-after-next options (10)	
* The number in parentheses after each step refers to the chapter in which the step is described	

311

Step*	Result
12. Select solution-after-next target (10)	Target solution-after-next
13. Modify target for irregularities (11)	
14. Choose recommended changes (11)	Recommendations
15. Prepare proposal (12)	Proposal
16. Inform people not involved to date (12)	
17. Detail recommendations (12)	Complete recommendation specifications
18. Prepare installation plan (13)	Installation plan
19. Install recommendations (13)	Installed system
20. Standardize performances (13)	System performance measures
21. Review project at betterment timeline date (14-15)	Next recommended changes
22. Repeat step 21 (14-15)	Further actions and changes

* The number in parentheses after each step refers to the chapter in which the step is described

Installation, not implementation, is in the title of this chapter because it signifies the transition to the new as the end point of all the preceding implementation efforts. If you have followed the previous steps thoroughly (Chapters 6 through 12), people in your organization will be "warmed up" to what is coming, for they will have taken part in determining the focus purpose, selecting the SANT, and detailing the recommendation. The right people will have approved or bought into the proposed change, the most effective timing will have been established for its installation, and workers will be expecting training to meet the new system requirements.

The idea of implementation should not be left to the end of a project when conventional wisdom says you have to "sell" the solution. This is often too late. The process followed in developing the change is part of implementation in Breakthrough Thinking, making this step (installation) a naturally expected event for everyone.

All members of the project team should be directly involved with installation, rather than assuming someone else can do it or treating it as "beneath their dignity." Indeed, the group should be highly motivated to see their creation put into practice.

Involvement is needed even if the organization has an efficient transition mechanism to take the solution through the requisite departments or staffs—e.g., prototyping, tooling, start-up manufacturing, and production runs for a new product design. (Ideally, many people from these areas should have been involved all along in the project.) The recommended solution is bound to need modifications as the installation proceeds, no matter how well it is detailed. Installation may slow or stop, even though the difficulties may be trivial, unless the project team keeps abreast of happenings. They are the ones who know best how to modify the solution without altering it too much.

Of course, not everything can be planned and designed to cope with contingencies, external disturbances, and drifts of policy. But the continued involvement of the project team can significantly increase the likelihood of a successful installation.

Table 13-1 lists the steps you need to take when developing your installation plan. These steps, however, are far from sequential in performance or operational in details. Many of them, you will find, take place concurrently, while others are iterative. Still others refer to ongoing operations of the organization. In all cases, use the Breakthrough Thinking process to develop specific installation activities, outcomes, and personnel.

Table 13.1 **Installing the Solution** (Page 1 of 2)

- Test, simulate, or try out the solution.

- Set up an installation schedule.

- Develop procedures for presenting and "selling" the solution to anyone not yet involved.

- Prepare operational resources (equipment orders, location preparation, job descriptions, department specifications, train or shift personnel, etc.).

Table 13.1 **Installing the Solution** (Page 2 of 2)

- Install the solution (or proceed to next stage of protocol).

- Monitor the installation closely to follow-up on and solve operational problems.

- Establish operational performance measures to provide operators/managers with norms.

- Evaluate the performance of the installed solution in terms of its goals, objectives, and purposes.

- Get and celebrate success.

It often helps to put a "change master" or "installation transition manager" in charge. This person could be the facilitator or chair of the project team. Large and complex projects, however, may need someone more skilled in handling the numerous problems that can arise during installation. Such a person should be familiar with all of the work leading up to the installation (purposes, hierarchy, solution options, SANT, etc.).

Test, Simulate, or Try Out the Solution

Will the solution or "current release" actually achieve its targeted purposes? Nothing in the preceding steps guarantees this, although some preliminary testing has been done. Nor can an abundance of experience answer the question. The purpose of this step, therefore, is to test out the solution's workability, effectiveness, stability, and efficiency prior to its installation.

Many new questions concerning the solution and its components arise at this point: Will the equipment and input data perform as designed? Will clients or users provide the feedback needed to operate and refine the system? Will output items effectively achieve the purpose? Will the human agents perform according to the solution specifications?

Finding the answers now, before installation, will permit modifications at the most favorable time. It is not even too late to discover that the solution is unworkable.

Testing is a system that can be designed with the general flow of reasoning. The test system needs purposes, measures of effectiveness, alternatives, regularities, a FIST, and so forth. Following are the most frequently used testing systems:

- *Experiments.* Use the conventional research approach (especially in betterment projects when more time is available) to test a hypothesis on which a key part of the recommendation is based. Will people be able to read the highway signs in the time allotted? Will workers be motivated by a buy-back incentive? Several techniques listed in the Appendix, such as the Taguchi Method, can be used.

- *Physical Models.* These are usually reduced-scale replications of a physical item. A *pilot plant* is a full-scale but less comprehensive version of a process. So is an inexpensive *mock-up* of a workplace, or the preparation of a product *prototype.* Layout and *flow diagrams* as well as *two- and three-dimensional models* are possible substitute test methods. Actual *construction* of only one workplace may be desirable for cases that will require many similar workplaces (e.g., airline reservation desks or cashier stations in department stores).

- *Simulation.* Done with or without a computer, simulation can estimate performance (e.g., the number of workers, pieces of equipment, or inventory items), and explore various configurations (e.g., layout of facilities, flow of people, mix of products, etc.). Computer-based simulation models can range from very specific situations (the number of beds in a hospital recovery room) to very broad ones (the system dynamics of an entire firm or urban area). Paper-and-pencil models, such as a multi-activity chart, can simulate shifts of work among people and machines to "test" various methods.

- *Making Actual Changes in Existing Systems.* A solution involving a slight rearrangement of equipment, forms, or methods may be tested by actually making the changes. If they do not work, you can simply go back to the original arrangements.

- *New Machinery.* Tests of expensive machinery are desirable but usually not possible. However, you might be able to conduct tests in the manufacturer's plant, or visit other organizations that have similar equipment. If no equipment test is possible, try other techniques, such as simulation.

- *Scenario Writing.* By writing out a description of what would happen if the solution were used, a group or individual can "visualize" future conditions quite effectively.

- *Negotiation, Role Playing, and Other Behavioral Activities.* These are active forms of scenario writing, in which individuals or groups test the solution by acting it out in various ways.

- *Pilot Demonstration or Field Test.* This technique is similar to the physical models noted above; however, it is for solutions that do not involve hardware. It is usually limited to a few departments (people, locations, etc.) and a specific period of time. Normally, only parts of the solution are piloted at first, before resources are committed to a full pilot. The results of the partial pilot can be combined with other test methods (e.g., simulation) to increase the scope of the assessment.

- *Optimization and Theoretical Calculations.* Optimal conditions for physical items can often be tested on computers (vibration frequencies, material usage, stress concentrations, etc.), using known theories and principles in physics, mathematics, and statistics.

- *Quality Audit.* In this test an independent group reviews the solution (especially if it is non-technical, policy-based, or procedural) to assess its workability, acceptability, degree of improvement, achievement of performance specifications, ability to interface with other organizational activities, and so forth.

- *No Test Possible.* There may be many reasons why a solution cannot be tested: There is not enough time; it is a one-time system (e.g., a fireworks show); it does not lend itself to testing (e.g., social policies); it involves too many people (e.g., urban renewal); there is not enough money. In such cases, "testing" should involve at least an internal review and, as noted in #10, a quality audit.

Set Up Installation Schedule

More than just deadlines and due dates are involved in this step. Installing any project creates strains, uncertainties, role conflicts, and disruptions to ongoing activities, regardless of how completely the previous phases have been carried out.

There are many ways to deal with the stress and strain brought about by organizational change: parallel operations, in which the old is operated concurrently with the new; phased-in segments from either the beginning or end of the proposed system; complete "cold turkey" installation overnight or over a weekend; or pilot testing of the whole solution in one location or several similar locations.

With each of these installation strategies come certain questions that the organization needs to answer: What inducements, rewards, or incentives can be used to get people not involved with the project to accept it? How can as many people as possible participate in preparing the schedule? How will conflicts among various people and groups be resolved? What training should accompany the installation? How can the organization-at-large be kept informed about installation activities and developments? This step (along with the next step) addresses these questions.

Setting up an installation schedule means expressing in detail what was expressed in general terms in the original project timeline. For many projects this detailing is all that is needed.

The installation process for most projects, however, faces two difficulties. The first is that people at all levels of an organization may play "games" that delay, if not scuttle, the installation-even after agreeing that the solution is desirable. The second is that the character and degree of many implementation problems are unpredictable.

Playing games during installation is both a conscious and a subconscious response. It is subconscious to the extent that people react automatically to change because of individual and organizational realities. For example, the "not invented here" factor can surface at almost any time, even with excellent participation by many. This, in turn, may lead to the "massive resistance" game, especially when people are not completely informed about the installation details.

Games may take several forms:[1]

- Massive resistance, refusal, or defiance by those in secure enough positions to do so
- Tokenism, or publicly displaying support for a solution, while privately conceding only a small "token" of support
- Procrastination in contributing to the installation process, or substituting a contribution of inferior quality
- Bureaucrats playing out their reputation
- Deflection of goals for the problem area by raising others purported to be more important
- Non-supportive attitudes, such as "it's not our problem"
- The felt need to "keep the peace"
- End play, or acting in a way that ostensibly achieves the purpose being sought but actually "protects" existing power/authority/fiscal control arrangements

Games can take a variety of other forms as well: strikes, slowdowns, high turnover rates, grievances, and so on. Whatever their form, however, they all have the same effect, which is to "divert resources, especially money; deflect policy goals; and dissipate personal and political energies that might otherwise be channeled into constructive action."[2]

Delay is the principal peril of game-playing. While some delays can result from "legitimate" reasons, such as a vendor shipping products late, the ones at issue here all stem from people's unwillingness to accept

---

1. E. Bardach, *The Implementation Game*, Cambridge, Mass.: MIT, 1977. Also see Chapter 9 in G. Majone and E. S. Quade, eds., *Pitfalls of Analysis*, New York: Wiley, 1980.

2. Bardach, *op. cit.*

change. In short, the more games people play, the longer installation is delayed, and the lower the probability is for successful installation.

Delays caused by game-playing give rise to the second difficulty— that is, the unpredictability of installation problems. Because of the motives behind such delays, an installation schedule needs far more than slack time for external occurrences of delay. It needs to incorporate appropriate considerations for the whole range of factors that can cause delays.

The anticipated outcomes of this step are a timeline and activity schedule that take into account the major events, activities, and person(s) responsible for each activity. A written scenario can help to interrelate people and groups with activities, events, and decisions. These factors can then be built into a realistic schedule that effectively addresses "the problems of [disorganization] (incompetence, variability in the objects of control, and coordination), dilemmas of administration (tokenism, massive resistance, procrastination, monopoly conditions, deterrents, incentives, etc.), diversion of resources, deflection of goals, dissipation of energies, and delays."[3]

Time and costs can be set aside for finding ways to motivate people and to discourage game-playing. At the very least, time for *any* delays that are likely to arise can be incorporated. Extra blocks of time might also be built into the installation schedule for such activities as negotiating, revising priorities, instituting better control of installation activities and events, arranging top level support, introducing incentives, tracking delay tactics, appealing to authority, or otherwise "fixing the game."

Of course, your attentiveness to these factors should not detract from the first need to identify the critical events and activities for the actual installation of the solution. It is both embarrassing and counterproductive to do well at the art of game fixing but then have a "technical" failure when the solution is installed.

---

3. *Ibid.*

Given all these considerations, developing an installation schedule might be a sizable project in itself. Treating it as such leads to the major suggestion for *how* to set it up–i.e., follow the general flow of reasoning (Chapters 8 through 12).

Develop Procedures for Presenting and "Selling" the Solution

The word "selling" appears in quotations here because its interpretation at this point differs from the usual meaning. First, "selling" refers to obtaining organization-wide utilization of a solution that could not possibly have involved everyone in the project effort. For example, developing a service order system that affects 40% of the 60,000 employees in a telephone company covering five states could not involve all employees, even when a widely representative task force developed the recommendations. A second meaning concerns transferring a solution found effective in one part of an organization to other departments or locations. Some examples include a good inventory control and accounting system in one warehouse of fourteen in a company, and effective ways to screen people for heart disease in one county of twelve in a health care system. This meaning is often called *process institutionalizing* of the solution or system as soon as it has been proven successful.

This step continues the formulation of plans to get the recommended solution approved (Chapter 11). The goal now is to seek commitment to its installation. That is, you want to "actualize" the organization into utilizing the solution.

By this point, a constituency that favors the solution is probably well formed. Links to the various support services are mostly in place. Yet, even with an internalized search for continuing change and improvement, many projects require commitment to push for adoption of the solution. This step seeks to organize the constituency and its resources to secure the *continuing* sanction of all those who can influence the installation.

As the installation progresses, the solution will begin to affect new people, all of whom may have far different perceptions and concerns from those in the immediate project group or those already using the solution. Because of the realities that such people bring with them, they can cause added difficulties to the installation process. In effect, then, this step seeks to reduce the probability that the "new" people will deter installation efforts. Gauging the reactions of the "market" (customers, clients, users, and so forth) to the solution, predicting who will play what "games," and estimating the intensity of their commitment to such games all come into play in this step.

Addressing these difficulties through the Breakthrough Thinking process will probably take place concurrently with setting up the installation schedule. This will result in an installation plan that identifies the key actors, changes their perceptions and behavior (in a positive fashion, it is hoped, rather than a coercive one), and retains flexibility even at this stage for changing the solution. If some of the key actors can be identified earlier, they should be involved in developing the installation plan. By asking for their advice and having them help identify factors that might impede the installation, you will cultivate their sense of "ownership" in the solution that will go far to ensure a successful installation.

The plan that results from this step will most likely contain a list of whom you should meet with regularly, who is responsible in the other departments, what is to be covered, when operational resources should be ready (see next step), who is to be responsible for actual changes, what monitoring methods are to be used, and so on.

Prepare Operational Resources

The virtual impossibility of being prescriptive about this step is illustrated by comparing two widely different solutions. What human, physical, and informational resources need to be prepared for (1) installing the plans for a $180 million medical center, and (2) implementing a seventh grader's self-designed plan for studying a required text?

While we cannot specify the operational resources for every project (as the example above illustrates), we can offer two important generalizations. First, people must have the skills, abilities, and knowledge to do the required installation. Second, all of the materials, equipment, information, and human agents necessary to operate the installed solution must be ready before it can be successfully implemented.

The elements and dimensions of the system matrix (Chapter 12) provide a good way to map out the scope of the installation system. The following are only *partial* in number and *suggestive* of this scope:

Inputs. Introduce customers/clients/users to new ordering/ information/monetary requirements, order new forms, get new material specifications and quality levels, set up bills of material, establish continuing attitude survey of users and customers, establish line of credit for operating funds.

Outputs. Set up financial accountability methods, measure quality of product/service in users' perceptions, get regulatory clearances for services/products, organize distributors for new advertising campaign.

Sequence. Hire equipment movers to change layout, prepare locations for control information to be obtained, prepare advertising materials, determine optimal allocation methods for supervisors to use, set up methods for tagging products distinctively.

Environment. Change to new organizational structure, develop the political support for continued operation, set up departmental operating rules, prepare for letters "smoothing" the way, arrange for new organizational design.

Human Agents. Train personnel for new assignment(s), transfer/hire new personnel, set up job descriptions, establish and evaluate performance requirements, train troubleshooters to handle difficulties, obtain needed professional services.

Physical Catalysts. Order new equipment, arrange for refurbishing of tooling, obtain comparisons of equipment specifications.

Information Aids. Update maintenance manuals, establish regulations, set up implementation guides, reprogram software for monitoring activities.

(Note that almost each one of these items can be considered a small project, for which the general flow of reasoning could be used.)

The sequence of these activities should be fairly well established in the installation schedule, along with the procedures for presenting and "selling" the solution. Several items can occur concurrently, with layout changes taking priority, for example, over information or system modifications, while both are going on. Both would also have priority over, say, modifying the organization structure or developing new product designs, while work is still being done on the latter two. Techniques for prioritizing and establishing precedence are noted in the Appendix.

Many compromises and decisions regarding the recommended solution will be required as installation gets under way. You will need to refer continuously to the purpose hierarchy, measures of purpose accomplishment, major alternatives and components, the SANT, regularities, and other information as you make these decisions. These information resources will help you make choices that lead to the long-term effectiveness and workability of the solution.

Install the Solution. DO IT!

This step puts the installation schedule into operation. It starts the transition to real-world modes of operating. Installation is influenced by many of the same dynamic factors that affect the other steps—i.e., factors that "delay it, stop it, restart it." The factors cause a project to speed up, to branch to a new phase, to cycle within one or between two phases. . . There are six groups of dynamic factors: interrupts, which are caused by environmental forces; scheduling delays, timing delays and speedups, . . . feedback delays, comprehension cycles, and failure recycles."[4]

Monitor the Installation

The installation of a change almost always indicates that people are anticipating positive results. The steps in this chapter are intended to increase significantly the probability of achieving them. However, one phenomenon that can lead to disillusionment and doubts about the change is the initial downturn in performance that generally occurs just before and after the installation. That is, average performance tends to

---

4. H. Mintzberg, D. Raisinghani, and A. Theoret, "The Structure of 'Unstructured' Decision Processes," *Administrative Science Quarterly,* Vol. 21, No. 2, June 1976, pp. 245-275.

decrease in anticipation of the change. Then, the anticipated increase in performance after installation usually doesn't come for a much longer period of time than planned.

In other words, the costs of adjusting to the change, most often not even included in any cost estimates for the recommendation, balloon and far too frequently exceed the installation costs! New systems and equipment do not immediately perform as expected, and adaptation, debugging, retraining, reorienting departments, and clarifying information channels are needed—all adding to the costs and deterioration of performance.

Monitoring should therefore be viewed as a learning or research and development (R&D) experience, rather than a matter of strict adherence to a set of system specifications and an installation schedule. *A change is not a videocassette that can just be inserted and expected to perform.* The tests described in Section A above are critical learning and experimenting methods that should reduce these costs. Because it is impossible, however, to plan for every contingency in making an actual change, the best preparation is to build in a monitoring function to look for and solve problems, utilizing all the available information about purposes, solution options, and related details as guides.

This responsibility is ordinarily assumed by operating and supervising personnel, but the project group or facilitator with an excellent understanding of the solution's purposes, regularities, SANT, and other alternatives ought to "stay in bed with the manager" (and/or self-managed work team). This is one way the solution's benefits can be maximized to at least the level proposed in the recommendation. This also establishes a way to trade off long- and short-term considerations effectively.

Monitoring to provide troubleshooting and follow-up may involve several actions:

- Scheduling visits to the areas where the solution is installed until the new solution "habit" is formed.
- Providing a "tickle file" for periodic reminders that certain project areas must be visited for a check.

- Keeping close tabs on the triggers needed to activate contingency plans.
- Setting up a technical assistance committee.
- Including all levels of people in checking out solutions in their own and other departments.
- Establishing a separate group or designating an individual to follow up on all newly installed solutions.
- Scheduling a review of the newly installed system (in conjunction with the betterment timeline) earlier than usual.
- Reviewing performance data with the progress function or learning curve techniques.

In addition to time and cost per "unit," other performance data provide good monitoring indices: efficiency, productivity, budgetary control ratings, excess direct labor cost ratio, equipment utilization ratio, cumulative failures or failure rate, number of breakdowns, and so on. One point at which it may be desirable, and often profitable, to discontinue follow-up and debugging efforts occurs when the learning curve reaches a plateau, or when reliability or other factors reach the desired level and stay relatively constant for a while.

Operating personnel and external customers/users who have been involved in the effort make good monitors. Their enthusiasm for and understanding of the solution help assure its installation. One aspect of following-up people can focus on the appropriate utilization of time or money "saved" from what was being done before, especially in professional (engineers, nurses, architects, etc.) and nonprofit organizations (case workers, teachers, counselors, etc.). If the people and resources are not being channeled into the activities specified in the recommended solution, then the solution benefits are not being realized.

Many of the performance evaluation techniques that might be used in this step—learning curves and progress functions, control charts, index values, and exception reporting, to name a few—are highly interrelated with the performance measures to be developed in the next step. They are also prospects for operators and managers to use monthly after norms are established.

Establish Operational Performance Measurements

"Install the Solution" above started the actual installation of the solution. This step completes it by providing the norms needed for operating and supervising purposeful activities.

You should consider *operational requirements* that can lead to performance measurements for continuously doing the following:

- Adjusting equipment and people needs.
- Determining when equipment needs maintenance or replacement.
- Determining how work can be subdivided to achieve a balance of job enlargement, skill utilization, and minimum delay.
- Establishing the size of a crew for a particular operation.
- Estimating costs for submitting bids on special products or services.
- Determining the selling price of products and services.
- Establishing task measures for employees to guide their performance.
- Obtaining and updating control limits for quality assessment techniques and performance measurements output evaluation.
- Preparing budgets.

Many organizations already have data that could be used as performance measurements (e.g., elemental time standard data, standard costs per machine, historical records). Many norms, however, will need situation-specific data that can only be collected as the solution is installed. In many cases, estimates developed with the people involved are quite sufficient and quite often to be preferred. The agreement of those working in the system on an estimate is very often all that is needed to create an effective stimulus for accomplishing that level and more.

Performance measurements for the whole solution or its components are based on the measures of purpose accomplishment from previous steps (Chapter 8). They are expressed in various units: time per output unit, time per element, time per work component, output units per minute (or hour), number of people served per week, dollars per transaction, percentage of machine utilization, per capita complaints, productivity index, percentage of material utilization, hours of direct labor, cost per unit, and so on.

Two measures may be paired as a check and balance. When one gets better, the other should not get worse. Some examples of check-and-balance pairs are percent efficiency and percent downtime; percent weight utilization and number of rejects; percent of direct labor and amount of indirect labor. Picking any set of measures will involve trade-offs among criteria—accuracy compared to understandability, measurability compared to rigidity of conformance to organizational goals, process measures compared to outputs/results modeled.

A performance measure should be expressed as an expected value (mean, mode, minimum, etc.) with its associated variability and confidence levels. Variability limits are psychologically desirable for operators and managers who already know that each performance cycle will not take an exactly identical time. All parts of the performance measure need updating periodically as part of normal operating activities.

A performance measure must be associated with a well-defined activity, artifact, or outcome. The measure attains greater accuracy and precision (less variability) the greater the specificity of the real-world phenomenon to which it refers. Compare, for example, the accuracy and precision of possible performance measures for a regional planning unit in a developing country with those for a winter road-salting program for a city in the northern United States. In addition, the frequency of occurrence of a phenomenon influences accuracy and precision needs. A three-hour performance measure for the activity of preparing a training course outline once a year can tolerate far greater variance than the number of radios produced in an hour in a factory. Many techniques in the Appendix are available to collect and organize performance information so that a norm or performance measurement can be established.

Performance measures should be consistent among comparable jobs, tasks, departments, and so on. They also need to be similar with the organization's goals, meaning that the measurement processes "program" needs to be reviewed periodically. A betterment design project once every year or two is one way of doing this. A control model based on, say, the number of complaints per week is another.

Because a performance measure is always tied to a well described phenomenon (such as a job or department), there is a tendency to treat the phenomenon as rigid. But TQM encourages continuing improvements in the phenomenon, although this involves constantly updating the performance measures. Several methods may be considered in handling suggested improvements:

- Put the idea in the suggestion system.
- Let the person or group with improved output continue with the old performance measure for a specified period of time (i.e., earn whatever is possible, if on incentives) before changing the performance measure(s).
- Utilize non-financial incentives, such as newspapers and other publicity, providing psychic rewards to the individual or group.
- Give a merit increase to the individual or group.
- Determine the savings for a specified period of time, such as six months, and pay the individual or group that amount, then change the performance measure.
- Provide a methods incentive. An increase beyond, say, 140% performance means an incentive payment to the individual or group and a change in allowed times or performance measures.
- Determine if increased frequency of the measured activity signals a need for improving the accuracy and precision of the performance measure.

Performance measurements should motivate people and thus create favorable attitudes and performance. Three key essentials for doing this are (1) purposes, societal values, and TQM objectives should guide the establishment and use of performance measures; (2) people should know how the measurements are developed and preferably take part in setting them up; and (3) they should know as quickly as possible the results of their performance.

Evaluate the Performance of the Installed Solution

The project team or facilitator should periodically assess just how well the project purposes, TQM objectives, and overall goals are being attained. This goes beyond daily or weekly performance reports that an organization would normally have prepared. Goals, objectives, values, and purposes were agreed upon for each project, and a solution was selected to achieve them. How well are they being accomplished, now that a period of time (a year or so) has elapsed? In addition to providing an audit and review function, this evaluation may signify when betterment for a project should be set up (see next step) if interim reports about the project indicate no particular difficulties.

Critical to the evaluation are the perceptions of operating personnel and clients. These people need to feel comfortable with the solution and perceive its advantages. Clients and managers need to know that benefits are accruing through the changed "behavior" of the organizational personnel. Customers in particular should perceive the benefits and pleasures of a better-quality or lower-priced product or service.

One factor that may appear often in evaluation is the status of productivity achievement in the solution. Yet productivity for a specific solution/system is best measured by overall performance factors (see Section G) and the bigger purposes in the hierarchy, rather than by specific and limited terms. In other words, reducing waste or increasing the number of output units per day or decreasing delays in the specific system assume that overall productivity is being improved. This may not be so if bigger purposes and societal values are not being achieved; increasing the daily number of buggy whips produced is hardly the same as increasing productivity. Productivity measures or indices are really an aggregate concept (see Chapter 14).

Get and Celebrate Success

Everything in the general flow of reasoning pushes to obtain the biggest changes possible. As long as a change is being made, you might as well get the most benefits. Studies have shown that over twice the economic benefits are obtained with Breakthrough Thinking than with conventional approaches,[5] so getting big changes is a reasonable expectation for a project.

As promising as such results are, however, the reality is that *all* of the changes you seek may not be attained at one time. So welcome the small improvements (next version of the "current release") as they occur, as long as the installation process continues.

In addition, the people involved in developing, installing, and using the changed systems should have an opportunity to celebrate their successes. Small improvements or installations should have small celebrations, while the complete installation should be a more notable event. Chapter 15 will discuss several ways in which recognition and rewards can be given for getting results. There will be more formal mechanisms for the whole organization. Informal arrangements may be appropriate at this point for people directly involved with a project–a lunch or dinner, a picnic, a movie, a round of drinks after work, or a party. A lot of special effort is expended on such projects, so at least a little personal return is desirable early on.

Case Illustrations

Case A: Package Tracking

The testing phase of the recommended solution was the first item of business after initial approval of the solution was obtained. The results of the tests were included in the final presentation to top management to gain full approval of the solution. The four tests used to evaluate the system were:

1. Bar code integrity test
2. Package tracking system test
3. Label acceptance test
4. Concurrent on-line test

---

5. O. Friedman, "The Economic Effect of Cost Control Programs in the Mid-West Industry," Masters thesis, University of Wisconsin-Madison, 1973.

The schedule of these tests, along with the installation plan for the recommended solution, is shown on figure 13-1. The first line in the chart, "Gain Acceptance of Plan," goes beyond the approval step, for it included a series of meetings of all the people who would be users of the new system: line supervisors of the sorters, the engineers responsible for the maintenance of the line, the line sorters themselves, the managers in charge of the sorting areas, drivers, and customer service representatives. Also invited were the hub regional managers as well as experts in the development of long-term automated systems.

The remaining line items on the chart describe the four tests and installation plans.

Case B: Emergency Operations Center

The many steps needed to install the EOC are shown in figure 13-2. In addition to the immediate installation plans, the changeable nature of emergencies and the advances of technology required that major attention be given to the betterment timeline. The project team felt that planning a betterment program now would enable changes to be made rapidly in the future.

The betterment program they designed included a yearly simulated EOC exercise, followed by an evaluation and feedback session. In the simulated drill, people would be able to gain "hands-on" experience with the EOC facility, from which they could suggest valuable changes and improvements to the facility. Hence, the yearly exercise would be staged not only to train personnel but also to update and improve the EOC. With such a betterment program, the EOC facility will continue to adapt to the needs of the city well into the future.

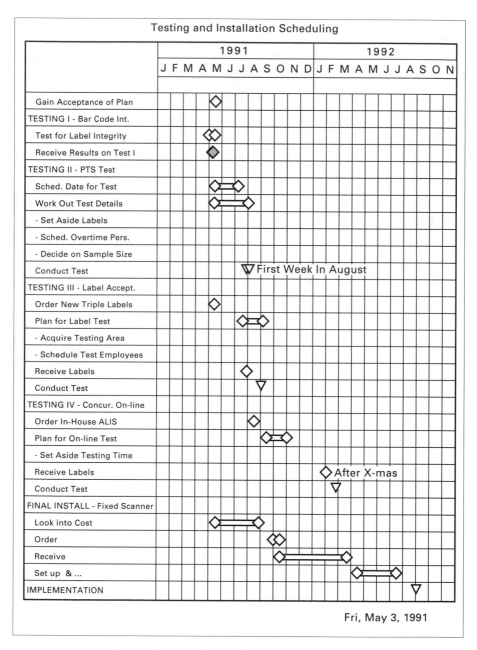

Figure 13-1. Testing and installation scheduling.

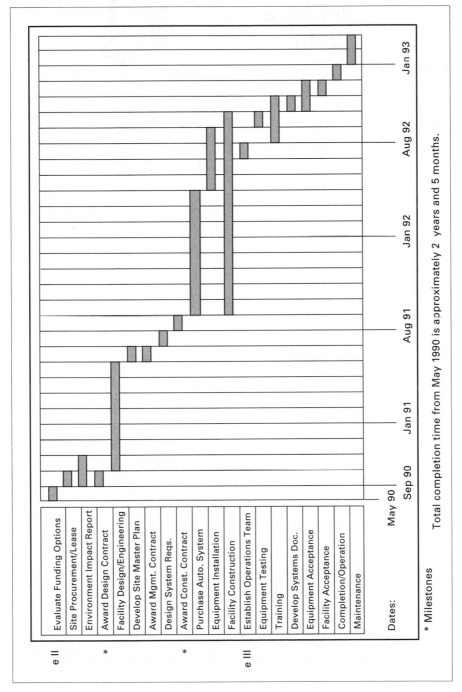

Figure 13-2. Installation Plan Timeline (Gantt Chart).

* Milestones   Total completion time from May 1990 is approximately 2 years and 5 months.

Incorporating the Solution into the Organization

14

Chapter 14 focuses on the steps in the Breakthrough Thinking process highlighted below. (The numbers in parentheses refer to the chapter in which the step is described. The Breakthrough Thinking process is detailed in Chapter 5.)

Step*	Result
1. Set up TQM program (6)	TQM mission, values, strategic plan
2. Identify primary projects and activities (7)	Initial plan of action and timeline
3. Set up TQM project (7)	Project system (purposes, people, etc.)
4. List possible purposes (8)	
5. Develop purpose hierarchies (8)	
6. Determine criteria to select purpose level (8)	
7. Select purpose(s) (8)	Focus purpose(s) in a hierarchical context
8. Establish measures of purpose accomplishment (8)	Success factors
9. Establish subgroups if needed (8)	Subgroups established
10. Generate many solution-after-next options (9)	List of viable alternatives
11. Assess solution-after-next options (10)	

* The number in parentheses after each step refers to the chapter in which the step is described

Step*	Result
12. Select solution-after-next target (10)	Target solution-after-next
13. Modify target for irregularities (11)	
14. Choose recommended changes (11)	Recommendations
15. Prepare proposal (12)	Proposal
16. Inform people not involved to date (12)	
17. Detail recommendations (12)	Complete recommendation specifications
18. Prepare installation plan (13)	Installation plan
19. Install recommendations (13)	Installed system
20. Standardize performances (13)	System performance measures
21. Review project at betterment timeline date (14-15)	Next recommended changes
22. Repeat step 21 (14-15)	Further actions and changes

* The number in parentheses after each step refers to the chapter in which the step is described

Every solution undergoes normal operating changes, even minimal ones, as time goes on. Most of these changes stem from individual proclivities, and represent people's ways of making the new system work more effectively for them (like taping down a switch, organizing files differently, or building a bookshelf at the back of a desk). In the U.S., these ideas are normally not recognized as suggestions; however, they should be. In addition, there should be a formal process for implementing such suggestions.

While some suggestions and changes certainly improve the solution and its operation, others can lead to deteriorating performance and even subversion of the solution. The evaluation step should detect these latter conditions, so that an effort can be made to correct them.

Betterment Efforts

The betterment timeline concept is intended primarily to improve *satisfactory* conditions, gauged by comparing system performance with operating norms. The first step toward betterment is to be punctual about following up on changes that are found to be needed as the solution ("current release") is installed. Delay in getting them incorporated can cause poor habits to form in the operation of the system.

A second betterment effort is to schedule performance reviews at short intervals (say, three to six months) to determine if small changes might move the solution closer to the measures noted in Chapter 13, Step G. Operating and supervising personnel are normally responsible for conducting these reviews. Of course, they also are pivotal in securing the continued assistance of all parts of the organization to assure good results.

A third betterment effort you might consider scheduling is a completely fresh project. This would occur every two to three years (or longer), and would approach the current system as if it didn't exist. It would be done even if all the measurements indicate the system is completely satisfactory. After all, the best time to develop changes in a system is at the height of its success. The idea is to search for a new SANT and recommended solution to determine if there is enough difference between the present system and the new recommendation to make it worthwhile to install a change.

Still another betterment effort is to update the FIST–yearly, for instance, suitable for year t_2, even as changes are being made today to move the solution closer to the FIST for year t_1 (see figure 12-14). A FIST that describes a renovated downtown area in a medium-sized city five years from now, for example, should be updated every two or three years to keep abreast of changing community needs, even as the area is now being modified in accordance with the recommended solution derived from the current FIST.

A key reason for emphasizing continual changes and betterment scheduling is to promote a "happy but dissatisfied" atmosphere. This kind of atmosphere induces the tension psychologists and organizational behavioralists claim needs to exist to achieve successful changes. Unsatisfactory conditions create their own tensions, so betterment efforts need scheduled events to start building the tensions that will prompt a search for change.

When TQM projects are undertaken within an organization or community, a yearly report summarizing the various activities and results provides a good way to assess the overall effectiveness of TQM efforts. Even if a project facilitator is independent and works for several different client organizations, it would benefit all the organizations if the facilitator were to compile a comprehensive report of project results.

Besides, information is always being collected about the performance of various systems and solutions. Why not combine all the data for an overall assessment? Such information would bring organizations up to date about the utilization of TQM resources, difficulties with achieving expected results on newly installed solutions, and possible bases for continual betterment changes.

If not through one yearly report, a series of reports could accomplish these ends.Use graphs and indices to portray various aspects of a system's performance. Videos might also be created to illustrate the performance of a new system. Bulletin boards, newsletters, workshops, annual conferences, quarterly reports, and budget review sessions provide other opportunities for transmitting information about the performance of new systems.

Productivity

Because increased productivity is a major objective of almost every project, the productivity index is a commonly sought aggregated measure. However, it is almost impossible to predict, for in most cases it is a descriptor of the past. Another difficulty is that the term "productivity" lacks a clear-cut definition that can serve as a basis for measurement and aggregation. What usually happens is that several other measures, singly or collectively, are usually *assumed* to be synonymous with productivity, such as time saved, number of shutdowns, waste improvement, total cost of quality control, per capita coverage with allowed times, dollars of cost, reliability, and rate of change in any of these or other measures. Some of the groups of data are called *process productivity* or *bounded productivity* (the relationship between actual and total capacity outcomes). All such measures and indices leave much to be desired, although they can be useful for making historical comparisons.

Productivity basically has to do with the creation of wealth or the addition of value to materials being used. This is done by utilizing human abilities (time, energy, skills, ingenuity) along with tools and equipment to modify the materials. Total outputs (products and services) available for purchase by others are divided by the total inputs (labor hours, investments, materials) to give a gross productivity index. Obtaining such a measure is difficult for an individual company.

What has emerged as a close approximation of "productivity" is a combination of factors that people in an organization identify as constituting desirable performance. For example, one manufacturing company uses five factors to determine its added-value idea of productivity: employee performance, money performance, material usage, level of activity, and growth. It then looks to internal contributors to all of these as the manipulable levers to improve the factors: product development, innovations, marketing, administrative efficiency, and resource utilization. The exact relationship among all these is not established, but knowing what is considered important and obtaining measures of them enables TQM efforts to be keyed to major productivity indicators in the organization.

Some of the tools and techniques in the Appendix could interrelate or combine factors (e.g., rate of return on investment, multi-attribute utility model, multiple regression), but nothing really significant is available. Information about individual factors remains most critical for organizations when studying ways to increase productivity.

Installation Stumbling Blocks

While defining and measuring productivity pose no small problems, incorporating a developed solution into the organization is by far the most difficult part of any project. There are many possible reasons for this, but the biggest stumbling block comes from traditional accounting systems. The vast majority of enterprises burden themselves with the traditional credit/debit accounting approach. This approach worked fine when it began in the early part of the century–a time when the direct work force accounted for the majority of expenses, overhead costs were minimal, and variances had little impact on calculated costs.

Today, these circumstances are no longer the case. Many enterprises, especially in the government, education, research, and service arenas, have a very low percentage of few, if any, direct labor employees. The majority of the work force in the service sector is indirect labor. Because of this, the traditional accounting approach focuses on the very smallest, least significant portion of the enterprise, and the true costs to provide any process are unknown. As long as these costs are not known, the organization will continue to resist change to Breakthrough Thinking and TQM methodologies, because these methodologies focus on improving processes that cannot be tracked through existing accounting methods. When overhead is lumped into one big account, for example, true process costs cannot be determined and so breakthroughs cannot be evaluated.

Variances in these organizations show up as another stumbling block to implementing breakthrough solutions and continuous improvement. Variances, the traditional short-term measure of failure, drive most organizations to make presumably "good" changes, which in fact frequently exacerbate the problems they are supposed to fix.

In today's organizations it is critical to know the real costs involved in conducting an activity or performing a process. Until these costs are known and understood, the enterprise will be at odds with itself, with the accounting department waging battles against everyone else because of outmoded accounting practices. Ironically, these battles are most often fought over creative breakthrough solutions and continuous incremental improvements because of the misunderstood financial impacts of such changes. These activities often show up as adding to overhead and additional variances. As a result, management cannot make effective decisions about these changes, since they are effectively comparing rutabagas to computers.

Another stumbling block to incorporating a solution into the organization is cultural entropy. Every organization is slow to respond to changes, but corporations are especially sluggish when the change threatens to disrupt the unique cultural blend of norms, values, and beliefs that has developed over time. Before installation ever begins, then, it is imperative that all those involved with the change understand the ramifications of the changes they are attempting. In particular, they need to understand the ramifications and impacts of altering how they approach strategic planning, problem solving, resource allocation, and continuous improvement.

The incorporation of the solution into the enterprise must be visual, gradual, and carefully structured. Both a betterment timeline and transitional timeline should be utilized and monitored closely to ensure that the installation process builds in solution-after-next elements at the proper time. Additionally, care must be taken to communicate the reasons, impacts, and ramifications of these changes with all those involved to assure their ongoing support. Even better, as many as possible of these people should be trained in Breakthrough Thinking, continuous improvement, and strategic planning techniques.

During the installation and incorporation phases, the more visual and graphic the presentations of breakthrough strategies, plans, and information, the more effective the installation will be. By making the plans visible, people are better able to augment the solution with additional creative ideas both to improve current strategies and to fine-tune the focus on the solution-after-next.

New challenges also arise at this point, such as how to ensure that installed cultural changes become standardized throughout the organization. These cultural changes will be required for the continued use of Breakthrough Thinking after the project is completed. Yet, as mentioned above, organizations tend to resist cultural changes, and there will be many obstacles forced into the path of those who try to impose them. However, by taking the time to define the purpose of the changes, the criteria for determining success in reaching that purpose, and the constraints imposed on the installation plan, the culture can be gradually changed and organizational entropy overcome.

The purpose hierarchy serves as an effective teaching tool for educating people about the changes needed. In fact, all of the Breakthrough Thinking principles can help facilitate such changes. However, it is also important that feedback be open and prompt. As noted in the opening of this chapter, formal feedback and suggestion mechanisms should be an integral part of the installation process.

It is perhaps needless to say that the installation plan should be based on the critical processes of the organization. Yet, in the past, all changes to these processes would remain within the confines of the system, and no one gave much thought to how the immediate changes in these processes affected other elements of the system, much less the organization as a whole. The Breakthrough Thinking process corrects this myopia by putting the *customers* in the forefront of all planning and decision making.

Organizations that focus on the customers' needs and consider other system elements can more easily focus on solutions that break out of the traditional way of solving problems. One of the best examples is the company in New Hampshire which today makes 80% of the fitted trunk liners for automobiles built in the United States. At the turn of this century, they could have maintained a focus similar to other companies of the day, restricting production to their original product, fitted horse blankets. Instead, they clearly understood their purpose of making other items for the burgeoning transportation industry; they wisely kept attuned to their customers' demands for functionality and looks; and so they modified the elements of their critical processes for fitted cloth products.

The third major stumbling block to installation is one of succumbing to the siren's song—that is, getting caught up in continuously creating new solutions and forgetting about implementing the developed solution. Frequently, organizational culture focuses on the creative and disdains the mundane part of actually installing the designed plan. The installation and succeeding standardization of new methods are often viewed as only required for "the workers," not the "planners" or managers. This fallacious idea must change dramatically.

The fourth stumbling block to incorporating the project into the organization is a lack of sufficient planning. Successful installation requires a significant amount of resources–including people, time, money, and equipment. Many areas of concern are often overlooked or budgeted for incorrectly (overhead or variances). The changes brought about by the new system will require significant training of individuals involved in it. Furthermore, system changes may impact all other areas of the organization. As the customers needs are better understood and breakthrough methods are devised to meet them, critical processes, methods, equipment, space, and time demands may all change as well. In addition, elements of the corporate culture–values, ideals, and beliefs–need to be factored into the installation plans. Given these numerous details, demands, and considerations, adequate planning is an essential part of successful installation. It must begin early in the process, and continue even as the solution is being installed and standardized.

The last stumbling block is an unrealistic or short-sighted assessment of what occurs during the installation process. When reviews are conducted (as scheduled on the transition and betterment time-lines), judicious information collection on how and what progress is being made can drive continuous improvement and lead to key breakthroughs. It is important, however, that these reviews also be guided by the purpose hierarchy in order to assess how well the organization is moving forward toward the FIST.

The information collected for each review should be incorporated at least annually into a comprehensive review to ensure the organization remains focused on the customer, under-stands its basic values, knows where the largest gaps are in its critical processes, and understands its competitive advantages. Once again, using the purpose hierarchy as a guide will keep the review process focused on the most critical issues.

Despite the stumbling blocks to installing a solution and getting the new system incorporated into the organization, there are overriding reasons to do so. As we continue to become more of a polyglot global marketplace, organizations throughout the world are changing. We cannot continue our current problem-solving approach and expect to remain at the forefront of competition. While we focus on what is preventing us from producing our products and services as well as we can, our competition is focusing on what the customer wants and what they have to do and change to meet those needs.

Right now there are enterprises all over the world that are changing their basic approach to problem solving and strategic planning. The ones who successfully synthesize Breakthrough Thinking and (as Chapter 15 discusses) Strategic Total Enterprise Management approaches into their everyday processes, while allowing their workforce to participate in them, will be the enterprises that leapfrog their competition in the years to come.

Managing our strategic daily processes for and around breakthrough changes is a must.

Part III
The Organization as a Whole

Integrating the Solution: Processes and Initiatives

Chapter 15 focuses on the steps in the Breakthrough Thinking process highlighted below. (The numbers in parentheses refer to the chapter in which the step is described. The Breakthrough Thinking process is detailed in Chapter 5.)

Step*	Result
1. Set up TQM program (6)	TQM mission, values, strategic plan
2. Identify primary projects and activities (7)	Initial plan of action and timeline
3. Set up TQM project (7)	Project system (purposes, people, etc.)
4. List possible purposes (8)	
5. Develop purpose hierarchies (8)	
6. Determine criteria to select purpose level (8)	
7. Select purpose(s) (8)	Focus purpose(s) in a hierarchical context
8. Establish measures of purpose accomplishment (8)	Success factors
9. Establish subgroups if needed (8)	Subgroups established
10. Generate many solution-after-next options (9)	List of viable alternatives
11. Assess solution-after-next options (10)	

* The number in parentheses after each step refers to the chapter in which the step is described

Step*	Result
12. Select solution-after-next target (10)	Target solution-after-next
13. Modify target for irregularities (11)	
14. Choose recommended changes (11)	Recommendations
15. Prepare proposal (12)	Proposal
16. Inform people not involved to date (12)	
17. Detail recommendations (12)	Complete recommendation specifications
18. Prepare installation plan (13)	Installation plan
19. Install recommendations (13)	Installed system
20. Standardize performances (13)	System performance measures
21. Review project at betterment timeline date (14-15)	Next recommended changes
22. Repeat step 21 (14-15)	Further actions and changes
* The number in parentheses after each step refers to the chapter in which the step is described	

Organizations are seeking—and adopting—many new "processes" and initiatives in response to the rapidly and dramatically changing competitive (and budget-squeezing governmental and non-profit) world of services and manufacturing. They have many names, and several are usually in place in the organization before a TQM program is considered—e.g., total employee involvement, just-in-time, total productive maintenance, productivity improvement, customer focus, lead-time reduction, kaizen, continuous improvement, strategic planning, performance management, human resources development, concurrent engineering, cycle time reduction, gains-sharing, and so on.

The all-inclusive nature of TQM, encompassing quality performance (customer focus, continuous improvement and employee involvement) in *all* parts, products, services and activities of an organization, means that such processes and initiatives have a relationship to every other quality effort. This interrelatedness is the key foundation of Strategic Total Enterprise Management, introduced earlier in this book (see Chapter 2). "STEM," you will recall, is the term we use to describe the new prototype of organizational management that integrates the TQM philosophy with specific programs and practices. All hinge on the principles of Breakthrough Thinking and are developed through the Breakthrough Thinking process.

Actualizing the STEM concepts depends largely on your success in achieving the focus of this chapter: integrating new solutions with the other processes and initiatives of the organization. It is also crucial that *all* the various projects, programs, and processes, both new and ongoing, be clearly linked to your overall TQM initiative.

If conflicts between TQM and any other process or initiative are perceived, there are several ways to resolve them:

- Design an overall customer-focused and quality-based plan that incorporates the worthwhile concepts of each endeavor, using the approach described in Chapter 6.

- Apply the Betterment Timeline principle to each program and initiative to determine their purposes and solution-after-next target as a means to identify what roles, if any, each one may serve in the TQM/STEM system.

- Make certain that the Breakthrough Thinking process (Chapter 5, with details in Chapters 8 through 13) is used for all projects, regardless of the program or initiative from which they arise. Because projects are always being set up within any process, it is most important to avoid using only the goals, values, and criteria of the specific process or initiative within the project. Otherwise, the results will be skewed toward just that set of measures instead of toward the overall organization and customers. The emphasis on purposes, ideal systems, and system matrices in the Breakthrough Thinking general flow of reasoning enables the project group to sort out the critical factors for the good of the whole organization and customers.

Incorporating new and ongoing processes and initiatives under the umbrella of TQM requires the system designers to give careful consideration to the following factors:

- Motivation of those in the system whom the TQM/STEM transformation will affect most directly
- The transitional time needed to phase out of the current culture and into the new one
- Specific training for those immediately involved in the transformation, and general education of everyone about the TQM/STEM philosophy
- Reward system for those who most successfully exhibit or practice new behaviors, or who otherwise serve as role models for the rest of the organization

Motivation of People

Vital to any organizational change is the motivation of the people involved, especially when the goal is TQM/STEM. Up to this point we have been discussing an approach to developing effective, high-quality solutions to bring about such organizational changes. Now it is time to concentrate on the people who make these solutions a reality. In order to prepare the people for change, you need to increase both their understanding of the transformation and their willingness to take the action necessary to accomplish it.

Increasing people's willingness to take the necessary action depends on four key factors:

- Perception of benefits
- Communication
- Energy
- Involvement level

The first factor, perception of benefits, is the one that initially entices people into the transformation process. Unfortunately, most organizations stress the short-term rather than the long-term benefits of the transformation. These benefits fall into three major categories:

- "What's In It For Me" syndrome
- Job-related benefits
- Organization-related benefits

The first category, the "What's In It For Me" syndrome, has to do with short-term motivation, since a sustained TQM/STEM transformation cannot exist very long on self-centered motivators, but needs motivators that promote the viability of teams. Once the "What's In It For Me" benefits are received, they lose their luster as motivators and are replaced with demands for more "Me" benefits. System and program designers must therefore use the Breakthrough Thinking process to cultivate a "We" or "Us" attitude among workers. Also, employees and employers alike need to view benefits from a long-term perspective.

The second category, job-related benefits, refers to career growth, simplification of work, training, reduced stress, clear direction, improved communication, involvement in the decision-making process, and so on. These benefits are usually invisible to the employee at first. Management thus needs to highlight and reinforce them to make these benefits real, tangible, and valuable to employees.

The third category, organization-related benefits, focuses on the long-term survival of the organization in the global economy. These benefits include lifetime employment, security, prestige, and the like. Alan S. Binder has rightly praised Japanese organizations for their success with such long-term benefits. In a recent article in *Business Week*, he writes that "the Japanese specialize in solving problems and motivating the work force by making their employees both principals and agents. To a degree that Americans would find astonishing, large Japanese companies are run for the benefit of their employees rather than their stockholders. That means providing extensive fringe benefits as well as training and job security.... It means comparatively narrow pay differentials between executives and ordinary workers. It means that managers begin their careers with a stint on the factory floor. And it may also mean the aggressive pursuit of corporate growth, even when growth is unprofitable, to guarantee job security and provide attractive career ladders for employees."

Binder explains that "all these things and more convince Japanese workers that companies are run for their benefit." As a result, "when an employee of Toyota thinks of 'us vs. them,' 'them' is more likely to be Nissan or General Motors than Toyota's management." Binder concludes that U.S. businesses should not be surprised that "such beliefs lead to high productivity," and he notes that only slowly are these attitudes coming to America, as "profit-sharing and employee involvement spread and as command and control give way to workplace cooperation."[1]

Even with all these benefits, we find that the perception of benefits alone will not sustain the transformation to TQM and STEM. This perception must be accompanied by the other three factors as well.

The second factor, communication, is a practice that must evolve beyond the standard model of two-way communications to an interactive communication system. Interactive communication is a fact-based system that facilitates decision-making and action-taking processes. In an interactive communications environment, whoever can solve the problem at hand is assigned to the team to work on it, regardless of his or her level in the organization. Interactive communications are thus an important reinforcement of job-related benefits.

The third factor, energy, refers to the psychological involvement of the people. It is the commitment of their hearts to the transformation, which grows out of their belief that the transformation serves both their personal best interests as well as the best interests of the organization. Important bolsters to this conviction come from management action, benefits, and interactive communication.

The fourth factor, involvement level, refers to the change in people's commitment to the transformation. This involvement can range from apathetic to fully involved. Ideally, of course, you want everyone to be fully involved, especially those most impacted by the TQM transformation. Lukewarm or halfhearted involvement does not provide the solid foundation needed for long-term success. Involvement level is closely

---

1. "How Japan Puts the 'Human' in Human Capital," *Business Week*, November 11, 1991, page 22.

related to and influenced by the third factor–energy. The Breakthrough Thinking process is a major contributor to having people exhibit and believe in these desired characteristics of involvement.

In order for people to have a high level of willingness to take action, it is necessary to have interactive communication, the perception of many benefits, a high level of involvement, and a psychological commitment to the whole process. "If there's an overriding lesson to be learned from the evolution of quality in Japan, it's that there are no easy answers. Total Quality 'is not a cookbook thing,'" says David K. Snediker, a vice-president who runs the quality process at Battelle Memorial Institute in Columbus, Ohio. "It's a culture-transforming approach."[2]

These four factors–perception of benefits, communications, energy, and involvement level–together effect change in the ingrained culture of the organization and work to overturn the status quo mentality. They build upon and reinforce each other in the transformation process.

Figure 15-1 details a list of "people" realities that designers of TQM systems should address in their solution details.

• People who do the work know more than the experts.

• People have good long-term information capacity.

• People are likely to accept problems as stated.

• People are likely to believe a function being performed should remain ("functional fixedness").

• People's individual decision making is constrained by rules and regulations of the organization and the position held by the person.

• People become defensive when confronted with information implying something is wrong with their performance.

• People look for one right solution.

Figure 15-1. People realities. (Page 1 of 2)

---

2. *Business Week*, Special Bonus Issue, October 25, 1991, page 11.

> • People have short-time horizons.
>
> • People experience conflicts in selecting solutions.
>
> • People tend to reject solutions invented elsewhere. ("Our situation is different.")
>
> • Each person displays a preferred method of understanding reality.
>
> • Each person's interest in or commitment to an issue, problem, or change is different.
>
> • People's goals change and vary with age and experience.

Figure 15-1.   People realities.   (Page 2 of 2)

Addressing these realities early on will help strengthen the installation of specific solutions as well as the overall transformation to TQM/STEM. These realities and motivating principles apply to people at all levels of the organization.

Time Factor/Transitional Timeline

Another factor to consider is the time it will take to integrate new and ongoing processes under the umbrella of TQM. Time is often the major pitfall of organizational initiatives. It would not be a factor if you could simply stop the organization and change over immediately. Instead, you must go through a blending process. You can imagine the chaos that would happen in an organization if, say, the Quality Department decided on a Friday that workers would inspect their own work while it would concentrate on audits, training, and TQM starting Monday. Without a planned transition, the organization would have extreme difficulty functioning on Monday morning.

Much of the transition deals with setting up and training various groups in the organization, such as a top management quality steering council, project leaders and facilitators, and employees. Each group should be set up and each training program should be developed with the Breakthrough Thinking process to achieve the most involvement and benefits, and to integrate all such efforts in the organization.

The transitional timeline concept is an attempt to address the time phenomenon. You need to recognize that the transformation of your organization to TQM is a long-term process, with a minimum range of three to five years. So its transitional timeline has a long axis until completion.

As a planning and resource allocation tool used in conjunction with the Betterment Timeline principle, the transitional timeline is used to identify milestones in the changeover process. These milestones pinpoint times when additional organizational resources will be available, having been freed up from the old way of doing business. Unfortunately, the freeing up of resources does not occur evenly across the organization. Instead, certain pockets of the organization will embrace the transformation while other pockets will take a "wait and see" attitude. Those pockets that embrace the transformation and adapt to the new philosophy should be monitored to make sure they do not retreat back to the old way of doing business. They should be constantly encouraged to continue on the transformation path, and the resources freed up from past wasteful activities should be directed towards increasing the pace of the changeover. Those areas with the "wait and see" attitude also need to be encouraged to start the process by showing them concrete examples of what the transformation can accomplish.

Figure 15-2 shows a conceptual transitional timeline. TQM designers need to keep this concept in mind as a guide for monitoring the transformation progress. "Institutionalization and impact–the two end points–are highly interdependent. Impact is the difference that TQM makes in organizational or work group performance; institutionalization is the extent to which TQM is integrated into ongoing activities of the organization. Impact cannot occur without institutionalization, and institutionalization is unlikely to take place without some observed positive impact."[3]

---

3. Kaluzny, A. D., McLaughlin, C. P., "Managing Transitions: Assuring the Adoption and Impact of TQM," QRB, November 1992, pp. 380-383.

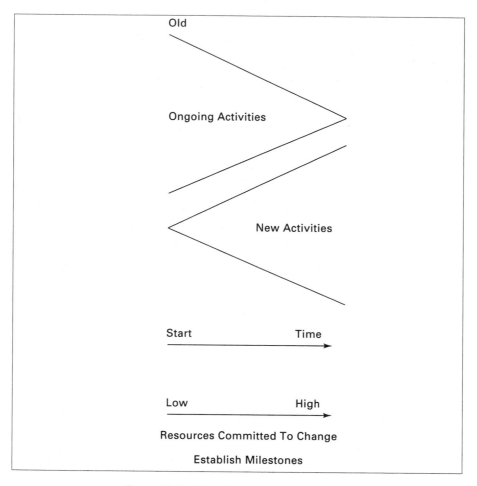

Old

Ongoing Activities

New Activities

Start   Time

Low   High

Resources Committed To Change

Establish Milestones

Figure 15-2. Develop transitional time line.

Change not only takes time, it also invites problems of its own. During organizational changeover, for example, it is possible for the organization to experience an identity crisis in defining its purpose. Doing things partly the old way and partly the new way, those involved in the transition may feel frustration and anxiety by being pulled in many directions and not having a clear identity.

To overcome this problem, you need a strong communication system to point out where you are and where you have to go. You need to keep your driving purpose alive and visible to all those involved. Utilizing the general flow of reasoning along with the purpose hierarchy throughout the transformation process will help ensure that the purpose is visible to all involved.

Another potential problem midway through the changeover is the tendency to mix what is left of the old with the new, and produce a hybrid which will not achieve your original purposes and may turn out to be worse than that which you are trying to improve.

An organization must change in an orderly manner to minimize such disruptions, but there will still be a tendency among those involved to seek safety in the old way and not change. This tendency to avoid change can threaten the progress made and cause slippage in what has already been accomplished. Staying attentive to the changeover process will ensure that everyone is kept informed about it, and as resources are freed up from the old system, they are concentrated on the new process in a planned, orderly manner.

Training of People

Once people are motivated to take action, they need training on what action to take and when to take it. In most organizations attempting transition to TQM, training is focused only on techniques of TQM. They land on a technique and train everyone in it. Then, when it does not take hold, they train everyone in something else. As we have observed repeatedly throughout this book, the results of an approach like this are usually less than spectacular. Normally, the team or individual utilizing this approach only develops a "band-aid" solution, and the problem reappears at a later time.

Strategic Total Enterprise Management entails a different training approach, requiring participants to start with a knowledge base. STEM's knowledge-based training begins by exploring the organization as a whole and looking into the future. It attunes workers to the needs and expectations of customers, and then helps in developing solutions that are both proactive and future-focused. Only after the people in the organization have this philosophical orientation is it time to introduce specific tools, techniques, and deployment processes.

In keeping with this approach, organizational training programs should teach people how to view systems with the Breakthrough Thinking principle before embarking on ways to improve them. That is, people need to understand what to improve before solutions are developed or techniques are thrown at them. Developing your training program through the principles of Breakthrough Thinking and Strategic Total Enterprise Management will help unfold key topics and strategies that lead to true cultural change in your organization.

Even the best training programs will need to be modified, or even revamped entirely, as the changeover to TQM progresses. Like any "system," they should be guided by an awareness of purposes and solution-after-next visions, and subject to restructuring through a betterment timeline. This approach to developing and refining training programs is perhaps best exemplified by what happened at Motorola when it changed over to TQM in the 1980s: "Our charter was not so much to educate people as to be an agent of change, with an emphasis on retraining workers and redefining jobs. Our first order of business was to analyze the jobs that existed [at the time] and try to anticipate what they would look like in the future. The first thing we learned was not to look too far ahead. If we made a two-year projection and trained people for that, then change didn't arrive quickly enough for people to make the shift. We had to anticipate, plan curricula, then train separately for each incremental change. We thought progress would be made in leaps, but it took place one step at a time."[4]

This new type of training needs to be widespread and introduced early on—not only during the changeover process within an organization but in the business world at large. Initially it should be taught in colleges and universities, and then expanded to high schools and even to elementary schools.

---

4. William Wiggenhorn, "Motorola U: When Training Becomes an Education," *Harvard Business Review*, July-August 1990, page 73.

In a recent article summarizing the results of the Total Quality Forum III, the following eight steps were noted as the best ways to incorporate TQM into the graduate curriculum of engineering and business:[5]

- Develop a total quality academic research agenda that excites the intellectual interest of management, engineering, and social science faculty.

- Identify a generic TQM core of knowledge.

- Educate and commit university leaders to total quality principles.

- Develop the terminology for, a common understanding of, and a commitment to total quality in academic and administrative sectors of the university.

- Achieve a comprehensive attitude change among faculty members to understand TQM so that they devote professional attention to quality management.

- Have school leaders, faculty, and staff "butt in" and begin implementing TQM.

- Focus faculty members on quality as a management objective and get them to address instructional strategies consistent with their own objectives and culture.

- Develop a process to assess and define TQM for application to engineering disciplines; build faculty and student awareness; and implement the process in education.

Our hope is that the academic community begins this process utilizing the principles outlined in this book; otherwise, the best we can hope for is just another education initiative with little impact in the long run. Unfortunately, the article cited above ends by announcing the creation of a National Quality Award for engineering schools. Just what we need–another award to encourage the adoption of TQM.

---

5. Chester Placek, "Academe, Industry Seek Approaches to Teaching and Researching TQM in Business and Engineering Schools," *Quality,* September 1991, pages 11-12.

Reward Systems

Designers of TQM cannot forget one final system: a reward system to recognize participants' efforts and program results. Once again, this system design should follow the same Breakthrough Thinking flow of reasoning that has been applied to every other design situation. In developing this system, it is important that you address both effort and results. Focusing on results only reflects a short-term viewpoint by management, while rewarding peoples' efforts reflects a long-term viewpoint that produces results.

One of the authors directed the successful implementation of Quality Circles at a Fortune 100 company for five years (from inception to maturity), and found that 20% of the teams produced results that saved real dollars. This organization had 200 participative teams (or quality circles) in operation, resulting in savings of $6 million a year. If the reward system had targeted results alone (hard dollars), only 20% of the participants would have been rewarded. Instead, the company took the long-term view and rewarded all teams for using the new process. This reward system was non-monetary and built on recognition through the following:

- *Annual President's Days.* Each site would send one of its teams (chosen by the teams involved at the site) as a representative at an all-day, off-site meeting attended by the top 100 managers in the company. Teams would present their process and results, showcase their site, interact with the top managers, and help set the priorities for the next year.

- *Site Recognition.* Each site would conduct a quarterly review for all employees, at which time teams would be recognized for both their effort and results. The recognition would end with an invitation to those not involved to become part of the process.

- *Thank-you Letters from a Corporate Officer.* Every year those involved in the participative process would receive a personal letter from the sponsoring corporate officer (with copies to the individuals' Division Managers and Supervisors) thanking them for participating and explaining how they were contributing to the long-term growth of the company.

- *Mugs, Baseball Hats, Pens, Etc.* At some sites, team members were given personalized items to build team spirit.

In a survey conducted by the Steering Committee, it was found that team members appreciated the local recognition along with the corporate recognition far more than small gifts. Feeling that they were a vital part of the organization and having that communicated through a number of channels helped sustain the momentum and increased peoples' willingness to take additional action.

Other organizations have built elaborate structures to provide rewards through gains-sharing, bonus systems, time off, and the like, only to find that they are short-term motivations. Longer-term inspiration seems to come when people are recognized on a number of levels—for both their individual and team efforts.

Even so, David Garvin, a professor at the Harvard business school, notes that "to get an effective quality process rolling," an organization has to have more than "symbolic" rewards. He cites companies like Allen-Bradely, Corning, and others that put quality objectives into the bonus plan of their top brass. Corning has monetary incentives for factory workers as well. And Teradyne CEO Alexander V. d'Arbeloff named a fast-track project manager the company's first quality director. Tangible incentives like these "tend to get [people's] attention," says Garvin.[6]

More and more, quality performance is being used as a criterion for compensating senior management. According to a recent article in *Quality Progress*, more than half of U.S. businesses plan to use this measure. German, Canadian, and Japanese businesses are using it more as well: "Currently, 20% of the Japanese companies, 19% of the U.S. companies, 15% of the Canadian companies, and 10% of the German companies indicated they use quality performance as a compensation criterion.

---

6. *Business Week*, Special Bonus Issue, October 25, 1991, page 38.

Fifty-one percent of the U.S. companies, 39% of the German companies, 35% of the Canadian companies, and 31% of the Japanese companies indicate they will do so in the future. The data indicate that quality performance as an essential part of organizations' strategic review process is going to increase dramatically in the next few years."[7]

It is possible to design or set up an effective compensation pay system by using the general flow of reasoning.

A Final Word of Caution

While, ideally, all organizational processes and initiatives should be integrated under the umbrella of TQM, they cannot simply be lumped together. It is a common, and serious, mistake to assume this can be done, and pressure to do so must be resisted. Before this "lumping" is done, a thorough review of the purposes of each process and initiative should be undertaken to be certain that they meet the criteria and targets detailed in Chapter 6. Only those processes and initiatives that meet the criteria should be retained under the TQM umbrella. Those processes and initiatives not meeting the criteria should either be terminated or upgraded through the Breakthrough Thinking process to meet the TQM criteria.

An Application of Breakthrough Thinking and TQM

The following is a slightly abbreviated report of one person's experience with integrating Breakthrough Thinking with TQM:

> I work as a manufacturing engineer in a large aerospace company. My company has started to use TQM as a quality improvement method for all processes. The effectiveness of the TQM method is debatable to those of us who are living with the direct effects of the decisions made. After reviewing Breakthrough Thinking, I decided that there is a better way to manage Total Quality Management.

---

7. Karen Bemowowski, "The International Quality Study," *Quality Progress*, November 1991, pages 33-37.

The current TQM method that is applied has a different structure than Breakthrough Thinking. "TQM consists of continuous process improvement activities involving everyone in an organization–managers and workers–in a totally integrated effort toward improving performance at every level. This improved performance is directed toward satisfying cross functional goals, such as quality, cost, schedule, mission need, and suitability. TQM integrates fundamental management techniques, existing improvement efforts, and technical tools under a disciplined approach focused on continuous process improvement. The activities should ultimately be focused on increased customer/user satisfaction."[8]

The preceding definition of TQM defines the application of continuous process improvement to a very broad area. There are more specifically focused areas including motivating improvements from within, satisfying the customer not just conforming to requirements, and emphasizing continuous process improvement not just compliance to standards that contribute to the TQM definition. The strategy claims that importance calls upon concentrating on prevention not correction. Although this is true that prevention is better than correction, the method of prevention is the focus of any improvement effort.

Breakthrough Thinking works more towards focusing on purposes/functions and goal statements to understand the problem situation; what can actually be done to not only change the situation, but to know what direction that solution is taking things. In defining the problem a project team can separate the major components such as needs, symptoms, goals, desires–in short all components important in defining the problem (defining the appropriate purpose/ function, i.e., listing possibilities, defining a hierarchy, selecting values, objectives, measures of effectiveness, goals, design specifications/constraints, and so on). Establishing things such as a planning horizon, system parameters, and

---

8. Support guide to DoD Directive 5000.51 on Total Quality Management, Office of the Deputy Assistant Secretary of Defense, Pentagon, Washington DC 20301 02/15/89 page 1.

key objectives are important. Listing potential solution ideas and paring these down to potential solution ideas and their alternates brings us closer to an ideal solution.

Breakthrough Thinking then goes on to evaluate these alternatives using decision methods, eventually getting down to the selection of a functional solution. Going further to convert this solution into something that can be implemented effectively and selling this solution to those in authority (if need be) lead up to implementation. Installation is not considered the last step but rather performance monitoring is the last continual loop going through why, how, whom, when; to establish the actual effectiveness of the solution and how that can be adjusted for optimum system performance.

The XYZ Co. Way

The following is a short description of the XYZ Co. TQM method application. I say this since the personnel who run the program make changes as they see necessary.

One of the first and foremost efforts of TQM is to know your customer. It is stated that user satisfaction is the ultimate requirement to which everyone must strive whether the user is an internal customer or an external customer. The only way the user can ultimately be satisfied is if the product or service meets the user's need or intended use at a reasonable cost. Secondly, TQM requires us to set true customer requirements. Knowledge of the user's needs and expectations is a prerequisite to satisfying them. It is critical that these requirements be understood and reflected accurately in specifications for products, services, and processes. "Quality is conformance to a set of customer requirements that, if met, result in a product that is fit for its intended use."[9] The pursuit of continuous improvement strategy is the last point of the TQM model that we will discuss here. As far as XYZ Co. is concerned, this is the TQM environment.

---

9. *Ibid.,* page 10.

Statement of the Problem

Communication of division and corporate policy established by those in the vice-president position (and higher) has trouble making it down to the regular employee. Policy statements and changes are usually general in nature with implementation rules set forth by the organization responsible for its realization (or oversight). This is much like the relationship citizens have with Congress passing tax laws with the IRS putting forth rules and clarifications to carry out these laws.

The problem arises from the employee not being aware of what has transpired and how it might affect them. It is very important for policy statements and changes to get to the employee as soon as possible. What can be done to get this information where it needs to go?

The communication that corporate would like to get through to the rank and file is QUALITY COMES FIRST. When building a product that requires precision manufacturing, a lapse in quality can affect not only that part or assembly but the entire function of the product. The organization, division, and corporate leadership desires quality to guide every effort of the manufacturing process. Right now the corporation is using the TQM method to resolve this problem.

Application of TQM to the Problem

To "kick-off" TQM, certain people were chosen to be trained in establishing TQM within each organization. An organization is generally comprised of 100-150 people with 15-18 managers within 3 levels of management to guide the whole mass.

The training consisted of company "experts" passing on the training and experiences they have received.[10] This took all of 3 hours. These "trained" people then got together in another meeting to discuss how to organize. What occurred was something of a "guided brainstorming" session yielding the notion that no one really knew how information was supposed to flow through the organization. People just found their niche

---

10. This information comes from an interview with several TQM facilitators in the company.

and showed up for work everyday. It was decided to send out questionnaires to everyone within the organization by individual department, to identify who is your customer, and who are you a customer for? This exercise was to address one of the major points of emphasis in TQM–"Know Your Customer/Customer Satisfaction."

This seemed to be generally effective in getting across the realization that there should be a customer/server relationship. What to do with this way of thinking wasn't conveyed at the time other than a form of the golden rule, i.e., "do unto your customers as you would want to be served."

The results of who was whose customer resulted in an interesting by-product. This was the documentation of the INFORMAL way business was being conducted. You can establish the formal structure of the company from the Division Operating procedures (DIVOPS). Within the DIVOPS, you can know who is the expected customer for any given function or product. It turns out that many more people were drawing information from informal sources in order to get a more complete information picture to allow them to do their jobs. Never mind doing them better, but just to accomplish what they needed to do. This more or less proved the point that people were not getting fully served as the customer.

An example of this could be the stacks of computer printout sent to someone in Production Control (PC) who is in charge of delivering the proper tool to the right location. The printout is a listing of all the tools and their status–usable or non-suable–for manufacture. PC is supposed to be aware of what is on this list to avoid getting the wrong tool. The only problem is the way that they choose the tool is by the instructions given them by the Manufacturing Engineers who incidentally is not sent one of the tool listings.

It turns out that the Manufacturing Engineers have been finding people who have this printout and use that copy to get the required information. Rather than doing the kicking and screaming necessary to get their own copy, they find some other way to obtain the information. This is the forming of an informal method.

Management about this time was beginning to feel the pinch of a program that is winding down and pressure to consolidate efforts and save money. Since the information about the informal service was available, the TQM facilitators decided to use it to formulate how they would consolidate some department functions and even some departments.

Since functions and departments were changing, it was recognized that it would be important to identify who the customer is or should be for a person or function. This began the second phase of trying to implement TQM–identifying the customer's needs. Bring out the surveys!

Using the survey tool to find out the customer's needs was again useful since it seemed to force people to get to know the actual people on the other end of their services. This gave rise to a general feeling of teaming to accomplish the job rather than just doing the minimum required. Groups headed by the TQM facilitators began the work of organizing all of this information. They decided to use groups made up of customers and servers to iron out the "gripes" and differences of each person. This brought about an easing of the pains of making a change. Unfortunately, no one was thinking of the future where downsizing and shifting responsibilities constantly forces a shift in the way a thing is accomplished. These groups locked in on things they wanted *at the time,* not taking into consideration what would be good for them in the future.

Points of Application of Breakthrough Thinking

Although the intent of TQM is a good one (it has its effective points), I would state that there are very useful points from Breakthrough Thinking that could have greatly enhanced the efforts put forth.

Breakthrough Thinking would have all of the stakeholders involved in any decisions on the process of solving this problem. As things happened, the very people who were giving out the changes in policy (the Vice-Presidents and higher) were not involved. They were merely reacting to the results of some surveys that collected the thoughts and judgments of the employees. This begs to ask:

- What were the inputs to the information system?
- Who was responsible for output to the masses?
- Who has the authority to make substantive changes in the way business is conducted?
- Who knows what the goals are for the company?

The people with the answers were not directly involved with the process. It seems a simple thing to talk about values, objectives, and goals, but without all of the affected parties involved you can't expect a complete solution. Especially the formulation of the Solution After Next: How can you have a SAN (or an Ideal SAN) without knowing these things? Having the stakeholders involved is very important.

Having identified and established the values, objectives, goals, etc., the group using Breakthrough Thinking is able to describe the direction of their efforts. This won't all be done by just asking for everyone's input and then formulating policy around the results or consensus. Having bona fide Measures of Purpose Accomplishment available for Quantitative Measurement of the process is invaluable for making proper decisions that lead towards an ideal solution.

Interestingly, there was never the mention of a deadline in the discussions about the TQM method (probably an interpretation of the word Continuous in CPI). The presence of a deadline in Breakthrough Thinking projects can affect the forming of potential solution ideas. The planning horizon is directly tied to the system parameters and key objectives to influence what choices are possible or desired.

Using decision methods would have also shown the comparison of the components of the Potential Solutions according to the importance (using weighting). This would certainly expose the nature of the components as they relate to the whole solution. It might turn out that it would be better to change the DIVOPS rather than restructure (or even eliminate) a department. Just because of downsizing, it doesn't make every department equal in vulnerability to change.

Using these methods will lead to, hopefully, one or two solutions. If there is not one solution that towers over all, maybe it is possible to combine details of each to form one. Once one is described and agreed upon, implementation can take place. My experience with Breakthrough Thinking tells me that implementation would probably be anticipated and welcome. With the efforts thus far with TQM no one can say for certain where things are finally going to end up. Are they getting the best solution? Who can say. They might eventually work something out but it is doubtful this will happen right away.

When trying to perform some follow-up on implemented ideas and solutions, TQM and the continuous process improvement (CPI) approach should do the job, ... but then maybe not. Breakthrough Thinking has Measure of Purpose Accomplishments already worked out as part of the process of finding a solution. It happens (hopefully) with the same people and same ideas so that the performance monitoring is focused on the proper measures. TQM banks on cycling through the Seven Step performance improvement model which is "Repeated as desired."[11] In other words, if things seem to be going smoothly, often there is no compelling reason to go through the complete cycle again. Knowing how often we humans get comfortable with our familiar circumstances, there is no need to wonder how effective this arrangement would be.

Some Results of TQM

The application of TQM within my company has brought about some interesting results. Some things are effective, yet many things are not. When we applied TQM to the problem of disseminating information from the vice-presidential level within our division down to the people working on the floor, the first step attempted from the management effort was to establish the "TQM cultural environment." This environment includes items such as vision statements, long term commitment,

---

11. Support Guide, TQM model, page 14.

people involvement, training, and the like. The focus was on providing the vision for what the organization managers needed to be and where they needed to go. A tangible target for this vision was chosen to be the Malcolm Baldrige National Quality Award. This award stresses quality through a corporation in its many facets and grades applicants on the individual facets of every section of business. Convincing management of the need for a different vision was difficult citing the "vision statements" already established through cooperation with the customer years before. They couldn't see a need for taking another look to see if it really applied any more.

Malcolm Baldrige did serve to point out many shortfalls of the organization as compared to that particular yardstick. What I don't think it accomplished was identifying why this was a shortfall and why it was important for *us* to worry about it.

Conclusions

It has been my intent to compare a few important points of TQM and Breakthrough Thinking as they are related to a current situation in my company. Having lived through the "application" of TQM and then having the experience of Breakthrough Thinking to a real problem, I wanted to emphasize some differences in the two methods. Breakthrough Thinking has some advantages that cannot be ignored. The fact that much of the informative phases occur as a part of the process, thus pointing out very important characteristics of the problem and your system, show immediate benefits to the problem solvers.

Although TQM is now considered a permanent part of our corporate fabric, I would recommend that we not follow the cookbook blindly, but rather endeavor to include Breakthrough Thinking within the framework of CPI and gradually teach its values and approach in all design and problem solving.

The Future for TQM

16

"*The failure of management is the single biggest factor in the lack of communications and poor performance in our organizations.*"[1]

– Representative George Brown (Calif.)
U.S. House of Representatives

Throughout the history of organizations, management has been looking for ways to improve the enterprise and guide it for short-term profit and long-term serviceability. Because of this multiple focus, a view of management might be best described as "kaleidoscopic"–composed of many segments that are differently colored, differently aligned, and frequently fragmented.

Total Quality Management imposes structure on this view, changing it from "kaleidoscopic" to "telescopic." TQM brings together all the pieces and fragments into an organization-wide pursuit of high performance and continuous improvement. It marshals the talents and skills of every employee in this pursuit, prompted always by the prospect of meeting and exceeding customer expectations. In short, TQM brings the mission of the enterprise–and the challenges of management–into clear focus. In doing so, it offers hope for correcting the "failures of management" that Representative Brown refers to in the opening passage. It is quality and performance, or else!

To take TQM from theory to practice, we have outlined the principles of Breakthrough Thinking and detailed the Breakthrough Thinking process–or "general flow of reasoning"–which we offer as a new and much needed problem-solving paradigm. The Breakthrough Thinking process provides the methodology for successfully implementing TQM

---

1. Second Annual Symposium on the Role of Academia in National Competitiveness and Total Quality Management, , July 24-26, 1991,USC, Los Angeles, CA.

371

in an organization. By reshaping the way we go about solving problems, it opens up possibilities for making significant breakthroughs in organizational planning and management, resulting in a Strategic Total Enterprise Management system (STEM).

As a model of planning and management, STEM offers significant advantages to organizations. It allows the organization to formulate future-focused strategic plans that can be deployed as needed. It enables the organization to eliminate waste by by-passing traditional planning and data gathering steps. It gives the organization flexibility in executing short-term, day-to-day operations while maintaining a fixed focus on its long-term goals. It allows the organization to optimize the use of resources, since the desired outcomes are known prior to implementation.

In addition, STEM has the advantage of frequent scheduled reviews. These reviews not only serve the purpose of continuous improvement; they also provide a way to make the TQM/STEM philosophy an integral part of the corporate culture. Of course, to become fully ingrained in the culture, Breakthrough Thinking and TQM need the commitment of top management. Still, the built-in reviews in a STEM system elicit constant feedback that amplifies positive occurrences while minimizing adverse ones.

Armand V. Feigenbaum's distinction between visible and invisible forms of competition explains our emphasis in this book on modes of thinking and patterns of reasoning. He defines "visible" competition as the quality of products and services themselves, while "invisible" forms of competition are how individuals and organizations think and act, how they approach their work and reach decisions, what kinds of training they provide, and so on. Although Feigenbaum says these factors are hard to measure, we have shown that there is a great deal of research and evidence indicating the structure of a more effective "invisible" mode of thinking (Chapter 3) and general flow of reasoning (Chapter 5).

The ultimate basis for quality is the actual design of the product or service (what Feigenbaum would call "visible" competition). But TQM goes beyond this by adding features to "delight" customers, not just meet their needs. The general flow of reasoning in the Breakthrough Thinking process leads to both types of results, since its focus on purposes and solutions-after-next calls equal attention to initial designs and future innovations.

One large organization we are working with is using the STEM model with the express goal of optimizing operations in all of its divisions. Since the company allowed the various divisions to design their own solutions, each division began the process by developing a purpose hierarchy, recognizing the gaps between their current status and their newly defined purpose. They then developed a plan to accomplish their purpose, which included carefully evaluating their division's needs based on a transitional timeline and solution-after-next target. At this time two of the twelve divisions have begun actual installation of their solutions, while the others are at various stages in the process.

The results achieved by the first two divisions have already caused them to begin to change the way they accomplish their basic purpose. For they have now established the long-term needs of their three primary customer segments, and so are no longer focusing on what the competition is doing—as they did in the past. In addition, their projects have shown them the value of working together to accomplish the clearly visible purpose to which all top management had agreed.

This one example of the effectiveness of the Breakthrough Thinking process can be matched by hundreds of other examples attesting to its benefits, including when it is used in conjunction with TQM. By itself, TQM has brought significant improvements to businesses, both large and small, in the service and manufacturing sectors alike.[2] Imagine what improvements TQM could make if it is augmented by the powers of Breakthrough Thinking.

The "marriage" of TQM and Breakthrough Thinking comes at a particularly critical time. A seminal article published several years ago in the *Harvard Business Review* describes the situation well:

---

2. GAO Report to the Honorable Donald Ritter, U.S. House of Representatives, May 1991.

"Today managers in many industries are working hard to match the competitive advantages of their new global rivals. They are moving manufacturing offshore in search of lower labor costs, rationalizing product lines to capture global scale economies, instituting quality circles and just-in-time production, and adopting Japanese human resource practices. When competitiveness still seems out of reach, they form strategic alliances–often with the very companies that upset the competitive balance in the first place.

"Important as these initiatives are, few of them go beyond mere imitation. Too many companies are expending enormous energy simply to reproduce the cost and quality advantages their global competitors already enjoy. Imitation may be the sincerest form of flattery, but it will not lead to competitive revitalization. Strategies based on imitation are transparent to competitors who have already mastered them. Moreover, successful competitors rarely stand still. So it is not surprising that many executives feel trapped in a seemingly endless game of catch-up–regularly surprised by the new accomplishments of their rivals.

"For these executives and their companies, regaining competitiveness will mean rethinking many of the basic concepts of strategy. As 'strategy' has blossomed, the competitiveness of Western companies has withered. This may be coincidence, but we think not. We believe that the application of concepts such as 'strategic fit' (between resources and opportunities) 'generic strategies' (low cost vs. differentiation vs. focus), and the 'strategy hierarchy' (goals, strategies, and tactics) have often abetted the process of competitive decline. The new global competitors approach strategy from a perspective that is fundamentally different from that which underpins Western management thought."[3]

The "fundamentally different perspective" which the writers refer to concerns the adoption of a management philosophy, not prescriptive methodologies. That philosophy must be a customer focus and TQM if

---

3. Gary Hamel and C. K. Prahalad, "Strategic Intent," *Harvard Business Review,* May-June 1989, pages 63-76.

organizations wish to continue to compete, especially in the increasingly competitive global marketplace.

Advocating TQM is not enough, however. A new philosophy about thinking and reasoning is needed as well. For *how* you go about translating the TQM philosophy into actual programs and practices is just as critical, as Chapter 6 detailed. The general flow of reasoning outlined in the Breakthrough Thinking process is the guide to developing this new "thinking" philosophy. It promises tremendous advantages to organizations—perhaps *the* advantage that will distinguish an organization in the future.

The issues described in the excerpt above raise other questions about the quality movement, particularly the strategic management of quality. The most pressing of these problems today are:[4]

- How do we combine the traditional and the marketing approaches?
- How do we relate the various reports linking price and quality?
- How do we draw together the various departments which are concerned with its strategic management: viz. production (including design, etc.), marketing, QA/QC, R&D, and finance, and provide a common "currency" for decision making?
- How do we decide on which strategy to adopt?
- How do we set up a suitable strategic control system?

Once again, the answers to these questions—and to others like them—reside in the Strategic Total Enterprise Management model, which combines the goals and ideals of TQM with the principles of Breakthrough Thinking. Organizations that adopt the STEM approach and deploy its consistent practice throughout the enterprise will not only be able to resolve these pressing issues; they also will be equipped to compete successfully on a global basis.

4. A. M. McCosh and M. Walsh, "The Financial Management of Quality as a Strategy," *Marketing Intelligence & Planning*, 1988 (Volume 6, Number 1), page 10.

We end with a few final words about an important component of TQM, and that is its focus on the customer. But, as Alan Scharf points out, we do not merely mean customer satisfaction. Customer *delight* has replaced the "old rule" of satisfying the customer. "Today, every customer expects to be satisfied. There is no delight in that. *Delight comes from the same root as delicious. When it happens, you smile, and remember.* A client makes quality molded plastic parts, such as telephone cases. To delight a major customer, the president gave them a copy of the results of the hundred internal quality tests they do on each product–voids, cracks, warpage, irregularities, color variations....

" 'We are delighted' said the customer. 'This test document is now a mandatory requirement for all future shipments.

" 'Now I'm delighted,' said the president. 'You see a similar letter went out to my competitors. We are the only company in the country capable of doing those tests. That gives us 100% of that market.'

"Customer delight leaves a delicious memory. It brings customers back along with new ones who heard the story. Customer delight is an enduring competitive weapon."

Customer delight must:
 • Meet the customer's needs
 • Deliver the unexpected
 • Deliver it with sincerity and enthusiasm
 • Satisfy a behavioral need of the customer
 • Create a memory and a story to tell

"It works. It is essential for success. Michael Shays, publisher of *Competitive Concepts* (EMS Network International, 858 Longview Road, Burlingame, CA) says, 'If during hard times you don't delight your customers, they may not stay with you when the good times return.'

"Customer delight comes from pro-acting to the marketplace–listening, testing, surprising the customer, responding to tomorrow's needs and to future competitors."[5]

---

5. Alan Scharf, "Customer Delight," *Creative Leap International Newsletter,* Fall 1991 (Scharf and Associates, 1137 Elliott St., Saskatoon, SK, Canada, STNOV4).

Epilogue

> "We believe that top management's caution reflects a lack of confidence in its own ability to involve the entire organization in revitalization–as opposed to simply raising financial targets. Developing faith in the organization's ability to deliver on tough goals, motivating it to do so, focusing its attention long enough to internalize new capabilities–this is the real challenge for top management. Only by rising to this challenge will senior managers gain the courage they need to commit themselves and their companies to global leadership."[6]

Each person must adopt the ideas of TQM and think with the general flow of reasoning in all activities. Although much of what this chapter describes appears to focus on the organization, the truth of the matter is that an organization cannot really *do* anything. It is the behavior of individuals who act in the name of the organization that give rise to this expression. If *you* are the organization, then you need to start thinking and acting in ways that reflect the new organizational model. Instead of looking for data and applying techniques, you must talk about purposes and solutions-after-next. Instead of telling people what to do, you must help them discover for themselves what to do, using the Breakthrough Thinking principles. Instead of keeping information secret, you must share it. Instead of following orders from above or handing them down to those reporting to you, you must obliterate communication barriers by asking the right questions as identified in the Breakthrough Thinking general flow of reasoning.

Above all, senior management today must adopt and practice the ideas presented in this book. Each one must practice the total quality ideas in all personal activities–starting times for appointments and meetings, office and desk organization, return of telephone calls, early response to letters and e-mail, and so on. Each must encourage everyone in the organization to begin using all the aspects of the Breakthrough

---

6. Hamel and Prahalad, page 76.

Thinking principles, STEM, and TQM to improve all facets of the organization. Senior management does not have the luxury to wait for the organization to get all the new processes into place. Change is slow in complex systems, and we need to find ways to speed up the process. Getting results as quickly as possible must be sought within the longer-term movement toward the solutions-after-next. The general flow of reasoning provides a vital process for doing this.

Senior management also must exhibit bold, proactive, and creative leadership that empowers the organization to change. The organization's very survival depends on this. Your organization can merely exist, or you can change it into a world-class competitor. Organizations that merely exist today will disappear in the future.

As you make the necessary changes in your organization to embrace the principles we have outlined in this book, keep in mind that one high-profile "victim" of these changes will be "the traditional American bureaucratic command-and-control" style of management. Remember, too, that in the future managers will have to learn to "cede power and responsibility to employees, the people who can do the most about quality."[7]

It is critical that, starting today, in all of our activities, we begin to practice the ideas in this book. Waiting is not suitable if we are going to be competitive in today's global marketplace. Time is of the essence. We all must change.

---

7. *Business Week*, Special Bonus Issue, October 25, 1991, page 8.

Appendix A

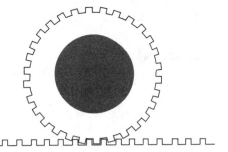

The marvelous ability of humans to develop symbols, signs, and abstractions has led to a huge number of models, techniques and tools. Most were proposed for the analysis and research methods of conventional planning and design approaches. Yet most of them can be converted into valuable aids for Breakthrough Thinking in TQM.

Appendix A provides:

- An alphabetical list of many, but not all, techniques, models and tools useful within a system design by Breakthrough Thinking in TQM.
- An alphabetical cross-reference index of techniques by purposes or functions to be achieved.

Each model, tool, or technique is described in these terms:

- *Results:* The specific outcomes and formats the technique produces or model presents.
- *Inputs:* The particular information, questions, or estimates needed to apply the techniques or build the model.
- *Purpose/Function:* The mission, aim, or primary concerns the results or outcomes help to achieve. More than one technique might achieve the same purpose.
- *Function:* Outcome help to achieve. More than one technique or model can achieve the same purpose.
- *Special Characteristics:* Special equipment, observation, recording, time factors, experts, skill levels or so on that are needed to apply the technique. If this category is not included in the technique description, no unusual characteristics appear to pertain.

ABSTRACT DIMENSIONING

RESULTS: An extraction of key dimensions from given correlations of a stated problem and several workable solutions.

INPUTS: Intensive probe sessions consisting of 8 to 10 consumer respondents, 2 - 3 client staff participants, and a trained moderator. Project's known dimensions (e.g., management direction, factors affecting product production, previously proposed client solutions, competitive products, etc.) and a list of relevant correlations.

PURPOSE/FUNCTION: To identify product opportunities in the consumer market.

SPECIAL CHARACTERISTICS: "Product opportunities" include repositioning established brands and services, new venture opportunities, etc.

REFERENCES: "Marketing Research Tool Defines New Product Opportunities, Repositioning Established Brands," *Food Product Development*, May 1979, pp. 58-60.

ACTIVITY NETWORK DIAGRAM (ARROW DIAGRAM)

RESULTS: Completion of project as quickly as possible and within budget.

INPUTS: Subtasks, their sequencing and duration.

PURPOSE/FUNCTION: Helps to determine likely time of completion of a project and assists in monitoring sub-tasks for conformance to necessary schedule.

REFERENCES: Mizuno, S. *Management for Quality Improvement*, Productivity Press, 1988, pp 249–281.

A FORTIORI ANALYSIS

RESULTS: Sensitivity of system performance and effectiveness beyond an already acceptable value of a particular attribute.

INPUTS: All the data (operational or test data, theoretical extrapolation, etc.), subjective opinions based on the judgment of experienced personnel.

PURPOSE/FUNCTION: To test/evaluate the sensitivity of the attribute whose value is uncertain (i.e., to find out how important even the range of values will be on the effectiveness of the result).

SPECIAL CHARACTERISTICS: Computer can be used to try many different quantities.

REFERENCES: E. S. Quade, *Analysis for Public Decisions*, New York: American Elsevier, 1975, pp. 41-44.

ACTIVITY BALANCE LINE EVALUATION (ABLE)

RESULTS: Updated network with built-in information of schedule time, expected completion date, latest completion time, etc. of the project.

INPUTS: Activities and their durations.

PURPOSE/FUNCTION: To evaluate the schedule and performance of a project.

SPECIAL CHARACTERISTICS: Often performed on a computer.

REFERENCES: R. I. Levin and C. A. Kirkpatrick, *Planning and Control With PERT/CPM*, New York: McGraw-Hill Book Co., 1966.

ACTIVITY SAMPLING (Work Sampling)

RESULTS: The estimation of the proportion of time spent by one or more persons or machines performing a given activity or function. A study also produces the proportion of time for all activities or functions.

INPUTS: Instantaneous observations of the activities in one of several sampling modes - - random, stratified random, systematic, sequential, etc.

PURPOSE/FUNCTION: To summarize and convert sample data on a proportional basis to the actual times for activities. An easy statistical check and verification.

SPECIAL CHARACTERISTICS: Some special skill in observing instantaneously. The organizer should be skilled statistically and familiar with sampling techniques and meaning of statistical inference.

REFERENCES: G. Nadler, *Work Design: A Systems Concept* (Homewood, Illinois, 1970) Chapter 7.

ADAPTIVE FORECASTING

RESULTS: Expected quantity (e.g., amount of sales, cost, etc.) in the next period determined by a weighted average of the quantity in the current period and the forecast of the quantity for the current period made during the previous period.

INPUTS: Last set of forecast quantities and current one-step-ahead difference between actual and forecast values.

PURPOSE/FUNCTION: To adapt forecasts from a previously established model in accordance with each difference between actual and forecast values as they occur.

SPECIAL CHARACTERISTICS: Also called "error learning." Forecasting model can be readily and simply updated. (See other forecasting technique.)

REFERENCES: C. R. Nelson, *"Applied Time Series Analysis for Managerial Forecasting,"* Holden-Day, Inc., San Francisco, 1973, pp. 157-159; R. J. Mockler, *"The Management Control Process,"* Appleton-Century-Crofts, New York, 1972, pp 57; E. Buffa, *Modern Production Management,* John Wiley and Sons, Inc., New York: Fifth Edition, 1977, pp. 323-325.

AFFINITY DIAGRAM

RESULTS: Summarizing and characterizing large quantities of data into related groups that identify hidden meanings and create a group consensus. Creates a descriptive series of header cards for each related grouping.

INPUTS: Individual participant's facts, feelings, opinions, hunches, and so on.

PURPOSE/FUNCTION: To create a group consensus as to what are the important factors that are influencing an issue.

SPECIAL CHARACTERISTICS: Facilitator often helpful for groups.

REFERENCES: Mizuno, S. *Management For Quality Improvement* (Productivity Press, 1988), pp 25-28, Hoffherr, G., Moran, J., & Talbot, R. Competitive Times (GOAL/QPC 1991).

ANALOGIES

RESULTS: A listing of alternatives and ideas, usually for possible solutions.

INPUTS: Noticing, perception, suggestions, association, questions, purposes/functions to be achieved.

PURPOSE/FUNCTION: To generate ideas by stimulating thoughts through analogies.

SPECIAL CHARACTERISTICS: Facilitator often helpful for groups.

RELATED STRATEGY STEPS: Steps 2 and 4 B.

REFERENCES: Leatherdale, W. H., *The Role of Analogy, Model, and Metaphor in Science* (North-Holl and/American Elsevier, 1974), pp. 1-32; J. W. Dickey and T. M. Watts, *Analytic Techniques in Urban and Regional Planning,* McGraw-Hill Book Company, New York, 1978, pp. 234-245.

ANALYSIS OF VARIANCE (ANOVA)

RESULTS: Summary of reject/do not reject condition of the hypothesis based on F-test/T-test.

INPUTS: The related data (e.g., amount of sales in stores, no. of customers in restaurant, etc.).

PURPOSE/FUNCTION: To test for the null hypothesis against the proposed hypothesis.

SPECIAL CHARACTERISTICS: One way analysis of variance evaluates one factor. Analysis of simultaneous and interaction effects of n-factors needs factorial design of experiments.

REFERENCES: B.A. Griffith, A.E.R. Westman, and B.D. Lloyd, "Analysis of Variance," *Quality Engineering* Vol. 2.2, 1989, pp 195-226.

ATTITUDE SURVEYS

RESULTS: A percentage statistical representation of attitudes and opinions (favorable/unfavorable, yes/no, etc.) on particular topics.

INPUTS: Interested participants or desired subject population, issues, requests by agencies or organizations, problem definition, measuring instruments and sample size.

PURPOSE/FUNCTION: To identify and measure population (or company, etc.) attributes or attitudes.

SPECIAL CHARACTERISTICS: Questionnaire or interview techniques are usually involved.

REFERENCES: Jaci Jarrett Maszta, "Survey says........employee survey as management tools," *Managers Magazine*, vol 66, page 8, May 1991; Ned Rosen, "Employee attitude surveys: what managers should know," *Training and Development Journal*, vol. 41, page 50, Nov. 1987.

AUDITING TECHNIQUE

RESULTS: Identification of good/poor performance regarding a system specification, department, division, system, firm, corporation, etc.

INPUTS: Complete business and performance data (e.g., accounting ledgers, bank statements, internal audit reports, models of expenditure allocations, etc.).

PURPOSE/FUNCTION: To review and evaluate the fairness and authenticity of the records, measurements, and financial reports prepared by the management or person responsible.

SPECIAL CHARACTERISTICS: Usually performed by external auditors, but more internal auditors being used.

REFERENCES: Kenneth W. Stringer, *Statistical techniques for analytical review in auditing*, Wiley, New York, 1986.

BISOCIATION

RESULTS: A list of ideas and alternatives, especially for achieving the purpose/function.

INPUTS: Purpose(s) and/or function(s) to be achieved. Sources of stimulators, principles.

PURPOSE/FUNCTION: To confront disparate concepts for stimulating the generation of ideas.

SPECIAL CHARACTERISTICS: The simultaneous mental association of a stimulator as one "plane" in space and the purpose plane. The two planes or fields ordinarily not regarded as related.

REFERENCES: A. Koestler, *The Act of Creation*, Hutchinson & Co. Ltd., London, 1965.

BRAIN RESTING

RESULTS: Individual(s) who have "rested" after engaging in non-project activities.

INPUTS: People who have been intensively involved in seeking creative ideas.

PURPOSE/FUNCTION: To aid in being creative.

SPECIAL CHARACTERISTICS: A process of variable time. A period of relaxation of sports, social activity, reading, working on another project, or idleness.

REFERENCES: G. Nadler, *Work Design: A Systems Concept* (Homewood, Illinois, 1970), pp. 673-674.

BRAINSTORMING

RESULTS: A wide range of alternative ideas (e.g., suggestions for addressing a specific purpose, identification of experts who will aid in the different phases of the approach).

INPUTS: A concise purpose or problem statement usually in the form of a question and seven to ten participants willing to focus on creativity without being critical.

PURPOSE/FUNCTION: To generate a large quantity of ideas. To enhance creativity through group discussions.

SPECIAL CHARACTERISTICS: Takes about one hour. Stress no criticism or evaluation is to take place at a session.

REFERENCES: R.A. Rusk and R.M. Krone, "The Crawford Slip Method as a tool for Extraction of Expert Knowledge," in G. Salvendy, Ed., *Human Computer Interaction*, El Sevier, NY, pp 279-282.

BRAINWRITING

RESULTS: A wide range of alternatives (e.g., ideas and suggestions for achieving a purpose or solving a problem).

INPUTS: A group of participants, a concise problem statement, and slips of paper on which to write each idea.

PURPOSES/FUNCTIONS: To generate a wide range of ideas about a specific topic.

SPECIAL CHARACTERISTICS: Ideas are written on slips rather than discussed as in brainstorming. Then ideas discussed (as per "nominal group technique") or put into pool from which group members select slip to further develop the idea (believing game). Avoids bias by exchanging slips.

REFERENCES: J. N. Warfield, *Societal Complexity: Planning, Policy, and Complexity*, John Wiley and Sons, (New York, 1976); H. Geschka, G.R. Schaude and H. Schlicksupp, "Modern Techniques for Solving Problems," *International Studies of Management & Organization*, Vol. 6, No. 4, Winter 1976/77, pp. 45-63.

BREAK EVEN ANALYSIS (Economics)

RESULTS: An equation or graph depicting the quantity of items at which total revenue equals total expense.

INPUTS: Fixed and variable cost estimates, revenue and price breaks (discounts, etc.)

PURPOSE/FUNCTION: To determine the minimum number of units of income needed to meet the costs (usually production, distribution and marketing); to perform sensitivity analysis on P&D cost and price assumptions.

REFERENCES: P.F. Ostwald, *Engineering Cost Estimating*, 3rd ed., Prentice-Hall (Englewood Cliffs, NJ, 1992); G.W. Smith, *Engineering Economy: Analysis of Capital Expenditures*, 4th ed., Iowa State University Press (Ames, 1987); J.A. White, M.H. Agee and K.E. Case, *Principles of Engineering Economic Analysis*, 3rd ed., Wiley (New York, 1989); H. Bierman and S. Smidt, *The Capital Budgeting Decision*, 7th ed., Macmillan (New York, 1988); J.R. Buck, *Economic Risk Decisions in Engineering and Management*, Iowa State University Press (Ames, IA, 1989); W.J. Fabrycky and B.S. Blanchard, *Life-Cycle Cost and Economic Analysis*, Prentice-Hall (Englewood Cliffs, NJ, 1991).

BUDGET (Economics)

RESULTS: A logical arrangement of income and expense data which represents reasonable operating expectancies for a given period.

INPUTS: A time period, data, and some knowledge of planning (can be cost estimates).

PURPOSE/FUNCTION: To consolidate many operational expectancies into a concise financial format (Also to cost out ideas).

REFERENCES: P.F. Ostwald, *Engineering Cost Estimating*, 3rd ed., Prentice-Hall (Englewood Cliffs, NJ, 1992); G.W. Smith, *Engineering Economy: Analysis of Capital Expenditures*, 4th ed., Iowa State University Press (Ames, 1987); J.A. White, M.H. Agee and K.E. Case, *Principles of Engineering Economic Analysis*, 3rd ed., Wiley (New York, 1989); H. Bierman and S. Smidt, *The Capital Budgeting Decision*, 7th ed., Macmillan (New York, 1988); J.R. Buck, *Economic Risk Decisions in Engineering and Management*, Iowa State University Press (Ames, IA, 1989); W.J. Fabrycky and B.S. Blanchard, *Life-Cycle Cost and Economic Analysis*, Prentice-Hall (Englewood Cliffs, NJ, 1991).

CASE HISTORIES

RESULTS: A clear recording of an instance of an actual problem.

INPUTS: The details of a problem (and possibly solution) from records, interviews, and reports.

PURPOSE/FUNCTION: To identify problem solving processes, causes of success or failures and actors for a previous problem.

REFERENCES: Richard E. Neustadt, *Thinking in time: the uses of history for decision makers,* Free Press, NY, 1986.

CASH FLOW ANALYSIS (Economics)

RESULTS: Summary of money flows over time as a result of installing a solution, graphical illustration for the project (optional).

INPUTS: Estimated costs and benefits over the life of the project, people who benefit from the project, etc.

PURPOSE/FUNCTION: To determine the amount of money available or the difference between the incremental costs and the incremental income or benefits for each month, year, etc. of a project in order to evaluate its financial viability.

SPECIAL CHARACTERISTICS: Familiarity with accounting. Doesn't consider benefits or disadvantages which can not be assigned a monetary value.

REFERENCES: P.F. Ostwald, *Engineering Cost Estimating,* 3rd ed., Prentice-Hall (Englewood Cliffs, NJ, 1992); G.W. Smith, *Engineering Economy: Analysis of Capital Expenditures,* 4th ed., Iowa State University Press (Ames, 1987); J.A. White, M.H. Agee and K.E. Case, *Principles of Engineering Economic Analysis,* 3rd ed., Wiley (New York, 1989); H. Bierman and S. Smidt, *The Capital Budgeting Decision,* 7th ed., Macmillan (New York, 1988); J.R. Buck, *Economic Risk Decisions in Engineering and Management,* Iowa State University Press (Ames, IA, 1989); W.J. Fabrycky and B.S. Blanchard, *Life-Cycle Cost and Economic Analysis,* Prentice-Hall (Englewood Cliffs, NJ, 1991).

CAUSE/EFFECT ASSESSMENT (MATRIX)

RESULTS: A statement of the relationships between events where they interact with each other. Sometimes in the form of a matrix.

INPUTS: A number of actions or events; a basis on which the assessment is performed.

PURPOSE/FUNCTION: To establish relationships between actions or events which are the results of the other or others.

SPECIAL CHARACTERISTICS: Must have rules by which to judge causes and effects.

REFERENCES: T. Brown, *Inquiry into the Relation of Cause and Effect,* Delmar, New York: Scholars' Facsimiles and Reprints, 1977, pp. 7-250; K. Iskikawa, *Guide to Quality Control,* 2nd ed., Asian Productivity Organization, Tokyo, 1982. G. Hoffherr, *The Tool Book, Decision Making & Planning for Optimum Results,* Markon, Inc., 1993, pp 25–26.

CENTRAL LOCATION TESTING

RESULTS: Attitudes and preferences expressed by the consumers for a new product suggested improvements.

INPUTS: Central location (e.g., shopping centers, transportation terminals, social group meetings, etc.), test facility equipped with testing and interviewing booths, and interviewer and consumers and their reactions.

PURPOSE/FUNCTION: To identify new-product opportunities to expose new products to potential users for testing, and to gather additional data for making and marketing a new product.

REFERENCES: E. P. McGuire, *Evaluating New Product Proposals,* A Research Report from the Conference Board, New York, 1973, pp. 41.

CHECKLISTS

RESULTS: The generation of certain information, ideas or opinions of others.

INPUTS: A statement of needs, or problem, for which ideas are desired; a solution or suggestion to be reviewed for presence or omission of ideas. A set of desirable principles for the locus content area or for various techniques and models.

PURPOSE/FUNCTION: To generate information, opinions or ideas; to check details of a solution.

SPECIAL CHARACTERISTICS: A special form of questionnaire to check for operationality of a solution. Checklists are often statements of principles.

REFERENCES: N. Cross and R. Roy, *Design Methods Manual,* London: The Open University Press, 1975, pp. 129-132; G. Nadler, *The Planning and Design Approach,* Los Angeles CA; The Centre for Breakthrough Thinking Inc., 1981; any book or paper about features to be desired in a good solution for a particular project area (e.g., regional planning, factory layout, curriculum development, computer system).

CLASSIFICATION

RESULTS: A large number of items divided into different major areas, categories, or groups or into a pattern.

INPUTS: An agreed upon criterion for classification. A general description for each. Alternatives to be classified.

PURPOSE/FUNCTION: To sort a number of separate items into a smaller number of groups. To define major areas.

SPECIAL CHARACTERISTICS: See techniques on categorization, ranking, rating, and weighting for specific methods.

REFERENCES: N. Cross and R. Roy, *Design Methods Manual,* London: The Open University Press, 1975, pp. 87-90.

CLIMATE ANALYSIS

RESULTS: Frequency and percentage of responses to questions about the environment, management style, readiness factors (Chapter 16), etc. of an organization. Sometimes displayed as a cognitive map of employees.

INPUTS: Questions about the organization's environment, judgment, and behavior; a target group from which responses are desired.

PURPOSE/FUNCTION: To identify and compare climates (attributes of an operating situation, department, company, etc.).

SPECIAL CHARACTERISTICS: Target group can be an organization.

REFERENCES: F. Fransella and D. Bannister, *A Manual for Repertory Grid Technique,* London: Academic Press, 1977.

CONTINGENCY ANALYSIS

RESULTS: An array of options which reflect courses of action based on conditional factors. A table to summarize the situation. The contingency conditions ranked in likelihood of occurrence.

INPUTS: Most expected condition and related option (e.g., budget for "normal" conditions), definition of goals, description of contingencies and plans evaluation criteria.

PURPOSES/FUNCTION: To analyze and differentiate alternative options based on their future outcomes in light of contingent conditions.

REFERENCES: G. A. Churchill, Jr., *Marketing Research: Methodological Foundations,* the Dryden Press (III. 1976) pp. 415-419; K. B. DeGreene, *Sociotechnical Systems: Factors in Analysis, Design and Management,* Prentice-Hall (Englewood Cliffs, N.J., 1973), pp. 194-195.

CONTINGENCY TABLES

RESULTS: A table which accounts for all combinations of the factors being investigated (e.g., level of marijuana use, dominant anti-social behavior, and actual frequencies), and accepting or rejecting the null hypothesis.

PURPOSE/FUNCTION: To determine if the variables in a cross-classification analysis are independent (e.g., whether or not the level of marijuana usage affects antisocial behavior).

REFERENCES: G. A. Churchill, Jr., *Marketing Research: Methodological Foundations,* The Dryden Press (III., 1976) pp. 415-419; H. D. Brunk, *An Introduction to Mathematical Statistics,* Xerox College

Publishing (Lexington, Mass., 1975), pp. 364-367; Lawrence L. Lapin, *Statistics: Meaning and Method,* Harcourt Brace Jovanovich, Inc. (New York, 1975) pp. 428-434.

CONTROL CHARTS

RESULTS: An indication of possible shifts in the expected population/mean within desired confidence limits as plotted on a chart.

INPUTS: Measurements from each time ordered subgroup, desired goals in terms of mean value and confidence/control limits.

PURPOSE/FUNCTION: To detect if desired mean (and variability of samples) is within desired limits, and to determine whether the process is performing in a consistent, satisfactory manner as set up in the goals.

SPECIAL CHARACTERISTICS: A statistical technique. Some illustrative types are: P - chart (control charts for fraction defective); C - chart (control charts for number of defects per unit); X and R charts (variables control charts); and CUSUM charts (cumulative sum control charts).

REFERENCES: G. Nadler, *Work Design: A System Concept,* (Homewood, Illinois, 1970), pp 130-134; W.A. Shewhart, *Economic Control of Quality of Manufactured Products,* American Society for Quality Control, Bookcrafters (Chelsea, MI, 1980); American Society for Testing and Materials, *ASTM Manual on Presentation of Data and Control Chart Analysis,* 6th ed., ASTM-MNL7 (Philadelphia, 1990); J.M. Juran, *Quality Control Handbook,* 4th ed., McGraw-Hill (New York, 1988).

CONTROL MODEL

RESULTS: A schematic representation of the means of measuring the performance of a specification in an operating system, comparing it with the desired measures, and taking action if a significant and practical difference occurs.

INPUTS: Operating conditions, measurement methods, desired specification(s), desired confidence.

PURPOSE/FUNCTION: To maintain the attribute(s) of a component or system within desired or designed limits.

SPECIAL CHARACTERISTICS: Many forms are available - timeline-based (see network techniques), mathematical, statistical, etc.

REFERENCES: T.J. Williams, *Analysis and Design of Hierarchial Control Systems,* Elsevier Science Publishers (Amsterdam, 1985); R.C. Dorf, *Modern Control Systems,* 3rd ed., Addison-Wesley (Reading, MA, 1980); G. Nadler, *The Planning and Design Approach,* The Center for Breakthrough Thinking, Inc. (Los Angeles, 1981), Chapter 15.

CORRELATION ANALYSIS (Regression Analysis)

RESULTS: A coefficient of relationship which explains linear variations between paired measures of two variables of the same phenomenon.

INPUT: Two measures about the same phenomenon or variable, a number of sets of measures about individual cases or occurrences of the phenomenon.

PURPOSE/FUNCTION: To measure the strength of the linear relationship between the two interval-scaled variables.

REFERENCES: R.W. Farebrother, *Linear Least Squares Computations,* Marcel Dekker (New York, 1988); A.J. Dobson, *An Introduction to Statistical Modelling,* Chapman and Hall (New York, 1986); I. Guttman, *Linear Models: An Introduction,* Wiley (New York, 1982); J.R. Rice, *Matrix Computations and Mathematical Software,* McGraw-Hill (Tokyo, 1983).

COST-BENEFIT ANALYSIS (CBA) (Economics)

RESULTS: An estimation and evaluation of net benefits (or statement assessing costs and benefits) associated with each alternative for achieving defined goals; rank-ordering of alternatives based on decreasing benefit-cost ratios.

INPUTS: Defined goals, alternatives, constraints (budgetary, legal, social, political, and institutional) on the project, control variables (location, starting time, number of installations, etc.), identification of the social and economic components of both costs and benefits.

PURPOSE/FUNCTION: To evaluate the merits of alternative solutions.

SPECIAL CHARACTERISTICS: The user must be familiar with the overall specification of the project. Careful analysis and weighting of alternatives may take from several days to several weeks.

REFERENCES: P.F. Ostwald, *Engineering Cost Estimating*, 3rd ed., Prentice-Hall (Englewood Cliffs, NJ, 1992); G.W. Smith, *Engineering Economy: Analysis of Capital Expenditures*, 4th ed., Iowa State University Press (Ames, 1987); J.A. White, M.H. Agee and K.E. Case, *Principles of Engineering Economic Analysis*, 3rd ed., Wiley (New York, 1989); H. Bierman and S. Smidt, *The Capital Budgeting Decision*, 7th ed., Macmillan (New York, 1988); J.R. Buck, *Economic Risk Decisions in Engineering and Management*, Iowa State University Press (Ames, IA, 1989); W.J. Fabrycky and B.S. Blanchard, *Life-Cycle Cost and Economic Analysis*, Prentice-Hall (Englewood Cliffs, NJ, 1991).

COST-EFFECTIVENESS ANALYSIS (Economics)

RESULTS: Rank ordering of alternatives in terms of effectiveness relative to costs.

INPUTS: Objectives, alternative means, cost data, and judgments to determine measures of effectiveness.

PURPOSE/FUNCTION: To evaluate alternative means for achieving specified ends, to evaluate and compare alternative projects or systems for the purpose of selecting the most cost-effective alternative.

SPECIAL CHARACTERISTICS: Cost-effective analysis is similar to cost-benefit analysis except that the non-monetary performance of the project is estimated.

REFERENCES: P.F. Ostwald, *Engineering Cost Estimating*, 3rd ed., Prentice-Hall (Englewood Cliffs, NJ, 1992); G.W. Smith, *Engineering Economy: Analysis of Capital Expenditures*, 4th ed., Iowa State University Press (Ames, 1987); J.A. White, M.H. Agee and K.E. Case, *Principles of Engineering Economic Analysis*, 3rd ed., Wiley (New York, 1989); H. Bierman and S. Smidt, *The Capital Budgeting Decision*, 7th ed., Macmillan (New York, 1988); J.R. Buck, *Economic Risk Decisions in Engineering and Management*, Iowa State University Press (Ames, IA, 1989); W.J. Fabrycky and B.S. Blanchard, *Life-Cycle Cost and Economic Analysis*, Prentice-Hall (Englewood Cliffs, NJ, 1991).

COUNSELING INTERVIEWS

RESULTS: Facts or ideas generated by the person/groups being interviewed or suggested actions for an individual or group.

INPUTS: A prepared list of questions to elicit personal insights, experiences, opinions, and facts from a selected or willing individual/group.

PURPOSE/FUNCTION: To generate ideas from an individual by directing and advising the individual into a specific train of thought.

REFERENCES: Neville B. Taylor, "How do careers counsellors counsel?" *British Journal of Guidance & Counselling*, Vol 13, page 166-67, May 1985.

COUNTERPLANNING

RESULTS: A revised decision, plan, problem, or perception.

INPUTS: A problem, decision, plan or design, proposed conflicting assumptions.

PURPOSE/FUNCTION: To examine the assumptions underpinning a problem, decision, plan or design.

SPECIAL CHARACTERISTICS: Based on the dialectical process.

REFERENCES: N. Cross and R. Roy, *Design Methods Manual*, The Open University Press, London, 1975, pp. 57-64.

COUPLET COMPARISON TECHNIQUE

RESULTS: The item from a list that best relates to the criterion (e.g., the most specific purpose, the most complex idea, the most intelligent person, the most regular or frequently occurring item).

INPUTS: A list of alternatives related to the criterion.

PURPOSE/FUNCTION: To select the item most closely related to the criterion.

SPECIAL CHARACTERISTICS: A modified pair comparison technique (PI). Compare the first two items to determine which is "best" for the criterion, compare it with the third item for same reason, compare it with the fourth item, and so on through whole list.

REFERENCES: G. Nadler, *The Planning and Design Approach*, The Center for Breakthrough Thinking, Inc. (Los Angeles, 1981).

CRITICAL INCIDENT TECHNIQUE (Focus Groups)

RESULTS: Record of critical (worst or best) incidents, cases, or worker requirements for success in a given job.

INPUTS: Factual descriptions of specific instances of occurrences or job behavior that are characteristic of either satisfactory or unsatisfactory situations.

PURPOSE/FUNCTION: To specify the critical requirements for a particular job (e.g., finger dexterity, computational accuracy, perceptual speed, and ability to work effectively under distracting conditions).

SPECIAL CHARACTERISTICS: Highlight the irregular but crucial occurrences for which a person, group or system should be prepared.

REFERENCES: R.A. Ash, E.L. Levine, and F. Sistrunk, "The Role of Jobs and Job-Based Methods in Personnel and Human Resources Management," in K.M. Rowland and G.R. Ferris, Eds., *Research in Personnel and Human Resources Management*, Vol 1, JAI Press (Greenwich, CT, 1983) pp 45-84; S. Gael, *Job Analysis: A Guide to Assessing Work Activities*, Jossey-Bass (San Francisco, 1983).

CRITICAL PATH METHOD (CPM)

RESULTS: Network with built-in information of earliest and latest start times, earliest and latest finish times; earliest and latest project completion time; the activities that are on the critical path.

INPUTS: A knowledge of project objectives and activities with their estimated time durations.

PURPOSE/FUNCTION: To identify critical activities of a project and the path of critical (no slack time) duration; to determine the best sequence of activities and their schedules in a project, to determine the shortest time for project completion; to evaluate alternative projects.

SPECIAL CHARACTERISTICS: CPM or precedence network planning uses deterministic time durations. (See PERT networks regarding probabilistic time estimates.) Computer programs are available.

REFERENCES: Moder, Phillips and Davis, *Project Management with CPM, PERT and Precedence Diagramming*, 3rd edition, Van Nostrand Reinhold Co., NY, 1983.

CROSS-IMPACT ANALYSIS (MATRIX)

RESULTS: A matrix identifying factors that interact, might also reflect probability of occurrence of interaction.

INPUTS: Future trend data from mathematical models, individual or group opinions of possible impact.

PURPOSE/FUNCTION: To explore future developments, to identify change not considered in mathematical models.

REFERENCES: J. W. Dickey and T. M. Watts, *Analytic Techniques in Urban and Regional Planning*, New York: McGraw-Hill Book Company, 1978, pp. 297-315.

DECISION WORKSHEET

RESULTS: Each cell of the worksheet matrix contains the measure of the amount of each criterion (rows) present in each alternative (columns). Each criterion is usually weighted to show importance, and states of nature and probabilities of outcomes may be incorporated in the measures. The alternative with the highest total of the measures is usually considered a prime candidate to be selected.

INPUTS: All of the relevant data: Desires of clients (discrete and variable criteria, weightings), estimates of states of nature, forecasts of the events, alternatives, and related performance estimates.

PURPOSE/FUNCTION: To select an alternative best suited to the purpose for which a decision is needed.

SPECIAL CHARACTERISTICS: Many other techniques might be used in the decision process, such as optimization models, utility assessments, ranking and weighting procedures, and probability estimation.

REFERENCES: R. L. Keeney and H. Raiffa, *Decisions with Multiple Objectives,* New York: John Wiley & Sons, 1976; G. Nadler, *The Planning and Design Approach,* The Center for Breakthrough Thinking, Inc. (Los Angeles, 1981); A. Rapoport, *Decision Theory and Decision Behavior,* Kluwer Academic Publishers, Norwell, MA, 1989.

DECISION TABLES (Decision Trees)

RESULTS: Tabular summary for information systems of conditions (Are work study funds available?), actions (request for funds, etc.) to be followed under different conditions in a given environment, and decision rules (yes/no).

INPUTS: Factors relevant to the decision and the specific possible action choices; analyst, decision maker, policy, etc.

PURPOSE/FUNCTION: To document (for programming a computer) a decision-making process by describing actions to be followed.

REFERENCES: B. Moret, "Decision Trees and Diagrams," *Computing Surveys,* Vol. 14, No. 4 (December 1982).

DECISION TREE (Decision Tables)

RESULTS: "Tree" shape representation depicting the components and sequential alternatives, along with probabilities of success for each "branch."

INPUTS: The decision-making situation, alternatives and possible events, and estimates of probabilities and payoffs.

PURPOSE/FUNCTION: To evaluate the priorities and feasibilities of different alternatives.

REFERENCES: B. Moret, "Decision Trees and Diagrams," *Computing Surveys,* Vol. 14, No. 4, December 1982.

DELPHI

RESULTS: A convergence of expert opinions about problems, purposes, criteria, recommendations, etc.

INPUTS: A two to five member team of investigators who prepare a series of three to five questionnaires to elicit opinions of 20 to 30 participants who never meet. Responses to one questionnaire are organized to form the basis for the next one.

PURPOSE/FUNCTION: To elicit, collate, and generally direct informed judgments toward a consensus on a specific topic.

SPECIAL CHARACTERISTICS: The process will take approximately one and a half to three months. Delphi enables participants to remain anonymous.

REFERENCES: A. Delbecq, A. Van de Ven, and D. Gustafson, *Group Techniques for Program Planning - A Guide to Nominal Group and Delphi,* Chicago, Ill.; Scott, Foresman Co., 1975; H. Sackman, *Delphi Critique,* Lexington Books (Mass., 1975); H.A. Linstone and M. Turoff (Eds.), *The Delphi Method: Techniques and Applications,* Reading, Mass., Addison-Wesley Publishing Co., 1975.

DELTA CHARTS

RESULTS: A flow chart-type portrayal depicting Decisions, Events, Logic, Time, and Activity for a project.

INPUTS: Purposes, resources, functional components, source of decisions, etc. for a project.

PURPOSE/FUNCTION: To portray an overall program concept.

REFERENCES: J. N. Warfield, *Societal Systems: Planning, Policy, and Complexity,* New York: John Wiley & Sons, 1976.

DEMAND ANALYSIS (Economics)

RESULTS: An allocation solution that satisfies the demand considering inventory and price.

INPUTS: Indifference curves, an understanding of the market.

PURPOSE/FUNCTION: To evaluate alternatives to find an optimum between supply and demand.

SPECIAL CHARACTERISTICS: Similar to Input-Output Analysis.

REFERENCES: P.F. Ostwald, *Engineering Cost Estimating,* 3rd ed., Prentice-Hall (Englewood Cliffs, NJ, 1992); G.W. Smith, *Engineering Economy: Analysis of Capital Expenditures,* 4th ed., Iowa State University Press (Ames, 1987); J.A. White, M.H. Agee and K.E. Case, *Principles of Engineering Economic Analysis,* 3rd ed., Wiley (New York, 1989); H. Bierman and S. Smidt, *The Capital Budgeting Decision,* 7th ed., Macmillan (New York, 1988); J.R. Buck, *Economic Risk Decisions in Engineering and Management,* Iowa State University Press (Ames, IA, 1989); W.J. Fabrycky and B.S. Blanchard, *Life-Cycle Cost and Economic Analysis,* Prentice-Hall (Englewood Cliffs, NJ, 1991).

DEMOGRAPHIC FORECASTING

RESULTS: Prediction of people's movement, consumption and purchase behavior.

INPUTS: People's attitudes, activities, interests, opinions, perceptions and preferences.

PURPOSE/FUNCTION: To forecast future life-styles and develop consumer preferences and profiles.

SPECIAL CHARACTERISTICS: Usually done with questionnaires and attitude surveys.

REFERENCES: Gilbert A. Churchill, Jr., *Marketing Research: Methodological Foundations,* The Dryden Press (Ill., 1976), pp. 561-564.

DIALECTICAL INQUIRY OR PROCESS

RESULTS: Exposition of differing points of view in hope of developing sound policy and decisions. Possible list of new ideas.

INPUTS: Debate of important issues by concerned and well-informed individuals. Often pits an assumption or an idea against its opposite.

PURPOSE/FUNCTION: To identify basic concepts on which agreement can be obtained. To engage in a deliberate scenario wherein each person proposing a perspective tries to play the believing game.

REFERENCES: R.D. Mason and L.I. Mitroff, *Strategic Assumptions Surfacing and Testing,* New York: John Wiley & Sons, 1981; J. N. Warfield, *Societal Systems: Planning, Policy, and Complexity,* New York: John Wiley & Sons, 1976; N. Cross and R. Roy, *Design Methods Manual,* London: The Open University Press, 1975, p. 58.

DIGRAPHS

RESULTS: A directed graph or structural model of a problem.

INPUTS: Two numerical sets and a partition with binary relations.

PURPOSE/FUNCTION: To visually state the relationships of variables - a structural model which carries no empirical or substantive information.

SPECIAL CHARACTERISTICS: See Interpretive Structural Modeling (ISM), see Interrelationship digraph.

REFERENCES: J. N. Warfield, *Societal Systems: Planning, Policy, and Complexity,* John Wiley and Sons, New York, 1976.

DYNAMIC MODEL

RESULTS: A time based representation of the performance of a system with suggested changes, improvements if any.

INPUTS: System variables and their interrelationships (e.g., equations, graphs).

PURPOSE/FUNCTION: To represent some aspects of the external world as a means of trying to influence, control or understand it more effectively; to explain the system's behavior in terms of its structure and policies, suggesting changes to structure, policies, or both, which will lead to an improvement in the behavior.

SPECIAL CHARACTERISTICS: Primarily concerned with feedback loops and supplementary variables which indicate system performance.

REFERENCES: R. G. Coyle, *Management System Dynamics,* London: John Wiley & Sons, 1977, pp. 5-19.

ECONOMETRIC MODEL (Regression)

RESULTS: A system of interdependent (usually regression in nature) equations that describes some sector of economic sales, monetary or profit activity. (Relationships among economic variables in mathematical equations.)

INPUTS: Complete economic data (several years' history) and their relationships, if available, in relation to a particular sector, region, firm, etc.

PURPOSE/FUNCTION: To analyze policy setting and economic forecasting variables.

SPECIAL CHARACTERISTICS: Modern computing facilities allow models of almost any size to be developed but for purposes of exposition the smaller and simpler the model the better.

REFERENCES: R.W. Farebrother, *Linear Least Squares Computations,* Marcel Dekker (New York, 1988); A.J. Dobson, *An Introduction to Statistical Modelling,* Chapman and Hall (New York, 1986); I. Guttman, *Linear Models: An Introduction,* Wiley (New York, 1982); J.R. Rice, *Matrix Computations and Mathematical Software,* McGraw-Hill (Tokyo, 1983).

END-MEANS CHAIN

RESULTS: Hierarchy chain or tree starting with an end. An end is identified with several means each of which can be viewed then as an end with several means, and so on.

INPUTS: Ends, objectives, purposes or goals to be achieved and a variety of possible means of reaching these ends.

PURPOSE/FUNCTION: To identify alternatives of policies and procedures which might be considered; to design and use a good value system.

SPECIAL CHARACTERISTICS: Developing a chain is a process, one end at a time.

REFERENCES: Pierre Valette-Florence and Bernard Rapacchi, "Improvements in means-end chain analysis using graph theory and correspondence analysis," *Journal of Advertising Research,* Vol. 31, No. 1, Feb/March 1991, page 30; J. Gutman, "A Means-End Chain Model Based on Consumer Categorization Processes," *Journal of Marketing,* Vol. 46, Spring 1982, pp 6-72.

EXPECTED FREE CASH FLOW MODEL (Economics)

RESULTS: Calculations of FCF's (future cash flows).

INPUTS: Net operating profit after taxes, new capital investment, expected rate of return on investment and the length of time in years for which high-returning projects are expected to exceed the blended cost of capital, dividend payout ratio and debt ratio.

PURPOSE/FUNCTION: To provide improved investor information (prospectus); to analyze and evaluate investment decisions.

REFERENCES: P.F. Ostwald, *Engineering Cost Estimating*, 3rd ed., Prentice-Hall (Englewood Cliffs, NJ, 1992); G.W. Smith, *Engineering Economy: Analysis of Capital Expenditures*, 4th ed., Iowa State University Press (Ames, 1987); J.A. White, M.H. Agee and K.E. Case, *Principles of Engineering Economic Analysis*, 3rd ed., Wiley (New York, 1989); H. Bierman and S. Smidt, *The Capital Budgeting Decision*, 7th ed., Macmillan (New York, 1988); J.R. Buck, *Economic Risk Decisions in Engineering and Management*, Iowa State University Press (Ames, IA, 1989); W.J. Fabrycky and B.S. Blanchard, *Life-Cycle Cost and Economic Analysis*, Prentice-Hall (Englewood Cliffs, NJ, 1991).

FACTOR ANALYSIS

RESULTS: The resolution of a large number of correlated variables into a smaller set of factors that underlie the variables.

INPUTS: A set of variables with a matrix of intercorrelations.

PURPOSE/FUNCTION: To establish major factors that portray major influences among all of the variables.

REFERENCES: Richard L. Gorsuch, *Factor Analysis*, L. Erlbaum Associates, Hillsdale, NJ, 1983; Roderick P. McDonald, *Factor analysis and related methods*, L. Erlbaum Associates, Hillsdale, NJ, 1985.

FAILURE ANALYSIS (FMEA - Failure Modes & Effect Analysis)

RESULTS: A strong, reliable alternative is determined which minimizes risk of failure.

INPUTS: Set of alternatives and comparison and/or tests.

PURPOSE/FUNCTION: To determine weaknesses and the reliability of each alternative.

SPECIAL CHARACTERISTICS: Similar to Reliability Analysis.

REFERENCES: W. Hammer, *Occupational Safety Management and Engineering*, Prentice-Hall, Inc. (Englewood Cliffs, New Jersey, 1988).

FAULT TREE ANALYSIS (FMEA)

RESULTS: A list or "tree" of the specific faults that could contribute to a specific breakdown and their probabilities of occurrence.

INPUTS: A thorough description of the system and the top undesired event(s) including the spatial and temporal bounds on the system.

PURPOSE/FUNCTION: To assess the reliability of complex systems; to model the system conditions that can cause the undesired event (analysis of chemical processing safety, fire safety, seismic risk, and other risks).

SPECIAL CHARACTERISTICS: Computer programs and operations research techniques are currently being developed to analyze large, complex fault trees.

REFERENCES: W. Hammer, *Occupational Safety Management and Engineering*, Prentice-Hall, Inc., (Englewood Cliffs, New Jersey, 1988).

FINANCIAL INVESTMENT APPRAISAL (Economics)

RESULTS: Future streams of capital and operating costs and revenues which will result from the implementation of investment projects.

INPUTS: Financial costs and returns; discounting factors.

PURPOSE/FUNCTION: To evaluate alternative investments.

SPECIAL CHARACTERISTICS: See cash flow analysis, free cash flow technique, break even analysis.

REFERENCES: P.F. Ostwald, *Engineering Cost Estimating*, 3rd ed., Prentice-Hall (Englewood Cliffs, NJ, 1992); G.W. Smith, *Engineering Economy: Analysis of Capital Expenditures*, 4th ed., Iowa State University Press (Ames, 1987); J.A. White, M.H. Agee and K.E. Case, *Principles of Engineering Economic Analysis*, 3rd ed., Wiley (New York, 1989); H. Bierman and S. Smidt, *The Capital Budgeting*

Decision, 7th ed., Macmillan (New York, 1988); J.R. Buck, *Economic Risk Decisions in Engineering and Management,* Iowa State University Press (Ames, IA, 1989); W.J. Fabrycky and B.S. Blanchard, *Life-Cycle Cost and Economic Analysis,* Prentice-Hall (Englewood Cliffs, NJ, 1991).

FISHBONE DIAGRAM (CAUSE AND EFFECT / ISIKAWA DIAGRAM)

RESULTS: Illustrates clearly the various causes affecting a process and help to cure the causes.

INPUTS: Causes obtained by brainstorming for every effect, problem statement.

PURPOSE/FUNCTION: Represents relation between some "effect" and all possible "causes" influencing it.

REFERENCES: K. Isikawa, *Guide to Quality Control,* 2nd. edition, Asian Productivity Organization, Tokyo, 1982; J. Moran, R. Talbot and R. Benson, *A Guide to Graphical Problem Solving Progresses,* Quality Press, 1990, p.s.

FISHBOWL PLANNING

RESULTS: A restructured plan at the point where it is acceptable to all.

INPUTS: Brochures, workshops, public meetings, citizens' committee techniques, and a concerned public.

PURPOSE/FUNCTION: To inform and involve public, to air opposition and support to alternatives.

SPECIAL CHARACTERISTICS: All Planning and TQM efforts are open to the public.

REFERENCES: J. B. Rosener, "A Cafeteria of Techniques and Critiques," *Public Management,* (December 1975), pp. 16-19.

FLOW CHARTS

RESULTS: A diagram or schematic representation (symbols, flow, layout, etc.) that indicates how an activity is to be carried out.

INPUTS: Process, decision, state, and connector symbols, ideas, conditions, unit operations, types of equipment and people, solution purposes to be achieved, etc.

PURPOSE/FUNCTION: To represent complex processes as a connected sequence of decisions and actions; to design, analyze, and debug them.

REFERENCES: C. Collett, J Collett: J. DeMott, G. Hoffherr, J. Moran, *Making Daily Management Work,* Goal QPC, 1992, pp 37–48; G. Nadler, *Work Design: A System Concept* (Homewood, Illinois, 1970); International Labor Office (ILO), *Introduction to Work Study,* 3rd ed., ILO Publications, Geneva, 1978.

FOCUS GROUP TESTING (Critical Incident Technique)

RESULTS: Data regarding reactions to changes in new product concepts package designs, advertisements, etc. to be used.

INPUTS: A group of six to ten people, prototype of the new product, and a representative of the client's company.

PURPOSE/FUNCTION: To identify preferred alternative of a limited group.

SPECIAL CHARACTERISTICS: Session may take one to two hours.

REFERENCES: E. P. McGuire, *Evaluating New-Product Proposals,* A Research Report from the Conference Boad, New York, 1973, pp 37-40;G. Guilfoyle and C.L. Mauro, "Integrating Human Factors and Industrial Design: Matching Human Factors Methods up to Product Development," *Proceedings Human Factors and Industrial Design,* Tufts University, Medford, MA, 1980.

FOCUSED GROUP INTERVIEWS

RESULTS: A wide variety of ideas and opinions.

INPUTS: Structured or guided interview questions, group of six to ten concerned participants.

PURPOSE/FUNCTION: To expose ideas and promote reactions. To gather information, opinions and ideas.

SPECIAL CHARACTERISTICS: Better suited to exploratory activities. Relies on group discussion as well as directed questions. A variation of the depth interview. Makes coding, tabulation and analysis difficult.

REFERENCES: D. L. Johnston and A. H. Mendleson, *Using Focus Groups in Marketing Planning;* West Publ. Co., 1982; J. B. Rosener, "A Cafeteria of Techniques and Critiques," *Public Management* (December 1975), pp. 16-19.

FORCED CONNECTIONS

RESULTS: Ideas suggesting new connections between components of a product or system, new innovations.

INPUTS: Interaction matrices, a system in need of innovation.

PURPOSE/FUNCTION: To generate innovations.

REFERENCES: N. Cross and R. Roy, *Design Methods Manual,* The Open University Press (London, 1975), pp. 93-96; G. Nadler, *The Planning and Design Approach,* The Center for Breakthrough Thinking, Inc. (Los Angeles, 1981)

FORCE FIELD ANALYSIS

RESULTS: A model/diagram showing forces for change (organizational crisis, product obsolescence, lowered productivity, quality, etc.), present balance point, and desired balance point.

INPUTS: All the elements and trouble spots or forces for change of an issue/process.

PURPOSE/FUNCTION: To analyze organizational factors for change and improvement; to diagnose factors affecting change potential.

SPECIAL CHARACTERISTICS: Helps promote "win-win" situations where all power bases in an organization cooperate and benefit.

REFERENCES: J. W. Moran, Richard P. Talbot, Russell M. Benson, *A Guide to Graphical Problem-Solving Processes,* ASQC Quality Press, Milwaukee Wisconsin, 1990; G. Hoffherr, *The Toolbook Decision Making & Planning for Optimum Results,* Markon, Inc., 1993, pp 35–36.

FORECASTING TECHNIQUES

RESULTS: Conjectures and predictions about specific conditions, performances, or factors in the future.

INPUTS: Data about the past status of conditions or factors, rough or approximate models that can be used to find relationships of data and time.

PURPOSE/FUNCTION: To anticipate, calculate and predict future happenings or conditions.

SPECIAL CHARACTERISTICS: Three types: Qualitative methods (Delphi method, Market research, Panel consensus, Visionary forecast, Historical analogy); Time series analysis & projection (moving average, exponential smoothing, trend projections); Causal methods (Regression model, Econometric model, Intention-to-buy and anticipations surveys, Input-output model, Economic input-output model, Diffusion index, Leading indicator, Life-cycle analysis). Computers are used in most cases.

REFERENCES: H. Levenbach and J.P. Cleary, *The Modern Forecaster,* Van Nostrand Reinhold, New York, 1984; S. Makridakis and S.C. Wheelwright, Eds., *The Handbook of Forecasting: A Manager's Guide,* 2nd ed., Wiley, New York, 1987; T.L. Saaty and L.G. Vargas, *Prediction, Projection and Forecasting,* Kluwer Academic Publishers, Norwell, MA, 1990.

FUZZY SETS

RESULTS: A class of objects or alternatives with a continuum of grades of membership concerning degree of fuzziness ranging between zero and one.

INPUTS: Classes of objects or alternatives which have poorly defined boundaries.

PURPOSE/FUNCTION: To classify objects for use in pattern recognition, prediction, communication of information, and abstraction.

REFERENCES: G.W. Evans, W. Karwowski and M.R. Wilhelm, Eds., *Applications of Fuzzy Set Methodologies in Industrial Engineering*, Elsevier, Amsterdam, The Netherlands, 1989; J. Kacprzyk and M. Fedrizzi, *Multiperson Decision Making Models Using Fuzzy Sets and Possibility Theory*, Kluwer Academic Publishers, Norwell, MA, 1990; H.J. Zimmermann, *Fuzzy Set Theory*, Kluwer Academic Publishers, Norwell, MA, 1991.

GAMING

RESULTS: Simulated effects (e.g., costs, time, waste) of an individual's or group's alternate decisions in a specific game.

INPUTS: Definition of the problem, statement of the purpose, a design team or individual, a participating team or individual, and specific starting values of variables.

PURPOSE/FUNCTION: To experiment in a non-real situation with alternative policies, programs, or plans to determine their impacts in a simulated environment.

SPECIAL CHARACTERISTICS: Often computerized. Development of games requires expert skill.

REFERENCES: M. F. Rubinstein and K. R. Pfeiffer, *Concepts in Problem Solving*, Englewood Cliffs, N.J.: Prentice-Hall, Inc., 1980; K.G. Ramamurthy, *Coherent Structures and Simple Games*, Kluwer Academic Publishers, Norwell, MA, 1990.

GANTT CHARTS

RESULTS: A chart of a project schedule. A series of bars representing the beginning, duration and end in time of job segments, plotted against a calendar scale; updated frequently to reflect the changing status.

INPUTS: Knowledge of activities necessary to complete the project, decisions of start/end dates and minimum durations, and availability of resources needed and a time scale.

PURPOSE/FUNCTION: To schedule, control and manage a project. Used for determining the project duration, and as a communication aid.

SPECIAL CHARACTERISTICS: Time to use is related to project complexity. Skill required to divide the project into tasks and to estimate durations.

REFERENCES: Cristopher V. Jones, The three-dimensional Gantt chart, *Operations Research*, Vol. 36. p89, Nov-Dec 1988; also see reference for CPM; G. Hoffherr, *The Toolbook, Decision & Planning for Optimum Results*, Markon, Inc., 1993, pp 41–42.

GRAPHICS

RESULTS: Painting, drawing, photograph, sketch, graph, computer printout or any form of visual or artistic representation.

INPUTS: Markers, a writing instrument, paper, computer program, a subject and ideas, and frequently mathematical rules.

PURPOSE/FUNCTION: To visually represent a relationship or object.

REFERENCES: John W. Moran, Richard P. Talbot and Russell M. Benson, *A Guide to Graphical Problem Solving Processes*, Milwaukee, WI, ASQC Quality Press, 1990.

GRAPH THEORY

RESULTS: A graphical representation of the organizational structure.

INPUTS: Points assigned for units or people of an organization, lines for relationships.

PURPOSE/FUNCTION: To provide a model for testing system arrangements, and to clarify formal requirements of the organizational system.

SPECIAL CHARACTERISTICS: Also a mathematical concept.

REFERENCES: J. N. Warfield, *Societal Systems: Planning, Policy and Complexity,* John Wiley and Sons (New York, 1976), pp. 29-264.

HISTOGRAMS

RESULTS: A graphical display of the number of occurrences of numeric data values in specified intervals or cells.

INPUTS: Values of the variable X and the frequency occurrence of X value.

PURPOSE/FUNCTION: To represent the distribution of the sample of data. Proves a basic understanding of the shape, location, and variability of the data.

REFERENCES: J. W. Moran, R. P. Talbot, R. M. Benson, *A Guide to Graphical Problem-Solving Processes,* Quality Press, 1990, pp 17–29.

HOSHIN PLANNING

RESULTS: Helps to control the direction of the company by orchestrating change within a company.

INPUTS:

PURPOSE/FUNCTION: Ensures that the direction, goals, and objectives of the company are rationally developed, well defined, clearly communicated, monitored, and adapted based on system feedback.

REFERNCES: Yogi Akao, *Hoshin Planning,* Productivity Press, 1992.

INDEX NUMBERS

RESULTS: A general composite numerical representation of a whole group of factors (e.g., consumer price index).

INPUTS: Past information about all the factors. A rough model of needed values.

PURPOSE/FUNCTION: To observe index changes and their influence, to judge the state of the phenomenon being indexed.

REFERENCES: W. R. Crowe, *Index Numbers,* London: Macdonald & Evans, Ltd., 1965; M. Bruckheimer and A. Steward, *Index Numbers,* Chatto & Winclus, London 1970; W. Eichhorn, R. Henn, O Opitz, and R. W. Shepherd, *Theory and Applications of Economic Indices,* Physica-Verlag, Wurzburg 1978.

INDIFFERENCE CURVE

RESULTS: A graph relating preferences for several levels of alternatives usually in terms of 0-100 scaling. The point of indifference of utility for the individual.

INPUTS: Preferences or utilities an individual has for differing amounts of a parameter or factor.

PURPOSE/FUNCTION: To identify the point at which there is a transfer of allegiance from one objective, amount, idea or product to another.

SPECIAL CHARACTERISTICS: Also known as the iso-utility line.

REFERENCES: J.R. Buck, *Economic Risk Decisions in Engineering and Management,* Iowa State University Press, Ames, 1989; D.V. Lindley, *Making Decisions,* 2nd ed., Wiley, New York, 1985.

INFLUENCE DIAGRAM

RESULTS: Display of changes in one variable as another changes by means of a direction at arrow to show direction of causation (e.g., an increase in production leads to an increase in inventory and vice-versa, and an increase in consumption leads to a decrease in inventory and vice-versa).

INPUTS: The names of the variables concerned and the causal relationship. Also a representation of delays and control actions.

PURPOSE/FUNCTION: To display interactions that are the basis of dynamic models.

REFERENCES: R. G. Coyle, Management System Dynamics, London: John Wiley & Sons, Inc., 1977, pp. 63-93.

INFORMATION CONTENT ANALYSIS (INCAN)

RESULTS: Amount of information processed by a person per unit time in a task. Determines complexity of information processed. May also identify how a person prefers to acquire information.

INPUTS: Factors of a task that comprise the basis for determining the "amount" that directly influence human information processing.

PURPOSE/FUNCTION: To determine relative difficulty or complexity of tasks. A possible job evaluation method. Based on information theoretic formulations.

REFERENCES: G. Nadler, *Work Design: A System Concept* (Homewood, Illinois, 1970).

INPUT-OUTPUT ANALYSIS (MATRIX)

RESULTS: A technical table or an inverse coefficient matrix relating sources (inputs) and users (outputs).

INPUTS: Inputs and outputs or a system and the phases in the production-consumption cycle; an investigation of needs.

PURPOSE/FUNCTION: To predict output levels, study impact of changes in demand levels, quantify the interrelationships and transactions among subsystems and explain flows in input-output conversion processes.

SPECIAL CHARACTERISTICS: "Intersectoral flow analysis" is an alternative which requires a less costly field survey.

REFERENCES: Ronald E. Miller and Peter D. Blair, *Input-output analysis: foundations and extensions*, Englewood Cliffs, NJ, Prentice-Hall, 1985.

INTERACTION ANALYSIS (DIAGRAM) (MATRIX)

RESULTS: Matrix diagramming of the relationships of elements.

INPUTS: A group of diverse backgrounds, set or sets or elements.

PURPOSE/FUNCTION: To describe complex relationships; identifies self interactions within members of a set and cross-interactions of members of different sets.

SPECIAL CHARACTERISTICS: Computer can be used, time is dependent on the number of entries.

REFERENCES: N. Cross and R. Roy, *Design Methods Manual*, The Open University Press (London, 1975), pp. 67-74.

INTERPRETIVE STRUCTURAL MODELING (ISM)

RESULTS: A hierarchical structure to organize the objectives, steps or processes of a system. Usually a "network" or semi-lattice looking portrayal.

INPUTS: Signed and weighted digraphs and matrices, computer technology and group processes, and a graphical representation of a directed network.

PURPOSE/FUNCTION: To serve as a basis for final documentation and as an outline for the communication of the substantive ideas of a complex system.

SPECIAL CHARACTERISTICS: Usually done with the assistance of a computer. Used to assist the policy maker in coping with organized complexity and as a social learning tool. See also DIGRAPHS.

REFERENCES: J. N. Warfield, *Societal Systems: Planning, Policy, and Complexity*, New York: John Wiley & Sons, 1976.

INTERRELATIONSHIP DIGRAPH

RESULTS: Maps out the logical or sequential links among related items. It allows for multidirectional thinking.

INPUTS: Header card outputs of Affinity Diagram or other similar process.

PURPOSE/FUNCTION: Breaks group out of linear thinking to multidirectional thinking. Forces the group to examine the effect one idea has on all of the others. This is not a straight line cause and effect approach.

SPECIAL CHARACTERISTICS: Usually done with the assistance of a neutral facilitator.

REFERENCES: Mizuno, S. *Management For Quality Improvement,* (Productivity Press, 1988), pp 23-25

INTERVIEWS (Critical Incident Technique)

RESULTS: Facts or ideas generated by the person/group being interviewed.

INPUTS: A prepared list of questions to elicit personal insights, experiences, opinions, and facts from a selected willing individual.

PURPOSE/FUNCTION: To generate ideas, comments, and information from an individual by directly posing relevant questions to that person.

REFERENCES: H.R. Booher, Ed., *People, Machines and Organizations: The MANPRINT Approach to Systems Integration,* Van Nostrand Reinhold, New York, 1990.

KANO MODEL

RESULTS: A list of customer needs captured in the actual words of the customer and categorized by what the customer must have, wants to have, and things that would delight them.

INPUTS: Customer verbatums.

PURPOSE/FUNCTION: To capture and analyze the actual words of the customer and translate them into substitute quality characteristics.

REFERENCES: N. Kano, *Attractive Quality & Must be Quality Abstract,* Japan Society of Quality Control (JSQC) 12th Annual Meeting, 1982.

LATTICE OR SEMI-LATTICE STRUCTURE

RESULTS: A numerical or graphical relationship with all values or modes connected to all immediate neighbors (lattice); only some connections with various neighbors (semi-lattice).

INPUTS: Factors, concepts or "locations" among which interconnections are thought to exist.

PURPOSE/FUNCTION: To portray relationships among ideas, concepts, or values; to establish partitions of complex relationships.

SPECIAL CHARACTERISTICS: No flow pattern number is assumed, as in "network models."

REFERENCES: T. Donnellan, *Lattice Theory,* Oxford: Pergamon Press, 1968

LEARNING CURVES

RESULTS: A graphic or mathematical representation of how repetitive production systems, human tasks, or team activities take less time per unit and involve less cost per unit as time goes on.

INPUTS: Repetitive task or production, some type of measurement of improvement from the beginning of performance.

PURPOSE/FUNCTION: To investigate individual (persons, department, etc.) performance, to compare the performances of several individuals, to estimate future times and cost per unit.

SPECIAL CHARACTERISTICS: Sometimes called progress functions, experience curves, or improvement curves.

REFERENCES: T.R. Gulledge, Jr. and B. Khoshnevis, "Production Rate, Learning and Program Costs: Survey and Bibliography," *Engineering Costs and Production Economics,* Vol. 11, 1987, pp. 223-236; R. Nanada and G.L. Adler, *Learning Curves, Theory and Application,* American Institute of Industrial Engineers, Norcross, GA, 1977; J. Smith, *Learning Curve for Cost Control,* Kluwer Academic Publishers, Norwell, MA, 1989.

LEXICOGRAPHIC MODELS

RESULTS: Ranking of the alternatives for the most important attribute. Those remaining are ranked for the next most important attribute, and so on.

INPUTS: Alternatives and attributes, decision maker, subjective weights provided by the decision maker.

PURPOSE/FUNCTION: To evaluate multi-attributed alternatives.

SPECIAL CHARACTERISTICS: The required information processing load is less for these models than for linear models. Lexicographic processes do not generate rating types of evaluations.

REFERENCES: W. D. Perreault, Jr., and Frederick A. Russ, "Comparing Multi-Attribute Evaluation Process Models," *Behavioral Science*, Vol. 22, No. 6, November, 1977, pp. 423-31.

LINE OF BALANCE (LOB)

RESULTS: Progress chart (e.g., production objective and actual production at a certain point in time) with the line of balance (LOB) indicated; all bars which fall below the LOB represent points which are behind the production plan; those above the LOB indicate points which are ahead of schedule.

INPUTS: Project objectives (e.g., number units/time period, number of units to be delivered, scheduled completion date, etc.), principal steps which must be accomplished en route to the objective (in the form of a process flow chart), and inventory of the Stock Status for all principal steps.

PURPOSE/FUNCTION: To evaluate (measure) the actual progress of a system against a scheduled objective.

REFERENCES: G. E. Whitehouse, *Systems Analysis and Design Using Network Techniques*, Prentice-Hall, Inc., Englewood Cliffs, New Jersey, 1973, pp. 90-4; A. L. Iannone, *Management Program Planning and Control with PERT, MOST, LOB*, Prentice-Hall, Inc., Englewood Cliffs, New Jersey, 1967, pp. 129-54.

MAINTENANCE CHART

RESULTS: A visual display of the defined actions, times, and supporting requirements necessary for maintenance of all equipment.

INPUTS: The steps and procedures of a system, its inputs and outputs.

PURPOSE/FUNCTION: To determine a schedule for maintenance.

SPECIAL CHARACTERISTICS: See also machine loading, Gantt Chart.

REFERENCES: S. Nakajima, *Introduction to TPM*, Productivity Press, Cambridge, MA, 1988; S. Nakajima, *TPM Development Program*, Productivity Press, Cambridge, MA, 1988.

MANAGEMENT OPERATIONS SYSTEM TECHNIQUE (MOST)

RESULTS: Network with built-in information of schedule time, expected date, latest allowed date, etc.

INPUTS: Project objectives, list of activities with their durations and costs.

PURPOSE/FUNCTION: To evaluate schedule, progress, and cost performance of a project.

SPECIAL CHARACTERISTICS: Combines CPM, PERT and LOB. The network differs from CPM and PERT in that it begins on the right side and works backwards. One time estimate (expected time) is used. The planning, scheduling, and cost effort is somewhat less than in PERT. Also see CPM, PERT, LOB.

REFERENCES: A. L. Iannone, *Management Program Planning and Control with PERT, MOST, and LOB*, Prentice-Hall, Inc., Englewood Cliffs, New Jersey 1967, pp. 83-126.

MANAGERIAL GRID ANALYSIS

RESULTS: A graphic portrayal of the types of leadership style based on one to nine scales for production orientation and people orientation (9,1 is production orientation, 1,9 people).

INPUTS: Manager's levels of concern for people and concern for task.

PURPOSE/FUNCTION: To identify several styles of management.

REFERENCES: R. R. Blake and J. S. Mouton, *The Managerial Grid III*, Houston: Gulf Publishing Co.

MARKOV CHAIN

RESULTS: A transfer model to analyze or symbolize the state of a given variable.

INPUTS: Number of conditions or alternatives the system or element can take.

PURPOSE/FUNCTION: To predict the future behavior of a variable.

SPECIAL CHARACTERISTICS: Mathematical.

REFERENCES: S.M. Ross, *Introduction to Probability Models*, 3rd ed., Academic Press, New York, 1985; R.W. Wolff, *Stochastic Modeling and the Theory of Queues*, Prentice-Hall, Englewood Cliffs, NJ, 1989.

MATHEMATICAL MODEL

RESULTS: Symbolic (e.g., algebra, calculus, probability) presentation showing pertinent factors quantitatively and portraying their relationships.

INPUTS: Precise data and possible formulas and theories.

PURPOSE/FUNCTION: To analyze collected data. To model a sample based on mathematical theories or relationships. To evaluate alternative models.

REFERENCES: I.D. Huntley and D.J.G. James, editors, *Mathematical modelling: a sourcebook of case studies*, Oxford{England}; New York: Oxford University Press, 1990; Dick Clements, *Mathematical modelling: a case study approach*, Cambridge {England}; New York: Cambridge University Press, 1989.

MATHEMATICAL PROGRAMMING TECHNIQUES

RESULTS: Explicit statements of allocations based on objectives, alternatives, resources, side effects, resource scarcities, and constraints.

INPUTS: Quantitative techniques, coefficients of alternatives must be quantified.

PURPOSE/FUNCTION: To state specific amounts (of resources, products) to be allocated to specific recipients.

SPECIAL CHARACTERISTICS: Types: Branch-and-Bound, Dynamic programming, Goal programming, Integer programming, Linear programming, Quadratic programming, Stochastic programming.

REFERENCES: F.S. Hillier and G.J. Lieberman, *Introduction to Operations Research*, 5th ed., McGraw-Hill, New York, 1990; A. Ravindran, D.T. Phillips and J.J. Solberg, *Operations Research: Principles and Practice*, second edition, Wiley, New York, 1987; G.P. McCormick, *Nonlinear Programming: Theory, Algorithms, and Applications*, Wiley, New York, 1983; R. Fletcher, *Practical Methods of Optimization*, 2nd ed., Wiley, New York, 1988; J.G. Ecker and M. Kupferschmid, *Introduction to Operations Research*, Wiley, New York, 1988; M. Minoux, *Mathematical Programming, Theory and Algorithms*, Wiley, New York, 1986.

MATRIX

RESULTS: Organizes large numbers of pieces of information into sets of items to be compared.

INPUTS: Variables, tasks, demands, solutions, resources, people, and so on. Any items that need to be compared or contrasted with other items are inputs.

PURPOSE/FUNCTION: Shows relationships between sets of data. Between sets of data it can show strength and direction of the relationship.

SPECIAL CHARACTERISTICS: Manyu types of Matrix Diagrams are available such as "L" shaped, "T" shaped, "Y" shaped, "C" shaped, "X" shaped and so on.

REFERENCES: Hoffherr, G. *The Toolbook*, "Decision Making and Planning for Optimum Results, 1993, pp 33; Mizuno, S. *Management For Quality Improvement* (Productivity Press, 1988), pp 33-36; D.I. Cleland, *Matrix Management Handbook*, Van Nostrand Reinhold, New York, 1984.

MEASUREMENT

RESULTS: A quantitative value to represent a condition about phenomenon of interest.

INPUTS: Attributes of phenomenon to be measured, a standard of the measurement process, and a means for measurement.

PURPOSE/FUNCTION: To assign numbers to objects to represent quantities of attributes.

SPECIAL CHARACTERISTICS: Four types of measurements are available - - cardinal (numbering), ordinal, interval, and ratio-scale.

REFERENCES:

MEDIA-BASED ISSUE BALLOTING

RESULTS: Statements of citizens' views and opinions based on voting from newspaper ads, television instructions, etc.

INPUTS: A questionnaire or survey concerning public problems administered through the media, a group of concerned citizens.

PURPOSE/FUNCTION: To inform citizens of public problems and to generate opinions and views.

REFERENCES: J. B. Rosener, "A Cafeteria of Techniques and Critiques," *Public Management*, December, 1975, pp. 16-19.

MEETINGS

RESULTS: Minutes or summary of proceedings, informed participants from the meeting.

INPUTS: Interested citizen groups or members of an organization or firm, a chairperson, rules of order, an environment which promotes open discussion, and a topic for discussion.

PURPOSE/FUNCTION: To inform people, or gather present information. To provide a forum for discussion.

SPECIAL CHARACTERISTICS: Takes a considerable amount of time. Should be well planned.

REFERENCES: A. Jay, "How to Run a Meeting," *Harvard Business Review*, Vol. 54, No. 2, March-April, 1976.

MODELING (Simulation)

RESULTS: A representation of an existing or planned system, a means to explain phenomena, a static form of information.

INPUTS: Constructs, linkages, data, structure, inputs dependent on type of model.

PURPOSE/FUNCTION: To gain increased comprehension of a system and to represent a system.

SPECIAL CHARACTERISTICS: Types: Casual, naive and simple correlative, forecasting. The modelling strategy is described in Table 4-9.

REFERENCES: J. N. Warfield, *Societal Systems: Planning, Policy, and Complexity*, John Wiley & Sons (New York 1976); J.A. Buzacott and J.G. Shanthikumar, *Stochastic Models of Manufacturing Systems*, Prentice Hall Publishers, Englewood Cliffs, NJ, 1992.

MORPHOLOGICAL ANALYSIS (BOX) (TREE)

RESULTS: A number of alternative solutions synthesized from different elements, usually identified within the locus content area.

INPUTS: A concise problem statement.

PURPOSE/FUNCTION: To generate a large number of alternative solutions to a problem.

SPECIAL CHARACTERISTICS: Employs matrices, boxes, or relevance trees. The time required depends on the complexity of the problem.

REFERENCES: N. Cross and R. Roy, *Design Methods Manual*, The Open University Press (London, 1975), pp. 99-102.

MULTIPLE ATTRIBUTE UTILITY ASSESSMENT

RESULTS: A mathematical model (utility functions corresponding to each attributes and an appropriate additive or multiplicative model) and ranking of alternatives based on decreasing aggregate utility.

INPUTS: Alternatives, attributes, objectives, the analyst, the decision-maker(s) and their preferences.

PURPOSE/FUNCTION: To evaluate alternatives requiring multi-attributes (e.g., buying a car, selecting a site for nuclear power plant location, selecting a research proposal for funding, etc.).

SPECIAL CHARACTERISTICS: Can be time consuming and complex. Serves as much as a guide and stimulator to effective decision making as it does a model that will "make" the decision.

REFERENCES: M. F. Rubinstein and K. R. Pfeiffer, *Concepts in Problem Solving*, Englewood Cliffs, N.J.: Prentice-Hall, Inc., 1980; R. L. Keeney and H. Riaffa, *Decisions with Multiple Objectives: Preferences and Value Trade-offs*, New York: John Wiley & Sons, Inc. 1976.

NEEDS ASSESSMENT (ANALYSIS)

RESULTS: The set of and justifications for needs or requirements. They lead to the search for a solution.

INPUTS: Definitions, arguments, and values of people whose needs or requirements are likely to become statements of needs.

PURPOSE/FUNCTION: To establish and justify the needs or requirements of a target population.

REFERENCES: Donald E. Johnson[et al.], *Needs assessment: theory and methods*, Ames, Iowa University Press, 1987; Roger Kaufman, "A needs assessment primer, "Training and Development Journal, Vol. 41, No.10, p78, March 1991.

NEGOTIATION

RESULTS: An agreement achieved as the result of bargaining between two or more parties.

INPUTS: A controversy, a group of people and representatives.

PURPOSE/FUNCTION: To confer, discuss, or bargain to reach an agreement; to improve the relationship between two or more groups.

SPECIAL CHARACTERISTICS: Each group entrusts its representative with a group position which can powerfully constrain him and his ability to try for new and innovative solutions.

REFERENCES: P. Vecchio, *Organizational Behavior*, Dryden, Chicago, 1988; D.A. Lax and J.K. Sebenius, *The Manager as Negotiator*, Free Press, New York, 1986; M.T. Jelassi and A. Foroughi, "Negotiation Support Systems: An Overview of Design Issues and Existing Software," *Decision Support Systems*, Vol. 5, No. 2, 1989; M.F. Shakun, *Journal of Group Decision and Negotiation*, Kulwer Academic Publishers, Norwell, MA, 1992.

NETWORK ANALYSIS (Gantt/PERT/CPM)

RESULTS: An optimal time flow for a project in interconnected graphic representation.

INPUTS: Linkages, jobs, length of time needed for job, knowledge of problems, objectives and activities.

PURPOSE/FUNCTION: To subdivide problems into smaller problems and identify branch relationships between them. To plan, schedule, control, and monitor a project, to evaluate project performance.

SPECIAL CHARACTERISTICS: Examples: PERT and CPM. Generalized activity networks do not take into account that (a) all activities preceding an event must be completed before any activities emanating from the event could be performed, and (b) all activities in the project must be performed.

REFERENCES: S. E. Elmaghraby, *Activity Networks: Project Planning and Control by Network Models*, John Wiley & Sons, New York, 1977; E. Minieka, *Optimization Algorithms for Networks and Graphs*, New York: Marcel Dekker, Inc., 1978; R. E. Woolsey and H. F. Swanson, *Operations Research for Immediate Application: A Quick and Dirty Manual*, New York: Harper & Row, 1975.

NEW-PRODUCT EARLY WARNING SYSTEM (NEWS)

RESULTS: Model establishing the relation between advertising plus promotional efforts, and new-product sales.

INPUTS: The amount of advertising dollars spent, number of persons exposed to advertising, number of exposures, brand awareness.

PURPOSE/FUNCTION: To predict a new product's probable performance (trial usage, gauge estimated awareness, market share by purchase cycle, short-term sales results, etc.) in a test market; to evaluate (analyze and predict risk, payoff, and other outcomes of) new-product ventures.

REFERENCES: L.G. Cooper and M. Nakanishi, *Market Share Analysis*, Kluwer Academic Publishers, Norwell, MA, 1989.

NOMINAL GROUP TECHNIQUE (NGT)

RESULTS: A list of problems, solution ideas, criteria, or whatever issues are being worked on in rank order.

INPUTS: An unstructured problem in the form of a questions and five to nine creative participants selected for knowledge to contribute.

PURPOSE/FUNCTION: To generate ideas and judgments from a group. To provide opportunity for sharing information and experience, for stimulating ideas, for critical evaluation, for applying relevant values, and for generating feelings of participation.

SPECIAL CHARACTERISTICS: A process which involves silent generation of ideas and some interacting discussion. Takes around three hours in complete form. Participants need not be familiar with the technique.

REFERENCES: A. Delbecq, A. Van de Ven, and D. Gustafson, *Group Techniques for Program Planning - A Guide to Nominal Group and Delphi*, Greenbrier (Middletown WI, 1986); P.C. Nutt, *Managing Planned Change*, Macmillan (New York, 1992).

OPERATIONS CHART

RESULTS: List of operations and their sequence of performance involved in carrying on a task, displayed against a time scale.

INPUTS: An analyst or group, principal steps required of the task.

PURPOSE/FUNCTION: To find the most efficient method of completing a given work task; to simplify methods and minimize motions; to document work methods.

SPECIAL CHARACTERISTICS: Geometric symbols usually used. Finer division uses "Therbligs" or descriptors of small motion activities in time scale on chart known as Simo chart or Therblig chart.

REFERENCES: P.F. Ostwald, *Engineering Cost Estimating*, 3rd ed., Prentice-Hall (Englewood Cliffs, NJ, 1992); P.F. Gallagher, *Parametric Estimating for Executives and Estimators*, Van Nostrand Reinhold (New York, 1982); P.F. Ostwald, *AM Cost Estimator*, 4th ed., Penton Publishing (Cleveland, OH, 1988).

OPERATIONS RESEARCH

RESULTS: Analytical or statistical models which constitute the optimal solution.

INPUTS: Purpose of operation, mathematical models, optimization techniques, input-output models, relevant data, precise statement of problem.

PURPOSE/FUNCTION: To bring together available data on a specific problem, process it, and prepare quantitative reports. To point out significant relationships of activities and predict consequences or events when certain actions are taken.

REFERENCES: F.S. Hillier and G.J. Lieberman, *Introduction to Operations Research*, 5th ed., McGraw-Hill, New York, 1990; A. Ravindran, D.T. Phillips and J.J. Solberg, *Operations Research: Principles and Practice*, second edition, Wiley, New York, 1987; G.P. McCormick, *Nonlinear Programming: Theory, Algorithms, and Applications*, Wiley, New York, 1983; R. Fletcher, *Practical Methods of Optimization*, 2nd ed., Wiley, New York, 1988; J.G. Ecker and M. Kupferschmid, *Introduction to Operations Research*, Wiley, New York, 1988; M. Minoux, *Mathematical Programming, Theory and Algorithms*, Wiley, New York, 1986.

OPTIMIZATION

RESULTS: The preferred set of specifications is identified based on a criterion being maximized or prioritized.

INPUTS: Measures of goodness and set of specifications, subjective judgment and formal models, a defined problem.

PURPOSE/FUNCTION: To determine set of specifications which should be selected.

SPECIAL CHARACTERISTICS: Can be done by the computer; many types of models.

REFERENCES: F.S. Hillier and G.J. Lieberman, *Introduction to Operations Research*, 5th ed., McGraw-Hill, New York, 1990; A. Ravindran, D.T. Phillips and J.J. Solberg, *Operations Research: Principles and Practice*, second edition, Wiley, New York, 1987; G.P. McCormick, *Nonlinear Programming: Theory, Algorithms, and Applications*, Wiley, New York, 1983,; R. Fletcher, *Practical Methods of Optimization*, 2nd ed., Wiley, New York, 1988; J.G. Ecker and M. Kupferschmid, *Introduction to Operations Research*, Wiley, New York, 1988; M. Minoux, *Mathematical Programming, Theory and Algorithms*, Wiley, New York, 1986.

OVAL DIAGRAMS

RESULTS: A symbolic representation of the variables and the relationships of a system.

INPUTS: A team of less than 5 members - all familiar with the problem and its relationships. Tree diagrams and interaction matrix diagrams.

PURPOSE/FUNCTION: To describe a problem as a set of complex relationships of variables of the system (each represented by an oval) and its environment.

REFERENCES: M. M. Baldwin, Ed., *Portraits of Complexity: Application of Systems Methodologies to Societal Problems*, Battelle Monograph, No. 9, Battelle Memorial Institute (Columbus, Ohio, June 1975); R. de Neufville and J. Stafford, *Systems Analysis for Engineers and Managers*, McGraw-Hill, (New York, 1969); J. N. Warfield, *An Assault on Complexity*, A Battelle Monograph, No. 3, Battelle Memorial Institute (Columbus, Ohio April 1973).

PAIR COMPARISON

RESULTS: A preferred alternative, or the top ranked ideas.

INPUTS: Set of alternatives or items, criterion of value, weighting values (if needed).

PURPOSE/FUNCTION: To evaluate alternatives in pairs.

SPECIAL CHARACTERISTICS: Each alternative is compared with every other alternative based on the criterion.

REFERENCES: G. Nadler, *Work Design: A Systems Concept*, Homewood, Illinois: Richard D. Irwin, Inc., 1970, pp. 196-197; J. Canada and W. Sullivan, *Economic and Multiattribute Evaluation of Advanced Manufacturing Systems*, Prentice-Hall (Englewood Cliffs, NJ, 1989).

PARETO ANALYSIS

RESULTS: Mathematical or graphical relationship between a measurement and items under consideration (parts, materials, products, etc.) arrayed from most to least in terms of the measurement, (costs, profits, frequency of occurrence, etc.).

INPUTS: Fixed set of resources, historical records, need for dealing with a limited number of items.

PURPOSE/FUNCTION: To identify those small percentage of items that constitute the largest percentage of the measurement (e.g., cost).

SPECIAL CHARACTERISTICS: A basic model of regularity. Also known as ABC Analysis.

RELATED STRATEGY STEPS IN CHAPTER 12: Step 1a, 3a, 3e.

REFERENCES: K. Ishikawa, *Guide to Quality Control, 2nd rev. ed.*, Asian Productivity Organization (Tokyo, 1976); D.C. Montgomery, *Introduction to Statistical Quality Control*, 2nd ed., Wiley (New York, 1991); H.M. Wadsworth, H.M. Stephens and A.B. Godfrey, *Modern Methods for Quality Control and Improvement*, Wiley (New York, 1986).

PARTITIONING TECHNIQUE

RESULTS: Division of a large matrix into smaller matrices or division of a large problem into sub-units which are more workable.

INPUTS: Mathematical based matrices of large size, or interrelated problems.

PURPOSE/FUNCTION: To establish the critical subparts of a problem first. Permits P & D to continue on a concurrent or priority bases.

SPECIAL CHARACTERISTICS: Many computer algorithms available.

REFERENCES: S. Anily and A. Federgruen, "Structured partitioning problems," *Operations Research*, vol.39, No.1, p130, Jan-Feb. 1991; Marshall L. Fisher and Pradeep Kedia, "Optimal solution of set covering/partitioning problems using dual heuristics," *Management Science,* vol.36, No. 6, p 674, June1990.

PATH ANALYSIS

RESULTS: A valid cause and effect model.

INPUTS: Variables, two-arrow models, knowledge on how the system functions, and statistical tests.

PURPOSE/FUNCTION: To validate causal models, to evaluate alternatives and to predict which statistical relationships hold for linear models.

REFERENCES: Thomas A. DeCotiis and Timothy P. Summers, "A path analysis of a model of the antecedents and consequences of organizational commitment," Human *Relations,* Vol. 4, page 445-470, July 1987; C. Winship and Robert D. Mare, "Structural equations and path analysis for discrete data" *American Journal of Sociology,* Vol.89, page 54-11, July 1983.

PERFORMANCE MEASURES TALLY

RESULTS: A visual count record for each of the observed activities.

INPUTS: A categorization of activities, the problems of measuring measurement unit, and an observer of the performances.

PURPOSE/FUNCTION: To gather data about the system performance.

REFERENCES: G. Nadler, *Work Design: A Systems Concept,* Homewood, Illinois: Richard D. Irwin, Inc. 1970, p. 570.

PERFORMANCE MEASUREMENT

RESULTS: Average time or percent of activities regarding the performance of the system or of an individual.

INPUTS: Details about the system; measurement specialist.

PURPOSE/FUNCTION: To establish allowed times and cost for the system, to predict system performance.

SPECIAL CHARACTERISTICS: Many techniques may be used (e.g., tallies, historical records, time study, standard data).

REFERENCES: G. Nadler, *Work Design: A Systems Concept,* Homewood, Illinois: Richard D. Irwin, Inc., 1970; J. Bernardin and R. Beatty, *Performance Appraisal: Assessing Human Behavior at Work,* Kent Publishing (Austin, Texas, 1984); *Quality Progress* (magazine), November 1989; G. Latham and K. Wexley, *Increasing Productivity Through Performance Appraisal,* Addison-Wesley Publishing, 1981.

PERSONALITY-TYPE ANALYSIS

RESULTS: Individuals grouped by dispositions.

INPUTS: Individuals, a measurement system and an experienced evaluator.

PURPOSE/FUNCTION: To evaluate, categorize, and compare the quality of behavior of individuals.

REFERENCES: M. H. McCaulley, "Psychological Types in Engineering," *Engineering Education,* Vol. 66, No. 7, April 1976, pp. 729-736.

PERSON-CARD SORTING TECHNIQUE

RESULTS: Several major alternative solution ideas synthesized from many for achieving the selected purpose(s).

INPUTS: All of the ideas developed by other idea generating and creativity techniques.

PURPOSE/FUNCTION: To sort, synthesize and organize alternative solution ideas.

SPECIAL CHARACTERISTICS: Each generated idea is written on a small card. Major alternatives are organized by moving and grouping these based on "playing" the game of asking what family each "person" (card) belongs to. Based on K-J method in Japan.

REFERENCES: S. Hibino and G. Nadler, "The Person-Card Technique," *Training and Development Journal,* Vol. 34, No. 11, November 1980, pp. 78–83; W. J. Walkoe, "Computer Methods for Qualitative Analysis and Planning," Dept. of IE., University of Wisconsin-Madison, 1513 University Ave., Madison, WI., 53705, WP 80-2, July 1980; G. Hoffherr, *The Toolbook Decision & Planning for Optimum Results,* Markon, Inc., 1993, pp 15–16.

PERT/COST

RESULTS: Up to date (or updated) network with built-in information of schedule time, expected cost, latest allowed time, etc.

INPUTS: Project objectives, list of activities with their durations and costs.

PURPOSE/FUNCTION: To evaluate schedule and cost performance to predict and control cost overruns, to determine the fastest and the most economical method of completing a project.

SPECIAL CHARACTERISTICS: Two options - the "time/cost option procedure" displays alternative time/cost risk plans for accomplishing project objectives; the "resource allocation procedure" determines the lowest cost allocation of resources among project tasks to meet a specified project duration.

REFERENCES: S. Sakamoto, *Methods Design Concept: An Innovative Way of Productivity Improvement,* Japan Management Association (Tokyo, 1990).

PHYSICAL MODEL

RESULTS: A representation accessible to the senses; possessing external characteristics (miniature or enlarged version).

INPUTS: Ingenuity, a complete understanding of the problem, and appropriate materials.

PURPOSE/FUNCTION: To represent a semblance of reality for testing or evaluation. Can be aided by computer.

REFERENCES: G. R. Terry, *Principles of Management,* Richard D. Irwin, Inc., Homewood, Illinois, 1972; J. W. Forrester, *Industrial Dynamics,* M.I.T. Press, Cambridge, Mass., 1961, Chap. 4.

PLANNING, PROGRAMMING & BUDGETING SYSTEM (PPBS)

RESULTS: Defined goals, alternative programs, an evaluation of costs and benefits of alternatives, a budget by programs, and a means of measuring the results for future evaluation.

INPUTS: Knowledge of purpose, resources and requirements.

PURPOSE/FUNCTION: To plan and evaluate alternatives, to prepare budget statement.

SPECIAL CHARACTERISTICS: Computer can be used. Time dependent upon the complexity of the alternatives. Systems analysis techniques useful (Objective Trees and Cost-Benefit Analysis).

REFERENCES: D. A. Krueckeberg and A. L. Silvers, *Urban Planning Analysis: Methods and Models,* John Wiley and Sons, Inc. (New York, 1974) p. 197; R. de Neufville and J. Stafford, *Systems Analysis for Engineers and Managers,* McGraw-Hill, New York, 1971; C.O. Glaister, " What's Happening to PPBS?," *Armed Forces Comptroller,* vol.26, pp. 4-5, Fall 1981.

POLICYGRAPHS

RESULTS: Graphical visual aid on how policy-option fields propagate upwards through the reality domain towards the goals domain.

INPUTS: Goal elements, reality elements and policy elements; influence of various policy options.

PURPOSE/FUNCTION: To establish paths whereby the influence of various policy-options is thought to propagate through the feasibility and acceptability filters of the reality domain to achieve the objectives identified within the goals domain.

REFERENCES: M. M. Baldwin, Ed., *Portraits of Complexity*, Columbus, Ohio: The Battelle Monograph Series, 1975, pp. 176-177.

PRECEDENCE DIAGRAM METHOD

RESULTS: Graphical representation of activities in a project; earliest start and finish times; latest start and finish times for all the activities of the project and completion time.

INPUTS: Activities and their durations.

PURPOSE/FUNCTION: To plan, schedule and control the work or project by employing the efforts of many separate organizations and persons; to evaluate alternative projects.

SPECIAL CHARACTERISTICS: Precedence diagramming is activity-oriented and focuses on showing lead and lag times. This method eliminates events which are of great importance in CPM, PERT, etc.

REFERENCES: H. Ahuja, *Construction Performance Control by Networks*, John Wiley and Sons, Inc., New York, 1976, pp. 65-78; P. J. Burman, *Precedence Networks for Project Planning and Control*, New York: McGraw-Hill book Company, 1972, pp. 29-118: also see reference for CPM.

PRIORITIZATION MATRIX

RESULTS: Prioritizes or ranks tasks, issues, and details based on one or more known weighted criteria.

INPUTS: Group participant's knowledge of the topics being prioritized or feeling biased.

PURPOSE/FUNCTION: Develop group consensus on prioritizing important decisions, tasks, issues or assignments from the individual participants diverse judgement.

SPECIAL CHARACTERISTICS: Use a known weighted criteria or nominal group technique as a weighting system.

REFERENCES: Saaty, T *Decision Making for Leaders* (RWS Publications, 1988), pp. 22-26.

PROBABILITY ASSESSMENT

RESULTS: A prediction of the best-alternative regarding its outcome possibilities.

INPUTS: An understanding of probability, Bayes' Theorem, alternatives, utility theory.

PURPOSE/FUNCTION: To evaluate alternatives and predict the chances of their occurrences.

REFERENCES: W. Mendenhall, R.L. Scheaffer and D.D. Wackerly, *Mathematical Statistics with Applications*, 3rd ed., PWS Publishers (Boston, MA, 1986).

PROCESS CHART

RESULTS: Geometric symbol representation of required operations and inspections, with estimates of setup and run times.

INPUTS: Drawings, quantities, material and equipment to be used.

PURPOSE/FUNCTION: To portray a plan for manufacturing a product. To analyze existing operations.

REFERENCES: B.W. Niebel, *Motion and Time Study*, 8th ed., Irwin (Homewood, IL, 1988); M.E. Mundel, *Motion and Time Study: Improving Productivity*, 6th ed., Prentice-Hall (Englewood Cliffs, NJ, 1985).

PROCESS DECISION PROGRAM CHART

RESULTS: Identifies feasible countermeasures in response to potential conflicts or problems.

INPUTS: Groups ideas or feelings about what can go wrong on a particular task.

PURPOSE/FUNCTION: Maps out conceivable events and contingencies that can occur with appropriate countermeasures.

SPECIAL CHARACTERISTICS: Can be presented in numerous fashions such as a tree diagram, matrix diagram, or outline form.

REFERENCES: Mizuno, S. *Management For Quality Improvement* (Productivity Press, 1988), pp 40-42; "Special Issue: Seven Management Tools for QC," *Reports of Statistical Application Research,* JUSE, Vol. 33, No. 2, 1986.

PRODUCT/SERVICE LIFE CYCLE ANALYSIS

RESULTS: The forecasted times in the life cycle of a product.

INPUTS: S-curves, phases of product acceptance by various groups, annual sales of similar products.

PURPOSE/FUNCTION: To analyze and forecast the growth of a new product.

SPECIAL CHARACTERISTICS: Poor accuracy, often done by computer.

REFERENCES: W.G. Ireson and C.F. Coombs, Eds., *Handbook of Reliability Engineering and Management*, McGraw-Hill (New York, 1988); J.L. Nevins and D.E. Whitney, Eds., *Concurrent Design of Products and Processes*, McGraw-Hill (New York, 1989); D. Brazier and M. Leonard, "Concurrent Engineering: Participating in Better Designs," *Mechanical Engineering,* January, 1990; J.W. Priest, *Engineering Design for Producability and Reliability,* Marcel Dekker (New York, 1988).

PROFIT/VOLUME (P/V) ANALYSIS (Economics)

RESULTS: P/V chart (weekly, monthly, etc.) describing the relationship of profit (or loss) at various sales levels, break-even point, and inventory margin of safety.

INPUTS: Each element of cost (fixed, variable, or mixed), past actual sales and profit (or loss).

PURPOSE/FUNCTION: To establish the relationship between costs and profits at various levels of volume, to evaluate alternative projects/investments.

SPECIAL CHARACTERISTICS: The relationship determines the break-even point, and the margin of safety due to changes in volume, fixed and variable costs, and product price.

REFERENCES: P.F. Ostwald, *Engineering Cost Estimating,* 3rd ed., Prentice-Hall (Englewood Cliffs, NJ, 1992); G.W. Smith, *Engineering Economy: Analysis of Capital Expenditures,* 4th ed., Iowa State University Press (Ames, 1987); J.A. White, M.H. Agee and K.E. Case, *Principles of Engineering Economic Analysis,* 3rd ed., Wiley (New York, 1989); H. Bierman and S. Smidt, *The Capital Budgeting Decision,* 7th ed., Macmillan (New York, 1988); J.R. Buck, *Economic Risk Decisions in Engineering and Management,* Iowa State University Press (Ames, IA, 1989); W.J. Fabrycky and B.S. Blanchard, *Life-Cycle Cost and Economic Analysis,* Prentice-Hall (Englewood Cliffs, NJ, 1991).

PROGRAM EVALUATION AND REVIEW TECHNIQUE (PERT)

RESULTS: Network of events with earliest most likely and latest start and finish times.

INPUTS: Project objectives and activities with their durations.

PURPOSE/FUNCTION: To determine the best sequence of activities and their schedules in a project. To determine the shortest time for project completion; to evaluate project performance.

SPECIAL CHARACTERISTICS: Activity duration estimates are probabilistic: optimistic, realistic, and pessimistic. These are weighted to obtain an "expected time" for an activity. Computer programs are available and necessary for large projects.

REFERENCES: S. Sakamoto, *Methods Design Concept: An Innovative Way of Productivity Improvement,* Japan Management Association (Tokyo, 1990); See "Critical Path Method" and "Network Analysis" for other references.

PROGRAM PLANNING METHOD (PPM)

RESULTS: A list of problems ordered in priority, specification of problem, and specification of possible programs to solve the problem.

INPUTS: Problem and target areas, and participation of users, experts, and decision makers.

PURPOSE/FUNCTION: To define the problem and identify and select the best alternatives.

SPECIAL CHARACTERISTICS: Requires a few weeks of time including preparation and three or more half days for sessions. Skill needed to direct the sessions as in Nominal Group Techniques.

REFERENCES: A. L. Delbecq, A. H. Van de Ven, and D. Gustafson, *Group Technique for Program Planning: A Guide to Nominal Group and Delphi Processes*, Greenbrier (Middletown WI, 1986).

PROGRESS FUNCTION

RESULTS: A graphic representation which predicts expected costs, times, etc.

INPUTS: Past performance records.

PURPOSE/FUNCTION: To identify expected levels of cost, production or time.

SPECIAL CHARACTERISTICS: See learning curves.

REFERENCES: G. Nadler, *Work Design: A Systems Concept*, Homewood, Illinois, 1970, pp. 229-30, 239-40, T.R. Gulledge.Jr. and B. Khoshnevis, "Production Rate, Learning and Program Costs: Survey and Bibliography," *Engineering Costs and Production Economics*, Vol 11, 1987, pp. 223-236; R. Nanada and G.L. Adler, *Learning Curves, Theory and Application,* American Institute of Industrial Engineers, Norcross, GA, 1977; J. Smith, *Learning Curve for Cost Control,* Kluwer Academic Publishers, Norwell, MA, 1989.

PROJECT TEAMS

RESULTS: A group of people, each of whom solves smaller concentrated problems while solving the larger encompassing problem.

INPUTS: Differently talented people, a leader-coordinator, and a complex problem.

PURPOSE/FUNCTION: To concentrate the abilities of different people on an involved, complicated project/problem.

REFERENCES: G. L. Lippitt, *Visualizing Change*, Fairfax, VA.: NTL-Learning Resources Corp., 1973; G. Zaltman and R. Duncan, *Strategies for Planned Change*, New York: John Wiley & Sons, 1977; W. G. Bennis, K. D. Benne, R. Chin, and F. Corey, (Eds.), *The Planning of Change*, Third Edition, New York: Holt, Rinehart and Winston, Inc., 1976; Allan Cox, "The power of team (teamwork in business)," *Chief Executive(u.s.)* No.5, page 52-56, March-April 1989.

PSYCHOLOGICAL SCALING

RESULTS: A comparison of attributes based on a scale.

INPUTS: Objects with attributes, measurement criteria and some scaling knowledge.

PURPOSE/FUNCTION: To compare attributes based on measurements of the attributes.

SPECIAL CHARACTERISTICS: Type of scale - see "Measurement."

REFERENCES: J. Kowalik, *Knowldege-Based Problem Solving*, Prentice-Hall (New York, 1986); D.A. Waterman, *Building Expert Systems*, Addison-Wesley (Reading, MA, 1983).

PURPOSE EXPANSION

RESULTS: A list of possible purposes of the system or problem area arranged in one or more individual or interrelated hierarchies, and specifically selected focus purpose level (s).

INPUTS: People or person familiar with the system or problem area, a facilitator (if a group), and interaction with decision makers and others who may be involved (e.g., client etc.).

PURPOSE/FUNCTION: To identify the purpose that ought to be achieved; serves as a focus in P&D efforts.

SPECIAL CHARACTERISTICS: Time dependent on complexity of the system. Helps to ascertain the "right" problem (or purposeful activity).

REFERENCES: G. Nadler, *The Planning and Design Approach*, The Center for Breakthrough Thinking, Inc. (Los Angeles, 1981); M. Norton, W. C. Bozeman, and G. Nadler, *Student Planned Acquisition of Required Knowledge*, Englewood Cliffs, N.J.: Educational Technology Publishers, 1980.

PURPOSE NETWORK ANALYSIS

RESULTS: The target purpose of the P&D effort is displayed in a network which shows the parallel purposes as well as the components and bigger level purposes.

INPUTS: The initial purpose list and hierarchies from the purpose expansion technique.

PURPOSE/FUNCTION: To determine possible relationships between the P&D effort and parallel systems with which it may interact.

SPECIAL CHARACTERISTICS: An interpretive structural model of original and additional purposes is developed, using the ends-means relationship.

REFERENCES: See the references for Couplet Comparison, Purpose Expansion, and Interpretive Structural Modeling.

QUALITY FUNCTION DEPLOYMENT (QFD)

RESULT: Achieve customer satisfaction through incorporation of his/her needs in the product developed.

INPUTS: "What" are the customer wants, customer attributes desired in the product being developed.

PURPOSE/FUNCTIONS: provides means for identifying and carrying the customers voice through each stage of product and service development and implementation.

REFERENCES: J. Moran, G. Hoffherr, et al., *Training and Facilitating in QFD*, 1991, GOAL QPC, Yoji Akao, *Quality Function Deployment: Integrating Customer Requirements Into Product Design*, Cambridge, Mass., Productivity Press, 199; John R. Hauser and Don Clausing, "The House of Quality," *Harvard Business Review*, No. 3, pp 63-73, May-June 1988.

QUESTIONNAIRE

RESULTS: The generation of opinions, facts, and/or ideas of others. Also determine other data collection sources available.

INPUTS: A list of open or closed questions to elicit ideas and opinions of a pre-identified set of participants.

PURPOSE/FUNCTION: To generate ideas, opinions, or facts from a large number of individuals.

SPECIAL CHARACTERISTICS: Takes several weeks. Needs a skilled questionnaire developer. Low rate of return.

REFERENCES: M.A. Campion, "Interdisciplinary Approaches to Job Design," *Journal of Applied Psychology*, Vol. 73, 1988, pp. 467-481; M.A. Campion and C.L. McClelland, "Interdisciplinary Examination of the Costs and Benefits of Enlarged Jobs: A Job Design Quasi-Experiment," *Journal of Applied Psychology*, Vol. 76, No. 2, 1991, pp. 186-198; J.R. Hackman and G.R. Oldham, *Work Redesign*, Addison-Wesley (Reading, MA, 1980); *Applied Ergonomics*, special issue on questionnaires, Vol. 6, No. 2, June 1975.

QUEUEING THEORY

RESULTS: Probability models which describe the waiting and servicing system.

INPUTS: Arrivals (a probability distribution), the queue, and service (often probabilistic), and the nature of the decisions which need to be made.

PURPOSE/FUNCTION: To study waiting lines to minimize time loss, unused labor, and excessive cost; to evaluate queueing systems.

SPECIAL CHARACTERISTICS: Only very simple systems can be modelled to provide any utility.

REFERENCES: R.W. Wolff, *Stochastic Modeling and the Theory of Queues*, Prentice-Hall (New Jersey, 1989); J. Walrand, *An Introduction to Queuing Network*, Prentice-Hall (New Jersey, 1988); S. Asmussen, *Applied Probability and Queuing*, Wiley (New York, 1987).

REGRESSION ANALYSIS

RESULTS: Regression equation (e.g., sales or dependent variable expressed in terms of "independent" variables, such as GNP, price, costs, advertising, etc.).

INPUTS: All the data regarding the process (independent and dependent variables, past history, etc.).

PURPOSE/FUNCTION: To identify the main features of hidden or implied relationships from masses of data for any given process.

SPECIAL CHARACTERISTICS: Based on least square technique; efficient computer programs are available. Single factor and multiple regression models are available.

REFERENCES: R.W. Farebrother, *Linear Least Squares Computations*, Marcel Dekker (New York, 1988); A.J. Dobson, *An Introduction to Statistical Modelling*, Chapman and Hall (New York, 1986); I. Guttman, *Linear Models: An Introduction*, Wiley (New York, 1982); J.R. Rice, *Matrix Computations and Mathematical Software*, McGraw-Hill (Tokyo, 1983).

REGRESSION FORECASTING

RESULTS: A regression equation which predicts a change in dependent variable as related to change in an independent variable.

INPUTS: Knowledge about the variables and 20-50 sets of data points.

PURPOSE/FUNCTION: To forecast a future condition based on the relationships of the variables.

SPECIAL CHARACTERISTICS: Time dependent upon the amount of data needed to be gathered. Past behavior must be expected to continue into the future.

REFERENCES: R.W. Farebrother, *Linear Least Squares Computations*, Marcel Dekker (New York, 1988); A.J. Dobson, *An Introduction to Statistical Modelling*, Chapman and Hall (New York, 1986); I. Guttman, *Linear Models: An Introduction*, Wiley (New York, 1982); J.R. Rice, *Matrix Computations and Mathematical Software*, McGraw-Hill (Tokyo, 1983).

REL CHART

RESULTS: Activity relationship diagram (half-matrix) indicating the closeness rating of each paired combination.

INPUTS: All the activities, departments, and areas (e.g., carton storage, unloading area, raw milk storage, filling machine, cooler, rest room truck loading area, laboratory, etc. in a dairy) and a closeness desirability rating given to each paired combination.

PURPOSE/FUNCTION: To aid in the optimal placement of the facilities. To evaluate the space requirements for the layout.

REFERENCES: J.A. Tompkins, "20 Strategies for Successful Warehousing, Parts 1-4," *Material Handling Engineering*, March-June, 1989; J.A. Tompkins and R. Reed Jr., *Facilities Planning*, Wiley (New York, 1982).

RELIABILITY THEORY

RESULTS: The probability that a system will perform the intended functions in the predetermined environment for a predetermined time interval.

INPUTS: Independent but comparable performance measures, a measurement methodology, and objects, traits or constructs to be measured.

PURPOSE/FUNCTION: To have a system or solution provide similar results.

SPECIAL CHARACTERISTICS: Similar results are obtained by redundant components in a system, or measures are deemed reliable when independent but comparable assessments of the same object, trait, or construct are obtained.

REFERENCES: W.G. Ireson and C.F. Coombs, Eds., *Handbook of Reliability Engineering and Management*, McGraw-Hill (New York, 1988); H.A. Rothhart, Ed., *Mechanical Design and Systems Handbook*, McGraw-Hill (New York, 1984).

REPLACEMENT MODEL (Economics)

RESULTS: A set of decision rules (usually optimal) for the replacement of facilities that wear out, deteriorate, or fail over a period of time.

INPUTS: State of the equipment (operationality, likelihood of breakdown); costs of replacement and maintenance; dollar contribution (depreciation) to annual charges of the original price of the equipment.

PURPOSE/FUNCTION: To determine the optimal replacement policy, to evaluate alternative systems.

SPECIAL CHARACTERISTICS: This model constitutes a two-action Markov Decision Model in which action 1 is to replace and action 2 is not to replace. The assumptions are that the maintenance cost is an increasing function of the state; and the probability of a transition into any block of states is an increasing function of the present state.

REFERENCES: P.F. Ostwald, *Engineering Cost Estimating*, 3rd ed., Prentice-Hall (Englewood Cliffs, NJ, 1992); G.W. Smith, *Engineering Economy: Analysis of Capital Expenditures*, 4th ed., Iowa State University Press (Ames, 1987); J.A. White, M.H. Agee and K.E. Case, *Principles of Engineering Economic Analysis*, 3rd ed., Wiley (New York, 1989); H. Bierman and S. Smidt, *The Capital Budgeting Decision*, 7th ed., Macmillan (New York, 1988); J.R. Buck, *Economic Risk Decisions in Engineering and Management*, Iowa State University Press (Ames, IA, 1989); W.J. Fabrycky and B.S. Blanchard, *Life-Cycle Cost and Economic Analysis*, Prentice-Hall (Englewood Cliffs, NJ, 1991).

RESOURCE ALLOCATION AND MULTIPROJECT SCHEDULING (RAMPS)

RESULTS: Schedule of the activities of a multiproject organization.

INPUTS: Projects, their due-dates and sequence of the activities (e.g., CPM or PERT results can be used here), and resources.

PURPOSE/FUNCTION: To schedule activities for the several operating facilities of a multiproject organization in order to minimize due-date slippage.

SPECIAL CHARACTERISTICS: A heuristic system based on juggling slack activities. Computers often used.

REFERENCES: G. E. Whitehouse, *Systems Analysis and Design Using Network Techniques*, Prentice-Hall, Inc., Englewood Cliffs, N.J., 1973, pp. 97.

RETURN ON INVESTMENT (ROI) (Economics)

RESULTS: Average annual rate of return, (rank-ordering) of alternatives on the basis of the return expected from each; comparative net yearly cash flow chart including capital costs for all projects.

INPUTS: Life of the project, initial investment, average annual depreciation, net savings (cash flow, profit, taxes, etc.).

PURPOSE/FUNCTION: To evaluate alternative solutions.

SPECIAL CHARACTERISTICS: May fail to consider timing of capital outlays and benefits.

REFERENCES: J. R. Canada and J. A. White, Jr., *Capital Investment Decision Analysis for Management and Engineering*, Englewood Cliffs, N.J.: Prentice-Hall, Inc., 1980; P.F. Ostwald, *Engineering Cost Estimating*, 3rd ed., Prentice-Hall (Englewood Cliffs, NJ, 1992); G.W. Smith, *Engineering Economy: Analysis of Capital Expenditures*, 4th ed., Iowa State University Press (Ames, 1987); J.A. White, M.H. Agee and K.E. Case, *Principles of Engineering Economic Analysis*, 3rd ed., Wiley (New York, 1989); H. Bierman and S. Smidt, *The Capital Budgeting Decision*, 7th ed., Macmillan (New York, 1988); J.R. Buck, *Economic Risk Decisions in Engineering and Management*, Iowa State University Press (Ames, IA, 1989); W.J. Fabrycky and B.S. Blanchard, *Life-Cycle Cost and Economic Analysis*, Prentice-Hall (Englewood Cliffs, NJ, 1991).

RISK ANALYSIS (Economics)

RESULTS: (1) A calculation or judgment regarding the degree of uncertainty about future returns, as well as the likelihood of each value within a range of possible returns. (2) Assessment of probability of failure or possible harm to humans if technical system or product fails in some way.

INPUTS: Probabilities and consequences to possible courses of action.

PURPOSE/FUNCTION: To identify factors of risks; to provide a consistent means by which the various project outcomes and risks can be compared, especially in (1) for screening new product proposals.

SPECIAL CHARACTERISTICS: Primary elements are (1) technical uncertainty and cost schedule variability and (2) technological risks, societal risks, and conflict costs. Also see "multiple attribute utility assessment," "failure analysis," and "reliability theory."

REFERENCES: W.K. Viscusi, *Journal of Risk and Uncertainty*, Kluwer Academic Publishers (Norwell, MA, 1991); P.F. Ostwald, *Engineering Cost Estimating*, 3rd ed., Prentice-Hall (Englewood Cliffs, NJ, 1992); G.W. Smith, *Engineering Economy: Analysis of Capital Expenditures*, 4th ed., Iowa State University Press (Ames, 1987); J.A. White, M.H. Agee and K.E. Case, *Principles of Engineering Economic Analysis*, 3rd ed., Wiley (New York, 1989); H. Bierman and S. Smidt, *The Capital Budgeting Decision*, 7th ed., Macmillan (New York, 1988); J.R. Buck, *Economic Risk Decisions in Engineering and Management*, Iowa State University Press (Ames, IA, 1989); W.J. Fabrycky and B.S. Blanchard, *Life-Cycle Cost and Economic Analysis*, Prentice-Hall (Englewood Cliffs, NJ, 1991).

ROLE PLAYING

RESULTS: An activity out of an outcome or scenario prior to its occurrence.

INPUTS: A scenario similar to the one under study, group of concerned individuals willing to communicate with one another, extensive cooperation and background information.

PURPOSE/FUNCTION: To explore social preferences, to simulate a future event as a means of detecting areas of possible improvement.

SPECIAL CHARACTERISTICS: Information and "feelings" sometimes difficult to extrapolate to real situations.

REFERENCES: A. F. Klein, *Role Playing in Leadership Training and Group Problem-Solving*, New York: Association Press, 1956; F. W. Horton, Jr., *Reference Guide to Advanced Management Methods*, American Management Association, Inc., 1972.

RUN CHART

RESULTS: A graphic display of data used to assess the stability of a system over time.

INPUTS: Measurement parameters of a system.

PURPOSE/FUNCTION: Analysis of how a parameter of a system or process is behaving over time. This tool highlights trends, shifts, and possible cycles.

SPECIAL CHARACTERISTICS: Similar to Control Chart. Information generated from questionnaire studies and interviews might also be used.

REFERENCES: J. Moran, R. Talbot, and R. Benson, *A Guide to Graphical Problem Solving Processes* (Quality Press, 1990) pp. 16.

SAMPLING THEORY

RESULTS: A statistical estimate (mean, variance, significance of difference) of population parameters.

INPUTS: Small portion of what is being estimated, knowledge of statistics.

PURPOSE/FUNCTION: To estimate population parameters based on data from samples.

REFERENCES: J.M. Juran and F.M. Gryna Jr., *Quality Planning and Analysis*, 2nd ed., McGraw-Hill (New York, 1980); A.V. Feingenbaum, *Total Quality Control -- Engineering and Management*, 3rd ed., McGraw-Hill (New York, 1983); D.C. Montgomery, *Introduction to Statistical Quality Control*, 2nd ed., Wiley (New York, 1991).

SCALING, SUBJECTIVE

RESULTS: A ranking or rating representation of subject.

INPUTS: Individual knowledge of qualitative or nonmetric character.

PURPOSE/FUNCTION: To extract maximum amount of measures information from a given collection of judgments.

REFERENCES: See references for measurements.

SCENARIO WRITING

RESULTS: A narrative description predicting the future states of a system.

INPUTS: Analyst, decision maker, major dimensions and attributes of the present system, and goals.

PURPOSE/FUNCTION: To describe a future condition; to detail how a system is envisioned to operate.

SPECIAL CHARACTERISTICS: Useful for policy making (e.g., urban and regional planning, international political systems).

REFERENCES: E. Bardach, *The Implementation Game,* Cambridge, Mass.: The MIT Press, 1977, Chapter 10; J. Durand, "A New Method for Constructing Scenarios," *Futures,* December, 1972, pp. 235–330; F. Mobasheri, L.H. Orren, and F.P. Shioshansi, "Scenario Planning at Southern California Edison," *Interfaces,* Vol. 19, No. 5, September 1989, pp. 31–44.

SCHEDULING MODEL

RESULTS: The assignment of time values (start and completion dates) for carrying out the various operations in an orderly and synchronized manner. Usually in chart form.

INPUTS: Approximation of operation times, sequence of and interactions among operations.

PURPOSE/FUNCTION: To determine an operations plan. A forecast model, to predict and thus avoid shortages and minimize waste of time.

REFERENCES: K.R. Baker, *Introduction to Sequencing and Scheduling,* Wiley (Nnew York, 1984); M.A.H. Dempster, J.K. Lenstra and A.H.G. Rinnooy Kan, Eds., *Deterministic and Stochastic Scheduling,* Reidel (Dordrecht, The Netherlands, 1982).

SENSITIVITY ANALYSIS (Economics)

RESULTS: The change in a dependent variable resulting from a certain amount of change in one or more independent variables.

INPUTS: Possible changes in the model and/or criterion function, the parameters, or submodels.

PURPOSE/FUNCTION: To detect significant changes that may occur in the dependent variables from even small changes in independent variable(s). To identify the "sensitive" variables.

REFERENCES: F.S. Hillier and G.J. Lieberman, *Introduction to Operations Research,* 5th ed., McGraw-Hill, New York, 1990; A. Ravindran, D.T. Phillips and J.J. Solberg, *Operations Research: Principles and Practice,* second edition, Wiley, New York, 1987; R. Fletcher, *Practical Methods of Optimization,* 2nd ed., Wiley, New York, 1988; J.G. Ecker and M. Kupferschmid, *Introduction to Operations Research,* Wiley, New York, 1988; M. Minoux, *Mathematical Programming, Theory and Algorithms,* Wiley, New York, 1986.

SIMULATION MODEL

RESULTS: Forecast of a system's behavior under various assumptions; a better understanding of the system and its behavior.

INPUTS: Specifically stated purpose, necessary data gathered or estimated under defined variables and parameters.

PURPOSE/FUNCTION: To estimate the essence of a system that may operate in the future; to provide information to the detailing and decision-making processes.

SPECIAL CHARACTERISTICS: Usually computerized; many types of program languages (e.g., GASP, SIMSCRIPT, etc.). A simulation is an experiment.

REFERENCES: A. M. Law and W. D. Kelton, *Simulation Modeling and Analysis*, New York: McGraw-Hill Book Co., 1982; B.P. Ziegler, *Object Oriented Simulation with Hierarchical, Modular Models*, Academic Press (New York, 1990); H. Linhart and W. Zucchini, *Model Selection*, Wiley (New York, 1986); Also look for the journal *Simulation*.

SMOOTHING

RESULTS: Estimates of the present numerical values of the various coefficients and parameters that appear in the model or equation.

INPUTS: Set of data and a reasonable model to represent the phenomenon.

PURPOSE/FUNCTION: To develop a model that should fit current and very recent data very well; prepare short-term forecasts for a number of different items.

SPECIAL CHARACTERISTICS: Smoothing is a process similar to curve fitting, with two differences: (1) The model should fit current data very well, but data obtained a long time ago need not fit so well, (2) The computations are repeated with each new observation. Smoothing is essentially iterative, so computational procedures should be fast and simple. Three (or six or twelve, etc.) month moving averages is one illustration.

REFERENCES: R.W. Farebrother, *Linear Least Squares Computations*, Marcel Dekker (New York, 1988); A.J. Dobson, *An Introduction to Statistical Modelling*, Chapman and Hall (New York, 1986); I. Guttman, *Linear Models: An Introduction*, Wiley (New York, 1982); J.R. Rice, *Matrix Computations and Mathematical Software*, McGraw-Hill (Tokyo, 1983).

SOCIAL COST-BENEFIT ANALYSIS (SCBA) (Economics)

RESULTS: Comparison or rank-ordering of alternatives to aid in decision making.

INPUTS: Objectives; alternative means; cost data to determine the cost of each alternative; gains and losses of every member of society whose well-being would be affected by the projects or plans if implemented.

PURPOSE/FUNCTION: To evaluate the alternatives within single public sectors, such as transport, health, water supply, land use, or education; to rank order various projects competing for limited investment funds.

SPECIAL CHARACTERISTICS: Cost-effectiveness and cost-minimization are applications of SCBA in special circumstances. Cost-effectiveness seeks the best way of using a fixed budget allocation. Cost-minimization seeks the least cost way of undertaking a particular project, where the same benefits are assumed to result in each case.

REFERENCES: P.F. Ostwald, *Engineering Cost Estimating*, 3rd ed., Prentice-Hall (Englewood Cliffs, NJ, 1992); G.W. Smith, *Engineering Economy: Analysis of Capital Expenditures*, 4th ed., Iowa State University Press (Ames, 1987); J.A. White, M.H. Agee and K.E. Case, *Principles of Engineering Economic Analysis*, 3rd ed., Wiley (New York, 1989); H. Bierman and S. Smidt, *The Capital Budgeting Decision*, 7th ed., Macmillan (New York, 1988); J.R. Buck, *Economic Risk Decisions in Engineering and Management*, Iowa State University Press (Ames, IA, 1989); W.J. Fabrycky and B.S. Blanchard, *Life-Cycle Cost and Economic Analysis*, Prentice-Hall (Englewood Cliffs, NJ, 1991).

STANDARD DATA CHARTS, TABLES, & EQUATIONS

RESULTS: Established allowed times of a task, can be in different forms.

INPUTS: Reference material, time studies, past performances.

PURPOSE/FUNCTION: To determine allowed times on individual operations in advance of performance.

SPECIAL CHARACTERISTICS: Models: Elemental Standard data; predetermined motion time systems, etc. Most are now computerized.

REFERENCES: G. Nadler, *Work Design: A Systems Theory*, Homewood, Illinois: Richard D. Irwin, Inc., 1970, pp. 403, 437, 430.

STANDARD OPERATING PROCEDURES

RESULTS: Written manuals which tell employees at all levels the policies of the organization and described conditions.

INPUTS: Desired result(s), policies, practices to be followed, some historical data about similar problems.

PURPOSE/FUNCTION: To provide a reference for methods of problem solving in operating and supervising.

REFERENCES: B.W. Niebel, *Motion and Time Study,* Irwin (Homewood, IL, 1988); Y. Monden, *Toyota Production System,* Industrial Engineering and Management Press (Norcross, GA, 1983).

STATISTICAL MODEL

RESULTS: Mathematical relationship of the form (P) = f (x). A characteristic or measure representation of a sample.

INPUTS: Data, scale of measurement, underlying assumptions, and statistical knowledge.

PURPOSE/FUNCTION: To represent a sample based on the assembling, classification and tabulation of numerical facts; to analyze collected data; to establish relationship among variables.

SPECIAL CHARACTERISTICS: Some of these models are regression analysis, multi-variable analysis, curve fitting, distribution analysis, hypothesis testing, statistical inference, information theory, etc.

REFERENCES: R.W. Farebrother, *Linear Least Squares Computations,* Marcel Dekker (New York, 1988); A.J. Dobson, *An Introduction to Statistical Modelling,* Chapman and Hall (New York, 1986); I. Guttman, *Linear Models: An Introduction,* Wiley (New York, 1982); J.R. Rice, *Matrix Computations and Mathematical Software,* McGraw-Hill (Tokyo, 1983).

SUBJECTIVE PROBABILITY ASSESSMENT

RESULTS: A probability distribution or a probability density function.

INPUTS: A set of events and probability techniques or expert judgments.

PURPOSE/FUNCTION: To quantify the chance of events occurring. To evaluate alternative options, plans, policies, etc.

SPECIAL CHARACTERISTICS: Needs an analyst skilled to interview the assessor who has a basic understanding of probabilities. One's utilities can be calculated after assessing probabilities.

REFERENCES: W. Mendenhall, R.L. Scheaffer and D.D. Wackerly, *Mathematical Statistics with Applications,* 3rd ed., PWS Publishers (Boston, MA, 1986).

SYNECTICS

RESULTS: A number of possible solutions and the restatement of the problem.

INPUTS: A problem statement and 8-12 participants concerned with the problem.

PURPOSE/FUNCTION: An interacting group process for the generation of creative ideas in response to a problem.

SPECIAL CHARACTERISTICS: Seeks creative ideas through a process of analogies.

REFERENCES: G. Nadler, *The Planning and Design Approach,* The Center for Breakthrough Thinking, Inc. (Los Angeles, 1981).

SYSTEM MATRIX

RESULTS: The components of a system identified in terms of six dimensions for eight elements.

INPUTS: Part of a P&D group, familiarity with the system.

PURPOSE/FUNCTION: To identify and detail the components of a system or solution.

SPECIAL CHARACTERISTICS: Can be used with all other techniques by treating each of them as a system.

REFERENCES: G. Nadler, *The Planning and Design Approach,* The Center for Breakthrough Thinking, Inc. (Los Angeles, 1981).

SYSTEM PYRAMID

RESULTS: A representation of a system and its components in the form of a pyramid; interrelationships also shown.

INPUTS: A system, organizational unit, element or item of interest, a group of related and involved people.

PURPOSE/FUNCTION: To identify functional components of a purpose; to organize information into factors which contribute to it.

SPECIAL CHARACTERISTICS: Can be computerized. Can be used as a decision tree. Also see objective tree.

REFERENCES: G. Nadler, *Work Design: A System Theory,* Homewood, Illinois: Richard D. Irwin, Inc., 1970, pp. 200-204.

TAGUCHI METHODS

RESULTS: Production and design solutions such that their variation with respect to the desired quality is as small as possible.

INPUTS:

PURPOSE/FUNCTION: To minimize the loss a product causes to society after being shipped.

REFERENCES: G. Taguchi, *Introduction to Quality Engineering - Designing Quality into Products and Processes,* UNIPUB/Quality Resources (New York, 1986); G. Taguchi, *Introduction to Quality Engineering,* Asian Productivity Press (Tokyo, 1986); G. Taguchi and D. Clausing, "Robust Quality," *Harvard Business Review,* Vol. 68, No. 1, 1990, pp. 65-75.

TASK ANALYSIS

RESULTS: Task analysis worksheets, information summarization sheets, scoreable verification checklists.

INPUTS: Task elements, human factors involved in the performance.

PURPOSE/FUNCTION: To standardize work methods; to make work less difficult, less hazardous, and more comfortable; to design equipment compatible with human usage; to establish personnel selection requirements and training procedures.

REFERENCES: G. Salvendy, Ed., *Handbook of Human Factos,* Wiley (New York, 1987); L.E. Davis and J.C. Taylor, Eds., *Design of Jobs,* 2nd ed., Wiley (New York, 1979); M.S. Sanders and E.J. McCormick, *Human Factors in Engineering and Design,* 6th ed., McGraw-Hill (New York, 1987); B.W. Niebel, *Motion and Time Study,* 8th ed., Irwin (Homewood, IL, 1988).

TASK FORCE

RESULTS: An assemblage of people, assigned a charge by the organization or community that created it, which meets to accomplish the desired or better result.

INPUTS: A specific time period, a clearly-defined task, a specific group of people, many different techniques.

PURPOSE/FUNCTION: To engage in the planning process, sometimes analysis or "find causes" process.

SPECIAL CHARACTERISTICS: Small group of members (8-20), weak accountability to the general public.

REFERENCES: M. Michael Markowich, "Using task forces to increase efficiency and reduce stress" *Personnel,* vol.64, No. 8, page 34-39, August 1987; William J. Altier, "Task forces- an effective management tool," *Sloan Management Review,* vol.27, No. 3, page 69-77, Spring 1986.

TEAM BUILDING

RESULTS: Cohesiveness of individuals in a group in working toward an end.

INPUTS: Each member's feelings, attitudes, and perceptions of the team's effectiveness.

PURPOSE/FUNCTION: To help the members of a group to willingly cooperate for the common good (mutually acceptable work goals); to surface member's feelings and attitudes.

SPECIAL CHARACTERISTICS: Many different techniques to team building require a skilled process observer to increase the effectiveness of the group's task and maintenance roles.

REFERENCES: Donald E. Carter and Barbara S. Baker, *Concurrent Engineering: the product development environment for the 1990s,* Reading, Mass., Addison-Wesley, 1992.

TECHNOLOGICAL ASSESSMENT

RESULTS: Policy options based on the assessment of new technological developments.

INPUTS: Several (up to twelve) individuals and new technology.

PURPOSE/FUNCTION: To anticipate the likely consequences of developing technologies and to formulate policy options.

SPECIAL CHARACTERISTICS: ISM (Interpretive Structural Modeling) may be used.

REFERENCES: T. Forester, Ed., *The Information Technology Revolution,* M.I.T. Press (Cambridge, MA, 1980); S. Zuboff, *In the Age of the Smart Machine: The Future of Work and Power,* Basic Books (New York, 1988); S.S. Roach, *America's Technology Dilemma: A Profile of the Information Economy,* Morgan Stanley Special Economy Study (New York, 1987).

TECHNOLOGICAL FORECASTING

RESULTS: Estimates of the likelihood of radical technological developments, predictions of what the developments mean.

INPUTS: Strong research efforts and policies, periodic evaluation of technological successes and failures of competition, human judgment, knowledge (equivalent of a system matrix) of the technological field under study, and an understanding of its economic, social, and political implications.

PURPOSE/FUNCTION: To take into account technological changes in P&D efforts.

REFERENCES: T. Forester, Ed., *The Information Technology Revolution,* M.I.T. Press (Cambridge, MA, 1980); S. Zuboff, *In the Age of the Smart Machine: The Future of Work and Power,* Basic Books (New York, 1988); S.S. Roach, *America's Technology Dilemma: A Profile of the Information Economy,* Morgan Stanley Special Economy Study (New York, 1987).

TIME SERIES ANALYSIS

RESULTS: Set of chronologically ordered points of raw data (sales, inventory, theatre attendance, etc.) identified and explained on a time optimal curve and mathematical model.

INPUTS: Several years of data for a product or product line and clear and relatively stable relationships and trends.

PURPOSE/FUNCTION: To forecast based on past performance. To analyze past data.

SPECIAL CHARACTERISTICS: Can be in graph form with demands or volumes plotted on the ordinate against time intervals on the abscissa; could be moving averages where each point is the weighted average of a number of consecutive data points.

REFERENCES: B.L. Bowerman and R.T. O'Connell, *Time Series Forecasting,* Duxbury Press (Boston, 1987); M.B. Priestly, *Spectral Analysis and Time Series,* Academic Press (New York, 1982); H. Levenbach and J.P. Cleary, *The Modern Forecaster,* Van Nostrand Reinhold (New York, 1984); S. Makridakis and S.C. Wheelwright, Eds., *The Handbook of Forecasting: A Manager's Guide,* 2nd Ed., Wiley (New York, 1987).

TIME STUDY

RESULTS: The amount of time required to perform a task.

INPUTS: Breakdown of movements to perform a task, stop watch or timing device, an experienced rater of operator performance and allowances.

PURPOSE/FUNCTION: To determine the amount of time required to perform a task. To determine a fair day's work.

REFERENCES: B.W. Niebel, *Motion and Time Study,* 8th ed., Irwin (Homewood, IL, 1988); G. Nadler, *Work Design: A System Concept* (Homewood Illinois, 1970); G.E. Whitehouse, *Work Measurement IIE Microsoftware,* Industrial Engineering and Management Press (Atlanta, 1985).

TREE DIAGRAMS

RESULTS: A diagram in tree shape which identifies the relationships of the variables being portrayed.

INPUTS: Factor to be subdivided into branches.

PURPOSE/FUNCTION: To describe and interrelate the system structure.

SPECIAL CHARACTERISTICS: A brief process. Group can do effectively. Also see system pyramid, objective trees, and decision tree.

REFERENCES: "Special Issue: Seven Management Tools for QC," *Reports of Statistical Application Research,* JUSE, Vol. 33, No. 2, 1986; J.M. Juran and F.M. Gryna, *Quality Planning and Analysis,* 2nd ed., McGraw-Hill (New York, 1980).

TREND ANALYSIS

RESULTS: A trend extrapolation which seeks to forecast the future.

INPUTS: Time-series data, knowledge of regression analysis, selected technological parameter.

PURPOSE/FUNCTION: To make technological forecasts, new product forecasts (particularly intermediate and long-term).

REFERENCES: H. Levenbach and J.P. Cleary, *The Modern Forecaster,* Van Nostrand Reinhold, New York, 1984; S. Makridakis and S.C. Wheelwright, Eds., *The Handbook of Forecasting: A Manager's Guide,* 2nd ed., Wiley, New York, 1987; T.L. Saaty and L.G. Vargas, *Prediction, Projection and Forecasting,* Kluwer Academic Publishers, Norwell, MA, 1990.

UTILITY ASSESSMENT (CURVES) (Economics)

RESULTS: A curve from which normative statements and positive predications can be made concerning the choice an individual would make from different alternatives.

INPUTS: Measures of utility, data, and a model structure.

PURPOSE/FUNCTION: To define the value of a set of goods in terms of their quantity or of the attributes, to rank order alternatives (options, policies, plans, etc.).

SPECIAL CHARACTERISTICS: Three methods: direct estimation, certainty equivalent, and standard gamble.

REFERENCES: P.F. Ostwald, *Engineering Cost Estimating,* 3rd ed., Prentice-Hall (Englewood Cliffs, NJ, 1992); G.W. Smith, *Engineering Economy: Analysis of Capital Expenditures,* 4th ed., Iowa State University Press (Ames, 1987); J.A. White, M.H. Agee and K.E. Case, *Principles of Engineering Economic Analysis,* 3rd ed., Wiley (New York, 1989); H. Bierman and S. Smidt, *The Capital Budgeting Decision,* 7th ed., Macmillan (New York, 1988); J.R. Buck, *Economic Risk Decisions in Engineering and Management,* Iowa State University Press (Ames, IA, 1989); W.J. Fabrycky and B.S. Blanchard, *Life-Cycle Cost and Economic Analysis,* Prentice-Hall (Englewood Cliffs, NJ, 1991).

UTILITY THEORY (Economics)

RESULTS: An equation or relationship or factors which will maximize the probability of selecting an alternative to a certain level of utility or "goodness."

INPUTS: A structure (objective function) - inputs vary with the classification of the theory.

PURPOSE/FUNCTION: To evaluate how outcomes and alternatives are or should be made.

SPECIAL CHARACTERISTICS: Can be classified as (a) normative or descriptive, (b) cardinal or ordinal, or (c) probabilistic or nonprobabilistic. Also used in policy capturing.

REFERENCES: P.F. Ostwald, *Engineering Cost Estimating,* 3rd ed., Prentice-Hall (Englewood Cliffs, NJ, 1992); G.W. Smith, *Engineering Economy: Analysis of Capital Expenditures,* 4th ed., Iowa State

University Press (Ames, 1987); J.A. White, M.H. Agee and K.E. Case, *Principles of Engineering Economic Analysis*, 3rd ed., Wiley (New York, 1989); H. Bierman and S. Smidt, *The Capital Budgeting Decision*, 7th ed., Macmillan (New York, 1988); J.R. Buck, *Economic Risk Decisions in Engineering and Management*, Iowa State University Press (Ames, IA, 1989); W.J. Fabrycky and B.S. Blanchard, *Life-Cycle Cost and Economic Analysis*, Prentice-Hall (Englewood Cliffs, NJ, 1991).

VALUE ANALYSIS (Economics)

RESULTS: A ranking of alternatives based on value as translated to monetary worth for a function to be achieved.

INPUTS: Interest groups, list of alternatives and proposals.

PURPOSE/FUNCTION: To evaluate which alternatives have the most value; to identify unnecessary costs; to substitute different materials and methods to obtain equal value (or performance) at lower cost.

SPECIAL CHARACTERISTICS: Often presented as an approach to problem solving (see Chapter 5).

REFERENCES: P.F. Ostwald, *Engineering Cost Estimating*, 3rd ed., Prentice-Hall (Englewood Cliffs, NJ, 1992); G.W. Smith, *Engineering Economy: Analysis of Capital Expenditures*, 4th ed., Iowa State University Press (Ames, 1987); J.A. White, M.H. Agee and K.E. Case, *Principles of Engineering Economic Analysis*, 3rd ed., Wiley (New York, 1989); H. Bierman and S. Smidt, *The Capital Budgeting Decision*, 7th ed., Macmillan (New York, 1988); J.R. Buck, *Economic Risk Decisions in Engineering and Management*, Iowa State University Press (Ames, IA, 1989); W.J. Fabrycky and B.S. Blanchard, *Life-Cycle Cost and Economic Analysis*, Prentice-Hall (Englewood Cliffs, NJ, 1991).

VARIANCE ANALYSIS

RESULTS: An explanation and interpretation of the difference (positive or negative) that did occur from the original estimate of the factor involved.

INPUTS: Sample of data, performance records, minimal limits of variation which do not need explanation.

PURPOSE/FUNCTION: To measure the dispersion from the mean, and estimate conditional expectations.

SPECIAL CHARACTERISTICS: Used primarily in explaining performance differences from budgets on a monthly or quarterly basis.

REFERENCES: J.L. Devore, *Probability and Statistics for Engineering and the Sciences*, 2nd ed., Brooks/Cole (Monterey, CA, 1987); E.R. Dougherty, *Probability and Statistics for the Engineering, Computing, and Physical Sciences*, Prentice-Hall (Englewood Cliffs, NJ, 1990).

WE AGREE TECHNIQUE

RESULTS: A group of people meeting for the first time have a list of factors, items, concepts, assumptions, etc. on which they *all* agree.

INPUTS: Topic or need which brings the people together, whether voluntarily or by assignment. Different perspectives about the topic(s).

PURPOSE/FUNCTION: To develop guidelines for group operation; to enable the group to have effective meetings; to build a team concept.

SPECIAL CHARACTERISTICS: People meeting around a table each propose "we agree that..." statements. Discussion modifies each statement as made until all agree or statement crossed off the list.

REFERENCES: J. R. Kinghorn and B. Benham, *The We Agree Workshop*, Dayton, Ohio: Institute for Development of Educational Activities, Inc., 1973; J. C. Thomson and K. M. Koritzinsky, *Guidelines for Facilitating Change in Secondary Schools*, Madison, Wisconsin: Wisconsin Research and Development Center for Cognitive Learning, 1025 W. Johnson St., Jan. 1976.

WORK MEASUREMENT

RESULTS: The establishment of the time for a qualified worker to carry out a specific job at a defined level of performance.

INPUTS: A given task and/or operation, an operator with the necessary skill and sufficient training.

PURPOSE/FUNCTION: To determine the time an operation or element of operation should take.

REFERENCES: B.W. Niebel, *Motion and Time Study*, 8th ed., Irwin (Homewood, IL, 1988) G. Nadler, *Work Design: A System Concept*, (Homewood, Illinois, 1970); G.E. Whitehouse, *Work Measurement IIE Microsoftware*, Industrial Engineering and Management Press (Atlanta, 1985); also see "standard data charts, tables and equations," "time study," "activity sampling (work sampling.)"

WORKSHOPS

RESULTS: An understanding of an issue or idea's role, nature and/or importance.

INPUTS: Structured working sessions, interested participants, an issue or idea.

PURPOSE/FUNCTION: To inform and involve interested participants.

REFERENCES: J. B. Rosener, "A Cafeteria of Techniques and Critiques," *Public Management* (December, 1975), pp. 16-19.

ZERO-BASE BUDGETING (ZBB) (Economics)

RESULTS: Decision packages each justifying its existence from the beginning (zero budget in previous years). Each package includes a description of actions, achievement from actions, consequences of not approving package, quantitative package measures, resources required, alternatives, source of funds, etc.

INPUTS: Entire budget request in detail (e.g., cost-benefit analysis, resources, projections, etc.).

PURPOSE/FUNCTION: To develop a budget procedure for effectively allocating limited resources; to effectively evaluate the decision packages and rankings to establish a funding level.

SPECIAL CHARACTERISTICS: Computers needed in large organization involving thousands of decision packages. Taps a large reservoir of program knowledge and analytic resources: the operating managers.

RELATED STRATEGY STEPS IN CHAPTER 12: Steps 1b, 3f, 4d, 5d.

REFERENCES: P.F. Ostwald, *Engineering Cost Estimating*, 3rd ed., Prentice-Hall (Englewood Cliffs, NJ, 1992); G.W. Smith, *Engineering Economy: Analysis of Capital Expenditures*, 4th ed., Iowa State University Press (Ames, 1987); J.A. White, M.H. Agee and K.E. Case, *Principles of Engineering Economic Analysis*, 3rd ed., Wiley (New York, 1989); H. Bierman and S. Smidt, *The Capital Budgeting Decision*, 7th ed., Macmillan (New York, 1988); J.R. Buck, *Economic Risk Decisions in Engineering and Management*, Iowa State University Press (Ames, IA, 1989); W.J. Fabrycky and B.S. Blanchard, *Life-Cycle Cost and Economic Analysis*, Prentice-Hall (Englewood Cliffs, NJ)

CROSS-REFERENCE INDEX OF TECHNIQUES, MODELS, AND TOOLS BY PURPOSES/FUNCTIONS TO BE ACHIEVED IN A PROJECT

Analyze Alternative Options/Plans/Policies/
Programs/Contingencies/Functions

> Contingency analysis
> Contingency tables
> Function analysis diagram
> Gaming
> Goals-achievement analysis
> Implementation, planning, and control technique (IMPACT)
> Judgment analysis technique
> Judgment policy analysis
> Mathematical model
> Mathematical programming technique
> Multiattribute utility (MAU) models
> Nominal group technique
> Planning council
> Planning, programming, and budgeting system (PPBS)
> Queuing theory
> Utility assessment
> Value analysis
> Voting technique
> Zero-base budgeting (ZBB)
>> *Also see*   Appraise/assess alternative options/plans/policies/ programs/contingencies/ functions

Analysis Investments
> Break-even analysis
> Mathematical model
> Operations research
> Optimization
> Proforma cash flow analysis
> Risk analysis
>> *Also see*   Appraise/assess investments

Analyze Job Methods and Motions
> Control charts
> Critical incident technique
> Job evaluation
> Maintenance chart
> Operations chart
> Process chart
> Productivity circles
> Relationship (Rel) chart
> Simultaneous motion (Simo) chart

> Task analysis
> Task timeline
> Time study
> Training
> Work measurement

Analyze Policy Setting and Decision-Making Variables
> *See*   Analyze investments
> Analyze projects
> Analyze systems
> Appraise/assess investments
> Appraise/assess projects
> Appraise/assess systems

Analyze Product Quality
> *See*   Identify (Product) opportunities

Analyze Projects
> ABC analysis (Pareto model)
> Critical path method
> Feasibility studies
> Gantt chart
> Map of activity and thought chains (MATCH)
> Management operations systems technique (MOST)
> Mathematical model
> Milestone chart
> New business project screening summary
> Network analysis
> Precedence diagram method
> Program evaluation and review technique (PERT)
> Purpose network analysis
> Resource allocation and multiproject scheduling (RAMPS)
> Risk analysis
>> *Also see*   Appraise/assess projects

Analyze Project Impacts on Society
> Cost-effectiveness analysis
> Cross-impact analysis
> Delphi
> Environmental impact statements
> Multiattribute utility (MAU) models
> Nominal group technique
> Planning balance sheet analysis
> Social cost-benefit analysis
> Utility assessment
> Voting technique

Analyze Systems
> Curry's model

Decision worksheet
Decision tree
Function analysis diagram
Gaming
Gravity model
Index numbers
Linear models
Mathematical model
Mathematical programming technique
Opportunity identification
Optimizing model
Path analysis
Physical model
Planning balance sheet analysis
Planning council
Planning model
Planning, programming, and budgeting system (PBBS)
Queuing theory
Recursive programming model
Relative space model
Resource constrained scheduling heuristics
Simulation model
Value analysis
Zero-base budgeting (ZBB)
Also see Appraise/assess systems

Appraise/Assess Alternative Options/Plans/Policies/Programs/Contingencies/Functions
Contingency analysis
Contingency tables
Failure analysis
Failure analysis diagram
Gaming
Goals-achievement analysis
Index analysis
Indifference curves
Force field analysis
Judgment policy analysis
Measurement model
Multiattribute utility (MAU) models
Needs analysis
Nominal group technique
Pair comparison
Planning council
Planning, programming, and budgeting system (PPBD)
Probability assessment
Program planning method
Psychological scaling
Subjective probability assessment

Utility assessment
Utility theory
Variance analysis
Value analysis
Voting technique
Appraise/Assess Investments
Cash flow model
Expected free cash flow model
Financial investment appraisal
Profit/volume (P/V) analysis
Return on investment
Risk analysis
Sensitivity analysis

Appraise/Assess Projects
Cash flow analysis
Critical path method
Demand analysis
Impact analysis
Input/output analysis
Map of activity and thought chains (MATCH)
Multiattribute utility (MAU) models
Network analysis
New product early warning systems
Observation model
Pair comparison
Precedence diagram method
Program evaluation and review technique
Purpose network analysis
RAMPS
Resource constrained scheduling heuristics
Risk analysis

Appraise/Assess Systems
A fortiori analysis
Cost-benefit analysis
Cross-impact analysis
Decision worksheet
Environmental impact statement
Gaming
Pair comparison
Planning balance sheet analysis
Planning council
Planning, programming, and budgeting system (PPBS)
Relative space model
Replacement model
Resource constrained scheduling heuristics
Sensitivity analysis
Simulation model
Social cost-benefit analysis

Utility theory
Value analysis
Zero-base budgeting (ZBB)

Approach Problems
    Case histories
    Conference
    Counterplanning
    Delphi
    Digraphs
    Function analysis diagram
    Feasibility studies
    Flow chart
    Group process technique
    Interviews
    Meetings
    Negotiation
    Nominal group technique
    Project teams
    Purpose expansion
    Questionnaire
    Task force
    Workshops

Categorize/Classify Alternatives
    Abstract dimensioning
    Classification
    Control charts
    Data dictionary
    Fuzzy sets
    Hierarchical clustering
    Index analysis
    Multiattribute utility (MAU) models
    Pair comparison
    Partitioning
    Person-card sorting technique
    Task timeline
    Utility assessment

Collect and/or Organize Performance
Information
    Case histories
    Cash flow analysis
    Control charts
    Critical incident technique
    Delphi
    Flow chart
    Gantt chart
    Histograms
    Learning curves
    Multiattribute utility (MAU) models
    Management operations system technique

(MOST)
Nominal group technique
Person card technique
Progress function
Time study
Training
Work measurement
    Also see   Analyze job methods and
                             motions
                            Collect data and/or information
                            Identify new product opportu-
                            nities

Collect Data and/or Information
    Activity sampling
    Attitude surveys
    Case histories
    Central location testing
    Charrette
    Checklist
    Citizen referendum
    Climate analysis
    Computer graphics
    Counter planning
    Critical incident technique
    Data base system
    Delphi
    Ends-means chain
    Environmental impact statements
    Interviews
    Job interviews
    Learning curves
    Managerial grid analysis
    Media-based issue balloting
    Meetings
    Numbering/identification schemes
    Nominal group technique
    Observation model
    Opportunity identification
    Questionnaire
    Standard data, charts, tables, and equations
    Standard operating procedures
    Telecommunications
    Telephone polling
    Time study
    Training
    Use testing
    Wage scale
    Work measurement
    Workshops

Describe/Establish/Measure Relationships
    Cause/effect assessment
    Computer graphics
    Correlation analysis
    Data dictionary
    Data transformation
    Digraphs
    Dynamic model
    Factor analysis
    Fault-tree analysis
    Flow chart
    Interaction analysis
    Interpretive structural modeling
    Mathematical model
    Modeling
    Network analysis
    Oval diagrams
    Pareto analysis
    Physical model
    Planning model
    Profit/volume (P/V) analysis
    Purpose network analysis
    Statistical model
    System matrix
    Tree diagram

Detail Proposed Solution
    See   Analyze job methods and motions
            Analyze systems
            Collect data and/or information
            Describe/establish/measure
            relationships
            Determining human ability and
            skill requirements for tasks
            Involve people
            Predict future conditions
            Provide graphic representations

Determine Human Ability and Skill Requirements
for Tasks
    Aptitude test
    Critical incident technique
    Information content analysis
    Interviews
    Job evaluation
    Operation chart
    Performance/time measurement estimate
    Role analysis
    Task analysis
    Therblig chart
    Training

    Tree diagram
    Work measurement

Develop and Analyze Structure
    Computer graphics
    Critical path method
    Interpretive structural modeling
    Network analysis
    Precedence diagram method
    Program evaluation and review technique
    System matrix

Develop (Enhance) Creativity
    Bisociation
    Brainstorming
    Delphi
    Nominal group technique
    Morphological analysis
    Person-card sorting technique
    Synectics
        Also see   Generate alternatives/ideas

Establish Priorities
    See   Categorize/classify alternatives
    Organize alternatives
    Rank alternatives
    Rate conditions
    Weight criteria or factors

Establish Project Schedules and Basis for
Measuring Progress and Performance
    Activity line balance evaluation (ABLE)
    Gantt chart
    Learning curves and progress functions
    Line of balance (LOB)
    Management operations systems technique
    (MOST)
    Milestone chart
    Network analysis
    PERT/cost
    Precedence diagram method
    Resource constrained scheduling heuristic
    Task timeline

Estimate Budget and Dollar Requirements
    Budget
    Cash flow analysis
    Expected free cash flow model
    Planning, programming, and budgeting
    system (PPBS)
    Zero-based budgeting
        Also see   Analyzing investments

Evaluate Alternatives
  See   Analyze alternative options/plans/
           policies/programs/contingencies/
           functions
           Analyze investments
           Analyze job methods and motions
           Analyze policy setting and decision
           making variables
           Analyze product quality
           Analyze project impacts on society
           Analyze projects
           Appraise/assess alternative options/
           plans/policies/programs/contingen-
           cies/functions
           Appraise/assess investments
           Appraise/assess projects
           Appraise/assess systems

Evaluate Interpersonal Relationships, Performance,
and Effectiveness of an Organization
  Auditing
  Force field analysis
  Index analysis
  Organization mirror
  Organizational sensing
  Role analysis
  Training

Generate a List of Possible Purpose/Function State-
ments
  Brainstorming
  Brain writing
  Function analysis diagram
  Nominal group technique
  Purpose expansion
           Also see   Generate alternatives/ideas

Generate Alternatives/Ideas
  Analogies
  Bisociation
  Brain resting
  Brainstorming
  Brain writing
  Case histories
  Charrette
  Citizen advisory committee
  Conference
  Counseling interviews
  Delphi
  Dialectical process
  Fishbowl planning

Focused group interview
Forced connections
Interviews
Judgment analysis technique
Meetings
Morphological analysis
Nominal group technique
Productivity circles
Purpose expansion
Questionnaire
Random selected participation groups
Synectics
Team building
Telephone polling
Use testing workshops

Identify Management Styles
  Attitude survey
  Auditing technique
  Interviews
  Managerial grid analysis
  Questionnaire

Identify (Product) Opportunities
  Abstract dimensioning
  Central location testing
  Employee panels
  Focus group testing
  New-product early warning system
  Opportunity identification
  Product/service life cycle analysis
  Substitution analysis
  Use testing

Identify Problems, Overlaps, Conflicts
  Bisociation
  Brainstorming
  Data dictionary
  Delphi
  Group process techniques
  Interviews
  Meetings
  Morphological analysis
  Nominal group technique
  Person-card sorting technique
  Purpose expansion
  Questionnaire
           Also see   Approach problems
                         Identify management styles

Identify Project Opportunities
  See   Analyze projects

Identify (product) opportunities

Identify Regularities
    Classification
    Person-card sorting technique
    Priority setting
    System matrix
        Also see   Weight criteria or factors

Inform and Involve Citizens
    Citizen honoraria
    Drop-in centers
    Fishbowl planning
    Group process technique
    Judgment policy analysis
    Media-based issue balloting
    Meetings
    Negotiation
    Ombudsman
    Open-door policy
    Planning balance sheet analysis
    Planning council
    Public hearing

Involve People
    Activity matrix
    Brainstorming
    Conference
    Delphi
    Interpretive structural modeling
    Judgment analysis technique
    Judgment policy analysis
    Nominal group technique
    Opinion polling
    Planning council
    Planning model
    Productivity circles
    Program planning method
    Purpose hierarchy development
    Scenario writing
    Telecommunications
    Utility assessment
    Value analysis
        Also see   Inform and involve citizens

Measure Error
    Control charts
    Sensitivity analysis
    Variance analysis

Measure Project Progress and Performance
    See   Establish project schedules and basis

for measuring progress and performance

Organize Alternatives
    Classification
    Couplet comparison technique
    Data dictionary
    Data transformation
    Decision tables
    Fuzzy sets
    Hierarchical clustering
    Hierarchical structures
    Intent structures
    Logical framework
    Numbering/identification schemes
    Objective tree
    Person-card sorting technique
    Program planning method
    Purpose expansion
    Psychological scaling
    Scaling, subjective
    Scheduling model
    Specification listing
    System pyramid
    Team building

Plot and Analyze Data about the Performance of an Existing Installaion
    Budget analysis
    Control charts
    Index values
    Learning curves and progress functions
    Variance analysis

Predict Future Conditions
    Adaptive forecasting
    Budget
    Contextual mapping
    Control charts
    Cross-impact analysis
    Demographic forecasting
    Econometric model
    Forecasting
    Index numbers
    Learning curves
    Markov chain
    New-product early warning system
    Operations research
    Path analysis
    Performance measures tally
    PERT/cost

Person-card technique
Probabilistic system dynamics
Probability assessment
Product/service life cycle analysis
Progress function
Queuing therory
Resource constrained scheduling heuristic
Regression analysis
Regression forecasting
Reliability theory
Risk analysis
Role playing
Sales force composite
Scenario writing
Scheduling model
Simulation model
Smoothing
Sociological projection technique
Subjective probability assessment
Substitution analysis
Technological assessment
Technological forecasting
Time series analysis
Trend analysis

Preserve an Image
Computer graphics
Data dictionary
Graphics
Modeling
Photographs
Physical model
Planning model

Portray an Order of Events
Critical path method
Decision tables
Delta charts
Flow chart
Gantt charts
Interpretive structural modeling
Machine-loading charts
Maintenance charts
Milestone chart
Network analysis
Operations chart
PERT/cost
Precedence diagram method
Process chart
Program evaluation and review technique
Resource constrained scheduling heuristic

Specification listing
Task timeline

Produce Consensus
Arbitration and mediation planning
Group process technique
Judgment analysis technique
Meetings
Negotiation
Nominal group technique
Ombudsman
Team building
Voting technique

Provide Graphic Representations
Computer graphics
Decision tree
Delta charts (cell 19)
Digraphs
Flow chart
Graphics
Graphy theory
Histogram
Influence diagram
Intent structure
Interpretive structural modeling
Network analysis
Objective tree
Oval diagrams
Partitioning technique
Performance measures tally
Physical model
Policy graphs
Progress function
Purpose network analysis
System pyramid
Templates
Tree diagram
        Also see   Preserve an image
                       Portray an order of event

Rank Alternatives
Contingency analysis
Cost effectiveness analysis
Goals-achievement analysis
Multiattribute utility (MAU) models
Measurement model
Nominal group technique
Pair comparison
Scaling, subjective
Social cost-benefit analysis

Index

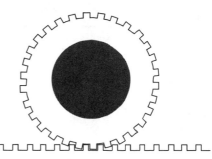